PENGUIN BOOKS

PSYCHOLOGY AT WORK

Peter Warr was educated at Cambridge and Sheffield Universities and is currently Director of the MRC/ESRC Social and Applied Psychology Unit at Sheffield University. As a visiting professor he has also taught at the Universities of Princeton, Colorado and California, USA, Canterbury in New Zealand, and Curtin in Australia. In 1969 he was awarded the Spearman Medal of the British Psychological Society for distinguished research, and in 1982 he received the Presidents' Award of the same society for his outstanding contributions to psychological knowledge.

Professor Warr is a member of several professional associations and has served on many editorial boards for journals and books to promote the understanding of psychology. He has published sixteen books, including *Thought and Personality* (1970) and *Work and Well-being* (1975), both also published by Penguin, and *Work, Unemployment and Mental Health* (1987). He is the editor of *Personal Goals and Work Design* (1976) and a contributor to *The Experience of Work* (1981).

Psychology at Work

Third Edition

EDITED BY

PETER WARR

PENGUIN BOOKS

PENGUIN BOOKS

Published by the Penguin Group
Penguin Books Ltd, 27 Wrights Lane, London W8 5TZ, England
Penguin Books USA Inc., 375 Hudson Street, New York, New York 10014, USA
Penguin Books Australia Ltd, Ringwood, Victoria, Australia
Penguin Books Canada Ltd, 2801 John Street, Markham, Ontario, Canada L3R 1B4
Penguin Books (NZ) Ltd, 182–190 Wairau Road, Auckland 10, New Zealand

Penguin Books Ltd, Registered Offices: Harmondsworth, Middlesex, England

First published in Penguin Books 1971
Second edition 1978
Third edition published in Pelican Books 1987
Reprinted in Penguin Books 1991
1 3 5 7 9 10 8 6 4 2

Printed in England by Clays Ltd, St Ives plc
Typeset in Linotron Times

Contents

Contents

Contents

Contributors

Jen Algera is an Associate Professor in the Department of Industrial and Organizational Psychology, Free University, Amsterdam, and a Professor of Personnel Psychology in the Department of Industrial Engineering and Management Science, Eindhoven University of Technology. He has worked for ten years in the Dutch steel industry as a consultant and researcher in the area of personnel and organizational psychology. His current research interests are in task analysis, personnel selection and the impact of new technologies.

Peter Allen is a Research Fellow at the Health Services Research Unit at the University of Kent, and was until recently a Fellow at the Social Psychology Research Unit at that University. He has directed research projects on intergroup processes in organizations and is currently engaged on a study of the implications of community care for health care staff working with mentally handicapped people. He has published in the fields of sociology, industrial relations and social psychology.

Donald Broadbent is a member of External Staff of the Medical Research Council, working in the Department of Experimental Psychology, University of Oxford. From 1949 to 1974 he worked in the MRC Applied Psychology Unit, being Director between 1958 and 1974. His current research is primarily on styles of attention in relation to the probability of developing symptoms in stressful jobs.

Marilyn Davidson is a Lecturer in Organizational Psychology in the Department of Management Sciences at the University of Manchester Institute of Science and Technology (UMIST). She has wide lecturing, consultancy and research experience, specializing in problems faced by women at work and all aspects of occupational stress. Projects have been undertaken for the World Health Organisation, the Commission of the European Communities, the Manpower Services Commission, and the Home Office.

Pieter Drenth is Professor of Work and Organizational Psychology at the Free University, Amsterdam. He previously worked as an organizational psychologist with the Royal Dutch Navy and with the Standard Oil Company in the USA. He is the author of many books and articles in the field of test theory, test development, selection and appraisal, and on more general organizational subjects, such as leadership, decision-making, participation and the meaning of working. At present he is serving a four-year term as Rector Magnificus (Vice-Chancellor) of the Free University.

Stephen Fineman is a Senior Lecturer in Organizational Behaviour in Bath University's School of Management. For some years he has been consulting and writing in the areas of organizational change and stress. These projects have developed into studies of social workers and the middle-class unemployed. His current interests are in terms of multidisciplinary, qualitative approaches toward understanding employment and unemployment, and new directions of thought about alternatives to conventional employment.

Simon Folkard is a Senior Research Fellow at the Medical Research Council's Perceptual and Cognitive Performance Unit at the University of Sussex. Since joining this group in 1971, his research has primarily concerned circadian (about 24-hour) rhythms in psychological functions and in their practical implications in a variety of situations, including the scheduling of periods of work. He has collaborated extensively with other European groups in this field, and spent 1985–6 working at the Institute for Medical Research and Occupational Health in Zagreb.

John Fox gained his B.Sc. and Ph.D. in psychology at Durham and Cambridge Universities. He then spent two years at Carnegie-Mellon and Cornell Universities carrying out research into artificial intelligence. After returning to the UK, he worked for the Medical Research Council on medical decision-making and the clinical uses of expert systems. He is currently Head of the Biomedical Computing Unit at the Imperial Cancer Research Fund, London, and is a member of the Knowledge-Based Systems Advisory Group of the Department of Industry's Alvey Directorate.

David Guest is Senior Lecturer in Industrial Relations at the London School of Economics, where he is currently responsible for the M.Sc. programme in Industrial Relations and Personnel Management. His research interests include the role and effectiveness of personnel management and work motivation in the context of changing patterns of work. He is Editor of the *Journal of Occupational Psychology*.

Peter Herriot is Professor of Occupational Psychology and Head of the Department of Occupational Psychology at Birkbeck College, University of London. He is particularly interested in all aspects of the assessment of employees for selection and career development within organizations. Recent research has included investigations of the decision-making process at assessment centres and of the use of biographical data for selection purposes. A current project is investigating within-organizational predictors of managerial performance.

John Long is Professor of Ergonomics and Director of the Ergonomics Unit, University College London. He worked initially as a manager for Shell International in Africa and the Far East. Subsequently, he became a senior scientist at the Medical Research Council's Applied Psychology Unit in Cambridge. His main research interests lie in the area of human–computer interaction, although he has also published papers on divided attention, typing, second language use and interpreter training.

Iain Mangham is Director of the Centre for the Study of Organizational Change and Development and Professor of Management Development in the School of Management, University of Bath. He is a social psychologist with over twenty years of experience in organizations. Immediately before taking up his appointment in Bath, he was Area Director in Southern Europe, the Middle East and North Africa for a large American pharmaceutical company. Current interests centre on top management decision-making, organization design and the management of creativity.

Nigel Nicholson is a Senior Research Fellow at the MRC/ESRC Social and Applied Psychology Unit at the University of Sheffield. He joined the Unit in 1972 after undergraduate and postgraduate studies at University College, Cardiff, and since that time he has also been a visiting scholar at American, Canadian and German universities. His research interests have been in three main areas: absence from work, trade-union behaviour, and work-role transitions. Current work in the last of these areas is placing increasing emphasis on organizational culture, innovation processes, and personality.

Roy Payne is Professor of Organizational Behaviour at Manchester Business School. Since graduating in psychology at Liverpool University he has held research posts at Aston University and at the London Graduate School of Business Studies, where he completed his doctorate. For a considerable portion of his career he was at the MRC/ESRC Social and Applied Psychology Unit at Sheffield University. His research interests include organizational structure, climate, occupational stress and the management of innovation in research and development organizations.

Rob Stammers is a Lecturer in Applied Psychology at Aston University in Birmingham. He completed his Ph.D. in training psychology at the University of Hull in 1975, and has maintained a strong interest in that field, carrying out projects for government departments and industry. His current research activities are in task analysis, computer-based training and simulation. He is also involved in inquiries into the broader human factors, issues of command and control, and process-control tasks.

Geoffrey Stephenson is Professor of Social Psychology and Director of the Institute of Social and Applied Psychology at the University of Kent at Canterbury. Before moving there in 1978, he had spent twelve years at Nottingham University, where he developed his interest in the application of social psychology to problems of industrial relations. While maintaining his teaching and research interests in that area, he is now investigating collaborative memory processes in the police and other organizational settings.

Toby Wall is Assistant Director of the M R C/E S R C Social and Applied Psychology Unit at the University of Sheffield. He is interested in attitudes, mental health, motivation and performance at work, applied research design, and psychological aspects of employee participation, job design, and new technology. His current research is concerned with the implications of advanced manufacturing technology for the well-being and behaviour of shop-floor employees, and with the psychological and clinical consequences of using information technology during medical consultations.

Peter Warr is Director of the MRC/ESRC Social and Applied Psychology Unit. He has been Editor of the *Journal of Occupational Psychology*, and is a member of the editorial board of several journals and book series. He is currently Vice-Chairman of the Industry and Employment Committee of the Economic and Social Research Council, and a member of the Neurosciences and Mental Health Board of the Medical Research Council.

To the memory of Sir Frederic Bartlett

Editor's Introduction

Previous editions of *Psychology at Work* were published in 1971 and 1978. Their objectives were much the same as those of the present edition, but circumstances surrounding the book have changed substantially. In those earlier years, applied psychology of the kind illustrated here generally lacked the maturity, theoretical incisiveness and practical power which it now has. The profession in the late 1980s is firmly established and strongly expanding, both outside and inside academic institutions.

Applied psychology in work organizations has a long history, but its early achievements were typically of a practical problem-solving kind. Those were of little interest to the academic community, and students of psychology were rarely exposed to the methods and findings of applied research. Around the time of the first edition of this book, few students looked for careers in the area, and there was very little interchange between psychologists working in pure or basic research and those whose interests were more applied.

It was that absence of interaction which gave rise to the first edition of *Psychology at Work*. In the late 1960s, introductory psychology books appeared to be of two quite different kinds. On the one hand were student texts, packed with experimental findings, and infused with enthusiasm for a single 'scientific method' defined in restricted, laboratory-oriented terms. Practical issues of everyday concern found no place there, and readers were presumably expected to conclude that applied psychology had no academic interest or relevance. On the other hand, several books described applications of psychology in popular terms, very much of the 'how to make friends and influence people' variety. Whatever their value to the lay reader, these made no scholarly contribution, and they were excluded from student reading lists.

This situation was characterized in the Introduction to the 1971 edition as follows:

> It is extremely easy (and correspondingly common) for academic teaching and research to become divorced from problems which

1

are important outside the university environment. Inside the academic culture a sort of serious-minded game-playing has become valued as the norm . . . Able students within the cultural framework which rewards laboratory investigation tend to develop into able teachers in that same framework; and the selection and assessment of students is undertaken within a value-system which remains stable and reassuring.

Meanwhile, back in the world there are some 'applied' psychologists who are trying hard to tackle the pressing human problems of the day. These . . . lack status and influence within the profession, so that they are rarely in a position to get at the root of this problem of imbalance – the teaching and the climate within university departments.

In brief, pure psychology is too pure and applied psychology is too applied; and much academic psychology is barricaded within its fortress of purity.

The 1971 volume set out to help remedy that situation. The goal was to communicate the intellectual excitement of applied research, and to make the point that applied psychologists can be as concerned to develop and test theories as their 'purer' counterparts. Applied investigators are by definition primarily concerned with problems arising in a particular setting of everyday life, work organizations in the present case. However, individuals within this group attach differing importance to practical versus theoretical objectives. Some applied psychologists (employed within an industrial company, for instance) are valuably engaged entirely in solving problems and seeking practical innovation. Many other applied psychologists, especially those within academic institutions, are in addition concerned to develop reliable generalizations and systematic theories. Their inquiries are addressed to real-life situations, but they set out to understand and influence these through the creation of models and through empirical testing of detailed predictions. Their concern for conceptual development and soundness of research method is thus very similar to that of their counterparts in basic research.

The first edition of *Psychology at Work* argued that a healthy, pure psychology was unquestionably needed, but it deplored the fact that academic psychologists overvalued pure research to the detriment of applied work. The chapters were therefore written to complement the two categories of book described above: practical issues were addressed by applied psychologists, who set out to illustrate theoretical development as well as the empirical richness of their field.

And that remains the present aim. There have been enormous advances in knowledge and method since 1971, and the present material is considerably different from that in the first edition. Marked improvements have occurred in the specification and measurement of variables, in the refinement of procedures and the conduct of longitudinal research, in the creation of specific models and broad conceptual frameworks, in the application of statistical procedures, and in the sophisticated use of novel computing power.

The book's environment has also changed, with widespread acceptance of the scholarly importance of applied research. Many more students of psychology and their teachers now take it for granted that energy and creativity should be directed toward issues of the kind described in the chapters which follow. They have no doubt that their discipline requires strong applied researchers in continuous interaction with 'purer' colleagues. Professional bodies and scientific networks are firmly established, with applied psychologists in demand as advisers, consultants, lecturers and trainers. Employment opportunities are expanding, and new entrants to the field are of a generally high calibre. Psychology at work has come a long way since 1971.

SIR FREDERIC BARTLETT

Yet the field still owes a major debt of gratitude to a figure who was influential some forty years ago. This is F. C. Bartlett, the Professor of Experimental Psychology at Cambridge University. The third edition of this book, like its predecessors, is dedicated to his memory.

Bartlett's career has been well summarized in several published tributes (e.g. Broadbent, 1970; Conrad, 1970; Buzzard, 1971). He saw that the development of psychology depended upon its involvement in day-to-day problems, arguing forcibly that the major theoretical advances were likely to come from those researchers whose prime concern was with genuinely practical problems. The juxtaposition of 'theoretical' and 'practical' here is most important. Bartlett's notion was

3

that we certainly need a theoretical structure, but that this has to be built upon a foundation of practical importance rather than solely on the basis of what academics happen to find interesting.

This can be emphasized through a pair of quotations. The first comes from a symposium held in 1947, in which Bartlett asserted:

> No matter what 'kind' of psychologist a person is, he is a student of human behaviour. To my mind the history of psychology shows that if he shuts himself up narrowly in any particular small sphere of conduct inside or outside the laboratory (but specially inside), he will tend to get over-immersed in a terrific lot of detail about behaviour problems which he cleverly imagines for himself, and will approximate to a sort of puzzle solving which is often ex-tremely interesting and, in a debating sense, intellectually attract-ive, but which leaves him revolving round and round his limited area. This works both ways, and if it is true that the general, or the laboratory, psychologist must be prepared to keep his problems alive by going outside the study or beyond his immediate ex-perimental settings, it is equally true that the field psychologist must seek his executive solution[1] with loyalty to that rigour of scientific method and that honest sense of evidence which only the study and the laboratory appear to instil (Bartlett, 1949, pp. 215–16).

The second quotation comes from an appreciation written after Bartlett's death in 1969:

> He would sometimes say that no good psychologist should be interested only in psychology. This made him friends outside his own subject, and also guaranteed to his professional writings a realism and contact with life sometimes lacking in academic psychologists. His ideas concerning psychology stemmed not from the criticism and development of abstract ideas, but from pondering on the mechanism which could produce an efficient stroke at cricket or explain why an African tribesman could

[1] In the context of the discussion from which this is taken, an 'executive solution' was a set of practical activities to solve a problem. This was contrasted with a 'fundamental solution', an explanation in terms of cause and effect.

remember perfectly the details of a number of cows sold a year previously. From a purely scientific point of view this made his ideas more original and more productive than those of the abstract theoretical schools, and from a worldly point of view he doubtless made psychology more acceptable to the representatives of other fields (Broadbent, 1970, pp. 1–2).

The present volume is a contemporary assertion of Bartlett's philosophy. Many of the authors have emphasized the links between general psychology and psychology in work settings, and they have tried to show how investigations into jobs and organizations can be as intellectually stimulating and theoretically challenging as research from a starting point which is 'pure' in academic terms.

WORK AND EMPLOYMENT

People 'work' in a variety of settings, inside and outside paid employment. Examples of unpaid work include housework, voluntary work, and domestic repair and decorating work. Definitions of the term in its general sense vary across time and between cultures, but most often they contain the assertion that work is an activity directed to valued goals beyond enjoyment of the activity itself. (That does not mean that work cannot be enjoyed; merely that enjoyment is not part of the definition.) In addition, there are suggestions that it is required in some way, and that it implies difficulty, a need to labour or exert oneself against the environment.

An important but restricted meaning of the term is illustrated in the title of this book. We are here primarily concerned with people in their jobs, when they are working for financial gain. This usually means being employed by someone else, with terms and conditions embodied in an explicit or implicit employment contract. 'Self-employed' people are in the minority in most developed countries, comprising between ten and twenty per cent of the work-force.

Jobs may be considered as 'socially acceptable means of earning a living' (Garraty, 1978, p. 10), thus excluding activities which are defined as illegal. Those which are referred to as 'full-time' typically take up between thirty-five and forty-five hours in a week, but travelling to and from a place of employment adds, on average, a further ten per cent. 'Part-time' jobs may of course vary in their weekly duration, but thirty hours per week is often taken as their upper limit for statistical and survey purposes.

Paid work has long been a cornerstone of society. It is a source of social cohesion and material welfare; and for the individual it is often crucial to both physical and mental health. It warrants study by psychologists for its enormous societal importance, but also for the contribution which increased understanding of job activities and relationships can make to the development of psychology itself.

TYPES OF PSYCHOLOGY

The subject-matter of psychology is wide-ranging, and some specialization into branches has naturally occurred. For example, individual psychologists may be principally interested in child development, in perceptual or cognitive processes, in animal behaviour, or in statistical models. Others devote their attention mainly to physiological correlates of behaviour, or to personality studies, the structure of attitudes, mental illness, or features of social interaction.

That branch of psychology which deals with people at work has been variously labelled as industrial, occupational, work or organizational psychology. Each of these terms has merit, but each has its own limitation. 'Industrial' excludes the large number of non-industrial settings in which people are employed (hospitals, schools, government departments, etc.); in the United States this difficulty is circumvented by use of the term 'industrial/organizational' (I/O) psychology. The second term, 'occupational' psychology, is mainly applied within the United Kingdom, and it is unfamiliar or unknown elsewhere. Despite that, the label is an appropriate one to cover all employment settings and processes. The third description, 'work' psychology, widely used in certain countries of continental Europe, is also a useful one; but, as we have seen, 'work' has wider reference than merely paid employment. Finally, 'organizational' is often applied primarily to issues at the level of groups, institutions or entire organizations, with an emphasis on social interaction and group structure. Additional forms of designation for people who investigate workers in job settings include ergonomists, human factors specialists, applied experimental psychologists, applied social psychologists, behavioural scientists, organizational behaviour (O.B.) specialists and industrial sociologists. This book covers the achievements of all these groups.

CONTENTS OF THE BOOK

The chapters which follow have been specially prepared for this volume. They are directed at students of psychology, industrial relations, business and management, but members of educational, professional and trade-union study groups are also likely to find material which arouses their interest. So will the many managers and administrators who are not 'students' in a strict sense, but who share a curiosity and concern for the developing science of psychology and for what it can offer them in their day-to-day work.

The diversity of topics to be covered is quite considerable. As a result, each reader is likely to find certain parts of the book more interesting than others. The material is arranged in a sequence which roughly speaking moves from an emphasis on the individual, through the study of groups, to the examination of complex organizations as a whole. This sequence is a straightforward one, but it is not necessarily the most suitable path for all readers to follow. Course teachers may wish to emphasize certain features or recommend a particular sequence, and the general reader may prefer to dip into a selection of individual chapters.

The authors are all experienced and influential in their fields. They have provided substantial and up-to-date summaries, but have written in a style which makes clear their personal approach and their preferred interpretations. Topics have been chosen because of their importance for the field and in order to reflect developments occurring within psychology and within society more broadly. In general, the book seeks to identify growth points and to anticipate some future developments.

This means that considerable changes in content have been made since the last edition. There is of course a general up-dating, with new perspectives and findings taking priority. In addition, much greater attention is now paid to jobs which require interaction with computer-based equipment, those which embody so-called 'new technology' or 'information technology'. This shift is associated with a growing concern for cognitive processes; jobs in new technology primarily require workers to handle information rather than materials. Chapter 4 thus examines equipment design and usage from a primarily cognitive standpoint. Chapter 3 considers training from a similar perspective. Chapter 13 extends an account of important job characteristics to look specifically at new technology work. Chapter 5 considers the importance for applied psychologists of 'expert' computer-based systems.

Three other major developments are captured in sections which were not present in earlier editions. Women are spending increasing proportions of their life in paid employment, in jobs and with problems that differ in important ways from those of men. Issues raised by this change are addressed in Chapter 11. Unemployment has also risen markedly since previous editions of the book, and its processes and effects now require examination; this is included as Chapter 16. A third new chapter reflects the increased pace of change more generally. Shifts in employment patterns and job content have brought into focus the need to study transitions between jobs and also more extended patterns of career development. These are examined in Chapter 8.

Authors throughout the book provide examples of the interplay between research and practice. For example, Chapter 1 examines the nature of skilled performance to identify optimum forms of workload; Chapter 2 draws implications from physiological and behavioural studies for the design of shiftwork schedules; and Chapters 6 and 7 are rich with suggestions about how to improve personnel selection procedures.

We hope that readers will come to share our enthusiasm. Applied psychology within work organizations is exciting, expanding, and of great practical importance.

1

Skill and Workload

Donald Broadbent

In everyday life, we divide jobs into unskilled manual, skilled manual, and white-collar; so that skill seems to be something unique to the work of, say, carpenters or motor mechanics. We do not use the word to describe workers whose job consists only of feeding metal plates into a press. Yet if their patterns of action were truly stereotyped and predictable, they could easily be replaced by a machine. The movements they make, and the visual patterns they can distinguish, are very subtle, variable, and yet lawful and organized. In this chapter, we shall mean by 'skill' the whole process of organizing a flexible series of actions. We shall see that the process is essentially the same for work that uses everyday knowledge which has not been formally learned (such as the machine-feeder) and for work that takes advantage of a deliberate history of training (such as the carpenter). Indeed, we shall also see that the same principles govern white-collar work also. Skill in this sense appears in all jobs; it is the control system that makes work effective.

'Workload' is also a term in everyday use, and usually implies 'having too many things to do'. If one watches somebody at work however, there is no obvious limit to the number of actions that they may take. A pilot may be executing numerous simultaneous movements of both hands and feet while talking, and yet seem relaxed; an executive may be sitting motionless thinking and yet complain of overload. The problem lies in the system that controls their actions, and workload has to be discussed in relation to their skill. By analysing their actions in this way, we can hope to improve conditions of work; and also see why general principles of controllability, feedback, clarity, and autonomy become so important when we go on in later chapters to think about the social organization of work.

9

FROM INTENTION TO ACTION

Feedback Control of Movement

Let us start with people who are packing chocolates. They want to pick up a piece of chocolate, move it towards a box, and drop it in. Even if this intention is present, there is still a problem of translating it into muscular movements.

One might think that something in the brain, corresponding to the intention, simply launches the correct series of contractions. That view is certainly wrong, however. If the room went dark just after the movement had started, the hand would go roughly to the neighbourhood of the chocolate; but not to the exact place (Beggs and Howarth, 1970). The muscular movements are guided and corrected by visual information, to make them correspond to what is intended. The start of the movement is fast, and unaffected by the light being on or off. As the hand gets nearer the target, it moves more slowly, while the eye picks up information about the remaining distance to go. The more accurately the final adjustment has to be made, the longer the total process takes. While the hand is in motion, therefore, the pattern of muscle contractions is guided by visual 'feedback' about what is happening (Beggs and Howarth, 1972).

The importance of feedback is even more noticeable at the next stage, when the fingers grasp the chocolate. Too tight a grip, and it will squash; too slack, and it will drop. Yet the chocolate is unlikely to be exactly the same size on every occasion. So holding it with exactly the correct pressure depends on a mechanism in the nervous system that compares the tension in the muscles with the tension that was intended; and corrects it if necessary. It is this adjustment that is often hard to achieve with sufficient delicacy in a machine, and therefore, despite the spread of automatic machinery, one will still find some jobs, such as handling fragile chocolates, that need human fingers rather than a robot.

Motor Programmes

All this sounds as if a movement has to proceed in a series of twitches, each contraction of the muscles being followed by a pause while the effects are being compared with the intention. Of course that is not so; the next movement can be started before the first is completed. Instead of a chocolate-packer, think of a typist or a piano-player. When one finger is reaching towards a key, the next finger starts to rise into the air before the first has arrived at its target (Rumelhart and Norman, 1982). Similarly, if the action calls for a rapid oscillating movement, as in polishing a shoe or shaking out a wet cloth, the limb starts to move back as soon as it reaches the far end, without waiting for feedback to be analysed. In fact, if the person is told to stop the action, several further wiggles will run off before the movements stop. The intention sends out a whole series of instructions for a series of movements, not one by one (Pew, 1966).

The effect of the whole programme is still monitored by feedback, though. If somebody is trying, say, to oil a moving crank, their hand will travel back and forth roughly in time with the crank. At times they may get slightly behind, so that they drip oil in the place the crank has just left. Every half-second or so, however, there will be a jerk in their movement to try and match the position of their hand with that of the crank. The intention starts a programme of commands to the muscles. The eyes and the feedback pathways within the limbs then check whether the right things are happening, even while that programme is still being issued, and occasionally correct the workings of the programme.

Chunking and Hierarchization

Thus far we have been talking mostly about the kinds of actions that all of us use; reaching, grasping, shaking. The example of typing, however, began to introduce the changes that happen within an individual after practice. Somebody with no knowledge of a typewriter keyboard might well finish pressing one key before starting the next movement. It is repeated experience of typing the word 'the', for instance, that creates the motor programme and launches the second and third fingers towards the keys for 'h' and 'e' before the key for 't' has been struck. As people learn to type, we find that their average speed increases for a time, then there is a pause with little apparent progress, then another spurt, and so on. The first stage may correspond to learning the location of each key; the next stage corresponds to common groupings of letters into whole words, and then to cliché phrases such as 'Dear Sir, In reply to yours of . . .'. The whole sequence of movements then emerges as a unit, with few of the pauses and hesitations between letters (or, later, words) that were common at the novice stage. In a practised person, the intention apparently launches a larger unit of action (Leonard and Newman, 1964; Shaffer, 1973).

The same grouping or chunking of muscular movements can be seen by interrupting the process and seeing how long the action continues. For instance, reading aloud is a skill of this kind; and if the room becomes dark while a person is reading familiar English sentences, the voice will continue for a while. If the sequence being read was random numbers, however, only a few more numbers would be spoken after darkness blotted out the text. The increase in size of the 'eye–hand' or 'eye–voice' span can be picked up also by measuring the actual eye-movements and seeing where the point of fixation is in relation to the motor output.

Similar hierarchic stages could appear in more complex skills, such as learning to use a computerized hotel reservation system. First the person learns the individual commands for displaying existing bookings, for moving to a certain date, or for changing to an 'entry' mode. Then they do complete operations such as answering a query about space on a certain day, or entering a person's requirements; but they still pause to think before each operation. Finally, a whole dialogue with a customer can run off with very little hesitation at each stage.

Notice that the larger units are made up of smaller ones, and those in turn of even smaller ones. The same lower-order units may appear in different higher-order groupings, as in reading aloud the sentences 'Dog bites man' and 'Man bites dog'. Further, the successful execution of the lower-order units is being monitored by feedback in the way we have discussed already. So, if there is some slip or fumble in the detailed movements, people often show a pause in the flow of the action, may try to correct the error, and may be able to tell you afterwards that they knew they had typed 'hte' in the middle of a sentence-chunk.

We must not think therefore of a practised action as a chain of muscle contractions with each triggering off the next. Rather, the original intention sets up a goal, that in turn sets up sub-goals, and those in turn sub-sub-goals. The whole arrangement creates an assembly of levels, such that several units at one level serve to achieve the goal of the next higher level. That is, the arrangement is hierarchical. At each level, what is achieved by the next lower level is compared with the goal, and further movements are produced if the outcome is incorrect. However, practice allows the execution of the lower levels to be monitored by simple, low-level, and therefore fast-acting, feedback loops. Thus, the practised person can execute quickly the whole action of typing a letter, bringing an aircraft to the correct height, or sewing a seam.

Anticipation

This saving of time is one of the advantages of building up large units of action. It allows actions to be started before the need for them has appeared in the outside world. Suppose we are building, say, a machine which shows letters to a postal worker, whose job is to press the correct keys to dispatch each letter to the right destination. The obvious way to build the machine would be to show one envelope at a time. But that would be wrong, because the eye–hand span will make it smoother and easier for the sorter to look at the *next* envelope while pressing the keys for the present one (Leonard, 1953; Conrad, 1960).

In that example, it would be possible (even though slower) for the sorter to react to each envelope when it arrives. But in many tasks the action must be started before it is needed. When a pilot starts to flatten out the descent towards the runway, the inertia of the aircraft will mean that the machine continues to go on downwards for quite a time after the controls are moved. The pilot needs to start action early, in anticipation of the state of the world at a future time. Similarly, if a tennis player waits to launch a stroke until the ball is within reach, he or she will be too late. The motor programme, started ahead of time, allows the action to produce its effect at the moment when it is needed (Poulton, 1957).

In the laboratory, one can carry out experiments on tasks similar to the job of oiling a moving crank. Inexperienced people fail to reverse their movements when the crank reverses; they act as if it was still going in the same direction as when they started their action. As their motor programme builds up, they begin to reverse movements at exactly the same time as the crank reverses. In fact, they are no longer needing to look at the crank all the time, only an occasional glance to check that all is well. One can interrupt their vision of the scene without affecting their tracking.

The established skill therefore unburdens the person of a number of problems that were very serious for the novice. Instead of each keypress or knob-turn being a separate event requiring a fresh intention, a single decision will unleash a sequence of rapidly successive movements. The sequence will be modified at intervals because of some idiosyncratic event or because of failure to achieve a sub-goal; today the ball is bouncing a little less than usual, or the player slightly lost balance when turning. Yet the sequence can be started ahead of time, and it can continue with a fair chance of success even without taking in any fresh information from the outside world.

All this depends of course upon the extent to which the task itself is made up of meaningful units. If the job is made up of a string of disconnected events, with no regularity or predictability, then even the practised person will have to think about each event as it happens.

THE CASE OF COGNITIVE ACTIONS

This is the point at which we should emphasize the continuity between tasks like typing or driving on the one hand, and tasks within white-collar jobs such as accountancy, production management or sales on the other. In driving or flying, it is obvious that the actions of the person may include operations that go on purely internally. The good driver checks if a road-sign warns that a road is slippery when wet, but no external action follows at once. All that happens is that the driver puts something into memory; later, he or she may accelerate if there has been no sign of hazard, but keep going slowly if there was a warning sign.

Holding information temporarily can be done in a number of ways; people can say it to themselves, form a picture in their mind's eye, and so on. We shall give all these kinds of temporary storage the general name of 'working memory' (Baddeley, 1986). Using working memory may be essential to hold the intention that the person is now pursuing, to remember interrupted tasks, as well as to remember bits of local knowledge as the car driver did in our example. In all cases, however, an outside observer cannot see directly what is happening.

In white-collar work, purely internal operations may form a higher proportion of the whole job, but the principles are the same. The intention to check on the non-delivery of an order will, in the experienced person, smoothly produce a sequence of sub-goals such as 'phone our stores reception people, phone the suppliers, phone British Rail, exit if the item is located'. The first of these will produce a sub-sub-goal of checking the internal extension number, this in turn a hand movement towards the directory, which is corrected when the book slips out of reach; once the number is found, the next movement is towards the phone, then to dial the stores. Only when the first call is over does the next sub-goal of contacting the suppliers come into play. The person who is new to the job will stop and think at each point, but the experienced one will begin the preliminaries of each stage even before the previous one has been completed.

As in purely motor skills, the novice feels that there is less time available than the expert does; and the number of separate actions to be considered is greater. If the situation is predictable and repetitive it will be easier for the experienced person to launch an appropriate sequence of actions without needing much monitoring of the consequences; conversely, if there are many random events, and uncertainty about the effects of actions, the load will be increased even for the expert. Notice also the importance of feedback; complex and abstract intentions such as 'ensuring adequate component supplies' cannot guide action if the person cannot find out whether or not the action is successful; information about the progress of one's actions is essential.

The hierarchy of actions extends therefore from low to high levels; from the grasping of an object to the meeting of a production schedule, the units getting larger at each level. At the higher levels, just as at the lower ones, problems are created by high external demand and by low control over the effects of actions.

AUTOMATICITY

Implicit and Explicit Knowledge

When we regard an action as intentional, we usually mean that the person can tell us what the purpose of the action was. There are cases when this does not apply, however. As practice builds up a structure of goals and sub-goals, the lower levels become less and less accessible to somebody's inquiry about what is going on. Novice typists know that they are trying to type first 't', then 'h', then 'e'; highly practised ones will say that they are typing 'the usual letter to Head Office', and may have difficulty in remembering whether or not they made some error at the key-stroke level. Thus, practised actions become less and less dependent upon an intention that the person can report, even if they were originally produced by such an intention. Rather, such actions trigger off when the sense-organs detect a particular pattern, simply because the situation is appropriate.

For some detailed acts, people cannot tell you what will be achieved by the act. This is most easily seen in the case of manual skills; very few people know that, when turning a bicycle to the left, they should start by moving the handlebars slightly in the opposite direction. When you first visit a country where the custom is to drive on the opposite side of the road from your own home, you will be shaken to find that you have a habit you did not know about, of stepping off the kerb while glancing last towards the direction from which traffic would come in *your* country. In the same way, workers who have operated a machine for many years may be able to secure higher output from it than the person who designed it; but not be able to say quite what it is that they do.

It is not only blue-collar work that shows these characteristics, however. A familiar example is the ability to produce grammatical sentences in your native language. You can do so without being able to give a formal statement of the rules of the grammar; and in fact even experts dispute what the rules are. The same effect can be shown in the laboratory (Reber, 1967). Again, in a business game one can show that somebody takes the correct decisions about raising a selling price or decreasing the size of a work-force, to achieve certain goals. Yet in the different context of being asked verbal questions about the task, the same person may not do well (Berry and Broadbent, 1984; Broadbent *et al.*, 1986).

In other words, some situations seem to call up familiar actions without needing the person to formulate a purpose that can be talked about to other people. Experienced managers, faced with a pile of paper describing the business game they are about to play, may start 'automatically' to search out the alternative possible decisions they can take, or to think of past situations from real life or previous games that showed one policy to be better than another. Yet they may not be able to put these strategies into words. Actions called up by a situation in this way will show all the usual hierarchic characteristics; to find the possible options may require a sub-goal of skimming the written instructions, or of contacting the supervisor of the game to explain a point, and so on.

However, such automatic actions can be started much faster than those that depend on working out the problem intellectually. If the person's experience has been appropriate, so that each complex situation calls out the correct action, such intuitive or 'seat of the pants' decisions may have considerable advantages. Correspondingly, it is dangerous to assume that one can learn decision-making, management of people, or interviewing by acquiring the ability to answer formal questions about those topics. It is also necessary for the person to call up the right information into working memory and act upon it when the appropriate situation arises. Acquiring that skill is a rather different kind of learning, usually based on practice in either real or simulated situations. (See Chapter 3.)

Slips of Action

Because familiar actions are released unintentionally by the context in this way, there can be spectacular and embarrassing disasters when an experienced person does something that is quite unintentional. For example, a pilot who suffered a failure of one engine on a propeller-driven aircraft has been known to reach out quickly and shut down an engine; but it was the *surviving* engine rather than the defective one. The right general action had taken place with a small detail wrong (Reason and Mycielska, 1982). Similarly, a train-driver may cancel a warning signal, as he is used to doing when passing early warning signals; but *this* time he should have taken the necessary steps to slow down. Less drastically, many of us will have had the experience of starting to drive forward at a traffic light when the neighbouring lane moves; until we notice that they are filtering down a side-turning and our lane is still stationary. Putting the kettle on the table and the teapot on the stove is minor by comparison, but it illustrates the same principle.

Errors due to automatic actions are probably impossible to eliminate completely, because usually it is very adaptive for actions to occur automatically and without requiring a pause for thought. The error only happens when the situation is not quite the usual one. Typically, the slip is an act that would often be correct, but not on this particular occasion. The action is similar to the action that would have dealt correctly with the situation, but there is some minor difference; the teapot goes on the stove, not out of the window, and the pilot shuts down an engine rather

17

than loosening his tie. Commonly, one part of the action changes places with a similar act that should come earlier; this is very noticeable in saying the kind of sentence that makes a 'tongue-twister'. Above all, the frequency of the slips is greater when the person is faced with a large number of demands in a short time.

These characteristics help to suggest ways of combating slips. The design of tasks ought to maximize the differences between actions and between successive parts of the same action. Actions needed in emergency should be practised to raise their probability; and one ought not to assume that a task people can do under normal conditions will still be error-free when a panic is on.

THE SEARCH FOR RELEVANT INFORMATION

Whether an action is started by an internal purpose or by some outside context, it is rare for the person to have immediately available all the information that is needed. As we have seen, a common first step in the action will be to set up a sub-goal of finding something in the surroundings; what is the phone number, what options are available for choice in this game, where is the invoice for this customer? As an alternative, there may be a sub-goal of finding something in memory; did I cancel the alarm, what did they tell us in training school about a low pressure indication in the containment vessel? These searches may present serious problems for people.

External Search, as in Visual Scanning

Suppose a novice looks for a particular object in a visual scene, such as the square that symbolizes a certain type of aircraft on an air-traffic control radar. The time taken to find the target will increase with the number of irrelevant items being displayed, and may become very great. It is almost as if some bit of the brain had to examine each object in turn until it found the right one. There are ways of arranging the search that are easier, however. Suppose the searcher knows that the target is coloured red and that most of the irrelevant ones are green. In that case the time will depend only on the number of red objects on the screen.

Objects of irrelevant colour do not count (Green and Anderson, 1956; Carter and Cahill, 1979). In general, giving the target some simple feature that is shared by no non-targets will help a lot. The same rule applies to hearing as well as to vision; if you want to hear what one voice is saying in a confused mixture, it is better to have that voice coming from one direction in space and all the irrelevant voices coming from a different direction.

Notice, though, that using a single feature to search in this way depends on your knowing *which* colour, or place, contains the information you want. It is no help to have a display unit covered with telephone numbers in various colours, until you know that customers are in green, suppliers in red and your own company numbers in blue. The single feature selects other information for further action, rather than simply working by grouping the material.

Quite often, a single feature cannot be used; but most of us have from our past experience learned sets or combinations of features that fall into common categories. For example, visual numbers and letters form such categories. We can find a number on a page of letters faster than we could possibly identify all the letters (J. Duncan, 1983). It follows therefore that we must be using some very undemanding analysis of the letters to set them to one side. This method of search is different from single-feature search, and we can call it 'categoric' for convenience. It is surprisingly efficient. One can show people very quickly a whole series of words, at rates of more than ten a second so that they cannot possibly read them all. Yet if before the list arrives people are asked to say the names of any animals in the series, they can quite often spot them. They must be learning enough about each word to know that it is not an animal name, even though they cannot identify every word (Lawrence, 1971).

Outside the laboratory, a similar mechanism can be seen when one scans a newspaper to find the football results. When one is designing the forms, displays, or reports that will be used in a job, it is important to allow this kind of search to operate. It is helpful, for instance, to use letters to refer to customers, numbers to suppliers, and mnemonic names for own departments, rather than just using numbers for all of them.

An even more important principle to ease the search task is that of 'constant mapping'. That is, the task is easier if possible targets on one occasion never occur as possible non-targets on another, and vice versa. If you *always* look for the occasional number in a large display of letters, then with enough practice you can reach a level of training where the letters hardly trouble you. If however you sometimes have to look for letters among numbers, and sometimes for numbers among letters, then practice has a less beneficial effect. Cluttering a visual display with things you always ignore is less harmful than misguidedly showing lots of information that you sometimes want and sometimes do not (Schneider and Shiffrin, 1977).

Naturally, even with constant mapping there will be some cases where the experienced person may still find it difficult to locate what is wanted among the irrelevant material. One obvious factor is the sheer degree of difference between the target and the irrelevant. It is harder to find a Q on a sheet of paper full of Os than it is on a sheet full of Xs. A more subtle point is that it is particularly hard to find a red Q amongst green Qs and red Xs. That is, when the target is defined by a combination of features, each of which can occur in an irrelevant item, then the number of irrelevant items remains important even after much practice (Treisman and Gelade, 1980). This kind of search should be avoided whenever possible. Suppose you are searching for the number of a particular order form among a pile of others. Do not expect to find the order number easily if it is *both* for a particular item *and* from a particular customer, in circumstances where the item and the customer also occur separately on other order forms! In such a case, you would do better to sort out all the forms from one customer and then search only those, looking for the item.

Internal Search Through Memory

It is important to distinguish the working memory we mentioned earlier, which holds things that change quite frequently, from memory for things that stay the same throughout long periods of your life. For example, the answer to the question 'How do you dismantle a Model X carburettor?' remains the same; the answer to 'What was the last carburettor you dismantled?' may change from day to day. In the former case, one wants the memory to endure and to be easily accessible; and this is primarily a matter of training and of the way the material has been organized in memory. In the case of working memory, one wants to forget the old answer as soon as it is inappropriate. Each type of memory has fairly sharp limits. Some of these limits cannot be much assisted by training, and only the arrangement of the job can help.

For example, a common method of holding something temporarily is to say it over and over again until it is needed, 'rehearsing' it. However, this method of storage only seems to work for as many words as one can say in a time of one to two seconds (Baddeley *et al.*, 1975). If, therefore, one is asked to transcribe, from a screen to a keyboard, code numbers consisting of twenty random digits, the use of internal speech can only succeed if one splits each number into several groups and keys each group separately. However, this then creates a problem of finding one's place after each group. A job that puts too much demand on working memory needs redesign.

There are other examples of jobs that may involve such problems. In air traffic control the controller has to retain the height, airspeed, and identity of a set of aircraft that may be changing. In using computers, the operator may have to hold in mind the mode currently in use, or the variable names that have been allocated. In the control of large process plants, the readings on distant instruments must be borne in mind after they have been checked. In conversation between people, the understanding of one sentence may depend on temporary storage of the content of earlier ones.

Because of the restriction on the length of time taken by a rehearsal, recall from the internal speech form of working memory is less reliable for long words than for short ones. Apart from this point, however, the extent of working memory seems to be limited by the number of items or units that have to be held, rather than by their nature. Thus the error rate on a six-letter group is not much higher than that for a six-digit group (Miller, 1956; Conrad, 1962, 1964). This can be useful; there are only a million different groups of digits of that length, but over three hundred million groups of letters. As the error rate goes up steeply with increasing length, it is a mistake to design a code number that is longer than you need for the number of different people, addresses, stores items, etc. that you want to reference. A typical credit-card number allows for the issue of cards to ten thousand million different people; fortunately, human beings (as opposed to machines) rarely have to recall them. When a bank asks a customer to give a personal identification number, to check that the customer does truly own a particular credit card, then they usually ask only for a number with a more modest four-digit length.

Training and experience play an important part in creating the units or 'chunks' that form this limit on working memory. The number of letters that can be held temporarily goes up if they form familiar units; twelve random letters would be a formidable load, but not the sequence FBI, UNO, EEC, WHO (Miller, 1956; Bower and Springston, 1970). People experienced in particular jobs build up similar units that are unknown to novices, so that a large number of separate radar echoes on a screen may be recalled as 'stacked aircraft over the beacon, safe situation to the South, converging tracks to the East'. The same principle of hierarchization seems to be operating here as in the building up of units of action, and indeed the two may be connected. There is the same danger that detail may be lost, coupled with the advantage that such detail is normally unimportant.

Other ways of increasing the amount in temporary memory include the use of particular sensory paths; a message that is spoken rather than written has an advantage in recall. This advantage is reduced when some later irrelevant speech sound arrives (Martin and Jones, 1979). Such findings make it look as if our neural systems for taking in speech can hold some extra information on top of that available from reading. Again, memory for images, pictures in the head, tends to interfere more with spatial activities such as tracking a target than memory for words does (Baddeley and Lieberman, 1980). If there is a danger that the job will involve temporary holding of information from one task while another is dealt with, then the two tasks should be arranged to differ from each other in this kind of way.

A particularly serious load on temporary memory may arise if tasks are interrupted, since the state of one task must be held in mind until it can be resumed. This is particularly true if the second task is itself interrupted; as can well happen if writing a letter is interrupted by a visitor and that in turn by a phone call. Very few such embedded interruptions can be tolerated; the rehearsal system and other important parts of working memory seem to be adapted to holding a single stream or package of information rather than separate units. In a rather similar way, the difficulty of understanding a sentence goes up rapidly as one goes from 'The sale that the bank arranged has been completed' through 'The sale that the bank that the boss chose arranged has been completed' to 'The sale that the bank that the boss that the takeover management that recently arrived appointed chose arranged has been completed' (E. Martin and K. H. Roberts, 1966; Herriot, 1968). Less blatantly, discussions in committees and interviews sometimes stray from the intended topic because repeated digressions take place. The original purpose has gone from the temporary memory of the participants; until perhaps the next day.

CHOICE

Once a person has set up goals, and after memory and the environment have been scanned for information, there comes the point of decision between several possible actions. Each of these might be appropriate in the general situation, but the particular details of this occasion make a single option the most correct. One can see this process particularly sharply in cases where one of several keys has to be struck, depending on which lamp or instrument is showing a signal on a display; or where a verbal message has to be passed that depends on what has been heard. Several factors are known to make the selection of the correct action difficult (Wickens, 1984):

Number of alternatives. When there are more possible actions, the time taken to react is greater, and the chance of an error greater.

Relative probability. If some actions are rarely required, but others often, then the rare ones will be slow in happening when they do occur. There is a high risk that one of the common actions will be incorrectly substituted instead, while the reverse does not often happen. (This is of course related to the 'slips of action' mentioned earlier.)

Compatibility. Some actions are much more natural in response to certain signals than others are. For example, think of a gas stove, on which one wants to turn off the left-hand rear burner because a saucepan of milk is boiling over. A vertical row of taps on the front of the stove, with perhaps one marked in small letters 'L R', to indicate 'Left Rear', is likely to cause a large problem of choice! Taps each adjacent to the burner controlled, or at least arranged in the same spatial pattern, reduce the time and chance of error (Shinar and Acton, 1978).

Similarly, it is better to move a lever left to make some controlled object go left, and right to go right, rather than the opposite. These relationships may result from practice throughout life, or possibly from better connections in the nervous system even without practice.

It seems plausible to think of an innate nervous connection to explain some facts. For example, it is much easier to repeat aloud a word that is heard than to press an appropriate key; and it is easier to press down a finger in response to a vibration on the tip of that same finger than on some other one. Some cases however are clearly due to social convention; in Britain, most people find it easier for an electrical switch to go down for on and up for off, whereas in the USA the reverse is the case. The conventions in house wiring systems have been opposite in the two countries for many years, and the general population have different experiences and expectations. Special care needs therefore to be taken in cases such as aircraft cockpits where both nationalities use the same equipment.

Lack of practice exaggerates other effects. As the light-switch example shows, people who have much experience of a certain choice are faster than those without. It is important to note that the other factors mentioned are more important if the level of practice is low. That is, the benefits of practice are larger when there is a choice between many different actions, and when the action was originally rather incompatible with the signal (Fitts and Seeger, 1953). It is of course important that one should practise the same action to achieve the same purpose, and not mix up experiences with different relationships. After riding a motor-cycle with a gear pedal that moves down for a higher gear and up for a lower gear, a new machine with the opposite relationship will seem hard to use at first. Practice will in that case greatly reduce the problem. To practise alternately on two machines with opposite relationships is however *not* recommended. Hence the importance of standardizing different pieces of equipment that may be used by the same worker.

TOTAL WORKLOAD

The Problem

We have seen a number of factors that will make a task go slowly or produce errors. Most actual jobs involve a mixture of more specific tasks. Pilots may have to control the height and heading of an aircraft, but also to talk to ground control, to keep an eye on the state of the engines, and to decide whether a storm requires a change of course. Equally, a shop assistant may have to enter the cost of purchases at a check-out keyboard, and give the right amount of money in change; but also to monitor a TV for shop-lifters, and when possible make suggestions to hesitating customers. A teacher may be discussing the project of one child, but also trying to find out the reason for a recent fall-off in that child's work, while keeping an eye on the activities of the rest of the class. Do difficulties in one task have any impact on another?

At one level, it is clear that some factors will cross over from one task to another. As we saw in the case of 'slips of action', one act may incorrectly replace another similar one. Hence if a task involves a set of push-buttons, adding a second task that also uses push-buttons will be more confusing than a task that uses sliding levers. On the display side also, adding visual signals for a second task to a visual display will be more confusing than adding an auditory task. Further, given the limits of the internal speech form of temporary memory, an overload could be produced by two tasks that both use internal speech. This could be true even though each task alone would produce no difficulty.

On top of these factors, however, extra tasks seem to interfere with each other in some way other than the use of similar actions or signals. Thus pilots may be worse at controlling aircraft height when a simul-taneous speech task is harder to hear, despite the lack of apparent similarity in the two tasks (Broadbent, 1958). Interference of this kind has been shown a number of times under better-controlled conditions in the laboratory. Each of the factors we have mentioned as increasing the difficulty of one task also increases the interference with other tasks. Unlikely things happening in one activity produce a disruption in the other, while likely events are less disruptive. Natural or compatible links between signal and action not only make a task easier, but also reduce the amount of disruption of another task (Broadbent and Gregory, 1965). Chunking actions into higher-order units makes them easier to combine with other activities; a motor programme that is highly predict-able can be carried on while producing only a minimum of interference with anything else that the person is doing. As one would expect from these facts, practice reduces the extent to which one task disrupts another, usually limiting the impairment to those moments when a true choice between actions is needed in each task.

We need therefore to think about the total amount that the person has to do, and not simply about each sub-task. A job may be impossible despite the fact that each of the component actions is within human limits.

Unfortunately there can be no simple rule for deciding when overload is present. It is no use looking at the number of signals on the display or the number of limb movements that are required. Interference depends on the probability of such events, and the degree of practice of the person. It also depends on other events that are not at present happening; because the worker is keeping an eye out for other signals, and that is a load even when the signals are absent. Further, one cannot evade the problem by assuring the worried pilot, shop assistant, or teacher that long exposure to the situation will make anything possible. Some tasks go on interfering with each other despite practice. We need methods of assessing each particular situation.

Methods of Assessment

Rating scales. One obvious approach is to ask the person. The best way to do this is through a standard set of questions that have been used on other groups and for which one knows the pattern of answers from various typical jobs. The difficulty is that people's stated opinions may be affected by things other than the job itself. They may be trying to impress you with their toughness, or with how unfairly they are being treated, and their answers could therefore be biased either way. Also, explicit knowledge is limited; customers may be complaining that they keep dialling your telephone number without getting an answer, but the operator may simply not know! Nevertheless, one can get useful information from comparing the answers to questions of different types to see if they are consistent (Rehmann *et al.*, 1983; Gopher and Braune, 1984).

Physiological measures. Measurements of heart rate, of the level of certain substances in the urine (Cox, 1978), or of the size of the pupil of the eye (Beatty, 1982), are known to change when people are working hard. One should beware of thinking that such measures are automatically free from the problems of rating scales; tense industrial relations, temperature, drinking coffee, and many other factors may well alter physiological measures when the workload remains the same. It is also rather difficult as yet to know whether a change is good or bad; heart rate or catecholamine excretion will change in pleasurably challenging situations as well as in those of overload as judged by performance or rating. On the other hand, such measures may reveal differences between situations that the person regards as identical, so they may well be useful.

Secondary task and trade-offs. A third method is to ask the person to treat their main work as primary, but also to do some other unimportant task as and when they can. For instance, to tap at regular intervals with a foot or hand that the main task does not use, or to try and say letters of the alphabet in random order. Occasional reaction signals can be presented, which workers are to acknowledge when they can. The argument is that any overload in the main work will be shown by impaired performance on the secondary task. However, some difficulties and precautions need to be noted (Ogden *et al.*, 1979).

First, it obviously will not do to have a secondary task that shows some local or mechanical interference with the main task, quite separate from any central overload. A supervisor, using speech a lot for the job, cannot say random numbers. Equally, a sewing machine operator cannot tap regularly with a free hand.

Second, a difficulty in the main task may increase rather than decrease the possibility of doing the secondary task. To take the simplest example, if a person is reading and the light goes out, that difficulty will not make it *harder* to answer heard speech messages. It might well make it easier. (This problem is known as that of 'data limitation' in the academic literature on attention.)

Third, people being studied may well change the way they do the main task because of the presence of the secondary one. For instance, if they normally remember something by saying it to themselves, but are asked to do a speech task as well, they may hold the information for the main task in a different part of working memory.

A partial, but still incomplete, solution to some of these problems is to ask the person to do the tasks several times with different degrees of priority for each. Sometimes saying the random numbers is the main task rather than a secondary one, sometimes the two are to be equal, sometimes the random numbers are of minor importance. From the shape of the resulting 'Performance Operating Characteristics' (the relative performance on the two tasks) one can draw rather more confident conclusions. It is very unsafe to compare a secondary task alone and in combination, without looking at the effects of priority (Norman and Bobrow, 1975, 1976).

After-effects. Finally, one may look in various ways at the state of the person at the end of the working day. This is a newer technique than the others and still under development; but there seems to be some sign that questionnaire answers of various kinds change if people have previously been exposed to higher job demand. There are also changes in some objective measures of performance. In the future this may be a useful addition to the tools available for measuring workload, but for practical purposes not yet (Broadbent, 1979, 1985).

SUMMARY

This chapter argues that even the least 'intellectual' forms of work require flexible achievement of sets of goals and sub-goals. All tasks therefore need clear feedback about the degree of success; and each action calls for processing of the current situation, of memory, and of the options for action. The need for such processing is reduced by consistency in the sequences of actions needed, high probability of occurrence of the correct action, low similarity of the signals for one action and those for another, or of one action to the next, and high naturalness or compatibility of the action to the particular signal. Good job design will therefore consider all these factors; but no job can be totally free from demand. On the one hand, a job without a processing requirement could be done by machine; on the other hand successful achievement is itself a higher-order goal for human beings.

Dangers of overload of processing can be assessed by a combination of methods, such as workers' opinions, physiological measures, secondary tasks, or after-effects; all of these must be treated with some caution, though all of them have their uses.

FURTHER READING

Many of the topics of this chapter are discussed in much more detail, and with the supporting evidence, by C. D. Wickens in *Engineering Psychology and Human Performance* (Merrill, 1984). The general organization of skilled performance is well covered in D. H. Holding, *Human Skills* (Wiley, 1981), and the detailed academic problems of motor output by C. R. Gallistel in *The Organization of Action* (Erlbaum, 1980). Specific methods of improving displays and controls appear in D. J. Oborne, *Ergonomics at Work* (Wiley, 1982), or E. J. McCormick and M. S. Sanders, *Human Factors in Engineering and Design* (McGraw-Hill, 1982).

Visual search and its theoretical relation to attention have been reviewed by R. M. Shiffrin in a chapter for the eagerly awaited second edition of *Stevens' Handbook of Experimental Psychology* edited by R. C. Atkinson and others (Wiley, in press). A review from a different point of view is given by D. E. Broadbent (1982). For those wanting highly technical detail on attention, *Varieties of Attention*, edited by R. Parasuraman and D. R. Davies (Academic Press, 1984), provides it. The different types of working memory are described by A. D. Baddeley in *Working Memory* (Oxford University Press, 1986).

Relations between implicit and explicit knowledge are considered in the chapter on process control in the volume by Wickens (1984). A chapter by J. Reason in the volume edited by Parasuraman and Davies (1984) discusses slips of action; and *Absent-Minded?* by J. Reason and K. Mycielska (Prentice-Hall, 1982) is a very readable account of recent approaches to the topic.

Workload, and particularly its assessment, are considered in *Mental Workload*, edited by N. Moray (Plenum, 1979). The approach to action stemming from studies of skill is now of considerable interest to psychologists in general; see, for example, W. Prinz and A. F. Sanders *Cognition and Motor Processes* (Springer, 1984). The possibilities opened up by studying action in terms of goal hierarchies are discussed in *Goal-Directed Behavior*, edited by M. Frese and J. Sabini (Erlbaum, 1985). Chapters by W. Hacker and by D. E. Broadbent in that volume consider particularly applications to industrial work.

2

Circadian Rhythms and
Hours of Work

Simon Folkard

Humankind has evolved as a diurnal species that is habitually active during daylight hours and sleeps at night. Since the Industrial Revolution, however, an increasing proportion of our workforce has attempted to overcome this natural bias, and to work at night. This colonization of the night can result in a number of problems for both the individuals concerned, and for the organizations employing them. This chapter summarizes these and the manner in which researchers from many disciplines, including psychologists, have attempted to solve them. Following an account of variations in psychological variables over the normal day, the concept of an underlying 'biological clock' is introduced. The characteristics of this clock are then considered in some detail to provide a framework within which the major problems associated with shiftwork are subsequently considered.

TIME OF DAY EFFECTS IN PERFORMANCE AND AFFECTIVE STATE

Psychologists have long recognized that people's efficiency at performing various tasks is not constant, but varies over the course of the day. Early theorists ascribed these variations to either a build-up of 'mental fatigue' with increased time awake (e.g. E. Thorndike, 1900) or to an underlying 'sleepiness rhythm', which was independent of whether people had actually slept (e.g. Michelson, 1897). As we shall see below, recent evidence suggests that both time awake and an underlying rhythm contribute to variations in 'alertness' or 'fatigue' over the day.

Task Demands and the Arousal Theory

Many of the early studies in time of day and performance were concerned with the optimization of work schedules in industrial and educational contexts. These, and subsequent studies, have indicated that at least for some types of task there are fairly consistent trends in efficiency over the day, but that the nature of the trend varies according to task demands. This is illustrated for three different types of task in Figure 2.1, in which the normal curves in body temperature (top curve) and in subjectively rated alertness (bottom curve) are also shown. In the case of performance, the efficiency at each time of day has been expressed as a percentage of the overall mean for the day.

Inspection of Figure 2.1 suggests that the performance trend over the day for a given task may depend on the short-term memory load involved in carrying out that task. Simple serial search performance (the second curve) involves little, if any, memory component and reaches a maximum in the evening. On more complex, 'working memory' tasks, such as logical reasoning, performance tends to improve to about midday and then declines (the middle curve). These require the use of a working memory system which involves a number of different cognitive sub-systems (e.g. short-term storage, processing throughput, etc.). It is likely that the pattern observed for this type of task is the outcome of a combination of different trends associated with the different cognitive mechanisms involved. When the task is one of 'immediate retention' which emphasizes memory mechanisms, such as that required to memorize digit strings or passages of text, then immediate recall of this material tends to be best early in the day and then steadily declines (see the fourth curve in Figure 2.1, and Folkard and Monk, 1980).

The apparent parallelism between performance on simple tasks and the temperature rhythm led to an early view that the diurnal variation in temperature was responsible for diurnal variations in performance (Kleitman, 1939). However, this link between performance and temperature was discredited when it was discovered that correlations between temperature and performance disappear when time of day is controlled for (Rutenfranz et al., 1972). It was then thought that the results could be explained in terms of an underlying rhythm in arousal or sleepiness that tended to parallel the diurnal variations in temperature (Colquhoun, 1971).

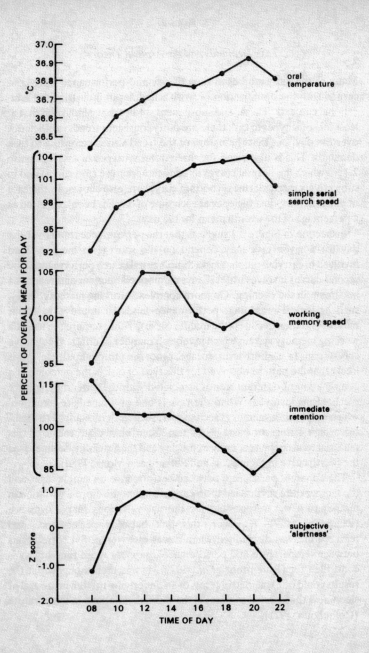

One reason why this arousal model was so enthusiastically adopted was that it could account for the many different trends observed. It assumes an inverted U-function relating performance to arousal such that, as arousal increases, performance on a given task improves until some optimal level of arousal is reached. Further increases in arousal result in a decline in performance due to 'over-arousal'. In addition, the model allows for different inverted U-functions for different levels of task difficulty, so that as task difficulty increases, the optimal arousal level declines. Thus the arousal model can account for the three performance trends shown in Figure 2.1, if it is assumed that task complexity increases from 'serial search' through 'working memory' to 'immediate retention'. In fact, although immediate retention is better in the morning, the available evidence indicates that delayed (seven days or more) retention is generally better following afternoon or evening presentation (see Folkard and Monk, 1985a). The arousal model can also account for this interaction, since there is some independent evidence that high arousal at presentation, while impairing immediate retention, may benefit delayed recall (Eysenck, 1982). Unfortunately, this explanatory power of the arousal model was also its downfall: many sets of data could be explained by invoking a particular point on the inverted U, and, as we shall see below, this model cannot account for the results of recent shiftwork studies.

Individual Differences

The arousal model also encounters problems in coping with individual differences in the trend in performance over the day. It has long been known that the trends for individual subjects may differ considerably from one another, and attempts have been made to link these differences to scores on personality tests, etc. There is some evidence that the performance of introverts on simple tasks may reach a maximum somewhat earlier than that of extroverts, and that this is paralleled by similar differences in body temperature (Blake, 1971). However, rather

Fig. 2.1   Average time-of-day trends from independent studies for temperature, three different performance measures, and subjective ratings of alertness. (See Folkard, 1983, for details of the individual studies.)

greater differences in the performance trends for simple tasks are associated with the dimension of 'morningness–eveningness', and these are *not* paralleled by a similar difference in the temperature rhythm as the arousal theory would suggest (see the review by Kerkhof, 1985).

'Morning' and 'evening' types are usually identified by means of a self-assessment questionnaire (e.g. Horne and Ostberg, 1976). This type of questionnaire attempts to distinguish between those who wake early and quickly, but who also feel tired relatively early at night ('Morning types') and those who take some time to get going properly in the morning but happily stay up late at night ('Evening types'). The performance of extreme morning types on a simple detection task has been found to deteriorate over most of the day, while that of evening types tended to improve (Horne *et al.*, 1980). In contrast, the time of the maximum body temperature of these two groups only differed by about one hour, which is insufficient, if it reflects arousal level, to account for the difference in the performance trend.

There is some question as to whether 'morningness–eveningness' is truly a stable trait rather than a reflection of recent habit, and there is a general, but as yet unproven, impression that both females and older people may show a greater tendency to be morning types. While it has yet to be established whether there are consistent sex differences in the trend in performance over the day, there is some suggestive evidence that females may be rather better in the morning (Baker *et al.*, 1984). Further, if these various individual differences reflect different trends in arousal level (despite the failure of the temperature rhythm to do so) then the nature of the differences in performance trends should depend on the demands of the task. Thus, if, in the morning, morning types are better than evening types on a simple detection task due to a higher level of arousal, they should be worse on a more memory-loaded task that is impaired by high arousal. This possibility has not been explored, although there is some evidence that differences associated with introversion are *not* dependent on task demands (Eysenck and Folkard, 1980).

Some Complications in Deriving Practical Recommendations

These differences in the performance trend over the day associated with task demands and individual differences complicate any recommendations for the scheduling of work over the normal day. Indeed, to some extent this complexity was recognized by early educational researchers in this area, who, on the basis of immediate memory and simple performance measures, suggested that more 'mentally taxing' school subjects should be taught in the morning (e.g. Gates, 1916). This recommendation is clearly questionable in the light of the superior delayed retention following afternoon presentation (Folkard *et al.*, 1977). The situation is further complicated by two other factors. First, some, but not all, authors have found a temporary decrease in simple performance in the early afternoon that has been interpreted as reflecting a similar decrease in arousal (Colquhoun, 1971). This decrease appears to be only partially dependent on the ingestion of food (see Folkard and Monk, 1985a) and may thus affect early afternoon performance whether or not individuals eat at lunchtime. Secondly, there are a large number of jobs, such as those involving simple manual dexterity or complex decision-making, for which no consistent performance trend over the day has been established. Thus, although we know that task demands affect performance trends, we cannot as yet make specific recommendations as to the best time of day to perform most given tasks.

Finally, even for those tasks for which consistent trends have been established (e.g. as in Figure 2.1), it is important to consider the contribution to these trends of the 'mental fatigue' associated with the time elapsed since waking rather than by the underlying 'sleepiness rhythm'. Thus, for example, the trend for immediate retention shown in Figure 2.1 might imply that people should get up earlier than normal in order to perform such tasks at 08.00. However, if they did so, and the trend were largely dependent on mental fatigue, then their ability may have deteriorated by 08.00. Such considerations become far more important when people shift their sleep/wake cycle by up to twelve hours in order to work on a night shift. Before considering performance under these conditions, we thus need some understanding of the factors underlying trends over the day.

CIRCADIAN RHYTHMS

Life on earth has evolved in an environment subject to regular and pronounced changes produced by planetary movements. The rotation of the earth on its own axis results in the 24-hour light/dark cycle, while its rotation around the sun gives rise to seasonal changes in light and temperature. The combined influence of the moon and sun leads to variations in gravitational pull on the earth's surface that are reflected in complex but predictable tidal movements of the sea every ~12·4 and ~24·8 hours. These resultant tides themselves vary in magnitude every ~14·7 and ~29·5 days according to the phase of the moon.

During the process of evolution, these periodic changes have become internalized so that they allow the organism to anticipate changes in the environment. Such an anticipatory ability clearly has an adaptive value for most species, and has presumably been strengthened through natural selection (Cloudsley-Thompson, 1980). It is now widely accepted that living organisms possess 'biological clocks', such that the environmental changes mentioned above are not merely responded to by organisms, but are actually predicted by them.

This 'anticipation' of environmental events is mediated by regular cyclic changes in body processes. In humans, the most pronounced of these are the ~24h 'circadian' ('around a day') rhythms that occur in almost all physiological measures (Minors and Waterhouse, 1981a). The most important characteristics of such rhythms are (a) their *period*, which is the time taken for one complete cycle of the rhythm (normally 24h), (b) their *phase*, which is a measure of their timing with respect to some external criterion such as clock time, and (c) their *amplitude*, which is usually measured as the difference between the maximum value and the average value over a complete cycle.

The Endogenous Clock(s)

The best evidence that human circadian rhythms are at least partially controlled by an endogenous biological clock comes from studies in which people have been isolated from their normal environmental time cues, or 'zeitgebers' (from the German for 'time givers'). In their pioneering studies, Aschoff and Wever (1962) isolated individual subjects from all environmental time cues in a 'temporal isolation unit' for up to nineteen days, while Siffre (1964) lived in an underground cave for two months. In both studies, the subjects continued to wake up and go to sleep on a regular basis, but instead of doing so on a ~24h basis, they did so on average every ~25h.

The circadian rhythms in other physiological measures, including body temperature and urinary electrolytes, typically show an identical period to that of their sleep/wake cycle.

However, about a third of the subjects studied have spontaneously shown a rather different pattern of results that has important theoretical and practical implications. In these subjects, the sleep/wake cycle and body temperature rhythms have become 'internally desynchronized', such that they run with distinctly different periods from one another. The temperature rhythm continues to run with an average period of ~25h, while the sleep/wake cycle shows a much shorter or longer period than either this or ~24h (Wever, 1979). Interestingly, this phenomenon of 'spontaneous internal desynchronization' has been shown to occur more frequently in older subjects, and in those with higher neuroticism scores. Further, while female subjects are more likely to desynchronize by a shortening of their sleep/wake cycle, males are more likely to do so by lengthening it. These individual differences may relate to the dimension of 'morningness' (see above) and may have important implications for the adjustment to shiftwork (see below).

At a more theoretical level, the fact that the temperature rhythm and sleep/wake cycle can run with distinctly different periods from one another has been taken to suggest that the human 'circadian system' comprises two, or perhaps more, processes. The first of these is a relatively strong oscillator that is dominant in controlling the circadian rhythm in body temperature (and in other measures such as urinary potassium, and plasma cortisol) and is relatively unaffected by external factors. The second is a rather weaker process that is dominant in controlling the sleep/wake cycle (and other circadian rhythms such as those in plasma growth hormone and urinary calcium) and is considerably more prone to external influences. There is some debate as to whether this second process is oscillatory in nature, but there seems to be general agreement that some circadian rhythms are dominantly controlled by the strong oscillator, while others are more influenced by the weaker process.

These two processes are thought to be asymmetrically coupled such that the strong oscillator exerts a considerably greater influence on the weaker process than vice versa. Thus, for example, internally desynchronized subjects show such a strong tendency to wake up at a particular point of the temperature rhythm, irrespective of when they went to sleep, that their sleeps can vary in duration from four to sixteen hours (Czeisler *et al.*, 1980; Zulley *et al.*, 1981). Further readings in this complex but fascinating area are suggested at the end of the chapter. The important points to bear in mind are (1) that circadian rhythms in different measures are *not* all controlled by a single system, so that different rhythms may adjust at very different rates from one another when people work at unusual times of day, and (2) that sleep is likely to be disrupted unless the temperature rhythm has adjusted to such a change.

Entrainment by Zeitgebers

Under normal circumstances both processes will be entrained to a 24h period by strong natural zeitgebers, including the light/dark cycle, and, in the case of humans, knowledge of clock time and the behaviour of other members of society. As a result, our circadian rhythms normally show a fixed phase relationship to one another such that, for example, our urinary adrenalin level reaches a maximum around midday, while our body temperature peaks at about 8.0 p.m. Similarly, all other circadian rhythms will reach their maxima at their appointed time, allowing us to fall asleep at night and waking us up in the morning. The occasional late night may affect those rhythms controlled by the weaker process, but are less likely to upset the strong oscillator and hence our body temperature rhythm and the time at which we spontaneously wake up.

However, this inherent stability in the human circadian system can pose problems if a mismatch arises between our internal timing system and our external time cues. The simplest example of this occurs when people fly across time zones, since *all* the zeitgebers change. A flight from Europe to the USA involves crossing several time zones, so that on arrival our timing system is 5 to 9 hours too early for the local zeitgebers. Although people seldom experience problems falling asleep after their arrival, their body temperature rhythms usually take about a week to delay their timing by the appropriate amount (K. E. Klein *et al.*, 1972). For the first few nights, this often results in people waking up in the early hours of the morning and being unable to get back to sleep. The rhythms in other processes adjust at different rates, presumably depending on the degree to which they are controlled by the strong oscillator or weaker process. As a result, the normal phase relationship between rhythms breaks down and is only slowly re-established as the various rhythms adjust to the new time zone. This 'internal dissociation' between rhythms is thought to be responsible for the 'jet-lag', i.e. feelings of disorientation or general malaise, experienced by some people.

These feelings of jet-lag are normally worse following an eastward flight, that requires an advancing of the body's timing system, than following a westward one requiring a delay. This 'directional asymmetry' effect is thought to be related to the fact that the endogenous period of our circadian system is ~25h. Thus, in the absence of any zeitgebers our rhythms will tend to delay rather than to advance. This bias towards a delay will assist adjustment to westward flights, and inhibit it to eastward ones. As we shall see below, this difference has implications for the design of shift systems.

When shiftworkers go on to the night shift, most environmental zeitgebers do not change, and thus discourage adjustment of the circadian system. The natural light/dark cycle, the clock time, and most social cues remain constant. The timing of work for some shiftworkers can be delayed by up to sixteen hours, and that of sleep by up to twelve hours. From what we have learnt so far, it is clear that the adjustment of a shiftworker's timing system to these changes, if it occurs at all, will be very slow. We shall return to this and associated problems later in the chapter.

Experimental Manipulations of Zeitgebers

In view of their important theoretical and practical implications, a large number of studies have examined the role of different zeitgebers in entraining the circadian timing system. For most plants and lower animals, the light/dark cycle appears to be the most powerful zeitgeber. In humans, the situation is more complicated. In his pioneering studies, Wever (1979) provided subjects with an artificial 24h light/dark cycle by means of an illuminated panel in the ceiling of an isolation unit. Although the rhythms of some subjects were entrained by these artificial zeitgebers to a 24h period, those of others were not and free-ran with their endogenous period of ~25h. However, if subjects were requested to go to bed when the ceiling lights faded, and to get up at 'dawn', then their rhythms were entrained to this artificial 24h day. Indeed, simply giving subjects auditory signals requesting them to go to bed or to get up, without any time cues from a light/dark cycle, has proved sufficient to entrain their rhythms. Thus, it would appear that for humans the most effective zeitgebers are of an essentially informative or social nature.

These 'informative' zeitgebers can be used in experimental settings to simulate the abrupt changes associated with shiftwork and jet-lag, but their timing can also be changed gradually to determine the range of entrainment of different rhythms. Thus the subject can initially be exposed to 24h artificial zeitgebers, and then the period of these be progressively shortened or lengthened by a small amount each 'day'. The sleep/wake cycle follows these changes in the zeitgeber period very closely over a wide range of periods. However, the circadian rhythms in body temperature, and in various other physiological functions such as urinary potassium, have a far more restricted range of entrainment and can normally only be entrained down to a period of ~23h or up to ~27h. Beyond this, many rhythms 'break out' from the sleep/wake cycle and free-run with their endogenous period of ~25h. By this means, internal desynchronization can be induced in all subjects.

This sort of study is important for two reasons. First, it allows us to estimate the minimum and maximum period with which different rhythms can run, and hence the speed with which they could theoretically adjust to the abrupt changes associated with shiftwork and rapid time-zone transitions. Secondly, this type of study allows the behaviour of the rhythms in different functions to be compared. Thus rhythms dominantly controlled by the strong oscillator described above should behave in a similar manner to that in body temperature, while those more dependent on the weaker process should follow the sleep/wake cycle for longer.

Similarities in the behaviour of different rhythms may allow us to extrapolate from one to the other in shiftwork situations. Thus, for example, the rhythm in simple serial search speed has been found to behave in a very similar manner to that in body temperature (Folkard *et al.*, 1983), suggesting that both should adjust to shiftwork at the same rate. The importance of this is that body temperature measures, which are relatively easy to obtain, could be used as an indirect measure of simple serial search speed, which is rather more difficult to assess in most shiftworking situations. Conversely, the rhythms in performance on more memory-loaded cognitive tasks, and in subjective ratings of alertness, behave rather differently from that in body temperature, indicating that the latter may be a rather poor 'marker' for these processes (Folkard *et al.*, 1983, 1985a).

Finally, it is worth pointing out that this type of study may also have tremendous theoretical implications for psychology, by allowing us to assess the degree of relationship, if any, between different psychological and physiological processes (Folkard *et al.*, in press). Thus, if the rhythms in two processes always behave in the same manner, this would imply some relationship between them. Conversely, if they can be separated, then they cannot be causally related. Wever (1983) therefore views this type of study as a temporal analogue of surgical or chemical lesion studies, that, unlike the latter, can be performed on intact humans.

Exogenous Effects

Measurements of any physiological or psychological variable reflect not only the activity of our endogenous circadian timing system, but also a number of exogenous factors. These factors may themselves show a ~24h pattern and thus enhance or diminish the magnitude of the overt circadian rhythm, depending on their phase relationship to the endogenous component. Thus, for example, body temperature is known to fall when we go to sleep, and to rise as a result of physical (and perhaps mental) activity, quite independently of any endogenous circadian rhythm. This can result in spuriously fast estimates of adjustment of the body temperature rhythm to shiftwork.

Some rhythms, such as those in noradrenalin and pulse rate, appear to be entirely exogenous in origin, while others, such as those in body temperature and urinary adrenalin and potassium, are at least partially endogenous. In these latter cases the relative magnitude of the endogenous and exogenous components can be estimated from various types of temporal isolation studies. This is illustrated in Figure 2.2 for the temperature and alertness rhythms. While both these rhythms have an endogenous component, that of the temperature rhythm is relatively small in comparison to its exogenous component.

Thus some rhythms will be virtually entirely dependent on the timing of sleep and wakefulness, and the concomitant timing of activity and meals. Others will be relatively uninfluenced by these factors and will

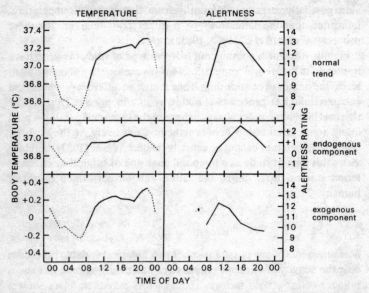

Fig. 2.2 The normal trends in temperature and alertness (top panels) broken down into their 'endogenous' (middle panels) and 'exogenous' (lower panels) components. The dotted line indicates readings taken when subjects were, or would normally be, asleep. (Derived from data of Minors and Waterhouse, 1981a, and Folkard *et al.*, 1985.)

depend more on the strong endogenous oscillator which, as we have seen, is likely to adjust rather slowly, if at all, to the shifts of the sleep/wake cycle associated with night work.

SHIFTWORK

There seems little doubt that shiftwork can result in a variety of problems for the individual worker. These range from difficulties with sleep that depend, at least in part, on a disturbed circadian timing system, through impaired subjective (and perhaps objective) measures of health, to an impoverished social life. These symptoms are often reflected in general feelings of malaise and may result in various consequences for both the individual and the employer.

It is generally assumed that disturbed circadian rhythms are central to the problems experienced by an individual shiftworker, and, indeed, Reinberg *et al.* (1984) have recently provided dramatic evidence to support this view. They found that workers who had medical and social problems as a result of shiftworking tended to show internal desynchronization between their body temperature rhythm and sleep/wake cycle, while those who were able to tolerate shiftwork better did not.

The problems of shiftwork do not arise equally in all individuals, or with all shift systems. Indeed, it has been estimated that some 10 per cent of shiftworkers positively enjoy their pattern of working, while about 60 per cent are able to tolerate it reasonably well. It is only a minority (20 to 30 per cent) of shiftworkers who positively dislike shiftwork and hence are presumably 'at risk' (Harrington, 1978). Nor do all shift systems result in problems for (some of) the individuals employed on them. As we shall see below, there is a great diversity of shift systems, and it appears to be only those that necessitate a change in the timing of sleep that may cause trouble (Kogi, 1985).

The Nature and Prevalence of Shiftwork

The prevalence of shiftwork has increased considerably over the past fifty years in most industrialized countries, and is currently rapidly increasing in the developing countries (Kogi, 1985). There appear to be three main reasons for this that can be broadly classified as social, technological and economic. Thus there is an increased demand for the provision of twenty-four-hour services such as medical care and transportation, while technological advances have resulted in the use of 'continuous processes' in, for example, the steel and chemical industries. However, the major reason for this increased prevalence appears to be economic, in that shiftwork can maximize the return on capital investment.

In view of this, it is not surprising that the prevalence of shiftwork varies dramatically with both the size and nature of the organization concerned. In France, the prevalence in 1974 varied from less than 10 per cent in companies with fewer than fifty employees to over 40 per cent in those with more than 500, and from less than 2 per cent in the building trade to over 70 per cent in metal processing (Rutenfranz *et al.*, 1977).

Comparisons between countries are complicated by inconsistencies in their criteria. Nevertheless, in most industrial countries about 20 per cent of those engaged in manufacturing industries work on some form of shift system. Statistics for developing countries are not normally available, but in Singapore in 1980 some 37 per cent of those in manufacturing industries worked shifts, apparently for purely economic reasons (Ong and Hong, 1982). These economic factors also appear to be resulting in the spread of shiftwork out of traditional shiftworking industries into white-collar jobs, such as computer operating, although there are few statistics on the prevalence of shiftwork in these jobs.

This sizable minority of the workforce is engaged on a wide variety of shift systems. These can be classified according to their key features (see Kogi, 1985), the most important of which is whether or not the system involves a displacement of normal sleep time. Other features include whether or not an individual always works on the same shift (e.g. evening or night) or rotates from one shift to another, and, if so, the speed and direction of rotation. However, even so-called 'permanent' night workers typically rotate from a nocturnal routine on work days to a diurnal one on their days off. Thus, in terms of our endogenous circadian timing system, the label of a 'permanent' shift system is somewhat misleading. Finally, it is also worth noting that the speed and direction of rotation of a shift system determine the mean period that an individual's circadian system would have to run at in order to stay adjusted to it.

Disturbed Rhythms and Sleep

Studies of the effects of shiftwork on circadian rhythms in physiological functions have been largely confined to the body temperature rhythm. This is mainly due to the ease with which temperature readings can be taken, and is perhaps unfortunate in view of the large exogenous component in this rhythm (see Figure 2.2). Nevertheless, there is considerable agreement that, whereas the body temperature rhythm is often disturbed by working at night, it rarely adjusts completely over a normal span of night duty and rapidly reverts to its normal state on 'days off'. Indeed, any adjustment to night work that is observed could simply reflect a shifted exogenous component and an unaltered endogenous one. Thus the temperature rhythm typically shows a 'flattening' or reduction in amplitude but little evidence of a real phase shift. An example of this is shown in Figure 2.3 from a simulated shiftwork study of Colquhoun *et al.* (1968).

On the sixth successive night shift (solid line), temperature continued to fall rather than rise over the work period. By the twelfth night shift (broken line) the rhythm had flattened to such an extent that any estimate of phase would be fairly meaningless. Further, large scale surveys in Germany and Japan indicate that it is extremely rare for people to work more than six or seven successive night shifts (Kogi, 1985). Studies of other physiological rhythms for which there is evidence of an endogenous component (e.g. urinary potassium and plasma cortisol) typically show a similar pattern of results to body temperature. In contrast, some rhythms, such as pulse rate and urinary noradrenalin, may show relatively good adjustment to night work, but this presumably simply reflects their largely exogenous origin (Akerstedt, 1985).

One of the major complaints of shiftworkers is that their day sleeps between successive night shifts are disturbed. They often attribute this to increased environmental noise (Rutenfranz *et al.*, 1981) and that may well be a contributing factor. However, it seems probable that the major cause of disturbed day sleeps is that they take place at an inappropriate

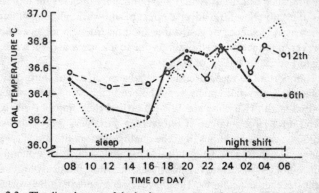

Fig. 2.3 The disturbances of the body temperature rhythm on the 6th and 12th days of a spell of 12 successive night duties. The dotted line shows the normal rhythm phase shifted to take account of the changed schedule, and thus represents a hypothetical 'totally adjusted' rhythm. (Derived from Colquhoun *et al.*, 1968.)

phase of the endogenous timing system (see above). Thus, unless this system has adjusted to night work, day sleeps will be of reduced duration compared to night sleeps. This has been confirmed by both polygraphic recordings and large-scale surveys (Akerstedt, 1985; Kogi, 1985). On average, the day sleeps of shiftworkers are between 1 to 4 hours shorter than normal night sleeps, and this is largely due to a reduction in Stage 2 and rapid eye movement (REM) sleep, rather than in the deeper slow wave sleep (SWS). Loss of SWS, but not that of REM or Stage 2 sleep, is typically 'made up' on recovery night sleeps taken on 'off days'. Thus night workers show a cumulative sleep deficit over successive night shifts, which is only partially restored on their rest days (Akerstedt, 1985).

Associated Medical and Social Problems

These disturbances of circadian rhythms and sleep undoubtedly contribute to the other major complaints of shiftworkers, namely impaired health and impoverished social life. The general feelings of malaise experienced by shiftworkers are similar to those associated with jet-lag and are reflected in an increased incidence of various psychosomatic conditions (Rutenfranz *et al.*, 1985). Objective measures of physical ill-health, such as cardiovascular and pulmonary diseases, or mortality rates, typically show little adverse effect of shiftwork, although there is an increased incidence of gastro-intestinal disorders in night workers. However, it is unclear whether this is due to the stress of night work, or to disturbed eating habits, or both.

It is important to recognize that the adverse effects of shiftwork are chronic, and may take many years before manifesting themselves in impaired health (Kundi *et al.*, 1979). Further, their impact is likely to depend on a large number of intervening variables, such as housing conditions, work conditions, and the quality of social life which is itself influenced by shiftwork. Thus shiftworkers are less likely to be members or office-holders in various organizations, including political parties and parent–teacher associations. They have fewer friends than day workers, and those they do have tend to be restricted to fellow shiftworkers (see J. Walker, 1985). Even contact with members of their own family tends to occur at unusual and often inconvenient times of day. The main advantage of night work, often cited by those 10 per cent who positively enjoy it (see above), is an enhanced ability to pursue solitary hobbies (e.g. gardening or fishing) during daylight hours.

Impaired Productivity and Safety

In view of the disturbed rhythms, partial sleep deprivation, general feelings of malaise, and impoverished social life of nightworkers, it is perhaps not surprising that most of the available evidence suggests that the night shift is associated with impaired productivity and safety! Unfortunately, this body of evidence is not large, since it has proved extremely difficult to obtain the relatively continuous and uncontaminated measurements of job performance necessary to assess the extent of this problem. Thus, in some shiftworking situations, impaired nighttime productivity could reflect the use of less efficient machines, since their maintenance is often confined to the day shift (see Meers, 1975). Most of the studies that have overcome this and related problems are summarized in Figure 2.4. In general, they agree that, when working on the night shift, performance speed is reduced, and error and potential accident frequencies are increased.

Laboratory studies, and field studies in which interpolated performance measures have been used, suggest that this impairment of performance efficiency at night is in part due to disturbed circadian rhythms, and in part to the cumulative sleep deficit that accrues over successive night shifts. Early researchers in this field emphasized the parallelism found between the circadian rhythm in body temperature and that in performance efficiency on some tasks (see above). They argued that poor night-shift performance stems from the fact that the circadian rhythm in temperature is at a low ebb at night and adjusts only slowly, if at all, over successive night shif's. Permanent shift systems were thus recommended on the grounds that these might maximize the adjustment of the temperature, and hence performance, rhythm. However, such a recommendation fails to take account of either the rapid readjustment that occurs on days off, or of the cumulative sleep debt that builds up over successive night shifts.

In addition, as we have seen, the concept of a single performance rhythm is erroneous. Like physiological rhythms, performance rhythms differ not only in their normal phase (see Figure 2.1) but also in the degree to which they are endogenously controlled. Indeed, there is

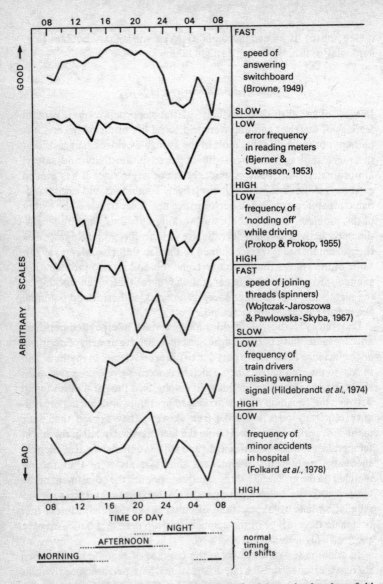

Fig. 2.4 The trends in various measures of productivity and safety from field studies of shift work. (See Folkard and Monk, 1979, for further details.)

evidence that the performance of memory-loaded, cognitive tasks, which are becoming increasingly common in paid employment, may be performed particularly well at night provided there is little adjustment of the individual's temperature rhythm (Folkard and Monk, 1980, 1985a). Further, and contrary to the arousal model (see above), the adjustment of this type of circadian rhythm which peaks at night has been found to occur relatively rapidly (e.g. Hughes and Folkard, 1976). Such adjustment will result in a progressive impairment of night-shift performance, and so suggests that, for this type of task, shift systems that minimize adjustment (i.e. rapidly rotating shift systems) may be preferable (see Monk and Folkard, 1985). It is thus noteworthy that the only field study to have found superior performance on the night shift concerned the logging errors of computer operators (a task with a high memory load) on a rapidly rotating shift system (Monk and Embrey, 1981).

From a performance point of view, such rapidly rotating systems also have the advantage of minimizing the cumulative sleep debt which can itself result in impaired performance (Tepas *et al.*, 1981; Tilley *et al.*, 1982; R. T. Wilkinson, 1965). Indeed, in a recent study Vidaček *et al.* (1986) have shown that even for a simple task, the beneficial effects of circadian adjustment may be outweighed by the detrimental effects of cumulative sleep debt after only three successive night shifts. There is also evidence that this sleep debt may affect productivity and safety, not only directly, but also indirectly through a short-lived temporary paralysis (probably a waking form of 'sleep paralysis'). The incidence of this paralysis increases in an approximately exponential manner over successive night shifts and may temporarily prevent workers from performing their job (Folkard *et al.*, 1984). In general, it would thus appear that, unless the shiftworker is engaged in a particularly crucial, but relatively simple, task, the advantages of permanent shift systems may be outweighed by their disadvantages. The alternative of using rapidly rotating shifts will minimize the cumulative sleep debt and may be particularly advantageous for the night-time performance of the increasingly common memory-loaded, cognitive tasks.

Possible interventions

There are three main forms of intervention that may help to alleviate the problems associated with shiftwork. First, the shift system can be tailored to suit the needs not only of the particular requirements of the job, as we have just seen, but also of the individuals and organization concerned. The earlier bias towards permanent systems that assumed complete adjustment of circadian rhythms would occur has now virtually been reversed to a bias in favour of rapidly rotating systems that should minimize the disruption of such rhythms. Theorists tend to agree that slowly rotating shift systems are probably undesirable, and that shifts should delay (i.e. morning–evening–night) rather than advance (night–evening–morning) (e.g. Czeisler *et al.*, 1982).

The choice between rapidly rotating and permanent systems needs to be considered, not only in relation to performance efficiency (see above), but also in relation to medical and social criteria. Unfortunately, there are insufficient medical data available for any valid comparison to be made, although it is arguable that the reduced sleep deprivation and undisrupted circadian rhythms associated with rapidly rotating systems may make them the lesser of two evils. Further, when social criteria are considered, a widespread resistance to change results in most shiftworkers favouring their current system. Nevertheless, when rapidly rotating shift systems *have* been introduced, they have proved highly acceptable, since they allow at least some normal social activity every week (J. Walker, 1985). However, some workers find them disorienting and, because of the difficulty of integrating them with the seven-day week, find it difficult to plan their social activities ahead.

The two other forms of intervention are more concerned with the individual, and are based on individual differences in tolerance to shiftwork, and on the development of appropriate coping strategies. These will undoubtedly prove to be interrelated, in that it seems unlikely that the same coping strategies will prove effective for all individuals. Further, our understanding of individual differences is limited by the lack of any *predictive* validity for the factors thought to be important. Thus there is some evidence from cross-sectional studies that morning types, introverts, those with rigid sleeping habits and those scoring high on neuroticism complain more about various problems associated with shiftwork (Folkard *et al.*, 1985b). What is not known, is whether these individuals have become morning types, introverts, etc., as a result of these problems, or vice versa. Clearly there is a strong need for longitudinal studies in this area to assess the predictive validity of these measures. However, even if their predictive validity can be established, they could not readily be used for selection purposes since candidates might well fake desirable scores on them. Rather, they might be useful in counselling individuals as to whether they would be likely to tolerate shiftwork and, if so, how best to develop adequate coping strategies.

Coping strategies are essentially concerned with the scheduling of various synchronizers that are under voluntary control. The most important of these is probably the timing of sleep. Sleeps taken at a regular time are likely to stabilize circadian rhythms, while an irregular sleeping pattern may disrupt them. Indeed, it has been shown that four hours' sleep taken during the night, in combination with an additional four hours taken at an irregular time of day, is sufficient to prevent the disruption of most rhythms (Minors and Waterhouse, 1981b). In practice, many shiftworkers *do* take a night-time nap (often unofficially) although this is seldom of four hours' duration (Kogi, 1985). However, there is some evidence to suggest that our endogenous timing system 'expects' a short sleep in the early afternoon, and it is possible that a regular four hours' sleep taken at this time might prevent the disruption of circadian rhythms. In fact, most nightworkers go to bed as soon as they can after their night shift, i.e. at about the time when most people are waking up, and this may well account for the sleep disturbances they experience. If they delayed their sleep until the early afternoon, this might reduce their problems considerably.

It has also been argued that the timing of meals may be an important synchronizer of circadian rhythms (Ehret *et al.*, 1978) but, whereas there is some evidence to support this suggestion from studies of lower animals, there is as yet no good evidence for this in humans (Reinberg, 1983). Finally, regular social and leisure activities at a relatively constant time of day will probably help to stabilize the circadian system, while irregular activities may disrupt it.

The importance of these various coping strategies should not be underestimated. In a recent exploratory study it was found that even those who, on the basis of individual difference measures, were apparently unsuited to shiftwork, could cope with it very well if they adopted appropriate strategies, while those whose test scores indicated that they were well suited to shiftwork failed to cope if they used inappropriate strategies (Adams *et al.*, 1986). Thus it would appear that individual differences in the potential to cope with night work may be over-ridden by the use of appropriate or inappropriate coping strategies. Clearly this is an important area for future research aimed at identifying appropriate coping strategies for different types of individual.

SUMMARY

A substantial proportion of our workforce is employed on some form of shift system. This can result in a variety of problems for both the individuals concerned and the organizations employing them. Central to these problems is the fact that we have evolved as a diurnal species that habitually sleeps at night, and this is reflected in our biological timing system. This system is disrupted when people work at abnormal times, and this disruption is thought to mediate the shiftworkers' problems. Consideration of the nature of our timing system allows a better understanding of these problems, and suggests ways in which they may best be alleviated.

FURTHER READING

Most of the topics covered in this chapter are considered in greater detail by various authors in S. Folkard and T. H. Monk (eds.), *Hours of Work: Temporal Factors in Work Scheduling* (Wiley, 1985b), which also has an extensive bibliography for those wishing to pursue this area.

General introductions to biological rhythm research include J. L. Cloudsley-Thompson's *Biological Clocks, Their Functions in Nature* (Weidenfeld and Nicolson, 1980), which also covers their adaptive significance, and D. S. Saunders' *An Introduction to Biological Rhythms* (Blackie, 1977). Human circadian rhythms and some of their practical implications are covered by both D. S. Minors and J. M. Waterhouse, *Circadian Rhythms and the Human* (Wright PSG, 1981a), and M. C. Moore-Ede, F. M. Sulzman and C. A. Fuller, *The Clocks That Time Us* (Harvard University Press, 1982).

3

Training and the Acquisition of Knowledge and Skill

Rob Stammers

Any discussion of training must make clear the context in which it occurs. The context chosen for this paper is an 'occupational' one. By making that explicit it becomes possible to clearly separate the present subject-matter from learning exercises conducted within an educational context. Early attempts at separating training from education tended to focus upon the specificity of objectives of training versus education, and also emphasized that training tends to minimize individual differences whereas education sometimes tries to maximize them.

Both training and education can be seen to be areas of the applied psychology of learning, and as such have a common theoretical base. The distinction made above in terms of objectives and individual differences can break down under close examination. In many educational exercises there will be very specific objectives, such as learning a particular mathematical procedure, or learning a specific set of dates and events. Similarly, in a training context there will be occasions when there is a need to maximize individual differences, for example in producing a team of people to carry out certain group tasks where a range of different contributions is expected. Thus some people prefer to speak generally of *instructional* activities, where the aim is to produce some degree of control over learning events whatever the context of these events.

While it might be possible in fairly general terms to separate education from training, it is clear that firm barriers do not exist. One current interest is in 'continuing' education, learning activities that can go on throughout life; there is also management education, where broad-based instructional activities are put forward to prepare managers for new situations, such as the impact of new technology. Having said this, it should be clear that in preparation for occupational tasks the objectives will be somewhat narrower than those of education. In the main, the learning will be directed towards specific tasks in specific contexts rather than the learning of bodies of knowledge for their own sake or as a basis for additional learning in the future.

Another theme central to this chapter is that of a distinction between knowledge and skill. A simplistic interpretation is that knowledge is knowing 'what' to do in situations, and skill is knowing 'how'. In many occupational situations the interest is in the competence that someone has in performing sets of tasks ascribed to them. As such there is a tendency to think of their activities as being 'skills', i.e. competent performance in relation to particular goals. An attempt might be made to separate skills from knowledge, the possession of concepts and rules that can be verbally described by the performer. Where physical performance is involved, tasks are again often typified as skills; and where the individual brings to bear higher-order cognitive capabilities, situations are often viewed as being more knowledge-based.

While the classical distinction can be maintained, it is suggested here that in most training situations what is communicated to the individual consists of knowledge in the form of concepts and rules. This knowledge may form the basis of the individual's competence in the situation, via its recall and use to meet certain task demands. Alternatively the knowledge may be taken and developed into skill in the sense that it will guide performance and become the basis of a competent interaction with the task environment to produce the desired results. Taken in this way it is possible to have a fairly broad view of skill (e.g. Singleton (ed.), 1978, 1981). Thus knowledge may be acquired in its own right, e.g. learning about a company's products and their specifications; or knowledge may be taken further in the performance of tasks, e.g. the operation of equipment and understanding its capabilities.

It is also important to keep a broad view of what skilled performance is. For example, the descriptive models that have been put forward to describe the patterning and organization of human perceptual motor performance have been extended to cover the situation of social skill (e.g. Argyle, 1983). Here the interaction of two people in, for example, an interview is likened to the interaction of the skilled performer in human–machine interaction or in a sports situation. Patterning of activity on the part of the performer is partly determined by the sequence of external events, with skilled performers adapting to the changing demands put on them by the environment. Occupational training situations therefore must be viewed broadly. Many textbooks take as their model the human–machine system, but with the growth of service industries and office-based jobs a broader view is needed. Indeed, many occupational tasks consist of human–human interaction.

Furthermore, training activities should not be viewed in isolation from other areas of occupational psychology and ergonomics. There are clear overlaps between personnel selection and training. A training programme cannot be produced unless something is known about the characteristics of the population from which trainees are being selected. Similarly, training activities can be much simplified if the ergonomics of the situation are appropriate. Training activities will be prolonged if the system has been badly designed. Many training problems may be eliminated by the adequate design of equipment and documentation, one example being written instructions and manuals. In any task area where the aim is to produce trained personnel, able to cope with the task demands, it must be assumed that a judicious mix of personnel selection, training and ergonomics activities will be at work to produce an optimum solution (see also Chapters 1, 4 and 6).

THEORETICAL ISSUES

In recent years there have been substantial developments in cognitive psychology. This has given rise to models of both the nature of knowledge and its acquisition. More recently, ideas from the study of motor skills have been extended into cognitive skills. It is now possible to provide a synthesis of this work that gives rise to a more satisfactory theory base for training activities than has been possible in the past.

All cognitive abilities must be based upon stored knowledge. Contemporary theories of memory draw upon the idea of items in memory being stored in the form of networks. A network consists of items as nodes, and the links between them represent the relationships between those nodes. For example, the human associative memory model (Anderson and Bower, 1973) holds that long-term memory is a highly structured set of associations. The basic component is the 'proposition', which is a set of associations and nodes. A proposition may be linguistic or non-linguistic. Each association is binary so that it connects two concepts. This may be on the basis of such relationships as subject to object, or spatial or temporal ones.

Network models have been used to accommodate the acquisition of new knowledge into a system. If the new information cannot be integrated into the present network, then retrieval of that information will be difficult. On the other hand, if it is well integrated then the new information is better understood and more easily retrieved. In discussing the acquisition of knowledge, Rumelhart and Norman (1978) have extended the acquisition model into a three-stage view of learning. The standard model of acquiring knowledge has always been one of *accretion*. However they see the need for additional *tuning* of acquired knowledge, and also *restructuring* of that knowledge. They use the term 'schema' (a concept for memory put forward by Bartlett, 1932) to refer to representations of knowledge in memory. Accretion involves new information being added to existing schemata, or the acquisition of new schemata themselves. Tuning involves the modification of existing schemata, inasmuch as the categories with which they deal are refined or elaborated with new information. The final stage, restructuring, involves the creation of new structures for interpreting information that comes in, or the creation of a new type of structure based on information already in memory. Although this theory has been described in terms of three stages, this should be not be taken to imply that the same information must pass through all these stages or that two or more of them must always be present in the learning process. Rather, different learners with different learning experience are expected to begin the learning process with a particular mix of these modes of acquisition.

A more recent learning theory is interesting because it begins to break down the traditional barriers between knowledge and skill. Anderson (1982) draws on the earlier skill-learning ideas of Fitts (1962), and proposes, as Fitts did, a three-stage model for the acquisition of cognitive skills. The objective is to be able to account for such phenomena as the speeding up of performance with practice, the loss of the ability verbally to describe performance, and an apparent increase in memory capacity.

The earlier theory of Fitts described three stages through which the learner passes as skill develops. There is an initial 'cognitive' phase, where instruction is conveyed to the learner, typically by a trainer. On the basis of a verbal analysis of the task, the learner attempts a conscious synthesis of the actions involved. The second phase is one of 'association'. Here the correct patterns of action are laid down by practice, and performance is shaped by the use of extrinsic feedback techniques. Errors are gradually eliminated, and performance eventually shifts from being under the control of extrinsic feedback to being under intrinsic feedback control. A final phase may be reached, termed 'automation'. Here the speed of performance is increased and very few errors occur. There is also a gradual increase in resistance to stress and interference from other activities. This is usually equated with the carrying out of activities in a subconscious way, whereby cognitive capacity is freed for other tasks. Thus people learning to play basketball initially find themselves tasked by the need to bounce the ball as they move around. Given sufficient practice this becomes a sub-skill that will run automatically, and the player is able to scan the court for other players and to move without consciously processing the bouncing activity.

Anderson's (1982) theory is also couched in terms of phases where the learner has different types of control over performance. Anderson is interested in how knowledge acquired at one point in time eventually supports skilled performance. A transition is seen whereby knowledge is transformed via a process termed 'compilation'. Skill learning begins with the communication of *declarative* knowledge. This can be seen as sets of rules and concepts about the area in which the skill is to be developed. Examples include the rules for writing computer programs in a particular language. The compilation process leads to this form of knowledge being converted into *procedural* knowledge. Procedural knowledge is used to guide performance in a more direct way. These 'productions', as they are called, are a different form of knowledge representation. They are used to pattern sequences of actions without recourse to previously stored information. Thus when a problem is presented, and a decision made, the appropriate production is selected and used to generate appropriate performance.

The transition between declarative and procedural knowledge comes about, typically, by practice. This is termed 'knowledge compilation', declarative knowledge becoming proceduralized. Similarities between this and Fitts' ideas should be apparent. In both theories there is an initial communication phase, where declarative knowledge is given to the learner (Fitts' cognitive phase). This can be termed the *instruction* phase of training. Following this there is likely to be a *practice* phase, where the knowledge gained is utilized and applied to the task in question. This would correspond to Fitts' association phase and be where Anderson's procedural knowledge is established.

The particular mix of these activities is more likely to enable the differentiation between what is called a cognitive task and what is called a motor task than is any arbitrary distinction based upon whether there is a manual output, or whether there is some degree of cognitive activity on the part of the performer. Identification of these phases of instruction and practice is also useful when we come to consider how material for training should be sequenced and structured and what are the functions of particular sorts of training devices.

TASK ANALYSIS

Any systematic approach to training must begin with an analysis of the task in question. This is an obvious statement, but nevertheless it remains the case that this essential first stage in training is one that is often poorly carried out, or in some cases not carried out at all. It is all too easy to assume that what is to be trained is 'obvious', or that experts in the area are best able to decide what the content of training should be. The systematic approach to training, however, takes as its starting point the fact that the training specialist needs to have a full analysis of the task in order to determine what the training content should be and what type of training activities will be involved.

Many different approaches to task analysis have been put forward. Some derive from work study techniques, with an emphasis on observable actions, others make a close examination of human perceptual-motor skills (Seymour, 1966). Some techniques take as their focus the abilities of the task-incumbent, while making reference to information-processing models (see Patrick, 1980; McCormick, 1976, for reviews). One technique that has had a fairly wide use in the United Kingdom is the hierarchical task analysis (HTA) method developed by Annett and colleagues (Annett *et al.*, 1971; Shepherd, 1985). This technique sets out to describe tasks in terms of hierarchies of operations. The initial step is specification of the task in fairly broad terms. This breakdown is then progressively redescribed in more and more detail to produce a hierarchy.

In breaking down a task using HTA it is suggested that, at each stage in the process, questions are asked about the relative costs of failure and its likelihood given the particular trainee population. If the product of these exceeds an accepted value, then the analysis is taken further; if not, then analysis ceases at this particular level. In this way, both the characteristics of the trainees (likelihood of failure) and the context of the training (costs of failure) are taken into account. The accuracy with which the assessments are made will depend upon the resources made available to the analyst (see Shepherd, 1985). The aim is to produce just sufficient information for adequate training without going into too much detail. The hierarchical diagram thus produced will show the analyst what activities have to be carried out. Missing from the diagram however is any statement about the task in detail or any statement about how the hierarchy is organized. At the same time as the hierarchy is being developed, the analyst also seeks to specify what 'plans' the task performer must have. By a plan is meant a rule or set of rules that guide the operator's activities in terms of how the sub-operations are carried out, how they are selected and in what sequence, etc. These rule structures are particularly important for tasks with a high cognitive load. They may be represented in simple verbal statements, or it may be necessary to represent them in complex decision-trees or algorithms.

As each operation is isolated, it is also necessary to specify where particular difficulties may lie for learners. Difficulties may occur on the perceptual side in terms of the input that determines whether or not that operation is performed, or in the feedback that results from the learner's own actions. Those actions themselves may represent difficulties for the learner to overcome, for example, in terms of novel actions or a large number of actions required to be carried out. Finally, difficulty may lie in learning the complex rule structure rather than in the individual actions themselves. A good example would be in a problem-solving task, where the rules for problem-solving are much more difficult to learn than the actions for problem-rectification.

The intention here has been to describe the general philosophy of hierarchical task analysis, rather than to provide a detailed account of how information is collected or represented in a particular form of analysis document. The reader is referred to the papers mentioned above for more details on implementation.

The output of the task analysis is twofold. Firstly there is the determination of training content. This is subsequently needed for the training design activities which will be discussed below. The second important role is that it should yield some specification of the performance required at the end of training. This is essential for the adequate evaluation of training, dealt with in the last section of the chapter.

TRAINING CONTENT AND SEQUENCING

The earlier theoretical analysis of the difference between knowledge and skill suggested that one way of viewing different training activities was to see an initial phase of *instruction*, where knowledge is typically communicated in a factual or declarative form, and *practice*, where that knowledge is put to use in task areas.

Task analysis will provide a specification of what the demands are. The translation of this into what an individual needs to learn in order to be able to carry out those demands remains a more problematic area. With task performance it is possible to specify the actions and decisions to be made. However, the form of conceptual underpinning that should be given before training is subject to debate. For example, questions have been asked on the extent to which the physics and chemistry of a process is appropriate training, as opposed to sets of generalizable rules about a system (K. D. Duncan, 1981). In learning to control a complex chemical process, theoretical descriptions of the process have been found less valuable than giving trainees generalizable rules that they can use in solving problems within those systems. In addition, studies by Berry and Broadbent (1984) have shown that under some conditions there is no clear relationship between effective task performance and the extent to which someone has explicit knowledge or is able to report on the knowledge content of the task. For example, practice can lead to an improvement in performance without any concomitant improvement in the ability to answer questions about what the task involves. This would tie in somewhat with the ideas of procedural and declarative knowledge, and with the suggestion that declarative knowledge becomes compiled into procedural knowledge, which is then less easily available for verbal report.

It is unlikely in any training situation that only task instructions would be given to individuals; some form of back-up statements, conceptual underpinnings or contextual information will usually be given. For some fairly simple tasks this background instruction can be minimal, whereas for cognitively oriented tasks more detail would be required. One approach to the problem of determining knowledge requirements reverses the process of task analysis as a 'top-down' activity and suggests a 'bottom-up' approach for determining training content. The background to this activity, as it is for task analysis, is some understanding of what knowledge the trainees already possess.

It is possible to think in terms of three categories of knowledge that need to be communicated to trainees for effective performance. Particular pieces of knowledge are not always classifiable uniquely in terms of one of these categories, but they provide a useful basis for the structuring of training material, as is demonstrated later. The three categories are 'general' knowledge, 'functional' knowledge and 'task' knowledge. Beginning at the third level, of task performance, questions may be asked about the human–system interface, and the set of rules governing the task elements that have to be carried out. Knowledge at the 'functional' level concerns reasons *why* the task is being carried out rather than *how* it is to be done. Knowledge of this kind is not essential for task activities to be carried out, but it provides a conceptual linking to other task areas.

'General' knowledge concerns the broad context of the task, the trainee's role within the system, and major components of the system itself. It is sometimes difficult to establish the purpose of this detailed underlying knowledge with any precision. It may be important as a supporting structure, which forms something like a schema or outline (Mayer, 1977), that enables more specific features of the task to be more readily learned. Provision of such a supporting structure could be defended as an appropriate training strategy, but questions must be asked about just how much of this type of content there should be, how much of it should be concrete or abstract, and how much of it is an essential prerequisite to learning.

Another justification that might be given for detailed background is that it will enable a better transfer of learning from one training situation to another. This is along the same lines as the notion of a supporting structure, but includes the possibility that a learner can move with minimum difficulty from one task to another, using previously established knowledge. Provision of supporting material might also be justified by the suggestion that it better enables an operator to adjust to the 'emergent' situation. By this is meant that, by possessing knowledge beyond the immediate situation, the operator may be better able to cope with events that are novel, and for which specific training has not been received. The important consideration in determining how much 'general' knowledge to provide is that its value should be empirically determined, rather than its use being based on established precedent or upon expert ideas about what knowledge is required.

In overall terms the *specification* of desirable knowledge-content is likely to proceed upwards from the task performance level. As it proceeds it will be seen that the functional knowledge will apply to a number of task-knowledge areas and that the general knowledge will form a structure for the complete task. However this knowledge is likely to be *communicated* in a reverse sequence in a top-down fashion, moving from the general to the specific.

Some examples of cognitive theories of instruction can now be described. Mayer's (1977) 'assimilation-to-schema theory' suggests that learning proceeds most effectively if the learner already possesses an adequate schema into which to assimilate new material. The underlying assumptions of the theory are that the individual is better able to receive the material which is to be learned if there is already a cognitive structure for assimilating this material and if the most appropriate structure is activated by the instructional task. Some empirical work has been done that supports these ideas, for example, work on 'advance organizers'. The idea here is that in advance of instruction the learner is given some outline of what is to be learned, in terms of a fairly abstract description of the subject-matter. This serves as an initial schema into which subsequent information can be incorporated. While the results are not unequivocal (e.g. Hartley and Davies, 1976), such approaches have a role to play within instruction.

Another widely discussed approach to training-content and sequence is the 'elaboration theory' of Reigeluth and Merrill (Reigeluth *et al.*, 1980). Here it is suggested that instruction should begin with a general outline of the topic to be covered. This is termed the 'epitome' or orientation structure. The material can then be divided into parts which are elaborated using supporting structures or 'elaborations'. These elaborations may in turn be sub-divided to give more and more detail on the knowledge to be acquired. This sub-division and elaboration continues until the desired level of learning is reached. The underlying approach is to allow learning to occur at the most meaningful level for the learner, while permitting the learner to be aware of the context and importance of what is being studied.

The above frameworks can be typified as being at a macro-level, that is, where large bodies of knowledge are structured to provide an adequate knowledge base for the task in question. Research has also been carried out on instruction at a more micro-level, at the level of the individual learning exercises. For example, Gagne (1977) suggests that before concepts are learned it is important that the learner has already mastered the necessary 'discrimination learning' that will make the acquisition of concepts easier. By discrimination learning is meant that the learner can perceptually discriminate between items to be categorized into concepts. In turn, the learning of rules should be preceded by the mastering of the concepts that they embody. Similarly, problem-solving activities should not be encountered until the necessary rules have been learned. This approach suggests good working solutions to the problem of instructional sequencing at the micro-level.

The above considerations apply, in the main, to what has been typified as the *instruction* phase of training. For the *practice* phase there is a greater reliance on procedures that have been established for the learning of physical skills. A central topic here is the importance of feedback for the acquisition and maintenance of skill (Annett, 1969). The importance of this variable cannot be overestimated; on the other hand the provision of appropriate feedback often requires an analysis of the subtleties of the learning situation and detailed decisions about which feedback is appropriate to the learning objectives.

Another topic in the practice area concerns the extent to which the learner should be confronted with the total task-demands from the outset of practice, or whether this should be approached through a number of learning exercises which individually tackle only parts of the task. This has been a classic issue within the psychology of learning, termed the part- versus whole-learning problem. The evidence in support of one approach or another is not at all clear (Stammers, 1982).

What evidence there is suggests that only in tasks where there is a great deal of cross-flow of information between independent parts will any particular benefits come from whole-learning. Part-learning will be most appropriate where the parts are sequentially organized and where poor performance in an earlier part will disrupt task performance in a later part. Where part-learning methods are used, evidence suggests that there is an optimal amount of part-practice before transfer to whole, but once this optimum is reached then synthesis of the parts into whole task performance does usually proceed quite rapidly.

Any training situation will differ from the real world, not least because there is usually an instructor on hand to make sure that errors, if they occur, are not disastrous. Thus any training activity can be seen in terms of the classic problem of transfer of learning (Annett and Sparrow, 1985). This topic comes to the forefront when it is hoped that particular training will lead to a generalization from one set of learning experiences to another. Issues of realism and transfer are also central to decisions about simulation in training, an area examined in a later section.

TRAINING MEDIA

Instruction and practice within the training process can be seen as involving communication. It should thus be possible to apply well-established principles to assess the effectiveness of different training media. In particular, ergonomic principles should be applicable to training media, in as much as their role parallels much of what goes on within other human–system interactions. The learner can be seen as an individual with a certain number of tasks to accomplish. These tasks are *learning tasks* that the instructional system demands, rather than tasks in the more general sense to do with the controlling or operating of systems. If this view is taken, then the ergonomic principles of good display-design and effective control-configuration can be applied to training systems. It is then possible to examine particular configurations and to determine their effectiveness. For example, is too much information displayed by a particular medium, is it displayed too quickly, is it in an ambiguous or unintelligible form?

Similarly, instructional systems can be criticized if the tasks that they present to the learners are extremely difficult to perform or leave people bored or poorly motivated. Training systems can be rejected if they do not allow for actions to be carried out easily by the learner. The trainee may know the answer, but if it is difficult to type this into a computer or to carry out an activity on a simulator, then the usefulness of the training device can be questioned.

In assessing training media along traditional ergonomic lines, a proviso is needed that the tasks to be performed are not fixed tasks but involve changing situations as the learners progress through different states of knowledge and skill. This puts a somewhat heavy burden on traditional ergonomics, since changing and developing environments have not usually been examined.

With these points in mind, it is possible next to assess various training media as communication devices. In doing so no attempt has been made to produce an exhaustive list of training media or to describe complete training systems made up of a variety of training methods and media. The more traditional training media should be well known to the reader. For example, in classroom training the learner is typically faced with an expert who will describe a body of knowledge. The audience may be small or large, ranging from a small tutorial group to the large mass lecture. The lecture, while an efficient way of communicating knowledge, is not without its faults or its critics. A number of principles exist for improving lectures, although these could be more widely applied. The advantages of hand-outs and visual aids are well known. Lectures that allow a two-way flow of information and other discussion-based learning situations are often seen as necessary complements to the one-way communication of information in the formal lecture. In fact a major criticism levelled at traditional teaching techniques is that they are open-loop in character, not allowing for feedback to the teacher.

As a back-up to most formal instruction there will be printed material. This will range from textbooks through to research papers and will also include hand-outs, instructional manuals and the like. The value of the printed word lies in its permanence and the opportunity to return to the source on a number of occasions. This medium can be extended to include electronic and photographic means of storing printed information. The strengths of this medium lie mainly in the *instruction* phase, but an instructional manual or procedural guide may be used in conjunction with *practice* in the operation of a piece of equipment. The complexity of that equipment will determine the extent to which the procedural guide will eventually be discarded as the learner masters the equipment. It may need to remain at hand to guide performance in a more complex or rarely practised task. Design of the printed material and its use in task performance in this latter context are good examples of an overlap of ergonomics and training. A fair amount of work has gone into the improvement of instructional text (Hartley, 1985) and the linguistic structure of instructions (S. Jones, 1968).

The value of individual methods of recording and storing instructional material is very context-specific. The instructional film has a long history and has particular applications for background information and safety training etc. The training film has some of the disadvantages of the lecture, in that it puts the learner in a passive situation and offers little opportunity for note-taking and pauses for questions etc. On the other hand, the visual medium can be a very powerful one for conveying ideas and may be quite effective in its propaganda or attitude-changing role, e.g. in the area of safety training. More recent developments in television recording techniques have led to more flexible systems; video tape is relatively easy to produce, play back, and to interact with.

Some of the disadvantages, in terms of speed of access to parts of a tape and quality of reproduction, are overcome with the high quality of recording available from video disc. This coupled to the high-speed, random access to images and the possibility of linking video disc systems to computers suggests some quite powerful training media for the future. With these media it is possible to cross the divide between *instruction* and *practice*. While a video tape may be used to communicate basic theory, it can be also used to demonstrate the operation of equipment. Another factor of importance in considering training media is their portability and the extent to which 'distance learning' can take place. Trainees at geographically remote locations can receive instruction from some central instructional facility, either directly by electronic means or by receiving individual packages of instruction that can then be played back locally.

The term 'closed-loop' can be applied to those training media which aim to provide a route for learners to make responses as they progress through the learning material. These responses are then assessed by the system in some way to determine the subsequent presentation of information. An example of this approach was seen in 'programmed instruction', which was widely discussed in the 1950s and 1960s (Kay *et al.*, 1968). The approach has been extended into the 1970s and 1980s via computer-assisted or computer-based learning, wherein the instruction medium is the ubiquitous computer terminal. The availability of micro-computers, and more recently specific 'authoring languages' for the development of instruction, has led to the principles of programmed instruction being more widely applied. Authoring languages are computer languages specifically designed for the writing of computer-based learning (e.g. PILOT).

Until recently, very little in the way of guidance has been available to the trainer who wanted to implement computer-based training. This has to some extent been rectified now (e.g. Beech, 1983), but trainers who wish to implement this form of instruction are still left with a complex task. They not only have to be experts in the subject-matter, but also have to have some ideas about instructional sequencing and need to be adept at computer programming. Despite the availability of authoring languages specifically devised for instruction, the trainer still has to learn to write computer programs. Apart from the enthusiast and those who are able to draw on fairly large resources, it would seem that there are still a number of barriers to developing computer-based instructional systems. However, this problem is increasingly recognized, and it is likely that future research and development in this area will move towards more sophisticated systems. This should enable the trainer to interact directly with the computer in terms of the subject-matter, the computer advising on optimal instructional approaches and producing exemplar sequences. In terms of the role of these media, they can be seen as equally useful for instruction and for the enablement of practice at task elements.

There are also a number of examples where the computer terminal has been used as a low-fidelity simulator (Stammers, 1981). Utilizing input devices such as touch screens and joysticks, the learner is able to interact directly with a representation of the task such as an aircraft's controls. The simulation may be low in terms of realism, but the trainee can receive fairly full feedback and guidance from the system and can work with a higher degree of instructional control via the computer. For certain task-areas there needs to be a carefully controlled and rich mixture of knowledge-communication and practice. A good example of this would be in training for problem-diagnosis, an area in which the computer has a particularly important role to play (Patrick and Stammers, 1981). Here the rules to be learned for problem-solving (for example in electronic fault-finding) can be communicated in instruction mode before the trainee switches to direct practice of those rules in a simulation of the task.

The discussion of computers as low-fidelity simulators leads naturally to a consideration of the role of simulators in general. A fairly broad interpretation of the notion of a 'simulator' is taken here. It can mean anything from a paper-and-pencil diagram of equipment through to the full-scale, highly realistic representations of a process plant or an aeroplane's flight deck. It is worth considering the reasons for the use of any form of simulation as opposed to direct training. Some of these concern safety and risk. Learning, in its early stages, is characterized by particular sorts of errors, such as inappropriate responses and errors of sequence. In some systems such errors are trivial in their consequences, in others they can be disastrous. In the latter case simulators can be important as media for learning that are forgiving and safe. Other reasons for the use of simulators concern cost. The use of a piece of real equipment for training purposes may be costly in terms of lost production or the consumption of resources, or the real situation may not be particularly efficient for learning purposes. Thus some form of simulation may be provided in order to allow for a more effective learning environment. The pacing of the task can be altered to speed up or slow down activities, and the learner can practise some parts of the task in isolation.

These reasons taken together suggest that in any complex task-situation a variety of forms of simulation can and indeed should be used. Low-fidelity simulators have their part to play in certain stages of learning and for certain tasks. For example, it has been demonstrated that for procedural tasks, low-fidelity mock-ups of real equipment are adequate for training purposes (Stammers, 1983). In other contexts, such as aircraft control, the question of degree of fidelity is still open. For example, how important is it to provide such features as vibration, motion or realistic visual displays? The evidence is equivocal, but there are strong demands from professionals in the area for high degrees of realism. This demand for realism may stem from reasons to do with more effective learning, or it could arise from the need to use simulators for testing or evaluation purposes as well as for training.

The complex simulator is most effectively used for the development of already existing knowledge and skill. It would be inefficient to learn the 'basics' in such an expensive device. It is also likely that the high-realism system simulator has an important role in what might be called confidence building. One problem in the development of skill, for example in the control of process plant, is the limited opportunity for practice of many of the important task elements. An advantage of the low-fidelity simulator is that it allows for extensive practice of task-relevant skills. On the other hand, the learner is put in the position of having very little opportunity to test out the validity and usefulness of what has been learnt. It seems, therefore, that the value of high-fidelity simulation may arise from a need on the part of the trainees to assess their state of knowledge and skill in a realistic environment.

Related to this is the importance of simulators in helping the trainee to cope with any stress which may accompany the task-performance. This could arise from low competence in relation to the task-demands. The controlled learning environment of the simulator enables some reduction of that source of stress through familiarization and the development of skill. At the same time the simulator can be used to increase progressively the demands on the individual, and thereby develop increasing resistance to the task-induced stress. An additional feature is the extent to which a simulator of high or low fidelity will enable extensive practice of particular task-elements; this can be used in attempts to combat the effects of stress. Another role involves the trainees in experiencing the demands of the task, and assessing their own level of competency in dealing with them. This latter point indicates the need for some degree of realism in the simulator, not for primary learning but for some form of personal assessment of the state of one's knowledge and skill. Whether this can be done only in a simulator of the highest technical fidelity is at the present time an open question. However, this factor probably lies behind a strong demand within a number of industries for higher realism in training devices, despite the fact that evidence from several psychological sources suggests that a lot can be gained from simulators of lower fidelity (Stammers, 1983).

The simulation topic is larger than can be fully discussed here. It is interesting in that it brings us face to face with the sorts of tasks presented by new technology. We should look to that technology as

one way of enhancing training by an appropriate use of simulators, recognizing that they can differ in fidelity in these several
ways.

TRAINING SYSTEMS AND THEIR EVALUATION

In the section on task analysis it was pointed out that the analysis should
yield not just information on the content of instruction, but also sets of
criteria for performance-evaluation during and after training. The importance of this is that it will enable a measure of effectiveness of the
chosen training activities. Evaluation is all-important for the training
specialist, but there is often reluctance on the part of those that have
spent many hours producing a training system to subject it to too close a
scrutiny in terms of performance-measurement. However, the only
systematic way to proceed is to assess the efficiency of training activities
as they occur, and there are a number of ways in which this can be done
(Hamblin, 1974).

The first concern should be to ask whether the training that is received
has actually produced effective learning. This can be termed 'internal
validation' of a training programme and should be possible on the basis
of the training-content information collected by task analysis and the
objectives that were set for the training programme. Measures can be
taken within the training programme itself. However, it may be that,
while effective learning occurred, it was not entirely relevant to job
performance. There is a need therefore for 'external validation', whereby individuals are measured in their job context to see if effective
performance is produced. If it is not produced, then certain shortcomings are suggested in the relevance of the information collected in the
task-analysis procedure.

The evaluation of training can be taken further to assess the extent to
which training received by individuals has an influence on the effectiveness of the organization or indeed upon the overall impact that that
organization makes on society. Training may also be assessed at a quite
different level, in terms of an individual's reaction to it and whether it
was found enjoyable or relevant to particular needs. This type of
assessment is sometimes called 'reaction evaluation', and may utilize
questionnaires asking for ratings on elements of the course. Such

information can provide useful pointers to the quality of training, but it is not necessarily predictive of performance changes.

It should be clear that a range of measures can be brought to bear in the evaluation of training. In the main there will be a temptation to use the most obvious measures of a trainee's reaction or performance. The measures of performance can be many and varied depending upon the type of activity involved, but for manual tasks they usually boil down to some derivation of speed and/or accuracy measures. In some situations it is difficult to relate this directly to productivity, but attempts can be made that are ultimately useful for assessing the cost-effectiveness of training activities.

A systematic approach to training will use such measures to determine whether activities within the task analysis or training design need to be revised. It is also important not to view training-evaluation as a once and for all activity, but to see it as one that continues throughout the life of the training programme. Attempts to determine whether the programme still matches up to the needs of the organization should be made periodically. It may be that the job demands will change over time, and training should be revised in the light of this. Alternatively the nature of the trainees might change, given, for example, changes in school syllabuses or a change in recruitment policy. The aim of evaluation is to build a closed-loop system, such that the measurements taken are used to assess and revise components of the system where necessary.

SUMMARY

The aim of this chapter has been to present an indication of the importance of training research to organizations. The theoretical base for training activities was described, seeking to indicate that exciting developments within contemporary cognitive psychology are being applied to the challenges presented by applied contexts. The key importance of task analysis to training activities was then given some emphasis: analysis should provide not only a determination of what the training problems are, but also indicate how to assess the extent to which those problems have later been solved by training. The next two sections directly addressed the question of training design; initially from the point of view of what the content of training should be, and then ideally how that content should be sequenced and how practice conditions can be organized. Training media were then discussed, illustrating the ways in which various technological innovations can be brought to bear upon the communication of training material and the provision of practice conditions. Finally, the importance of evaluation within a systematic approach to training was detailed and some comments made upon how the performance of a training system can be assessed.

FURTHER READING

Standard texts in this area are the *Psychology of Training* by R. B. Stammers and J. Patrick (Methuen, 1975) and *Training: Program Development and Evaluation* by I. L. Goldstein (Brooks/Cole, 1974). Research on perceptual-motor skills has been reviewed in *Human Skills*, edited by D. H. Holding (Wiley, 1981), and research related to cognitive psychology developments can be found in *Cognitive Psychology and its Implications*, by J. R. Anderson (second edition; Freeman, 1985).

A recent text looking at instructional sequencing is *Instructional Design Theories and Models* edited by C. M. Reigeluth (Erlbaum, 1983). A number of works assess the potential of computer-assisted learning. At a practical level, *Computer-Based Learning* by G. Beech (Sigma, 1983) examines the role of computers in basic instructional terms. A more critical appraisal, which suggests greater innovation, is *Learning and Teaching with Computers* by T. O'Shea and J. Self (Harvester, 1983). The area of simulation has been reviewed by R. B. Stammers (1983), and discussion of training media can be found in *Principles of Instructional Design* by R. M. Gagne and L. J. Briggs (Holt, Rinehart and Winston, 1974) and *Instructional Media: The New Technologies of Instruction* by R. Heinich *et al.* (Wiley, 1982). A standard text on evaluation is *Evaluation and Control of Training*, by A. C. Hamblin (McGraw-Hill, 1974).

4

Cognitive Ergonomics and Human–Computer Interaction

John Long

Ergonomics is one of the disciplines which seek to optimize the relationship between people and their work. The advent of the computer, together with changes in psychology, has given rise to a new form of ergonomics termed 'cognitive' ergonomics. The aim of this chapter is first to show how cognitive ergonomics relates to 'traditional' ergonomics, human–computer interaction and cognitive psychology, and then to describe some examples of cognitive ergonomics.

The chapter begins with a framework for viewing ergonomic activities, which is used to construct a model of 'traditional' ergonomics. Following a description of human–computer interaction, the response of traditional ergonomics to the challenge of the computer is illustrated, including its failure to address certain areas of difficulty experienced by users of interactive systems. These difficulties can be characterized in terms of the incompatibility between the computer's representations and those of the user. Developments within cognitive psychology are reviewed and the central importance of the user's internal representations identified. Cognitive ergonomics is then illustrated by three examples, whose aim was to help designers produce better interactive systems. The examples suggest how the concept of an internal representation can be exploited to increase the compatibility between users and computers. Finally, the approach of cognitive ergonomics, in which knowledge is acquired from and applied to the real world, is recommended more generally as a method for psychology.

FRAMEWORK FOR ERGONOMICS

Many disciplines are concerned with optimizing the relationship between people and their work, for example engineering, industrial medicine and personnel management. Ergonomics is one of these disciplines. The emphasis in ergonomics is on the person doing the work and the manner in which it is carried out, rather than on the technology or on the environment. The approach is to use scientific knowledge and techniques to achieve the optimization with respect to mental and physical well-being and productivity.

A framework for ergonomic activities showing the relationship between *work* and *knowledge* appears in Figure 4.1. In the framework, ergonomic activities involve a particular configuration of *tasks* and *sciences*. One configuration, traditional ergonomics, will be described in the next section. The configuration, however, may change, either because social or technological developments alter the tasks or because science itself moves on. Cognitive ergonomics is one such new configuration. The function of the framework is to characterize ergonomics in a sufficiently general form to accommodate the description of the different configurations of traditional and cognitive ergonomics offered in the following sections.

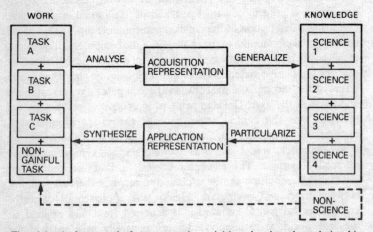

Fig. 4.1 A framework for ergonomic activities showing the relationship between work and knowledge.

The framework consists of a set of descriptions or *representations* and a set of activities or *transformations*, which originate and terminate in the world of work. Work is that function which changes an object or entity from one state into another state. The entities may be real or symbolic. The work-tasks of concern in this book are those carried out by people, for their own gain, and only these will be considered further. The purpose of the representations and transformations is to change tasks in the real world of work.

In Figure 4.1, work is decomposed into tasks. Knowledge consists of science and *non-science* (that is experiential knowledge, both craft and personal). Scientific knowledge is composed of individual sciences, each offering a potentially complete description and explanation of the tasks. Scientific knowledge is generally represented as data, reflecting regularities of occurrence, and as theories, embodying explanatory principles.

In the framework, scientific knowledge is acquired by two transformations. The activity of *analysing* the real world produces an *acquisition representation* which typically supports laboratory simulation for experimentation. The activity of *generalizing* the data from experiments produces the explanatory principles of the science knowledge representation. Scientific knowledge is applied likewise by two transformations. The activity of *particularizing* the science representation produces an *applications representation*, typically in the form of design principles for tasks, technology or the environment. The activity of *synthesizing* this representation with the real world of tasks in line with the criteria of well-being and productivity seeks to optimize the relationship between people and their work.

In terms of this framework, ergonomics consists of two main activities. One is an interdisciplinary research activity which acquires knowledge about people and their work: the transformations of analysis and generalization in Figure 4.1. The second is an operational activity: the transformations which apply the knowledge to the workplace, through particularization and synthesis.

TRADITIONAL ERGONOMICS

A model of traditional ergonomics expressed in terms of this framework appears in Figure 4.2. The model shows the configuration of tasks and

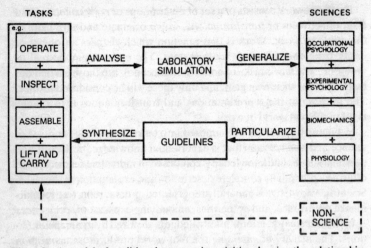

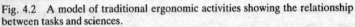

Fig. 4.2   A model of traditional ergonomic activities showing the relationship between tasks and sciences.

sciences typical of ergonomic practice since its origins at the end of the Second World War. Tasks such as these have been studied in coal mining, car assembly, glass manufacture and power-station operation. Of the particular sciences involved, physiology is concerned with the energic relations of the person with work in terms of cardiovascular response and homeostatic mechanisms. Biomechanics is concerned with the mechanical relations with work in terms of linked body segments and their musculature. Psychology is concerned with the informational relations in terms of mental processes. Last, occupational psychology is here concerned with organizational relations in terms of social factors.

In traditional ergonomics, the main acquisition representation is the laboratory simulation based on techniques of task analysis. The main applications representation is a set of guidelines for work design, often in the form of a checklist, for the equipment designer. The tasks shown in the model are typical of those from which scientific knowledge has been acquired and to which knowledge has been applied. Other tasks include monitoring radar displays, controlling cranes, driving cars and sorting letters.

Traditional ergonomics can also be characterized at a more detailed level in terms of the task-features, which describe tasks in terms of agent(s), functions, entities, instrument and location (derived from a description of language function by Clark and Clark, 1976). Concerning the agents of work, ergonomists have often been more interested in the people operating light or heavy industrial equipment than in office staff. Concerning the functions and entities of work, more effort has been directed at actions which control real processes directly, albeit at a distance, than at actions of symbol manipulation. Concerning the instrument of work, the traditional ergonomic interest has been in manual, mechanical and electro-mechanical technology. Concerning the location of work, the factory and the site have been of more interest than the office.

Most progress was made in the areas of: workstation analysis; displays; controls; layout of panels and machines; layout of workspaces; seating; thermal comfort; noise; lighting; and work organization (for example, Shackel, 1974). Last, concerning general approaches, emphasis was successively on: the optimization of the immediate task with respect to the then current technology of displays and controls ('classical ergonomics'); the optimal relations between all tasks and all design activities ('systems ergonomics'); and the need to reduce errors to improve both well-being and productivity ('error ergonomics').

To complete this section, let us consider an example of how work might be optimized in line with this model of traditional ergonomics (Visick *et al.*, 1984). The work is that of a post-office parcel sorter. It is a typical, routine and semi-skilled task, partly automated by electro-mechanical technology. The task is to: advance the parcels by activating a conveyor by means of a footswitch; pick up the parcel; rotate the parcel to read the destination; assign a destination code; press the appropriate key on a keyboard; return the parcel to the departure conveyor and restart the sorting cycle. In addition, the sorter has two other tasks: loading and unloading the sacks of parcels and tidying the workplace.

Within traditional ergonomics, different sciences can be used to address different aspects of the task. For example, (1) the sorter may be insufficiently challenged by such a simple and repetitive task. Research in occupational psychology suggests that performance might be improved by changing the organization of the work, for example from a one-person sorting station to a two-person one, which would permit task and social communication during sorting. (2) The sorter may make too many coding errors. Results from experimental psychology suggest the layout of the keys should reflect their frequency of use as well as their compatibility with the parcel destinations. Improving the keyboard might reduce the number of misdirected parcels. (3) The sorter may experience physical discomfort as the result of the posture required to return the parcel to the conveyor. Biomechanics research suggests that all parts of the workstation should be within easy reach to avoid awkward postures brought about by over-reaching. Changing the orientation of the seat might improve the sorter's posture by bringing the conveyor within reach. (4) The sorter may experience fatigue as a consequence of loading and unloading the sacks of parcels. Results from physiology suggest that heavy physical work requires a specifiable recovery time. Instituting an appropriate work–rest cycle or decreasing the size and hence the weight of the sacks might reduce fatigue. Attention to all these factors characterizes the practice of traditional ergonomics.

Cognitive ergonomics extends the practice of traditional ergonomics. However, before turning to this new development, it is necessary first to describe the technology of computers and second to consider the response of traditional ergonomics to this technology.

HUMAN–COMPUTER INTERACTION

The present widespread introduction of computers into the workplace continues and will increase. As a result, the computer is fast becoming the most influential machine of the twentieth century. For this reason, it is essential that ergonomics assimilates this new instrument of technology into its research and practice. In this section, the use of computers by people at work is characterized in terms of the task-features described earlier: agent(s), instrument, functions, entities and location.

New agents of work have accompanied the introduction and development of the computer. First, there are the computer professionals. Electronic engineers and computer scientists develop the basic hardware and software. Other computer specialists, including the programmer, the person who enters the data, and the operator, apply the technology to tasks. Then there are the non-specialists, or end-users, who operate the computer themselves. They need knowledge of computer operations to perform the task as well as knowledge of the applications domain to specify the task. These users of interactive systems are now a large and growing group of people including secretaries, engineers, teachers, designers, accountants and managers. They have a wide knowledge of their individual task-domains and variable knowledge of programming and computer operation.

As an instrument of work, computers essentially manipulate information, for example text for document creation, graphics for product design, records for accounting and positional and tracking data for machine control. The power of the computer lies in the speed of its operations and the increasing flexibility of its applications. To manipulate the information, the user needs to specify those parts of the task to be performed by the system, and to operate the computer. Operating the computer directly, rather than via specialists, allows the interactive user more control over the task. There are, however, disadvantages.

Operation involves new functions and entities not required by the pre-computer version of the task. For example, special 'query' languages may be necessary to enable the user to search databases for information. Artificial 'command' languages may be required to instruct the computer concerning which steps to perform. Alternatively, instructions may be issued by the use of entities such as 'menus' (sets of task-options), and 'icons' (symbols for objects and actions). Some functions and entities may require different procedures from non-computerized tasks, for example 'drawing' a circle in computer-aided design or deleting a sentence in word-processing. Task-relevant information may also be organized differently in the computer version of the task. In computer-aided design, the drawing may be treated as a set of overlaid sheets rather than the single sheet of the drafting board. In word-processing, the format of a letter on the display screen may be different from the printed version of the letter. In both cases, the user is required to adapt to the changes.

Concerning the location of work, computers can be found anywhere from the cockpit of an aeroplane to the reception room of a doctor's surgery. However, most computers are located in offices. The offices are both conventional, as in banks, and office-type environments created in factories.

In summary, the increased use of computers has resulted in the rapid expansion of the number of interactive users who are often required both to specify the task to be performed by the system and to operate the computer. Both activities may be associated with difficulties of task performance due to the computerized version of the task or due to differences between this version and the pre-computer version. Optimizing the relationship between interactive users and their work involves the minimizing of these difficulties. Their reduction constitutes perhaps the major challenge of computer technology for ergonomics.

TRADITIONAL ERGONOMICS AND HUMAN–COMPUTER INTERACTION

The initial response of traditional ergonomics to the advent of computer technology was to employ the same guidelines and scientific principles which had previously been applied to non-computerized tasks. These took the form of only the applications transformations shown in Figure 4.2 which had previously been applied to non-computerized tasks. For example, suppose preparing invoices on a typewriter were computerized by means of a word-processor. Invoicing might present the same problems as those described earlier for sorting parcels by means of a keyboard. These might include insufficient challenge due to simple, repetitive work; typing errors due to the incompatibility of the keyboard with the function or frequency of key usage; discomfort due to poor posture; and fatigue due to excessive typing. Solutions might include improvements in the organization of operators, the layout of keys, the design of the workstation and the cycle of work and rest.

Other problems, however, were not addressed by extant guidelines or scientific knowledge. Examples of such problems include the principles governing the location of electronic terminals to sustain social communication, the positioning of text on displays to facilitate the rapid finding of information, and the layout of special editing keys to avoid confusion. Also, the postural principles governing the use of document-holders to counter physical discomfort and the physiological principles governing fatigue in environments created by computers. The growing research literature addressing these problems (e.g. Grandjean, 1984) attests to the acquisition and application of knowledge by traditional ergonomics concerning computers and their effect on work (that is, involving all the transformations shown in Figure 4.2).

In the course of research, however, problems and difficulties of a novel kind were identified. These were associated with the differences between the computer's representation of the functions and entities of the task and those of the user. For the purposes of illustration, the problems may be divided into those related to the domain of application, those related to the task and those related to the computer interface.

The first source of difficulty is the computer's version of the 'domain', the range of the system's specific application. For example, the domain of a computerized shopping system is the set of goods available for purchase. Users may often experience difficulty in completing purchases successfully because the description of goods (that is, the computer's version of the domain) is inadequate for their purposes (Long and Buckley, 1984). The representation takes the form of short text descriptions, for example: 'Roses Red. Size 60 cm. Cost £10 a Dozen'. For one user, this information was inadequate to make a purchase. She wanted to know the kinds of roses, their names, whether they were floribunda, and whether they had a scent. Similar difficulties arose from the inadequacies of the system's crude graphics, which provide only a poor pictorial representation of the roses.

The second source of difficulty is the computer's version of the task. Computerization may leave many functions and entities of a task unchanged, although the procedures used to carry out the task will be different. For example, a product can be designed using a pencil and paper or a computer. Both media allow parts of the drawing to be modified, one by means of an eraser, the other by an instruction to the computer. However, other task components may be changed. Computer-aided design systems, for example, aid visualization of selected parts by permitting the 'layering' of drawings, that is the assignment of different parts of the design (for example, internal elements as opposed to the external casing) to different layers of the drawing. The layers have to be manipulated, that is selected, labelled and displayed. The computer version of the task thus contains an additional component. Many designers not only experience difficulty in layering, but, at least initially, often forget to select different layers, effectively treating the screen as a drawing board (Whitefield, 1984, 1985). As with the computer's version of the domain, therefore, the computer's version of the task, if inappropriate or different from the pre-computer version, may pose difficulties for the user.

The remaining area of difficulty concerns the computer interface. Users experience difficulties in communicating with the computer. In some systems, the user is offered a 'menu' of possible actions, in the form of a list from which one has to be selected before the machine carries out the action. In other systems, a special 'command' language is used to specify the action required. For example, in one information manipulation and inquiry system, data are kept in the form of 'blocks' (Hammond and Barnard, 1984). Blocks have names, and consist of 'entities', or rows, and 'attributes', or columns. Instructions to the computer are expressed as 'commands' (actions to be performed), and as 'arguments' (the attributes or blocks of data to be manipulated). Suppose the user wants to list young householders less than 25 years old who have children. The following must be specified: the name of the new block listing the young householders (YOUNG); the constraints on the age attribute (AGE < 25) and on the children attribute (CHILDREN > = 1); the name of the block from which the entries are chosen (HOUSEHOLDERS); and the command (SELECT, written as S). In addition, the instruction must be specified in the correct order: YOUNG ← <:S: (AGE < 25) & (CHILDREN > = 1): > HOUSEHOLDERS. The example is a simple one. Real inquiries are more complex, and produce more errors.

These examples indicate a wide and varied range of problems. However, they can be generally expressed as a mismatch between the computer system's representations and those of the user (see Morton *et al.*, 1979). This will be termed 'representational incompatibility'. Users experience difficulty in specifying and interpreting the computer's actions when the system's representation of the domain or the task differs from their own. Likewise, users experience difficulty in operating the computer, when the interface acts differently from the user's representation of it. The examples cited earlier suggest that many of the inappropriate user-representations may have their origins in the pre-computer version of the task, as in the shopping and computer-aided design examples, or more generally outside the context of work, as in the information manipulation and inquiry system.

The importance of representational incompatibility as a source of user difficulties derives in part from the recency of computer technology. New users have not had the opportunity to assimilate the representations embodied in the computer. Interface designers may not have been able to accommodate the task-specific or general representations of the users. Users, then, may have ill-formed computer-representations but well-formed non-computer-representations. Further, the complexity of computer systems and the open-ended tasks to which they are applied ensure that many different representations are involved in their use. Representational incompatibility, then, is widespread.

With hindsight, representational incompatibility was inevitable. Neither traditional ergonomics nor traditional design practice possessed either the knowledge or the techniques necessary to indicate how the computer-representations and the user-representations might be described and reconciled. This was because the reconciliation of representations for the previous technology had been brought about by emphasizing a single representation expressed in terms of knobs and dials, by restricting many tasks to specialist and highly trained operators and by structuring tasks as fixed sequences of actions. The widespread use of the new technology by non-specialists rendered these solutions inappropriate by themselves. Developments, however, were occurring within experimental psychology which suggested alternative ways in which the problem might be approached.

COGNITIVE PSYCHOLOGY

Any change in a science changes the model of ergonomics shown in Figure 4.2. In this way, the advent of cognitive psychology gave rise to cognitive ergonomics. The techniques and theories of the cognitive approach were found useful as a starting point from which to attack the problem of representational incompatibility associated with the new computer technology. The most general definition of cognitive ergonomics is thus the application of cognitive psychology to work. A characterization follows.

The cognitive approach to psychology emphasizes the acquisition and use of knowledge rather than conative aspects involving actions, their motivation and the will to carry them out, or affective aspects involving feelings and the emotions. In this sense, cognition reflects only one part of a particular division of the mind and its activities. The approach also emphasizes the so-called higher mental functions such as understanding, thinking and communication, rather than perceptual-motor functions. Much of the emphasis has come from the movement within psychology towards greater ecological validity (Long and Baddeley, 1981). So far and in general, these emphases have been carried over into cognitive ergonomics.

The cognitive approach also emphasizes the role of the internal representation in the explanation of behaviour. Here, cognitive psychology is contrasted with behaviourism or stimulus–response psychology. The latter approach attempted to explain human actions only in terms of variables which could be directly observed. Cognitive psychology using initially the language of cybernetics, recruited unobservable events inside the organism into explanations in terms of the flow of information (Broadbent, 1958). Later, cognition was assumed to include all the vicissitudes of stimulus information and to refer to any process by which the sensory input is transformed, reduced, elaborated, stored, recovered and used (Neisser, 1967). The conception of cognition as the successive transformations by the organism of information representing the real world has been generally carried over into ergonomics. Specific techniques such as cluster analysis and process-modelling have also been imported, where these have been found useful in characterizing and explaining representations and their transformation.

Since taking up the cognitive approach, psychologists have found it useful to import techniques and theories from other disciplines, in particular from linguistics and artificial intelligence. For example, linguistic structures have been invoked to trace the successive transformations needed to change a verbal representation of language into a semantic one (Clark and Clark, 1976). Likewise, artificial intelligence structures have been recruited to suggest how knowledge is represented and used (Minsky, 1975; see also Chapter 5). Structures from both disciplines are making a tentative appearance in cognitive ergonomics, either via psychology or directly, and these are illustrated in the next section.

The origins of cognitive ergonomics, then, are closely related to developments within cognitive psychology. At this time, most of the activity associated with these developments is centred on the acquisition processes illustrated in Figure 4.1. Activity related to the application processes is also developing, but more slowly.

COGNITIVE ERGONOMICS

Traditional and cognitive ergonomics can be contrasted in terms of the framework shown in Figure 4.1. They differ in terms of the tasks associated with the introduction of the computer and in terms of additions to the science base of psychology. Cognitive ergonomics, then, is a configuration relating work to science. In this context, its aim can be defined as the increase of compatibility between the user's representations and those of the machine. However, as a new development its definition and methods have not yet been agreed; even its name varies: 'software psychology'; 'interface ergonomics', etc. Further, its methods are not yet validated. For this reason, it will be instantiated by example.

Three approaches have been chosen to suggest how the system designer can be provided with information which will help improve cognitive compatibility. The examples relate to the three areas of difficulty identified earlier: domain, task and system interface.

The Domain of a Computerized Shopping System

The first example is taken from research on computerized shopping (Gilligan and Long, 1984; Buckley and Long, 1985a, 1985b). The research illustrates how compatibility between the system's representation of the domain and that of the user can be increased. The system offers goods for sale, such as groceries, clothing and consumer products. Information about the goods is transmitted by telephone cable, and is usually displayed on the user's domestic television set. Ordering of goods, to be delivered subsequently, is by keyboard. Users include the elderly, the house-bound and people without transport. The aim of the research was to help the system designers improve the usability of the system.

A general model of the shopping task, characterizing both conventional and computerized shopping, was constructed. Its main function was to structure the research and make explicit the scope. In the model, transactions are defined as the exchange of resources, between a vendor and a purchaser (the transactors). Resources are assumed to satisfy a need, for example buying a present (such as 'a vase'). They comprise any goods, including money, which can be bought or sold. The task as modelled consists of three basic activities: display, evaluation and exchange. 'Display' describes the making available of information about the goods, together with their transfer conditions. 'Evaluation' describes the matching of the features of the goods ('cut-glass'; 'good value') against those of the need ('cut-glass'; 'cheap'). 'Exchange' describes the giving and receiving of resources. For exchange to occur within the model, both transactors must successfully display their own, and evaluate the other's, resources.

A study was conducted to establish the errors and difficulties experienced by users attempting to purchase goods via the system. The data were generated by observing subjects making 'simulated' purchases, for example, a present; perhaps a cut-glass vase for a favourite aunt. The data consisted of video-taped recordings and transcribed verbal protocols. Difficulties in buying the vase might have originated in poor image quality, inadequate text description or incorrect interpretation of brand information. A model of the user, expressing the difficulties experienced, was then developed (extending Morton *et al.*, 1979). The model is illustrated in Figure 4.3. It consists of three components, each related to the domain, the task and the interface of the computerized shopping system:

1. *System variables* describe groups of discrete features of the technology, which were identified as contributing to users' difficulties. For example, the system variable 'Extent of Description of Goods' was identified as a source of the difficulty that subjects experienced in the 'evaluation' task-component. In the model, there are fourteen system variables, of which only three are illustrated in the figure.

2. *Knowledge variables* express the same difficulties as those attributed to the effects of the technological features, but in terms of the users' knowledge. Such knowledge was inadequate for task performance, since it led to difficulties and errors. For example, 'Knowledge of Brands' was sometimes inappropriately used to assess goods whose representation was inadequate to evaluate them for purchase. In the

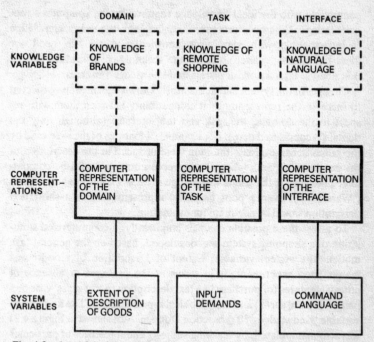

Fig. 4.3 A model of the difficulties experienced by users of the computerized shopping system. The difficulties are expressed in the form of knowledge and system variables.

model, there are seven knowledge variables, of which only three are illustrated in the figure.

3. *Computer representations* indicate 'ideal user' knowledge, that is, knowledge required by the system for 'error-free' shopping. In the example of the cut-glass vase, such knowledge could be described as knowing the features of the vase sufficiently well (given the computer's representation of it) to evaluate it for purchase. These representations are determined by the technology, that is, system features, but are expressed in psychological terms as 'ideal knowledge'.

In terms of the model, user-performance can be understood as follows. When performance is adequate, the user's knowledge is compatible with the ideal knowledge required by the computer's representations. When performance is inadequate, the user's knowledge is incompatible with ideal user knowledge. Since the need for ideal knowledge is determined by the technology, difficulties can be described as interactions of system and knowledge variables.

Changes in the system and in the user's knowledge might be expected to increase the representational compatibility between them with respect to the domain, the task and the interface (although only the domain is considered here). For example, if features of the vase used by the purchaser to evaluate the item were included in the description of the goods ('cut-glass'; 'cheap'), the representation would be compatible. Likewise, if the user's knowledge included knowledge of brands ('Waterford'), even a poor graphical representation or a short text description would be adequate for evaluation.

To assess these possible changes empirically, a computerized simulation of a shopping system was developed, based on the general task model. The system variable 'Extent of Description of Goods' was manipulated experimentally in terms of the presence or absence of criterial features for purchase in a text description (a 'cut-glass' vase or a pair of 'cotton' socks) and in a graphical representation. The knowledge variable 'Knowledge of Transaction Domain' (not shown in Figure 4.3) was also manipulated, by teaching subjects about features of particular goods. The effects of both experimental manipulations were statistically significant, as was the interaction. Including the criterial feature in the description of the items to be purchased aided faster and more accurate evaluation of the goods. Teaching subjects about particular features of items made the evaluation of the goods relative to those features faster and more accurate. However, the inclusion of the criterial feature in the text produced a stronger effect when subjects were not trained on the text item. Concerning the graphical capability of the system, visual images of the items to be purchased aided performance only when subjects possessed no specific knowledge, and when the information about the criterial feature was not included in the text.

The final step in the research was to communicate the findings to designers of computerized shopping systems. The information was intended to help designers produce more usable systems by identifying ways in which representational compatibility could be understood and increased. For example, in the case of a vase, the incompatibility between the user's representation and that of the computer might be reduced by including the criterial feature 'cut-glass' in the text, by providing the user with a separate, hard-copy catalogue containing high-resolution images, good enough to represent the visual features of cut-glass, or by making the vase a branded item known to the user, or by informing the user of the characteristics of the brand. In a different system, whose graphics are more accurate, the visual feature might be provided by the system images.

This concludes the first example of cognitive ergonomics. In contrast to traditional ergonomics, it involves a task based on computer technology, and uses a model of users' knowledge, in the manner of cognitive psychology, to identify and evaluate ways of increasing representational compatibility associated with the domain of the system's application.

The Task of a Computer-aided Design System

The second example of cognitive ergonomics is taken from research on computer-aided design (Whitefield, 1984, 1985). Design is the specification of an object, typically for manufacture, for example a bicycle frame or a chair. Computerized design systems allow designers to specify an object as a drawing they create by means of the system. The example illustrates how the compatibility between the system's representation of the task and that of the user (in this case, of the mechanical engineer) can be improved. The user's representation is here assumed to include mechanical engineering skills generally and in particular the application of design knowledge.

The framework for the research was derived from artificial intelligence in the form of the Hearsay-II speech-recognition program. Hearsay consists of a set of knowledge sources communicating via a central data structure called the 'blackboard'. The framework was modified to make it more appropriate for the design task. The final framework consists of a blackboard with dimensions of spatial location and information level, which is read from and written to by a number of different knowledge sources (see below). The blackboard contains parts of hypothesized solutions to the design problem with related parts linked together. The design is a result of the interaction between the knowledge sources and the constraints of the problem.

The framework was used to model a database of mechanical engineering design activity. The database was derived from an observational study in which designers using conventional drawing boards worked on layout designs for television and electronic-keyboard casings. To model the data, the verbal protocols of the designers were classified in two ways. The first classification concerned the activities and knowledge sources associated with the blackboard, for example 'generating' or 'evaluating' hypotheses about 'materials' or 'assembly'. The knowledge sources were divided into those involving the domain and those involving drawing. The second classification concerned the blackboard levels in the model associated with the knowledge sources, and hence also the number of levels. Analyses of the verbal protocols produced a total of twenty-three knowledge sources operating at three levels on the blackboard.

A second database, this time of users' activity on a computer-aided design system, was likewise generated and modelled. It was then possible to compare the two models because the same framework had been used to construct both. A qualitative comparison showed the two models to be very similar. However, the comparison suggested that the computer-aided group of designers used more drawing knowledge than the drawing-board group, largely at the expense of domain knowledge used to evaluate design solutions, but not of domain knowledge to generate them. This was partly because they required additional knowledge to use the system, for example how to 'navigate' around the drawing by selecting the partial view to be displayed on the screen. It was also partly because the knowledge was different in terms of the number of drawing options and their associated commands. In addition, the knowledge was more technologically determined, in the sense that designers spent much time on activities, such as the layering of drawings, which were not part of the non-computerized task. Overall, the comparison suggested that the computer-aided task increased the need for drawing knowledge which interfered with the designers' application of knowledge specific to the domain of mechanical engineering. In overall terms, it was thus lacking in compatibility.

On this basis, it was hypothesized that compatibility would be increased if changes either reduced the drawing knowledge required of the designer, or encouraged the greater use of domain knowledge. To test the hypothesis, two versions of a small, computer-aided design system

90

were devised. In the compatible version of the system, the need for drawing knowledge was reduced and the use of evaluative domain knowledge was encouraged by a total of four experimental variables. The two versions of the system were tested on a copying task requiring only drawing knowledge and a redesign task requiring both domain and drawing knowledge. The results were generally consistent with the hypothesis that compatibility would be increased by the changes made.

This concludes the second example of cognitive ergonomics, in which a framework from artificial intelligence was used to model the task of computer-aided design. The model was then used to improve the task-compatibility of an existing system.

The Interface of a Deciphering System

The third example of cognitive ergonomics is taken from research on an information manipulation and inquiry system (Barnard *et al.*, 1981). Such systems are becoming increasingly common in offices, where they are used to store and to access large databases of information, for example, census records, financial transactions, etc. This example will illustrate how the compatibility between the interface's representation of the system and that of the user might be improved.

A collection of errors and difficulties associated with the use of the system was generated. The collection consisted both of users' perceptions of the difficulties, and their experience in using the system documented by their performance. A framework was then developed to relate these difficulties to the kinds of change in system interface likely to lead to their elimination (Morton *et al.*, 1979). A very general model was constructed to reflect selected aspects of the data. The model's function was both to reflect the data and to permit further exploration thereof.

Hypotheses were then generated about the origins of selected difficulties and the ways in which a system might be structured to eliminate them. For example, users sometimes made errors in the ordering of command-language expressions. When asked to find the average age of entries in the block of data called PEOPLE, users sometimes entered AVG (AGE, PEOPLE) instead of AVG (PEOPLE, AGE), so reversing block and attribute orders. The model suggested two sources for the error: knowledge of natural language and general knowledge. In the absence of system-specific knowledge, using the order of the natural language expression of the inquiry 'what is the average age of the people?' would not have produced the correct order. Nor would the general knowledge assumption that block–attribute order was consistent across commands (in this system it was not consistent). The model also suggested two ways of modifying the interface to eliminate this type of error. The block–attribute order could be made compatible with natural language by making it the same as that used to express the inquiry. Alternatively, the order could be made compatible with general knowledge by making it consistent across all commands.

An experimental system capable of implementing both principles of ordering was developed to test the hypotheses. The supposed domain of application was spying, and subjects used the system to decipher coded messages, although in fact no knowledge of the domain was required. Subjects decoded messages using commands, for example DELETE and SAVE, requiring two numerical arguments, the number identifying the message (the recurring argument, incremented after each operation) and a number which differed with each operation (the variable argument). Each ordering principle involved two experimental conditions. The first was compatible with natural language, in that the direct object of the command preceded the indirect object (DELETE (digit) (message)), while the second was incompatible, that is, the reverse. The remaining conditions were compatible with the principle of consistent ordering. In the third condition, the message identifier (the recurring argument) always preceded the variable argument (DELETE (message) (digit)), while in the fourth, the message identifier always followed the variable argument (DELETE (digit) (message)).

The results of the experiment varied with the particular measures of performance. However, the results concerning the two ordering principles were clear enough for present purposes. Natural-language compatibility had no effect on performance, although individual commands suggested a small influence favouring the group with the direct object first. In addition, only the group having the recurring argument first was significantly better than the average of the natural-language groups. The results, then, support a restricted version of the principle of consistent ordering, that is the placing first of the recurring argument.

An account of the results was constructed on psychological and linguistic grounds and used to revise the initial ordering hypotheses. Neither compatible nor non-compatible natural-language groups appeared to be abstracting the common position of the direct object and using this abstraction as a general rule. In contrast, the group receiving the recurring argument first might have inferred the appropriate rule, whose use would have reduced the memory requirements of the task. However, it is unclear why the group with the argument placed second would not have acted similarly. Alternatively, the advantage might have accrued to the group receiving the recurring argument first, because the command structure is compatible with the way in which information is typically expressed in sentences. Information which is presupposed normally occurs before information which is novel. People's tendency to process novel information more thoroughly might have led to more attention being paid to the variable argument and so to better learning. No learning advantage would have accrued to the more thorough processing of the recurring argument, because its frequent occurrence would have ensured its easy and complete learning.

Concerning the initial hypothesis, then, the natural-language principle in the absence of any rule abstraction was revised from an ordering principle to a command-specific one. The principle of consistency was likewise revised from a simple ordering principle to one which was compatible with the structure of information presentation in sentences.

As in the other examples, the final step in the research was to inform designers of the findings in the form of principles, for example: 'placing a command argument first enhances performance only when the required command is prompted by the system or when the command vocabulary is relatively specific.' This concludes the third and last example of cognitive ergonomics, in which principles for increasing the compatibility of the system interface were developed on the basis of both cognitive and linguistic factors.

Taken together, the three examples illustrate cognitive ergonomics defined as the attempt to increase compatibility between the users' representations and those of the machine, where the machine is a computer. The illustrations cover the three areas of difficulty identified earlier (domain, task and system interface), and they recruit aspects of cognitive psychology, artificial intelligence and linguistics. The approaches have much in common: the practical aim of helping designers to produce better systems, and the use of theoretical structures and empirical methods to achieve this end. The approaches also differ between themselves, for example in the information offered to the designers, the type of theory used, the role of controlled experimentation, and the completeness with respect to the activities shown in Figure 4.1. Additional differences would have emerged had other examples been chosen. There exist alternative approaches whose aim is different from that of the examples. For instance, Card *et al.* (1983) sought to aid designers by suggesting ways in which the speed of performance of alternative system implementations may be predicted from a specification of their structure. If the performance of the user and the system can both be described in terms of time, the designer is presumed to be able to make trade-offs between their specific requirements.

In spite of the differences, however, and the limited achievement of any particular approach, cognitive ergonomics shows promise and has had some notable success. The emphasis on the real world of the workplace as the acquisition and the application domain of its activities, and the resultant strengthening of the science base (see Figure 4.1) recommend the approach more generally for psychology. In the absence of directed links with the real world, these are liable to weaken in favour of links which only relate the acquisition representation and the scientific one. The result is a poorer psychology.*

SUMMARY

This chapter has described and illustrated cognitive ergonomics as an attempt to increase representational compatibility between user and machine, where the machine is a computer. Cognitive ergonomics has two origins. The first is traditional ergonomics and its inability to cope with problems of representational incompatibility associated with the introduction of computer technology. The second is cognitive psychology and its use of linguistics, artificial intelligence and cognitive science more generally to develop the notion of the internal

* I would like to thank colleagues at the Ergonomics Unit, University College London, for useful discussion of issues raised in this chapter.

representation. The combination has produced a new configuration between work and science which shows both theoretical and applied promise.

FURTHER READING

Books on traditional ergonomics include *Ergonomics* by K. Murrell (Chapman and Hall, 1965), *Ergonomics at Work* by D. Oborne (Wiley, 1982), and *The Body at Work* edited by W. Singleton (Cambridge University Press, 1982). Books which address aspects of cognitive ergonomics include *Fundamentals of Human–Computer Interaction* edited by A. Monk (Academic Press, 1985), *Human Interaction with Computers* edited by H. Smith and T. Green (Academic Press, 1980), and *Software Psychology* by B. Shneiderman (Winthrop Publishers Inc., 1980). Other sources of both traditional and cognitive ergonomics are cited in the text.

5

Artificial Intelligence in the Workplace

John Fox

After years of predictions about its importance in industry, commerce, education and the home, information technology now affects most of us in some way. Several industries are being transformed by robot assembly techniques; commerce is increasingly reliant on electronic storage and transmission of information; many schools and colleges routinely teach computing as part of the general curriculum; home shopping and banking have arrived. Medicine, cinema, policing, transport, law; the penetration is wide. Skills too are affected; managers are increasingly expected to master information-management tools like database and financial planning packages; large numbers of teachers must at least understand the elements of computer technology; word-processing skills are demanded of office workers, and many factory workers must come to grips with computerized machine-tools, which change the pattern of their work and reduce the value of traditional manual skills in favour of mental ones (see Chapter 13).

However, although the use of information technology appears to be growing rapidly, it is growing less quickly than many people expected. In part this is only due to the fact that predicted rates of social change are often too high; we overestimate the speed at which a culture can assimilate new ideas and skills, and we underestimate the number of elements that have to change to accommodate a new technology. But one important reason for slowness in adopting information technology has less to do with the limits on people or societies, and more to do with the nature of the technology itself. Although the speed, reliability and versatility of computers in handling information cannot be matched by any human being, these information machines have one feature of all machines: they are totally unintelligent.

People are also information processors, and, although slow and prone to mistakes, they are good ones by some yardsticks. Even the least advantaged of us knows substantially more about the world and how to live in it than the most powerful super-computer. The small computer systems which we see in the office or factory possess little knowledge of the world, and are masters of few human abilities. Traditional computer systems cannot do something that we all take for granted: they cannot cope smoothly with the unpredictable, particularly when things go wrong. The most sophisticated computer systems must operate in routine situations, where the unexpected can only lie within narrow limits, as in robot welding and paint-spraying. If routine operation is not possible, the computer must rely on detailed executive control by a human being, as in word-processing or financial planning.

There are few industrial situations of the first, routine, kind. They can in principle be created (perhaps through a fully automated factory production line), but they are enormously expensive to achieve, and are subject to costly breakdowns and failures because of unanticipated events. The second possibility, on the other hand, requires difficult, and again expensive, creation of specialist skills for each and every new computer system.

It is not surprising then that the possibility of endowing future generations of computer systems with at least the rudiments of intelligence has attracted a great deal of attention. Images of intelligent robots capable of independently overcoming unexpected problems, like broken or incorrectly positioned tools, or successfully avoiding inattentive human beings wandering into their paths, are clearly attractive for design engineers. The thought of being able to bark instructions at a machine which is sufficiently intelligent to understand, however indistinct or ungrammatical those instructions, is endearing to many executives.

Both images are still far from reality. But the attention being given by technological nations to the subject of 'Artificial Intelligence', only lately an entirely academic subject, may lead to their realization. The first limited but practical body of techniques to emerge, 'knowledge engineering', is now being taken up widely by industry.

Knowledge engineering is immature, and arguably a long way from giving us really intelligent devices, but large numbers of people now assume that such devices can be built, and some believe that there are already examples of computer programs with capabilities which are reminiscent of natural intelligence. This chapter is about such knowledge engineering; the principles which underlie it and some uses to which it may be put. Issues of this kind are increasingly certain to confront the psychologist in work organizations.

THE EMERGENCE OF KNOWLEDGE ENGINEERING

Artificial Intelligence (AI) appeared as a recognizable discipline in the late 1950s and early 60s. At that time it was seen as a scientific subject, with close links to psychology. It was concerned with the principles of intelligence in people, animals and (its special contribution) machines. Like much modern cognitive psychology (which it influenced), AI used information-processing concepts as a theoretical framework for describing and explaining mental processes and the construction of computer programs to clarify and mimic the mechanisms of 'intelligence'.

Also like psychology, AI learned to avoid attempting a direct definition of intelligence. Instead it concentrated on specific abilities, but its scope was wide. It took in perception (simulating the mechanisms of vision and hearing), language (understanding the spoken and written word), decision making, problem solving and learning. Programs exist which can, to a degree, emulate these several human abilities (see Feigenbaum *et al.*, 1981, 1982). Some workers in AI have gone even further into the traditional territory of psychology, attempting to model attitude-formation, social behaviour, and even abnormal behaviour, using computer-based techniques (e.g. Boden, 1977).

Progress has been controversial and patchy, though in some areas rapid. Artificial intelligence work in visual perception and language has been very rewarding (and has had a major influence on psychological theories), while progress on learning has been slower, and some observers have questioned the viability of the whole enterprise (e.g. Dreyfus, 1979). But even within the field, few people expected a major development which occurred about ten years ago: the appearance of 'knowledge engineering'. By 1975, several AI systems had been developed that appeared to solve difficult, practical problems in medicine, science and engineering that were acknowledged to require high human expertise.

These systems came to be called 'expert systems'. Expert systems are computer systems which can cope with tasks which require expertise if carried out by people, and which exploit, at least in part, human understanding of the tasks. It was not that scientists now understood the fundamental principles or mechanisms of intelligent behaviour, but that symbolic programming techniques had been developed which were sufficient to solve specialist problems in ways that seemed comparable to human specialists.

I am going to concentrate on just one part of knowledge engineering in this chapter. This has to do with decision making. There are several reasons why it is natural to limit ourselves to decision making, largely leaving aside such problems as natural-language translation, robot control and so on, even though these may partly use expert-system techniques. First, the expert systems which can be routinely developed now are fundamentally decision-making or decision-supporting systems. Second, decision making is a key element of these more advanced capabilities. Finally, but not least, I will focus upon decision making because it is sufficiently simple to present the concepts of knowledge engineering clearly.

DECISION TECHNOLOGY AND EXPERT SYSTEMS

Many types of computer system can be used to help make decisions. Business, professional, public, and personal decisions can all be supported by data-processing techniques. Databases can provide information for stock-control decisions; statistical packages can identify significant situations or trends for public policy; accounting programs may help to plan personal spending, and so on. However I am not concerned here with data-processing techniques which simply inform decision-makers, but with a more complete decision technology which embodies a theory of what decisions are and methods for taking them.

Expert systems are not the first decision technology. For more than twenty years statisticians and others have developed mathematical techniques for medical diagnosis, educational assessment, personnel selection, staff allocation etc. This mathematical approach has often been very successful. However the numerical techniques used are very different from those used in expert systems.

We can illustrate this with a medical example; medicine is probably the largest non-military area of application for both expert systems and statistical methods. Suppose a patient comes to a doctor with particular symptoms. The doctor's aim is to consider these symptoms and perhaps to decide upon the most likely diagnosis. To take advantage of a mathematical technique in making this decision, a computer program like that summarized in Figure 5.1 could be used.

The three boxes represent the three essential components of the decision system. First, there are data for the particular patient; the symptoms and other information. Second, there is a database. Typically this contains a set of numbers; parameters such as mathematical probabilities, which represent the overall likelihood of particular symptoms occurring with particular diseases. The database may be compiled by asking specialists to estimate the correct values for the numbers, or more accurately by observing the frequency of symptoms in sufficiently large samples of patients. Finally, some mathematical formula (such as 'Bayes' rule', after the Reverend Thomas Bayes who invented it) is used, in conjunction with the database, to calculate the probability of each possible diagnosis for the patient given his or her particular symptoms. Many mathematical methods have been developed for

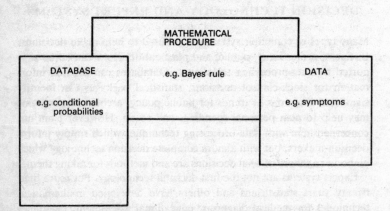

Fig. 5.1 A mathematical approach to medical decision-making.

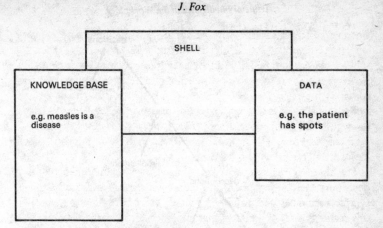

Fig. 5.2   An expert systems approach to medical decision-making.

carrying out this sort of calculation, but they all fall within the general scheme.

Figure 5.2 is an analogous, schematic diagram of an expert system. Its form is superficially similar, but this is deceptive. The distinctive characteristic of expert systems is that they emphasize qualitative, logical reasoning, not quantitative calculations. Consequently the database of an expert system does not contain numbers exclusively, and may not contain numbers at all. We call this material the 'knowledge base'.

A key feature of a knowledge base is that its contents are not abstract symbols like conditional probabilities or other numbers. Probabilities represent the *magnitude* of the relationship between a symptom and a disease, but not the *meaning* of that relationship. In expert systems the aim is to represent meaning explicitly, by recording concepts in a way that reflects people's understanding of them, but also in a form that a computer can exploit. For example, an important component of a knowledge base is often a body of facts which represent the way in which concepts are related to each other. Diseases *cause* symptoms; some symptoms are *side-effects* of treatments; some diseases are *specialized forms* of more general categories, and so on.

From Data to Decisions

Figure 5.3 is a schematic representation of many of the things that may be found in the knowledge base of an expert system. The most primitive

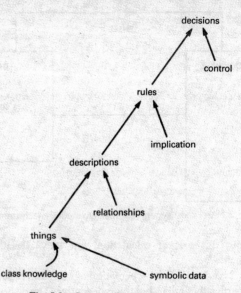

Fig. 5.3 Contents of a knowledge base.

element, shared with all other computer programs, is the symbol. By progressively adding more symbolic elements, the ability of the knowledge base to represent complex ideas increases. At the top of the figure is a simple kind of expert system that can make decisions. What follows is an explanation of the steps involved.

Computer programs manipulate *symbols*. Usually, however, these symbols are simply strings of letters and numbers like 'Mr Jones', 'measles', 'age' and '55' which have meaning for a human being looking at them but no explicit meaning for the computer. The first step in attaching meaning to these symbols is to say what kind of *things* they are, to say what *classes* of objects or concepts they are members of. Here are some medical examples:

Measles is a viral infection

Insulin is a drug

Chemotherapy is a kind of treatment

John Smith is a patient

Facts like this can be stored explicitly in a knowledge base for an expert system to use. Some programs permit the knowledge to be written directly in this sort of natural notation. The next step is to add more meaning by *relating* some things to other things. As more and more relationships between symbols are established, the contents of the knowledge base come to approximate the meaning of those symbols more and more closely. In these examples the main relationships are emphasized:

> John Smith *is* elderly
>
> Abnormalities of blood *include* leukaemia
>
> Poor hygiene *causes* infections
>
> Aspirin *reduces* inflammation

Descriptions alone are not sufficient for reasoning, making decisions or solving problems. We also need to be able to infer new facts or new data from existing ones. This is often done by *logical reasoning*, with 'if . . . then . . .' *rules*; the third step in the ladder in Figure 5.3.

> If spleen is enlarged
>
> > and asymmetrical enlargement of lymph nodes is confirmed
>
> then Hodgkin's disease is possible

Given data about a patient, rules of this kind are capable of drawing inferences about the patient, like inferences about possible diagnoses or treatments. However we cannot merely put a large number of rules in a pot and stir. When we have many rules (and a few knowledge-based systems already employ hundreds or thousands of such rules) we need to *control* the reasoning process. For example, some rules should take priority over others. Consider these two rules:

> If anaemia is present
>
> then iron supplement is required   (1)

> If anaemia is present
>
> > and spleen is enlarged
>
> then investigation for Hodgkin's disease is required   (2)

Rule 2 is more specialized than rule 1; if the patient data satisfy rule 2, then rule 1 will also be satisfied. But rule 2 refers to a situation where a significant disease may be present and an iron supplement might be quite inappropriate. A skilful decision maker does not apply rules blindly, but selectively. An expert system must be similarly controlled. The expert system program, the shell in Figure 5.2, often provides the necessary control, but in some cases knowledge about how to use knowledge is stored as part of the knowledge base.

If the knowledge base is sufficiently comprehensive it contains all the information that is required to make any *decision*. The shell makes sure that items are only retrieved when they are relevant to the decision or purpose at hand. Although many expert system shells are more elaborate than our description, and provide additional tools to make knowledge engineering practical, the power of these systems comes primarily from the quality and comprehensiveness of the knowledge base, not from the technical details of the program.

More Sophisticated Knowledge-based Systems

The first generation of practical expert systems were merely systems for making choices by the controlled application of general knowledge about problems to specific cases. For example one of the first expert systems, MYCIN, was designed to help decide what antibiotics to use for a particular patient with a particular infection, on the basis of general knowledge about organisms and infections (e.g. Buchanan and Shortliffe, 1984). The system called Prospector was designed to decide on profitable sites for drilling or mining, using general knowledge about geological formations and how they are associated with oil and minerals. These decisions, however, are really only the building blocks of more sophisticated skills, which have considerable industrial potential. Such skills include planning and design, and the capability to develop new skills for new situations.

Figure 5.4 illustrates the important new ingredients which can transform the simple decision maker into a system capable of more complex problem solving. Important problem-solving abilities are the ability to plan (e.g. planning a complex medical treatment or an industrial production schedule) and to design (e.g. designing a heart valve or a piece of electronic equipment). Although the two words are often used

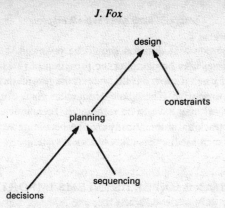

Fig. 5.4   Planning and design within an expert system.

interchangeably, they are used in knowledge engineering to refer to different kinds of problem solving.

A *plan* is usually thought of as a sequence of goals; to plan a drug treatment we must decide on a drug, then how to administer it, and then the dosage. The method of administration cannot be decided until the drug has been chosen, and in many cases the dosage can only be settled after it is decided whether to give the drug by mouth, injection, etc. In- dustrial planning often requires choice of materials before determining method of manufacture, and so forth.

Design requires an additional feature, the ability to take into account logical constraints which can affect decisions. In drug treatment again, some drugs must not be used if others are being taken, or if the patient is elderly, or suffering from certain conditions. In industrial design we must take into account the availability of components, the need for easy maintenance of the product, and so forth. The knowledge base of an expert system which is capable of planning or design must contain facts or rules to reflect these constraints.

Both these capabilities require another ability familiar to all of us, the ability to change one's mind. To make a choice, all that is in principle necessary is to consider the various alternatives (diseases, treatments etc.), weigh up the evidence or the desirable and undesirable features of the alternatives, and then choose the one that is most likely or desirable overall. When making a plan or a design however, we must build up the plan or design over a number of stages. During later stages it may emerge that an earlier decision was wrong, and therefore that everything based upon that decision should be reviewed. For example, a human designer may be planning the provision of raw materials for a new product when it turns out that one of the raw materials is unavailable or too expensive. The whole production plan, even the original product design, may have to be rethought. Techniques for doing this sort of 'backtracking' automatically are now becoming available and will significantly increase the versatility of expert systems.

WHY ARE EXPERT SYSTEMS IMPORTANT?

We are familiar with new technologies, almost blasé about communications, space technology, robots, word-processing, biotechnology and the rest. But expert systems seem to have attracted an interest which is unprecedented even for new technologies. Japan, the USA, the EEC and individual countries of Europe have committed huge public and private resources to research and development in expert systems and the parent discipline of artificial intelligence. Why?

Some of the reasons can be put down to politics and fashion. But these are surely not enough to explain the scale of investment and international consensus which appear to exist. I think that there are three main sources of the preoccupation with A I; the potential scope of the field; its expected penetration into our personal lives; and its implications for the way we see ourselves.

If knowledge engineering achieves all, or even most, of its objectives (still a big 'if'), then it is clear that its range of application will be huge. Other new technologies focus on specific activities, like the production of documents (word-processing), or assembling objects from parts (robots), or synthesizing new drugs (biotechnology). But even the first generation of expert systems seems to cut across activities, disciplines and industries. Table 5.1 illustrates just a few of the expert system projects started in the United Kingdom in the last year or two.

This list is limited by the decision-making capabilities of the first generation of knowledge-based systems, and yet it is still extremely wide. Once planning and design are added, the limits of application of expert systems become difficult to see. So the first reason for strong interest in A I is its potential wide scope. If the technology is as broadly applicable as predicted, then A I could prove to be a primary influence

TABLE 5.1 *Recent expert systems applications in the United Kingdom*

Commerce and trade:	harbour regulations; investment broking
Equipment maintenance:	fault-finding; fault-monitoring
Farming:	selection of fertilizers and timing of planting
Home:	gardening advice; baby management
Interpretation of law:	British Nationality Act, patents legislation
Manufacturing:	packaging of chemicals; assembly of computers
Medicine:	diagnosis; risk-assessment; treatment planning
Regulations advice:	pension and mortgage schemes; tax liability
Social services:	detection of child abuse; social security entitlements

on social, industrial and commercial change; it could affect the way we do everything, not just within specific industries or particular activities across industries.

The second reason for interest in expert systems concerns not what they can do but who they are likely to reach. Again it will be obvious from Table 5.1 that the kinds of activities they perform are of use to ordinary people, not just specialists and technicians. Word-processing is primarily for office workers, biotechnology for scientists, robots for production engineers. But expert systems can give advice on medical, tax, legal, and a host of other problems of potential value to everyone.

The final reason for interest in AI perhaps has something to do with human vanity. For centuries we have imagined making machines in our own likenesses; the idea of making systems in our own intellectual likeness is merely a modern form of this. Machines that are capable of formulating and solving problems for themselves, without referring to human controllers, both fascinate and terrify us. We find ourselves involved in a way that would be unthinkable for other branches of technology.

ARTIFICIAL INTELLIGENCE IN THE WORKPLACE

So what does all this have to do with work? It has to do with the changes that the introduction of A I could bring about. As pointed out in several other chapters, innovations produce changes well beyond the special-ized technicalities of the innovation. Assembly robots do not simply improve the finish of cars or the consistency of welding, or reduce the need for skilled labour. All these changes may happen, but experience shows that there are many other side-effects, often major ones. The labour force may find that its activities change, and the skills required for the new regime may be different, perhaps with different implications for the young and the old. Patterns of prestige and reward can be affected. Unaffected groups may be threatened. Apparently straightforward changes in how we do things can often take on a political dimension.

This section speculates about changes that could accompany the widespread use of A I techniques. Our purpose is not to look into the future and make certain and general predictions – long-term and wide-ranging social prediction is unreliable – but to explore the kinds of change that A I could bring about. If A I is to have a major influence, and we are to have any degree of choice about the nature of that influence, we must establish in advance the more likely developments. The areas that I shall look at are two rather general ones; the availability of work and changes in patterns of skill.

Effects on the Availability of Work

The primary motivation for any kind of industrial or commercial innova-tion is usually economic; perhaps to reduce production costs, increase service efficiency or establish a competitive edge. The adoption of A I is unlikely to be different in this respect. The ability to replace decision-makers, planners, designers and so on with their machine counterparts will probably be as attractive to future managers and investors as the replacement of skilled machinists with numerically controlled machine-tools was to earlier industrialists.

Initially the process is likely to be slow, because the cost of installing A I systems will be high for some while, as it has been with many new technologies. But as the technology becomes routine and costs fall, and as the long-term advantages become accepted, the investment will be made. This pattern is evident in other parts of information technology. Computer-aided design reduces the need for routine drafting work; word-processing reduces or eliminates the need for repetitive typing; electronic publishing removes work from typesetters, layout departments and artists.

But A I could cut deeper than these other computer applications. The ability of the machines to solve problems autonomously without having recourse to human discretion can only amplify the existing trend to displace labour. It is no longer fanciful to imagine computer systems working from rough functional requirements to produce detailed designs and manufacturing plans for new products, or for 'intelligent' office systems to translate documents from one language to another and even to generate memos, letters and technical documentation without human participation.

So A I will increase the rate of depletion of jobs in many areas. But history again suggests that cannot be the only effect. The technology will create its own industry; perhaps fifty companies already have a significant A I activity in the U K alone at the time of writing. This means new jobs. Many jobs may also be relatively immune because the cost of the technology is too high or the problems of its introduction intractable. Most hopeful of all may be the possibility that A I leads to entirely new activities rather than merely displacing old ones. A whole range of additional software products like expert systems, with new companies to provide and maintain them, may be introduced for the home, school and workplace which do not threaten any existing activity. However, the balance of creation and depletion will not be clear for a long time to come.

The Need for Human Skills

If jobs are depleted and/or created, then the requirements for the skills they employ will be increased or decreased. Knowledge engineering presently offers most to those activities which depend on routine intellectual skills, particularly those which exploit knowledge that can be written down; less to those which require physical dexterity and coordination; little for problems involving rapidly changing or novel circumstances, and almost nothing at all in situations which require wide appreciation of the world and its affairs. An optimistic interpretation of these observations is that (as was said about earlier waves of automation) A I will take the drudgery out of intellectual work, leaving people to do the interesting things; dealing with the new and exciting, the artistic side of life, working with people, and so on.

Well that may be, but it would be unwise to be complacent; the reasons that knowledge engineering is limited may not be quite the ones you would expect. It is an odd paradox of research in A I that the executive skills and activities widely desired and admired in many industrial societies (those based on knowledge, judgement and intellectual prowess) have proved to be most tractable to A I techniques, while the ordinary faculties of perception and language and commonsense which most of us take for granted have been the hardest to simulate by machine. A pessimistic interpretation, then, is that the computer will do more and more of the prestige work, leaving people to fill in the details. Machines will design the product; people will switch on and service the machines. Computers will plan the production schedule; human workers will operate it. Electronic doctors will decide what is wrong and what the treatment will be; the real ones will give the injections.

Like me, you may doubt both the optimistic and the pessimistic images of the future, but both may be true in part. Some things that we enjoy and find rewarding will be easy to automate and will be lost to us, while in other cases we may be glad that we are no longer required to do repetitive correspondence, keep up to date with turgid government regulations, or carry out routine examinations of an unending stream of items on a production line.

Without a deeper understanding of what people are good at and machines are not there will be damaging mistakes in the introduction of A I. Some mistakes will be merely expensive failures, others may be economically acceptable but encourage the fragmentation of skills and the consequent dehumanization of work. This is not new with A I; it happened with the introduction of factory methods and mass production, and again with automation. But the scope of A I methods may mean it goes deeper and wider.

Most people who read this might expect to be exempt from the negative side of industrial change. No longer. The doctor, the lawyer, the teacher, the psychologist . . . the manager, the scientist, the farmer . . . there are projects in A I which are aimed at developing expert systems for use in all these fields. The one group you might have expected to acquire an élite immunity, that of the computer scientists, is vulnerable too. An active branch of AI research is concerned with automatic programming.

SUMMARY

Information technology is having a substantial and rapidly growing influence on our lives. The ingenuity of software designers and the changing economics of computing are the driving forces of this growth, but there is an important limit to the conventional developments. This limit is that conventional systems are narrowly specialized and overly rigid in their interactions with the world and with people. To use them we must either make the world very predictable, or ensure that a human being provides executive problem-solving capabilities.

It is now plausible, though it remains to be convincingly demonstrated, that the techniques of AI could change this pattern. In a few years' time computer systems could have the ability to solve a wide range of decision problems without human intervention. This superficially simple capability requires further technical and theoretical advances in the field, but sufficient progress has been made to suggest an unprecedented range of applications.

The current generation of knowledge-based systems is useful but limited; the next generation is likely to be much more competent and flexible in processes of decision making, planning and design. Looking further into the future, it is likely that it will be possible to design systems that can not only solve problems, but also learn how to solve them. The key concept which distinguishes these systems from their mathematical and algorithmic predecessors is the explicit application of knowledge. Knowledge-based techniques are beginning to yield systems with something resembling human expertise, though whether we can achieve true intelligence remains to be seen.

FURTHER READING

Knowledge engineering emerged from the academic study of machine and human intelligence. M. Boden's book on *Artificial Intelligence and*

Natural Man (Harvester Press, 1977) is still a good and readable introduction, while for the technically minded the three volumes of *The Handbook of Artificial Intelligence* (Pitman, 1981, 1982) by E. A. Feigenbaum and his colleagues is a good survey up until about 1982. In contrast, H. L. Dreyfus's book *What Computers Can't Do* (Harper and Row, 1979) might be read for balance. J. F. Sowa's attempt (1984) to bring together cognitive psychology, artificial intelligence and classical computer science makes delightful reading, though is rather technical in places.

R. O. Duda and E. H. Shortliffe (1983) provide a short but authoritative description of research in expert systems, focusing on some of the better-known systems of 1983, while F. Hayes-Roth and colleagues provide a useful tour of concepts and problems in *Building Expert Systems* (Addison-Wesley, 1983).

Although expert systems are being developed for a wide range of industrial and commercial applications, medicine was the first, and still one of the largest, areas of application. *Readings in Medical Artificial Intelligence, The First Decade* (Addison-Wesley, 1984), edited by W. J. Clancey and E. H. Shortliffe, reprints a number of classic papers in the field. Another useful book, edited by B. G. Buchanan and E. H. Shortliffe (1984), describes ten years of the MYCIN project; MYCIN was the first recognizable expert system and almost defined the subject in its first years.

The journals *Artificial Intelligence* (North-Holland) and *Expert Systems* (Learned Information) are prime sources of academic and practical work in their fields, and the proceedings of the biannual International Joint Conference on Artificial Intelligence (published by Kaufmann) are a rich source of new ideas and developments.

6

Personnel Selection

Pieter Drenth and Jen Algera

In view of the wide differences between jobs and between people it would be surprising if a group of applicants for a number of vacancies measured up completely and exactly to the psychological demands of the positions. In many cases one has to try to remove person–job discrepancies, and three types of procedure have been applied with this aim. One can try to compensate for individual deficiencies through training (see Chapter 3), or one can modify the task so that it becomes adapted to the individual (see Chapter 4). The third approach is through selection, attempting to choose the most qualified person for each post. Selection methods may of course be applied in conjunction with the other two approaches, but they do require one important condition to be met, namely that the characteristics or personality traits which are responsible for success or failure in the position can be identified.

Before examining this question more deeply, a few points of definition need to be considered. Although the word 'selection' is sometimes used with a very broad reference, it is preferable to distinguish it from 'placement' procedures. One should only speak of selection when it is a question of the organization's accepting or rejecting an individual. A further distinction can be made between 'threshold-selection' and 'comparative-selection' (Hofstee, 1983). The former refers to accepting or rejecting an individual on the basis of passing an absolute, 'threshold', qualification, as can be the case in admission to higher-education systems. The latter type of selection, which is customary in work organizations, means that the organization picks the best candidate for a vacancy, then the next best, and so on until all vacancies are filled. In other situations we may not be concerned to accept or reject but rather to distribute employees over several levels or over qualitatively different posts that lie on the same level ('placement' or 'allocation').

However selection is defined, it is clear that the process should be part of a general policy in which the management and care of personnel is integrated. In other words, one cannot isolate selection and placement from total personnel policy. It is preceded by advertising and recruitment, and followed by induction, training and education, career planning and general management of personnel.

The contribution of psychology to selection has been influential on the one hand through the introduction of new psychological measuring instruments (tests and other types of predictors), and on the other hand through an evaluation of the contribution of interviews and other procedures to the selection process. As selection psychology developed historically, it gradually broadened its outlook. Four aspects can be distinguished which illustrate this gradual expansion: predictor orientation, criterion orientation, prediction models, and decision orientation. While these are not historical phases which exactly follow each other, they do broadly represent the main changes which have come about. They may be considered separately, although they necessarily overlap to some extent.

PREDICTOR ORIENTATION

The goal of selection procedures is to predict future behaviour of applicants in the job. Several types of predictors can be used. Undoubtedly, the most widely used procedure by work organizations is the employment interview. The next chapter (Chapter 7) specifically deals with interviewing, so in this chapter we will concentrate on other types of predictors.

Two approaches for predicting future behaviour can be distinguished (Wernimont and Campbell, 1968): the 'sign' approach and the 'sample' approach. In the 'sign' approach, a relation between personality traits and work behaviour is hypothesized. Both traits and work behaviour (the 'criterion' in this case) are defined at a theoretical, conceptual level, and have to be made operational by means of specific measures. The latter require a test score as a measure of the conceptual predictor (for example, intelligence) and an assessment of work performance as a measure of the conceptual criterion (for example, quality of work output). In the 'sample' approach, the job is considered as a universe of

114

tasks, from which a sample can be presented to the applicant in order to predict his or her future performance in the job. For example, a typing task might be used for the selection of secretaries. A main question in this approach has to do with the representativeness of the sample of tasks from the universe of tasks in the job.

Several reviews on the predictive power (predictive validity) of different types of predictors (e.g. general mental-ability tests, personality tests, biographical information, work samples) for different types of criteria (e.g. performance ratings, tenure, productivity) have appeared (Ghiselli, 1966, 1973; Schmitt *et al.*, 1984). In general, personality tests tend to have lower validity than other types of predictors such as cognitive ability tests and work samples.

The most salient contribution of psychology to personnel selection procedures started with the use of psychological tests. The characteristics of these will now be considered.

Psychological Tests

Initially, the selection psychologist worked in an isolated way. He stood, as it were, at the entrance of the company or institution and determined who could enter and who had to remain outside. It is not strange that the psychological test was relied upon to a large extent, since this instrument differs from other methods of assessment in a number of qualities that make it very suitable for its predictive task. A good test is characterized by the following features:

1. It is sufficiently reliable; that is, its results are not influenced too much by chance factors; it is a relatively consistent and constant, not too 'elastic', measuring staff.

2. It is normative; that is, norms have been determined on the basis of relevant and circumscribed samples.

3. It is sufficiently valid; that is, there is enough empirical evidence for two claims about the test; firstly that it measures the capacity or personality trait which it is supposed to measure (construct-validity), and secondly that it predicts with reasonable certainty the future performance or behaviour of the tested individual (predictive validity).

In the phase of predictor orientation, attention was directed primarily and often exclusively to the instrument as such. Numerous forms and specimens were constructed, modified, and adapted to particular circumstances. For a review we may refer to one of the many manuals on the subject (e.g. Anastasi, 1976; Cronbach, 1984; Guilford, 1959; Heiss, 1963; Meili, 1961; Vernon, 1956). The most illustrative for the extent of test production are the periodical Mental Measurement Yearbooks (1938, 1941, 1953, 1965, 1969, 1972, 1978) issued by Buros, in which thousands of tests are mentioned and discussed.

In addition, test theory and psychometrics also began to develop. Since Thurstone's (1931) publication on the reliability and validity of tests, many books and articles have appeared; and there now exists (for this development has continued to the present) a sizeable psychometric bibliography.

The Structure of Intelligence

An important side-effect of the emphasis of selection psychology on the test has been a concentration of attention on the nature and structure of intelligence. The extremely pragmatic, empirically oriented selection psychologists have recognized that mere attention to the question 'does it work?' (in this case – 'does the test correlate significantly with the criterion?') proves to be fruitless. Not only is there no scientific progress with this narrowly empiricist approach, but also the practitioner reaches a stalemate when he is merely interested in the practical question of predictive validity. Knowledge of a more theoretical kind, about the psychological meaning of what the test measures, is necessary to improve predictions, to make a sound choice of tryout tests, and to be able to make statements about an individual in a new situation.

After the spectacular successes of Binet, who was the first to successfully identify intelligence through the famous Binet–Simon test (1905), but who concerned himself less with mental processes themselves, it took a long time before there was again interest in the nature and structure of intelligence. It was Spearman (1927) who continued where Binet's predecessors had left off, and renewed the discussion with his theory of the occurrence of a general and specific factor in every intelligence test. Additionally he attempted to find measures that would correlate with all kinds of intellectual performance, without becoming

116

specifically dependent on, for instance, verbal or numerical achievement. His g-factor (general ability) is accordingly close to the reasoning factor which is measured to a great extent by tests like the Raven Progressive Matrices and Cattell's Culture Fair Test.

In Britain, psychologists such as Burt and Vernon maintained interest in tests for more general factors, while attention in the USA became strongly directed towards the search for a number of group factors. A leading worker in the latter tradition was L. L. Thurstone (1930), who isolated seven main factors from a series of fifty-six tasks. These factors were called 'primary mental abilities' and were believed to be more or less elementary in the chemical sense of the word. All intellectual performances were considered to be a product of some kind of combination of these primary abilities. These seven factors were: V(Verbal), N(Number), S(Spatial), M(Memory), R(Reasoning), W(Word fluency) and P(Perceptual speed).

It is now generally recognized that the discussion about g-factors and/or group-factors and/or specific factors, besides being a partly semantic question, is also to a large extent a matter of taste. Nowadays more and more emphasis is being put on the so-called hierarchical view (e.g. Burt, 1949; Cronbach, 1984; Humphreys, 1962; Vernon, 1971). In this hierarchical thinking, one assumes several levels of factors; the higher the level of a factor, the broader its nature and the wider range of performances it is thought to account for.

According to Sternberg (1985) these 'psychometric' theories of intelligence, differing in the number of factors and their geometric structure, are more in agreement than it looks at first sight. They share the assumption that individual differences provide a basis for identifying the dimensions of intelligence. Further, these different theories can be incorporated in hierarchical models.

Cognitive tests measuring different abilities or aptitudes (e.g. the General Aptitude Test Battery (GATB)) still form the backbone of most predictor batteries, although other types of predictors (work samples, biodata) can do at least equally well (Schmitt *et al.*, 1984). Fleishman and his co-workers have defined many abilities, not only in the cognitive domain but also in the perceptual and motor domain (see Fleishman and Quaintance, 1984).

CRITERION ORIENTATION

A strongly increasing attention to the criterion, i.e. the future behaviour to be predicted, meant an important widening of the scope of interest. This occurred not only on theoretical grounds, but also for the practical reason that, despite the very considerable energy and ingenuity devoted to the instruments and tests themselves, the resulting correlations with criteria remained of only moderate magnitude.

Conceptual Problems

Some confusion exists about the notion of a criterion in relation to such concepts as norms, goals and values. There are two main problems: a temporal issue (how long does one have to wait to collect criterion data?), and a question of which level of abstraction is most suitable. As far as the temporal question goes, Thorndike's (1949) distinction between ultimate, intermediate and immediate criteria may be of help, but these levels can in practice become somewhat blurred.

With respect to the question of abstraction, three levels can be distinguished. First, the level of *goals*. At this level it is a matter of formulating the aim of the process in the framework of which a prediction is wanted. We are here concerned with terms such as 'the mental health of society', 'the survival of the company', 'the optimal development of the child' (ultimate goals); or somewhat more concretely with 'social adaptation of clients', 'sufficient capability for work' or 'possession of knowledge and skills in a number of areas' (conceptual criteria).

Second, the level of *criterion behaviour*. This refers to behaviour or performance that is considered to be representative of the ultimate goal or conceptual criterion. Parallel to the formulations just cited, we find at this level terms like 'therapist's rating of behaviour', 'work performance', and 'school achievements'.

Third, the level of *criterion measure*. This measure or score is nothing more than an operationalization of the criterion behaviour. 'Score on rating scale X', 'number of units per hour', 'score on achievement test Y' are examples of such a measure.

It should be emphasized that the relationship between level one (goal) and level two (criterion behaviour) is not primarily a matter for empirical investigation. The question of which criterion behaviour is the best translation of a goal which is formulated in abstract and often rather ideological terms (values, ideals, norms) is a matter of judged relevance and acceptability. The psychologist will always have to make this judgement in consultation with the persons responsible for the decisions. To mention a practical example: the question whether it is preferable to use a criterion in terms of success during training or one in terms of actual work performance (there can be a great difference between the two; see Ghiselli, 1966) is not an empirical question but a matter of choice.

A major problem is that the more reliable criterion measures can be the less relevant ones. A score on the final paper-and-pencil achievement test (at the end of training) is a reliable criterion for the selection of potential pilots, but it is probably not as relevant as an evaluation of their flying skill. A verbal test of cookery knowledge is a reliable criterion, but is less relevant than a more direct measure of quality of cooking.

Developments in the Criterion

The results of empirical validation research, in terms of observed correlations between predictor and criterion, are generally poor. In a number of studies of the validities of very many tests with numerous criteria (Ghiselli, 1966, 1973; Schmitt *et al.*, 1984) the conclusion is reached that the average correlations for the different criteria lie no higher than the 0·30s or low 0·40s.

However, a correlation with a criterion is not the only standard for evaluating the test. Seen from a decision-making viewpoint, one can find situations in which rather low correlations still make a very meaningful contribution to the selection decision, whereas in other circumstances even a very high correlation has hardly any effect. None the less, it is obvious that in any particular situation the higher correlations are preferable. And seen from this viewpoint the results, as already indicated, are rather disappointing. The consequences have been that interest in selection research has somewhat diminished, that the psychologist has concentrated on statistically significant rather than practically useful differences, or that he or she simply returned to selection without research, 'claiming near-miracles of clinical insight' (Dunnette, 1963b).

However, meta-analytical procedures have recently been developed and applied to validation studies (see e.g. Schmidt and Hunter, 1981). Meta-analysis refers to (statistical) procedures which try to integrate and combine findings from individual studies. Within the framework of personnel selection, the basic issue is whether outcomes from individual validation studies can be combined so that cumulative knowledge can be developed, i.e. whether validity information can be generalized to other situations. Results of research on validity generalization seem to suggest that a number of statistical artifacts, e.g. sampling error, differences between studies in criterion unreliability, are responsible for the rather low average correlations found, and that the 'true' validity (after correction for these artifacts) can be much higher. This issue of validity generalization will be elaborated more fully in the next section; we concentrate now on explanations for the rather low *observed* correlations.

In the analysis of possible reasons for these low values, part of the problem is with the *test*. Attempts to construct a test for socially relevant criteria have frequently failed. As an illustration, we might refer to the trouble it took, and still takes, to construct satisfactory tests of creativity or 'social intelligence' that are sufficiently independent from general intelligence tests.

Another part of the difficulty can be located in the design of the validation study. The groups used for validation research are sometimes much too heterogeneous. Ghiselli's work (1966) shows that the group to be studied can often be classified into sub-groups, for which test–criterion relationships differ from the relationship found for the group as a whole.

Another set of reasons for low validity coefficients rests in the *criterion itself*. In the first place, measures are often unreliable. All too frequently subjective classifications, arbitrary grades or unreliable performance ratings are gratuitously accepted. One cannot expect to obtain acceptable validities with unreliable criteria. Secondly, we should note that insufficient recognition of all kinds of external variables can have a distorting effect on the correlation between test and criterion. Ghiselli's book is surprising not only in the rather low average correlations, but also in the great variety in validities with respect to the same kind of criteria. To cite a few examples: the correlation of intelligence tests with administrative criteria in different studies varies from -0.4 to $+0.8$; spatial ability tests correlate with performance of machine operators from -0.55 to $+0.65$. These results can be explained by a repeatedly different nuancing of the criterion in question, due to all kinds of organizational or environmental factors; job performance is affected by extra-individual factors which vary from study to study. In the discussion on validity generalization we will return to this issue.

Thirdly, it should be noted that low correlations are often generated by too simple a model, namely one in terms of a predictor and a single criterion. More often than occurs in practice, it seems necessary to refine the criterion. Two suggestions may be offered:

1. *Multidimensionality*. Although one speaks easily about a 'successful student' or a 'good worker', this does not mean that one single criterion measure can be found in which the total criterion behaviour is reflected. Toops (1944), in his classic article on the criterion problem, points out that an individual can be good for diverse reasons. A secretary can be good because he or she types quickly, types neatly, is friendly to clients, maintains a comprehensive filing system, or for other reasons. This point has been repeatedly substantiated, and for such reasons Dunnette (1963a) has advised: 'junk *the* criterion'. Schmidt and Kaplan (1971) discuss the dilemma in validation research: for reasons of understanding why tests correlate with criteria, multiple criterion measures are needed; but, from an economic point of view, a single criterion, reflecting the economic value of job performance, would be called for. They advocate following both lines: for the former purpose, separate criterion elements should be analysed, and from the economic point of view a single composite criterion, irrespective of the intercorrelations between criterion elements, should be constructed.

2. *Timeboundedness*. A criterion is rarely a timeless, perpetually valid given. Every criterion choice is bound to the moment of determination, and definitely is not always generalizable. For instance, Fleishman (1954) has demonstrated marked changes in the factor analytic structure of human motor functions during learning. At the early stages of learning a complex coordination skill a large proportion of variance can be accounted for by (a) a cognitive factor (knowledge of rules, procedures, processes) and (b) a more general coordination

factor. Towards the end of a 100-minute practice, however, the cognitive factor is replaced by a large specific coordination factor and a smaller motor speed factor. It will be obvious that the moment at which the criterion is determined will have clear repercussions for the question of which tests will correlate highly with it.

Indirect Criterion Research

This section on criterion orientation may be concluded with a few words about a useful side-effect of this kind of critical analysis of the criterion. This side-effect has also arisen from the increasing attention to construct validity instead of the predictive validity of a test. We said previously that the choice of the criterion is ultimately the responsibility of the sponsor; but this does not mean that the psychologist must accept and try to predict any criterion which is suggested.

The kind of objectionable situation that the politics of 'hands off the sacrosanct criterion' can lead to is shown in the well-known example of Travers (1951), in which a questionnaire designed to measure leadership qualities was validated against a rating criterion. In analysis of the data it appeared that, for example, weights for alternatives such as 'from a large city', and 'from a merchant's family' were negative, while weights for 'from the country' and 'from industrial occupations' were positive. In an attempt to explain these facts, it emerged that these item weights clearly reflected the anti-semitic feelings of the judges in the company concerned. Taking over this criterion uncritically only perpetuates and sanctions such a prejudice. Indeed, a correlation reveals as much about the criterion (as seen from the predictor) as it does about the predictor (as seen from the criterion).

PREDICTION MODELS

After our discussion of some characteristics of the predictor and the criterion, we now come to the question how to relate these two concepts to each other, how to specify the relation between predictor and criterion. To illustrate the use of such 'prediction models' we start with a discussion of the classical model for realizing a predictive relation between tests and future job performance.

The Classical Model

The classical model of the construction and evaluation of a test or test battery in the framework of selection consists of the following phases:

1. *Job analysis.* An attempt to understand psychologically which requirements there are for success in the job for which selection is to be made.

2. *Choice of a criterion.* An effort to define job performance in operational terms.

3. *Choice of a tryout series of tests.* This choice is based on knowledge of the particular job. If there are no tests available, one can translate them or construct them anew. It is advisable to select more tests, and to have (some 50 per cent) more items per test than will be needed eventually. This is because a number of tests and items will turn out to be unsuitable and will have to be deleted.

4. *First tryout.* In this phase, an evaluation is made of the general applicability of the tests, the adequacy of the time limits, the reliability of the tests and the like. Tests are changed and improved.

5. *Administration on an experimental group of subjects.* Ideally a group should only be considered if it is completely representative of the class of individuals for which the test will later be used. This means that one should really test a group of candidates in an application situation, but at this stage the data should not be used for selection decisions.

6. *Validation of the test or battery of tests.* When the experimental group has worked in the company for a sufficient period of time, criterion data should be collected and the relationship between test results and criterion performance can be investigated. Weights can be determined on the basis of correlations with the criterion and intercorrelations with other tests.

7. *Make-up of the test battery in final forms.* Finally, one has to choose the tests themselves, determine the weight of the test scores, determine the sequence, and so forth.

In actual practice we are unlikely to find a perfect relationship between tests and criteria, but we do hope to find a better than zero correlation. If there is some significant correlation, even far from unity, it is still possible to predict the most likely criterion score with a higher-than-chance probability of success. Figure 6.1 gives an illustration of this relationship and of the prediction process. In this figure the statistical relation between test performance (X) and criterion performance (Y) is presented visually: a simple, linear prediction model is used to describe the relation between predictor and criterion. A linear function, summarized as the regression line *r* in Figure 6.1, is used to express which value of the criterion (Y) belongs to a certain value of the predictor (X). This relation cannot usually be predicted perfectly: persons with identical predictor scores can have (slightly) different criterion scores, which is illustrated by the elliptical scatter-plot around the regression line *r*. This means that there is some scatter of actual Y-scores about the predicted value for each X.

This account is of course a somewhat idealized one, but the classical model in general presents a number of dangers and difficulties. At least four important points may be raised.

Firstly, it is often impractical to wait for the long period which in

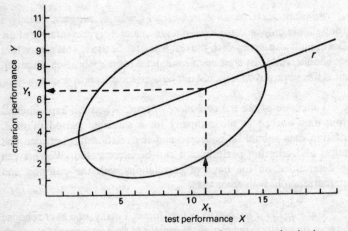

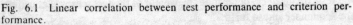

Fig. 6.1 Linear correlation between test performance and criterion performance.

principle is required before the success of members of the experimental group can be measured. In these situations a compromise procedure is sometimes adopted, administering the test battery to employees who currently occupy the position. By these means one has test data and criterion data available at the outset, so that validity can promptly be determined. This information is in terms of 'concurrent' validity as distinct from 'predictive' validity.

The disadvantages of this compromise procedure are twofold. In the first place, only the group that remains after selection, training, and a number of years' work is available. This group is smaller and often more homogeneous than an original group of applicants, and such a difference may have a substantial negative effect on the validity obtained. However, one can eliminate this difficulty by applying one of the several correction formulae for this so-called 'restriction of range' (e.g. Campbell, 1976). A second disadvantage is more serious. Too often it is impossible simply to transfer the results of a concurrent validity study into a predictive validity model.

A second danger in the classical model is that accidental relationships (the result of chance characteristics of the sample) are taken to be true and generalizable. And this danger becomes greater to the degree that one bases the choice of experimental tests on a 'shotgun' approach. This approach involves trying a large number of tests and other predictors in the hope that at least some of them will turn out to correlate significantly with the criterion. Especially with such a purely empirical procedure, the danger is not inconsiderable that chance correlations will be found. A solution is to repeat the validation of the test on a second experimental group. Correlations that survive in this so-called 'cross-validation' can be considered to reflect true relationships.

A third problem is that investigators often make unjustified use of the simple product–moment correlation. Underlying assumptions are that the relationships are linear and homoscedastic, but these assumptions are not always met. Sometimes the relationships are curvilinear, so that, for example, low motivation is paired with low achievement, relatively high motivation with good achievement, but very high motivation again with lower achievement. Deviations from a homoscedastic relationship can also be found, when, for instance, low intelligence is associated with low school achievement, while the higher the level of intelligence becomes, the less clear is the relationship; the scatter diagram is in this case pear-shaped. Kahneman and Ghiselli (1962) have shown that these kinds of deviations from linearity and homoscedasticity occur with some frequency. For these cases non-linear prediction models can be used. However, there should be stability in the pattern of non-linear relations and also some theoretical explanation for it, because in general in science one should strive for economy in explanation. This means that the more simple linear models are usually to be preferred.

A fourth point is the manner of combination of tests, in the case of more than one predictor, in an optimally predictive test battery. There are several statistical possibilities.

A distinction can be made between (a) conjunctive and (b) compensatory relations between test scores. These are illustrated in Figure 6.2, where the simplest, two-predictor situation is exhibited. With a conjunctive relation (represented by (a) in the figure) a candidate who is to be

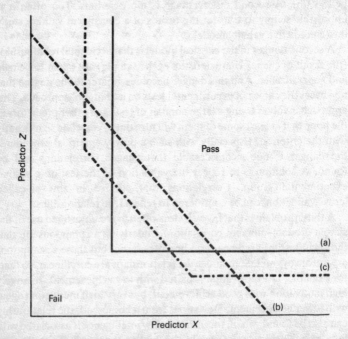

Fig. 6.2 Conjunctive (a), and compensatory (b), relation of test scores, and a combination of both methods (c).

acceptable has to pass the minimum requirements on both test X and test Z. Technically this is called the multiple-cutoff procedure. With a compensatory relation ((b) in the figure) a low score on test X (one which would be too low for acceptance in situation (a)) can be compensated for by a high score on test Z (and vice versa). In addition we could employ a combination of both methods, where there is a possibility of compensation but within certain limits. This is illustrated in Figure 6.2 by situation (c). As a more complex example we might take a school examination with five separate subjects. In order to pass the examination overall the requirement may be set that no score lower than 4 (on a 10-point scale) on any of the five tests is permitted, whereas in addition a total score of, say, 30 points is needed.

Parameter Determination

A prediction model is complete when its parameters have been 'determined', that is, when the weights of different predictors and constants in a formula have been established. Several procedures can be followed (see Roe, 1983):

1.   Traditionally, weights for predictors are determined *empirically* as is indicated in phases 5 and 6 in our example of the classical model. This procedure implies that much effort has to be invested in tryout studies.

2.   Instead of using empirical procedures, the weights and choice of the variables in a prediction formula can also be based on a *rational* procedure. For example, expert judgements may be used, in which outcomes of previous studies and/or theoretical considerations are taken into account.

3.   A combination of rational and empirical methods can be used. Starting with rationally determined parameters, subsequent modifications on the basis of empirical data can be made.

In all procedures it is necessary that empirical validation studies are performed on the test battery in its final form.

Validity Generalization

Probably the most discussed issue in the last five years in the area of personnel selection is the possibility of validity generalization. Traditionally, validity information has been considered situation-specific, so that for each situation the relation between predictors and criteria must be established anew. This position has been based on the findings that validity coefficients for similar job-test combinations have shown substantial fluctuations, as was illustrated in the two examples from Ghiselli's (1966) book which we mentioned in the previous section. Especially from the studies of Ghiselli (1966, 1973) it was concluded that in every single situation empirical validation is necessary because validity is determined by a unique set of factors.

However, in the early 1980s a number of researchers (Schmidt and Hunter, 1981; Pearlman *et al.*, 1980) claimed that, contrary to former views, observed differences between validity coefficients can be explained in terms of statistical and methodological artifacts, such as sampling error and differences between studies in criterion reliability, test reliability and degree of range restriction. Such a claim would imply that test validities are not specific to the situation, and that a validity study is not necessary in the case where validity information on similar job-test combinations is available. Schmidt and Hunter (1981) have developed a method for validity generalization which consists of three components:

1. *A procedure for compiling and classifying observed validity data.* Validity studies have to be classified according to test type and job category. To give an example, one cell of the test-type/job-category classification scheme in the Pearlman *et al.* (1980) study was verbal ability in conjunction with occupational groups 201–209 in the standard Dictionary of Occupational Titles. To get an impression of the broadness of this scheme to classify validity studies, it should be noted that the following job categories are included: 201, secretaries; 202, stenographers; 203, typists and typewriting machine operators; 205, interviewing clerks; 206, file clerks; 207, duplicating machine operators and tenders; 208, mailing and miscellaneous office machine operators; 209, stenography, typing, filing, and related occupations, not elsewhere classified. With regard to test type, each category contained different predictors

(item types) considered as measures of that factor or test type. The verbal ability test category included such item types as reading comprehension, vocabulary, grammar, spelling, and sentence completion. Within this particular test-type/job-category cell, 215 validity coefficients referring to criteria of overall job proficiency were compiled, from published and unpublished studies.

2.   *A statistical procedure for testing the homogeneity of a set of data classified as homogeneous.* The validity coefficients brought together within a single class in the previous step are evaluated in terms of statistical homogeneity and/or a minimum level of validity, in order to establish generalizability. To this aim, the average and variance of the 'residual distribution' of validities are computed, i.e. of the distribution that remains after the effects of artifacts like sampling error have been statistically removed.

3.   *A procedure for making generalizations from such sets of observed validity data.* After the statistical corrections, it may become apparent that a very large percentage, say 90 per cent, of all values in the distribution lie above a 'minimum useful level' of validity. In such a case, according to the Schmidt–Hunter approach, one could conclude with 90 per cent confidence that true validity lies at or above this minimum level in a new situation involving this test type and job, without carrying out a validation study of any kind. All that would be required in their procedure is sufficient job analysis information to ensure that the job in question is indeed a member of the occupation or job family on which the validity distribution was based.

On the basis of a series of analyses of published validity data, Schmidt and Hunter (1981) come to far-reaching conclusions. For example, 'professionally developed cognitive ability tests are valid predictors of performance on the job and in training for all jobs in all settings' (p. 1128).

   However, the Schmidt–Hunter procedure and its findings have been criticized on several grounds (Algera *et al.*, 1984; Burke, 1984; Schmitt *et al.*, 1984; Sackett *et al.*, 1986; James *et al.*, 1986) and it seems that the debate on the proper procedures for validity generalization has not ended yet. Algera *et al.* (1984) point out some methodological problems in all three steps in the Schmidt–Hunter procedure. For example, in their view the rules for classifying tests and jobs result in looser classification than the underlying psychometric model would allow. Sackett *et al.* (1986) investigated the statistical power to detect true differences between studies and concluded that statements attributing observed variation across studies to statistical artifact should be made with caution, especially when small sample sizes and small numbers of individual studies are included in the validity-generalization procedures. James *et al.* (1986) suggest that alternative models may explain variation in validity coefficients as well as the cross-situational consistency model of the validity-generalization approach. But nevertheless, it is to be expected that further research on proper procedures for the cumulation of findings from individual studies will have a major impact on personnel selection methodology in the future.

DECISION ORIENTATION

Another more recent orientation in thinking and writing about selection has emphasized the decision aspects of working with and advising through tests, particularly since the appearance of Cronbach and Gleser's *Psychological Tests and Personnel Decisions* (1st ed., 1957; 2nd ed., 1965). Interest in these features had naturally been present before; after all, the use of a regression formula for the prediction of satisfactory performance already involves working with probabilities and chances of success. But the advantage of a systematic and explicit decision orientation is that the various assumptions and elements in the decision process are exactly identified, and that the place and contribution of the test becomes clearer. One is compelled to make a clear distinction between several decision strategies in which the test plays a different role and fulfils different demands on different occasions.

In decisions of all kinds, two elements can be identified: first, the probabilities of certain outcomes, and second, the values of these outcomes (the utility or pay-off of outcomes). In order to reach a decision, it is in principle necessary for the decision maker to be able to attribute a value to the different possible outcomes and to try to compare the evaluated outcomes on some sort of quantitative scale. Of course this is not always an easy task. It is very difficult to compare on a scale a slow but accurate worker with a fast but less accurate one, or an efficient but not well-liked head of department with a somewhat less productive but very pleasant leader. Nevertheless, a decision approach brings out the need for an explicit evaluation and quantitative comparison of these outcomes. The probabilities of each outcome next have to be determined, perhaps by conducting predictive test research to allow calculation of the probabilities of a particular person reaching different levels of criterion performance. It is naturally very important to distinguish between the evaluations placed on different outcomes and the probability of these outcomes; a decision will be based on some form of combination of these two pieces of information, for example, by means of a formula where the probability of an outcome is multiplied by its value.

When we try to *classify* the decisions in which tests may play a part, a first important distinction to be made is that between individual and institutional decisions. With the first kind of decision, the focus is on the individual who makes the decision or for whom the decision is made. Each decision is made once, and the pay-off from the decision may vary between individuals even when they have the same chance of a certain outcome, since the perceived value of an outcome can vary between them. Examples of such individual decisions are occupational, career and school choice, as well as individual career planning within a company.

Within an institutional framework, on the other hand, a whole series of repeated decisions may occur. The value of the outcomes is determined here by the institution (the school, company or society) and is constantly the same for each particular decision. If the value is expressed in financial terms, human resources accounting methods can be used to assess the standard dollar deviation, a parameter for differences in job incumbent output. These accounting methods tend to be rather complex and costly, but recently more simple estimation methods have been presented (Schmidt *et al.*, 1979; Bobko *et al.*, 1983). The utility of the whole decision-making strategy is determined by the average pay-off of all decisions separately, so that it becomes a matter of maximizing this total yield or minimizing the loss. Examples of these institutional decisions are admissions to a school, selection for a company, examination for military service.

The decision approach places emphasis on the fact that the test is only 'responsible' for the determination of probability of success; since a lot more has to be taken into consideration in order to reach real decisions about people, the role and contribution of the test becomes more realistic and modest. Making decisions is more than using tests!

As an example of this line of thought, let us return to the selection situation in which a test predicts a criterion performance with a certain validity as summarized in Figure 6.3.

The vertical axis embraces the critical criterion score: above this value an applicant is judged satisfactory, below it he or she is deemed unsatisfactory. The horizontal axis extends around the critical test score, above which an applicant is accepted and below which he or she is rejected. The meaning of selection lies in the fact that the ratio of satisfactory to unsatisfactory people (the so-called 'success ratio') is more favourable (72/84 = 86 per cent) for the group on the right of the

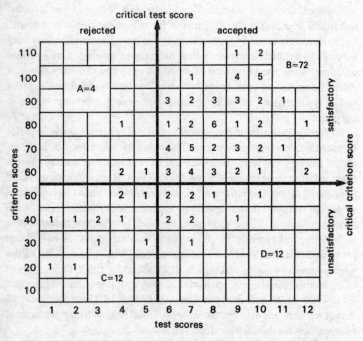

Fig. 6.3 A hypothetical selection strategy for a group of 100 applicants.

critical test score than it is for the group as a whole (76 per cent) or any randomly selected group.

But, as Figure 6.4 brings out, there are many factors besides validity alone which determine the magnitude of this success ratio. This figure represents variations in four features by contrasting two possible situations in each case. The first illustration (diagram (a)) is the customary example about changes in validity: the narrower scatter-plot yields a higher correlation. A second feature affecting the success ratio is the average level of ability of the group of applicants (diagram (b)); this may be viewed in terms of differences in the antecedent probability of success. Diagram (c) shows how changes in the definition of what is satisfactory criterion performance affect the ratio; and diagram (d)

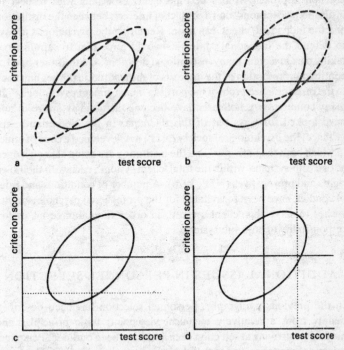

Fig. 6.4   Inter-relationships between validity, antecedent probability, selection ratio and success ratio.

makes a similar point about variations in the number of candidates to be accepted (the so-called 'selection ratio').

Which decision must be taken depends on the evaluation of the various elements relevant to this decision-making process. Cronbach and Gleser (1965) and Rulon *et al.* (1967), among others, have developed several formulae for determining the optimal strategy for selection, and for placement and classification decisions as well. For a complete treatment, we refer to these books. The point to be made here is that this line of thought has provided a scientific and rigorous basis for decision making which in selection, as elsewhere, is a complicated and intricate process.

A final remark should be made about the role and responsibility of the psychologist, which also has become more pertinent as a result of the decision approach. It has become clear, especially with respect to institutional decisions, that a conflict of interests between the institution and the individual 'client' can arise. Requiring the psychologist always to defend the individual's interests would force him to refrain from taking part in a great many institutional decisions. On the other hand, a continuous promotion of the interests of the institution pushes him back to the often criticized role of the partisan 'management psychologist'. In many countries psychologists have become increasingly aware of and have looked for ways out of this dilemma. In the Netherlands, for instance, the psychological society (NIP) has developed a code of ethics in which both the individual and the institution are being acknowledged as two 'sub-systems' within the total 'client system', each with their own rights and prerogatives (NIP, 1976). A number of conditions and rules of conduct have been formulated for the professional psychologist who wishes to serve this 'client system', in order to guarantee his or her responsibility to both sub-systems.

ADDITIONAL ISSUES IN PERSONNEL SELECTION

In the previous paragraphs, personnel selection has been described mainly from a relatively technical viewpoint; basic principles and models for arriving at selection decisions have been outlined. Personnel selection in practice means that decisions concerning individual persons have to be made. This implies that ethical issues are inevitably involved.

In several countries many passionate debates on the use of psychological tests and on selection procedures in general have resulted in some kind of regulations or guidelines.

In the USA the Civil Rights Act acquired the force of law in 1964 and included an article on personnel selection procedures. The Equal Employment Opportunity Commission has established a number of regulations to prevent discrimination in personnel selection. These guidelines also apply to psychological tests. In the Netherlands in 1977 a National Commission reported on the proper procedures to be followed in personnel selection.

Roe (1983) formulates four basic principles which should be followed by organizations that are selecting applicants:

1. The organization should respect the personal dignity of the applicant, e.g. by protecting his or her privacy.

2. The organization should acknowledge the negotiating role of the applicant, e.g. by providing correct information, or by providing the possibility of appeal.

3. The organization should be able to justify its selection decisions. For example, the procedures should have the highest possible validity.

4. The organization should prevent discrimination and fight against it, e.g. by resisting procedures by which persons are discriminated on the basis of characteristics, such as religion or race, that have nothing to do with bona fide job qualifications.

This last issue, fairness of testing versus test-bias, has received a good deal of attention lately. In the USA the Equal Opportunity Act and the great and increasing variety of minority groups have forced psychologists to look more seriously into possible discrimination in selection. Also, in European countries, with an increasing heterogeneity of the population (immigrant groups, guestworkers), bias and discrimination in selection have become a salient issue. Research and experience in cross-cultural testing have been very stimulating in finding ways not only to define and analyse the problem but also to indicate possible solutions (Irvine and Berry, 1983; Drenth *et al.*, 1983).

From a technical viewpoint, discrimination can be defined in many different ways (Van der Flier and Drenth, 1980). Considering two sub-groups which differ on some characteristic, non-discrimination can, for example, be expressed as equal quota from both groups, as equal representation of satisfactory people from both groups, or as equal success ratios in both groups. Figure 6.5 presents the situation where two sub-groups have different regression lines and differ in their average test score (X) but not in average criterion score (Y).

This figure illustrates how the use of one and the same critical test score below which applicants are rejected would discriminate against group I and, therefore, would be unjustified.

The three definitions of non-discrimination mentioned above imply different actions in practice. It is a matter of choice, based upon one's value orientation, which definition (or other possible definitions) should be followed. Discussions on discrimination have often focused on psychological tests, and some people would like to abandon their use. This is like killing the messenger who brings the bad news. Because psychological tests are more objective than other predictors, they lend themselves more easily to research on discrimination. Abandoning

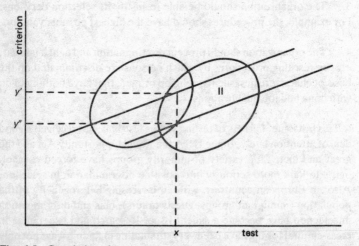

Fig. 6.5 Correlations between test and criterion for two sub-groups with different regression lines.

psychological tests in favour of other, less objective and less transparent predictors will not improve the fairness of selection procedures.

SUMMARY

In this chapter, four orientations to selection were discussed: those directed to the test, to the criterion, to the prediction model and to the decision. Although it is possible to find psychologists and psychological agencies today that can be characterized by the central ideas described in the first and second sections, there is nevertheless a certain historical development between the orientations. It is probably best to say that a repeated broadening of attention occurred, but that this did not necessarily exclude the issues emphasized in the preceding phases.

This meant that selection psychologists began to occupy a more and more integrated position in personnel policy. Initially they were more or less scientific door-keepers. Later they also became involved in problems of performance appraisal and job- and function-analysis; still later, they were asked to contribute to broader questions of personnel policy. This is a favourable development. Selection psychology has developed from a marginal phenomenon to become a central contributor to the overall personnel function.

FURTHER READING

Of the several general introductions to selection theory, these four are representative: L. J. Cronbach, *Essentials of Psychological Testing* (Harper and Row, 4th ed., 1984); M. D. Dunnette, *Personnel Selection and Placement* (Belmont, 1966); R. M. Guion, *Personnel Testing* (McGraw-Hill, 1965); C. H. Lawshe and M. J. Balma, *Principles of Personnel Testing* (McGraw-Hill, 2nd ed., 1966).

In the more specific field of test theory, H. Gulliksen's *Theory of Mental Tests* (Wiley, 1950) has long been authoritative, and the second edition by R. L. Thorndike of E. F. Lindquist's *Educational Measurement* (American Council on Education, 1951; 2nd ed., 1971) is also valuable. Other useful texts are J. C. Nunnally's *Psychometric Theory* (McGraw-Hill, 2nd ed., 1978) and J. P. Campbell's chapter on psychometric theory in M. D. Dunnette (ed.), *Handbook of Industrial and Organizational Psychology* (Rand McNally, 1976). More advanced treatments of test theory are provided by F. M. Lord and M. R. Novick, *Statistical Theories of Mental Test scores* (Addison-Wesley, 1968) and F. M. Lord, *Applications of Item Response Theory to Practical Testing Problems* (Lawrence Erlbaum, 1980).

All these are American sources. Work in Britain is illustrated by the contribution of P. E. Vernon (*The Measurement of Abilities*, University of London Press, 1956; and *Personality Assessment*, Methuen, 1963). German texts include those by G. A. Lienert (*Testaufbau und Testanalyse*, Julius Beltz, 1961) and by G. H. Fischer, *Einführung in die Theorie Psychologischer Tests* (Huber, 1974). Volumes by R. Magnusson (*Testteori*, University of Uppsala Press, 1966) and M. Reuchlin (*Méthodes d'analyse factorielle à l'usage des psychologues*, Presses Universitaires de France, 1969) are from Sweden and France respectively. Developments in the Netherlands are exemplified by A. D. de Groot's *Methodologie* (Mouton, 1961; English version, 1969), D. N. M. de Gruijter and L. J. Th. Van der Kamp (*Statistical Models in Psychological and Educational Testing*, Swets and Zeitlinger, 1984), R. A. Roe's *Grondslagen der Personeelsselektie* [Foundations of Personnel Selection] (Van Gorcum, 1983), and P. J. D. Drenth's *Inleiding in de Testtheorie* (Van Loghum Slaterus, 1976). The latter is reprinted in German by Barth Verlag.

7

The Selection Interview

Peter Herriot

The interview is ubiquitous. Whenever applicants are being selected for employment by organizations, an interview is likely to form a central part of the procedure, and to be given great weight in the decision. For many applicants for jobs, the interview *is* the selection process. They are not present when application forms are sifted or when final decisions are arrived at, but they certainly get first-hand and often unforgettable experience of the interview.

POINTS OF VIEW

The interview can be considered from several different perspectives. From the organization's point of view, it is usually the first opportunity to meet the applicant face-to-face. Many organizations consider that such face-to-face meetings are the best (or perhaps the only) way to assess various personal qualities which they believe to be important. For example, an interviewer who is a professional personnel specialist may concentrate on whether the applicant is motivated to work in this specific occupation or for this organization in particular. Does the applicant appear likely to conform to the organization's values and culture? Does he or she seem to have long-term senior management potential? If the interviewer is a line manager, or especially if he or she is likely to be the applicant's immediate superior, other concerns may be paramount: specifically, can I get on with this person, and will he or she fit into my team?

Other considerations will additionally be affecting the interviewer's point of view. Is the job market a buyer's or a seller's one? Is it more important to avoid employing those who might fail, or to attract those who are risky but potentially high fliers? What are the organization's policies regarding equal opportunities? What is its longer-term strategy for acquiring and developing its human resources? Above all, what is the place and purpose of this interview in the recruitment and selection process as a whole: is it an intermediate screening stage or is it the final phase?

From the applicants' point of view, the interview is likely to be the focal point of the process. It will probably be perceived as the major hurdle to be jumped, the crucial test to be faced, even though a higher proportion of applicants may have been rejected on the basis of the application form alone. It may well be the first occasion that the applicants have had the opportunity to meet anyone from the organization. Consequently, they may be keen to form impressions of and gain information about both the job and the organization. The job market situation, of course, will affect the applicants' point of view as well. In some settings they may be little concerned to find out about the organization, since they are desperate for employment of any sort, having been unemployed for a year. On the other hand, they might have just completed a degree in computer science or electronic engineering, as a consequence of which several hi-tech organizations are competing for their services. They will in this case be eager to discover the prospects for career development and interesting work which each employer provides. The stage in their life career which applicants have reached is another determinant of their point of view. Are they currently coping with the onset of several major life-roles at the same time (wife, mother, daughter, daughter-in-law, for example), or are they at a point where some of these responsibilities are beginning to be phased out?

A final point of view is that of the psychologist. Many psychologists are employed by organizations to develop methods of assessing individuals, and hence they are more likely to consider selection from the organization's point of view than from the applicant's. On the other hand, psychologists have not been so concerned with the overall organizational effectiveness of selection procedures as with the properties of each of the assessment tools used. This preoccupation with specific tools arises from the conventional sequence of operations in developing a selection procedure (Lewis, 1985). First, decide what it is you want to predict. The usual criterion construct, as it is called, is an individual's job performance, various indices of which may be available. Next, a job analysis is undertaken to discover the key tasks in the job. From these tasks is inferred a set of personal attributes necessary to perform them satisfactorily; these attributes may be aptitudes or personality traits or other personal characteristics. At this point, various assessment tools may be considered as a suitable means of measuring such attributes. Among them are psychological tests, exercises, and the interview. Each of the tools used should be validated against measures of the criterion; that is, the extent to which it predicts, for example, supervisors' ratings of job performance should be discovered.

Hence the selection interview is usually seen by psychologists as an assessment tool, and has been evaluated by psychologists in terms of its capacity to predict job performance – its predictive validity (see also Chapter 6). Since any measurement has to be reliable in order to predict successfully, the reliability as well as the validity of the interview has been of key concern.

PSYCHOMETRIC PROPERTIES

The reviews of the predictive validity of the selection interview have established that, as usually conceived, it has very poor predictive power relative to other assessment tools. This conclusion has been reinforced by the recent use of the technique of meta-analysis, whereby data obtained from a number of studies are combined for statistical analysis. For example, Hunter and Hunter (1984) performed meta-analyses on two previously published reviews of the literature. They also analysed a data-set derived from articles published in the two foremost American journals of applied psychology.

The predictive validity for the interview in the studies in Dunnette's (1972) review was 0·16; and in those reviewed by Reilly and Chao (1982) it was 0·23. The overall validity for the data-set from the two journals was 0·14, while correlations with different criterion measures were as follows: with supervisor ratings, 0·14; with promotion, 0·08; with training success, 0·10; and with length of tenure, 0·03.

Various efforts have been made, with some success, to so structure the interview as to increase these low coefficients. The term 'structure' has been used ambiguously, and it is worth defining in more detail for the purposes of this review. First, contrary to usage in some other research areas, greater structure is used in the selection literature to refer to a *reduction* in the number of behavioural possibilities open to the participants. Among the variables which may be so reduced are the following:

1.   Functions of utterances; are the parties limited to asking questions and giving answers only, or are other functions permitted?

2.   Functions by parties; is the interviewer the only one permitted to ask questions, or may the applicant do so also?

3.   Content; are the topics, or indeed the precise questions, determined in advance?

4.   Order; are the orders of topic coverage and of the functions of utterances determined in advance?

Thus a highly structured interview would be one in which the interviewer asks the applicant a predetermined sequence of questions to which the applicant replies. An extremely unstructured interview would be a conversation in which the interviewer and the applicant both ask questions, give answers, utter opinions, make offers, etc., in no particular order, and about topics which are not predetermined. Clearly, in the first case the behaviour of the applicant is supposed to have no effect on the subsequent behaviour of the interviewer, and vice versa. In the second, unstructured, case each party is continuously adapting his or her behaviour as a consequence of the behaviour of the other. The feedback signals in this process would concern both the content of the other party's utterance and also other aspects of verbal and non-verbal behaviour. Thus the unstructured interview resembles normal social intercourse in all situations other than formalized or ritual events.

When we consider the research literature on the effects of introducing more structure, it will become evident that the interviews so conducted are more valid because they resemble other psychometrically proven selection devices. Before we review this research, however, it is worth explaining the criteria for including or excluding articles. Much early research included the word 'interview' in the title of the report, but in fact dealt only with paper descriptions of applicants and perhaps photographs. Not only is this far removed from the real situation

(Gorman *et al.*, 1978) but also it actually substitutes the contents of the application form for the interview. Thus the present review will only contain articles which have taped or live interviews as the material.

A second question relates to whether the interview is real or simulated. While preference and greater weight should be given to real interviews, there is some evidence that college students acting as selection interviewers do not differ markedly from real interviewers (Bernstein *et al.*, 1975). Students are more lenient, but the standard deviations of their ratings, their inter-rater reliability, and the main effects of the investigations are similar to those obtained by professional interviewers.

Turning to the effects of structure, early research by Maas (1965) showed greater reliability for his 'patterned expectation interview' than for a traditional procedure in which an applicant was rated for certain traits after the interview. Maas's procedure was to discover traits to be evaluated by asking a committee of interviewers who were familiar with the job. Examples of behaviour on the job which typified these traits were included on the rating scales at the appropriate points, providing a form of behaviourally anchored rating scale. Interviewers were required to draw inferences from an applicant's responses to questions to expected behaviour on the job, and check the point on the trait rating scale where this expected behaviour level fell. Trait ratings were thus derived, weighted for their importance to the job, and an overall rating was also derived. No validity data are reported, however, and the significant increase in reliability which was obtained may be attributed to the use of the same type of evidence by all the interviewers to arrive at their trait ratings.

Latham *et al.* (1980) and Latham and Saari (1984), however, avoided some of these pitfalls. They conducted a proper job analysis, using the critical incident technique. The applicant is asked how he or she would behave in specific situations on the job, these having been derived from the critical incident analysis. Responses are rated on a five-point Likert scale, with job experts having previously stated behaviour typical of a grade 1, a grade 3, and a grade 5 response to each situation. Inter-interviewer reliability was high (0.76 for hourly workers at a sawmill; 0.79 for foremen), and so was concurrent validity.

Latham and colleagues attribute their success to the identification of specific behaviours crucial to the job, on the basis of a systematic job analysis (see too Wiener and Schneiderman, 1974; Osburn *et al.*, 1981). The intervening inference of traits is abolished, thereby removing the effect of differences in the implicit personality theories of different interviewers. Rather, the behaviours sampled as predictors are the same as those used in the criterion measure of job performance (Wernimont and Campbell, 1968). In fact, the only difference is that in the interview the applicant is asked how he or she *would* behave, rather than being required to actually perform the task in question. In all other respects, this type of interview is the same as a work-sample test (Robertson and Kandola, 1982).

Another highly structured approach to the interview has been developed by Mayfield *et al.* (1980) in the American life-insurance industry. Applicants are given ratings on a series of highly specific questions. These questions have previously been factor-analysed (with the factors being reliably replicated) into the following factors: work experience, education, social contacts, own insurance coverage, own finances, and future plans. Thus, for example, a question regarding work experience would ask whether an applicant had direct contact with customers in his or her previous job. This procedure resembles an application form or a biographical inventory more than the traditional interview. Hunter and Hunter (1984) give a mean validity of 0·37 across a range of studies for biodata as a predictor for entry-level jobs. Thus we may suggest that the success of Mayfield and colleagues' technique is attributable to its resemblance to another psychometrically successful selection procedure, the use of standard items of biographical information.

To summarize the evidence on the validity and reliability of the interview, we may conclude that it is inappropriate to treat together all forms of interview. Where the interview is in its usual, relatively unstructured form, validity and reliability are poor. However, where a very high degree of structure is introduced, considerable improvements are found. This is hardly surprising, since the structured interviews actually possess those characteristics which give psychological tests their reliability and validity. These are standardized procedure and content, and similarity between predictor and criterion measures. Such highly structured interviews remove from the situation many of the interpersonal features which are valued by interviewers and applicants; they are, in effect, work-sample tests or biographical inventories rather than interviews in the generally accepted sense.

ATTRIBUTES OF APPLICANTS

Given the overall poor validity and reliability of the traditional interview, a great deal of research effort has been invested in trying to understand why this should be so. The basic strategy has been to try to specify aspects of the applicant, the interviewer, and the situation which affect outcomes. If the features observed to be influential have no relation to personal attributes which are considered appropriate for the job, then they are treated as unwanted sources of bias. Excellent reviews by Schmitt (1976) and Arvey and Campion (1982) list these features, which are extremely numerous. They include the age, race, sex, appearance, attitude, experience of interviews, and non-verbal behaviour of the participants, and the physical setting and job-market situation. However, theoretical perspectives which might be relevant have rarely been applied. Behavioural decision theory, person perception, and attribution theories are conspicuous by their absence. Instead, therefore, of a theoretical understanding of the interview process, we are left with a lengthy list of potential causes of bias. The implication is that if these can be reduced by training or exhortation, the interview can yet become a useful assessment tool.

Instead of reviewing this literature in terms of individual causes of bias, we will instead concentrate upon certain general areas of research on the interview which point towards the need for a new theoretical framework. The first of these areas is in terms of the applicants' attributes which are to be assessed. It will be recalled that the inference from the job analysis to desired personal attributes is crucial, since it permits development or choice of assessment tools devised to measure attributes of applicants. The attributes assessed at the interview are assumed to be among those derived from the job analysis, and therefore should be predictive of job performance.

One generalization which can be tentatively made is that interviewers differentiate little between jobs in terms of the attributes which are required. Typical research is that of Hakel and Schuh (1971), who found that two clusters of attributes were regarded by interviewers as favourable across all of seven different occupational categories. They were a personal-relations cluster (e.g. sociability) and a 'good citizen' cluster (e.g. dependability, conscientiousness). Posner (1981) demonstrated that there was little disagreement among recruiters, students, and faculty about what the desired applicant characteristics were.

On the other hand, personnel managers and non-personnel managers differ regarding the relative importance of achievement motivation, job and company knowledge and academic performance when recruiting for the same job within the same company (Keenan, 1976a). Even when encouraged to employ the same nine dimensions when interviewing, interviewers may use only two or three of them in their decision making, these being different across interviewers (Zedeck *et al.*, 1983). The only exception to these findings is the work of Jackson and his colleagues (Rothstein and Jackson, 1980; Jackson *et al.*, 1982). They found different profiles of attributes reliably judged suitable for different jobs, but their results may be partly attributable to the initial presentation of job descriptions to their student 'interviewers'. This leaves one with the nasty suspicion that the main reason for a failure to differentiate between jobs in terms of the attributes required for them may be that interviewers or their organizations have omitted to analyse the jobs in question.

There is, then, a general failure to differentiate between occupations in terms of which attributes are judged to be important. However, this finding tells us nothing about which attributes actually do determine the interviewer's decision about an applicant's suitability. When the two parties have similar biographical details, the applicant is rated as more suitable (Rand and Wexley, 1975). Although the applicant's rated similarity to the ideal employee predicts selection decisions better than his or her similarity to the interviewer (Dalessio and Imada, 1984), the two may not be so distinct; for Tom (1971) demonstrated that perceptions of oneself and of one's organization are closely related. Keenan (1977) found that the degree of the interviewer's liking of the applicant predicted the interviewer's overall evaluation of the applicant's suitability 0·51. Given the evidence from social psychology, that we tend to like those who are similar to ourselves (Byrne, 1969), the conclusion seems to be that the interviewer is likely to compare the applicant with him or herself rather than with a job-derived profile.

It seems that the occurrence of the face-to-face episode of the interview is crucial to these judgements. Herriot and Rothwell (1983) obtained graduate recruiters' impressions of the applicant after reading the application form but before the interview, and again after the interview. They found that impressions of personality and motivation had increased in number, while those of ability and interests had decreased. Negative impressions predicted judgements of suitability better than positive ones. Indeed, the application form seems to serve mainly as a source of hypotheses which may be rapidly confirmed (Snyder and White, 1981); although when interviewers were prevented from reading the application form, they reached a decision just as quickly in the interview and were equally confident in it, even though that decision was based on less information (Tucker and Rowe, 1977).

Perhaps the final word may be had by recent investigators of what actually predicts interview decisions: Kinicki and Lockwood (1985). They found that the applicant's attraction for the interviewer, the fact that both parties were of the same gender, and 'interview impression' were the only significant predictors of judged suitability, with gender less predictive than the other two. 'Interview impression' was a factor consisting of ability to express ideas, job knowledge, appearance, and drive. Thus there is a considerable amount of evidence suggesting that the social experience of the interview results in judgements based on immediate impressions of the applicant. The gathering of further information from which attributes may be inferred does not seem to be important. Indeed, ratings of attributes are likely to be *post hoc* rationalization of immediate impressions.

NON-VERBAL BEHAVIOUR

The mechanisms by which such impressions of attraction and liking are mediated are likely to be largely non-verbal. Recently, a considerable amount of evidence regarding the effects of non-verbal behaviour on interview outcomes has accumulated. Dipboye and Wiley (1977) had recruiters decide whether to invite or reject for a second interview two individuals who provided essentially the same information about themselves. One, the passive applicant, was shy and tense, often answered with only yes or no, and was hard to draw out. He or she spoke in a soft tone of voice, maintained poor eye contact, and often prefaced statements with words reflecting low self-confidence, such as 'I think', or 'I guess'. The moderately assertive applicant, on the other hand, behaved in exactly the opposite manner. Not only was he or she more likely to be invited for a second interview, but also was considered to have better qualifications, experience, training, and academic record, even though there was in fact no difference between the two applicants in these respects.

Imada and Hakel (1977) found that the impressions of applicants based upon the amount of their non-verbal behaviour were maintained whether the rater was the interviewer, an actual observer, or an observer of a video-recording. Washburn and Hakel (1973) discovered, most interestingly, that the interviewer's non-verbal behaviour affected other raters' judgements of suitability of applicants for a sales position. Raters may have taken their cue from the interviewer's supposed reaction to the applicant, or the interviewer's behaviour may itself have affected the applicants (Keenan, 1976b). When attributes of applicants judged to be critical to the decision to accept or reject were rated as a function of the amount of their non-verbal behaviour, there was a very high degree of correlation between the attribute ratings (McGovern and Tinsley, 1978), suggesting an overall reaction rather than differentiated assessments. Interviewers are unlikely to be aware of the effects of applicants' non-verbal behaviour on their decisions (Forbes and Jackson, 1980). Some caution must be attached to these conclusions, however, in the light of the failure of Sterrett (1978) to find an effect of non-verbal behaviour on ratings of eight traits, and of the finding of Hollandsworth *et al.* (1979) that content of utterance had greater influence than style on ratings. Nevertheless, the overall conclusion must be that aspects of the applicant's behaviour during interview do indeed have a profound effect upon interviewers' judgements.

ATTRIBUTIONS AND OTHER JUDGEMENTS

Although non-verbal aspects of behaviour result in an immediate impression on the interviewer, there is also evidence that more inferential processes of attribution may be involved. For example, Tessler and Sushelsky (1978) had interviewers rate applicants for a job requiring self-confidence. Where the applicants had a college education but made no eye contact with the interviewer, they were judged to be lacking in self-confidence and hence unsuitable for the job. The same did not apply to applicants with only a high-school education and therefore with supposedly less reason to feel confident; their lack of eye contact was less of a liability.

Perhaps this is typical of a more general tendency to make attributions on the basis of interview behaviour (Herriot, 1981). For example, if something in an applicant's record is unusual (Constantin, 1976), or if they fail to follow the unspoken rules of the interview, they may well have a range of enduring characteristics attributed to them. Furthermore, we must take account of the 'fundamental attribution error' (Ross, 1977), whereby we attribute people's behaviour more to themselves and less to their situation than is justified. This implies that the interviewer is likely to attribute too much of the applicant's interview behaviour to the characteristics of the applicant, and too little to the fact that he or she is in an interview. Moreover, when inferences are made to characteristics of the applicant, such inferences are likely to be different for different interviewers. First, different behaviour might be taken to be evidence of a particular characteristic; and second, inferences from the presence or degree of one characteristic to that of another may differ.

If features such as the attraction of the interviewer to the applicant are crucial in determining the interviewer's judgements, it follows that those stereotypes and prejudices which enter into our personal relations are apt to permeate such judgements as well. The evidence indicates that this is indeed the case. Much of Arvey's (1979) review of unfair discrimination in the employment interview relates to discrimination on the basis of differences between interviewer and applicant. Since we tend to like those who are like ourselves, it can be seen that the use of the interview is likely to perpetuate such discriminatory practices. Arvey discusses the psychological mechanisms whereby unfavourable reactions to those unlike ourselves may be made. First, we may create stereotypes of them in terms of an obvious feature (e.g. gender, race); these stereotypes may be negative, may not match the job, or may affect the selection criteria. Alternatively, it may be the case that applicants from minority groups behave in unusual ways in the interview (e.g. in terms of eye contact, tone of voice, perception of norms).

Arvey's review demonstrates clear evidence of discrimination against women, in that they are given lower evaluations than men when both have similar or identical qualifications. This effect is moderated by the nature of the job, in that women are rated lower for masculine jobs, higher for feminine ones. Since managerial positions are assumed to require masculine characteristics, however, the consequence is extensive discrimination against women with respect to higher-status jobs. Other research has confirmed this overall picture, and has added further factors which affect decisions. For example, Kalin and Rayko (1978) found that applicants with foreign accents (i.e. different from the accent of the establishment) were given lower ratings for high-status jobs, but higher ratings for low-status jobs, than those with the establishment accent (in this case, English Canadian). Clearly, the use of the interview to form evaluations based on interpersonal style is likely to result in continued unfair discrimination.

A second possible source of unfairness is impression-management. If the impression created by behavioural style is the crucial factor, impression-management by either party will affect outcomes. There is some evidence to suggest that certain forms of impression-management are successful in selection settings. For example, female applicants in more masculine styles of dress have a greater chance of being selected for management positions than females with less masculine dress (Forsythe *et al.*, 1985). Perfumed applicants of both sexes are more likely to receive higher ratings on job-related and personality characteristics when the interviewer is female, lower when the interviewer is male (Baron, 1983). Clearly, clever impression-managers carry their perfume into the waiting-room with them, ready to apply a quick squirt when they discover from departing applicants whether the interviewer is a man or a woman!

While impression-management may be effective, however, there is no evidence to suggest that it occurs on a large scale. Admittedly, such evidence would be hard to come by, since the psychologist investigating the interview could be managed in the same way as the interviewer. When Fletcher (1981) asked student applicants which actions they thought would give them the best chance of success, they replied that they should be honest and answer the questions fully; but they also considered it important to 'sell themselves', look at the interviewer, be enthusiastic, and be willing to argue but also to admit ignorance.

The interview, then, when it is considered by organizations and psychologists as a tool of assessment, has not worked very well. Various reasons for this failure to be a valid and reliable measure of personal attributes have been discovered by research and described in this chapter hitherto. Attempts to improve validity and reliability by training interviewers have seldom been demonstrated to be effective (e.g. Vance *et al.*, 1978). Where success has been enjoyed, the improvement obtained was in reliability rather than validity (Heneman, 1975); or the training programme was lengthy and aimed successfully at reducing certain highly specific forms of decision error; for example, the contrast effect, where the quality of the previous applicant(s) affects the interviewer's assessment of the present one (Wexley *et al.*, 1973).

APPLICANTS' EXPECTATIONS

A basic theoretical question therefore needs to be raised. Is the most appropriate psychological approach to the interview to treat it as an assessment tool? We started this chapter by considering the interview from two points of view; that of the organization and its representative, the interviewer, and that of the applicant. While most of the psychological research carried out on the interview has been from the organization's point of view, there has recently been increasing investigation of that of the applicant. After this research has been reviewed, I will argue that the findings point towards a different theoretical framework in which psychologists may place the interview: it should be considered as an episode of social exchange rather than as a tool of assessment.

Let us first consider applicants' expectations of the interview. It is clear that applicants do hold expectations, and that these differ to some extent from those of the interviewer. The applicant expects the interviewer to talk more about the job and the organization than the interviewer expects to; whereas the interviewer expects applicants to talk more about themselves than applicants expect to (Herriot and Rothwell, 1983). On the other hand, applicants believe it to be a bad sign if interviewers do most of the talking. They have no very great respect for interviewers, believing them on the whole to be untrained and no better judges of personality than most (Fletcher, 1981).

To the extent that applicants are satisfied with the interview, we may infer that their expectations have been met. Hence their reasons for satisfaction are further indications of what they expect. Applicants are more satisfied with interviews when the questions are open-ended, offering them the opportunity to talk (Jablin and McComb, 1984).

Similarly, when interviewers show interest in applicants, give them the opportunity to display their technical knowledge, talk about the job and the organization, and review the career progression of employees similar to the applicant, satisfaction is greater (Alderfer and McCord, 1970; Keenan and Wedderburn, 1980).

In summary, applicants expect interviewers to allow them to present themselves; they also expect to get indications of the nature of the job and the organization; and they hope that the interviewer will be interested in them. Whether this latter expectation is merely that they like to receive hints whether or not they will be favourably assessed, or whether it is treating the interest of the interviewer as typical of how the organization treats its employees, is a matter for debate (Rynes *et al.*, 1980). As will be shown, subsequent research suggests the second explanation; the interviewer stands proxy for the organization as a whole. Certainly, the interviewer's behaviour is crucial to the applicant's decision. Glueck (1973) found that in over one third of cases the behaviour of the interviewer was cited as the major reason why an applicant chose a particular organization, while for two thirds this was at least a major influence. Moreover, those student applicants who were most influenced by recruiters were those with the best academic records and the most work experience. Interviewers have credibility with applicants if they give negative as well as positive realistic job information and if they are fluent (Jablin and McComb, 1984; C. D. Fisher *et al.*, 1979). It helps if they are not too old but not too young, and if they have a clear job title (Rogers and Sincoff, 1978).

What determines whether the applicant will accept a job offer or an offer of a further stage in the selection process? If one makes the assumption that such a decision is the consequence of a rational weighing-up of information, then one would be looking for evidence that job information played a vital role. However, most of the evidence suggests that the style rather than the content of the interviewer's behaviour carries more weight. Early research by Sydiaha (1962) drew attention to the possibility that the emotional climate of the interview affected both applicants' and interviewers' decisions. Decisions to accept were more likely when there was more agreement, giving of suggestions and opinions, and tension release (using Bales' categories of utterances) than when there was disagreement, tension, antagonism, and requests for information, opinions and suggestions. In subsequent research, Schmitt and Coyle (1976) factor-analysed applicants' reactions to interviewers, and found by multiple-regression analysis three factors which predicted applicants' decisions. They were the personality of the interviewer as perceived by the applicant, the interviewer's style of delivery, and the adequacy of the job information provided. These factors also predicted the evaluation of the interviewer by the applicant.

One inference derived from these results is that applicants use interviewers' style, perceived personality, and provision of job information to decide whether or not they are in favour of them. If they are in favour, they infer the nature of the organization from this favourable reaction, and come to a favourable decision. The recent research of Harn and Thornton (1985) supports part of this model. They, like Schmitt and Coyle, obtained descriptions of interviewers from applicants following interview. Of the five factors derived from these descriptions, three predicted the extent to which the applicant considered the interviewer warm and thoughtful. They were the interviewer's non-directive counselling behaviour, listening skills, and interpersonal sensitivity ($R = 0.68$). Only one factor, the interviewer's listening skills, was related to the applicant's willingness to accept a job offer ($r = 0.36$). Most interestingly, the more the applicant saw the interviewer as typical of the organization's other employees, the greater the relation between the interviewer's behaviour and the applicant's willingness to accept.

Thus the link between the applicant's perception of the interviewer as typical and the applicant's decision is established. The link between the applicant's reaction to the interviewer and the applicant's decision is made by Keenan's (1978) finding that applicants were more willing to accept job offers when they liked the interviewer. The initial part of the model is still problematic, however. Do applicants like interviewers because they provide job information *and* because they have a friendly interpersonal style? Or do they like them solely for the latter reason, and base their decisions both on liking them and on the job information which they provide? The evidence of Rynes and Miller (1983) is apposite; they found that both the interviewer's non-verbal style and the amount of information provided influence how effective a representative of the organization the interviewer is judged to be; how likely the interviewer is to offer a second interview or a job; how well the organization treats its employees; and the applicant's willingness to attend a second interview. In a second experiment, on the other hand, these authors found that the content of the information, rather than its amount, had a powerful effect. When the information presented was of a very much more attractive job or a less attractive one, the interviewer's non-verbal style failed to predict how well the organization was perceived to treat its employees or the applicant's willingness to attend a second interview; attractiveness of the job, however, did predict these variables.

Perhaps it may be concluded that where very clear differences between jobs exist, decisions are related to such differences; whereas, where there are no such clear-cut differences, the interviewer's style has the major effect. In addition, for the new graduates who were investigated here, a lack of occupational and organizational knowledge might result in a greater willingness to judge by the interviewer's style. In general, we may say that the interviewer's style has a major effect on the applicants' decisions, and that this is at least partly consequent upon the applicants' resultant favourable impression of the interviewer.

SOCIAL EXCHANGE

It can be seen that there are clear parallels between the ways in which the applicant and the interviewer react to the interview. Both parties evaluate each other on the basis of the face-to-face encounter. Interviewers' evaluations may well be on the basis of how much they like the applicant, partly because the applicant is like themselves and therefore thought to be good for the organization. The applicants' evaluation is likely to be on the basis that the interviewer is typical of the organization as a whole, and that, since they like the interviewer, they will like the organization too. Interview style rather more than verbal content seems to be the mechanism whereby these evaluations are formed. Hence we may describe the interview as generally practised as a social episode of acquaintance formation from which evaluations of the other party are derived.

One's response to this conclusion need not be one of shock or surprise. Relatively unstructured social exchanges between people are our normal and regular method of forming and maintaining relationships. Part of the function of such social exchange with others is to enable us to decide initially whether we like them or not. It is therefore

154

hardly surprising that when this mode of social relation is transferred into the employment situation, the participants make the same sort of response as they do normally: they decide whether they like the other party or not. The next question is, therefore, whether the unstructured interview *should* have a place in the employment process, assuming that it is inevitable that it results in such feelings of attraction or rejection. One must surely conclude that the relatively unstructured interview should not form any part of the basis upon which selection decisions are made by the organization. Decisions so based are likely to reflect the prejudices of the interviewer, and hence be discriminatory; for they are founded upon behaviour and inferred characteristics unrelated to the job. They are consequently unlikely to predict job success.

However, this does not mean that the unstructured interview has no place in the recruitment process as a whole; nor that other forms of interview are to be excluded. On the contrary, it will now be argued that different types of interview can form a major component of the process. This argument depends, however, upon taking a new overall stance regarding the recruitment process and the function of interviews within it. This new stance requires us to view recruitment as a process of social exchange, in which the potential employee's future work role is negotiated. This process implies mutual acquaintance and disclosure, in which the expectations of both organization and applicant are communicated and modified (Katz and Kahn, 1978).

As has been demonstrated in our review of the research literature on the interview, the expectations of both parties are concentrated upon that particular episode, since it is usually the central point of the selection procedure. Yet it is functionally unsuited to such a task; instead of information about whether or not applicants are suited to and in favour of a particular role, the interviewer is likely to discover whether he or she likes them or not. Instead of learning what the organization will really expect of them, applicants make hazardous inferences about the nature of the organization from their reaction to the interviewer as an individual. If interviews are to be of greater use, they have to be specifically designed to fulfil a function within a process of social exchange. Instead of most employment decisions being taken after the initial face-to-face meeting, such a meeting should occur where it belongs: near the beginning of the process, when acquaintance is being made.

Before outlining the functions of interviews within such a social exchange process, however, we should note that there exists an inequality of power between the two parties, and that any successful design of a recruitment procedure will have to reduce that inequality to enable information to be exchanged more freely. One only has to consider the differential likely consequences of the applicant refusing to answer a question ('That's a personal matter I'm afraid') and the interviewer likewise ('I'm afraid I can't tell you that, as it's confidential company policy information'). It is quite possibly in organizations' best interests to give applicants a realistic job preview (Premack and Wanous, 1985); but whether or not they choose to do so is entirely up to them.

The overall recruitment procedure, then, should incorporate acquaintance-formation and role-negotiation phases. The use of the interview will not be decreased, but rather enhanced by this development. The different functions which interviews have at different stages will be reflected in different structures, however; and the arrangements will have to incorporate efforts to reduce the imbalance of power between the parties. There now follows an outline of a recruitment procedure designed to reflect these considerations.

First, it should be possible for organizations to produce brochures and videos which contain enough representatives of the organization and enough realistic job information to enable potential applicants to decide whether to complete an application form. Pre-selection on the basis of the application form is a difficult process (Herriot, 1984); let us assume that applicants have self-selected themselves out on the basis of the advertisement/brochure/video to such an extent that the pre-selection sift can exclude those obviously unsuited by lack of qualification or experience. The next step is a face-to-face meeting. One of the shortcomings of the present interview is that only one interviewer represents the organization. Applicants therefore have to make the huge inferential leap from the behaviour of one person to that of the organization. This first interview should therefore ideally be with several employees in turn, including some, at least, with whom the applicant can identify. Moreover, if some of these interviewers are like the applicant in age, gender and race, their responses are likely to be less discriminatory. There is no need for these interviews to be lengthy, since impressions are formed rapidly.

The use of this initial interview to enable the organization to reduce the number of applicants seems misplaced, given its low validity and discriminatory features. Its function is to enable applicants to make immediate evaluations of the organization, and consequently to self-select out or indicate continued interest in a job. If reduction in the number of applicants is still necessary, a highly structured job-sample interview of the type proposed by Latham *et al.* (1980) may be used; alternatively, assessment centres incorporating real job-sample exercises may be appropriate (Thornton and Byham, 1982). The advantage of both of these latter forms of assessment is that they offer applicants a further chance to find out more about the job and the organization, particularly since middle or senior managers are often used as assessors in assessment centres.

The final stage of the procedure would be a role-negotiation interview. Here again, steps must be taken to reduce the power differential. The organization knows well the nature of the organizational climate and the demands that will be made on the prospective employee's time, energy, and loyalty. It may well be less than fully frank in its declaration of these expectations. The applicant, on the other hand, may have little experience of similar jobs in other organizations with which to compare this job. Indeed, if the applicant is an immediate graduate or a school-leaver, he or she will have little idea of what organizations in general expect from their employees. Further, the applicant will have no way of knowing the veracity of the organization's account. One way in which this difficulty might sometimes be overcome is to conduct the role negotiation by means of a four-party discussion. A representative of the staff association or trade union might help the applicant, while a personnel officer and the prospective line manager would represent the organization. The staff association representative would know the organization well, and would also have knowledge of comparable jobs elsewhere. Both sides would be expected to compromise in their expectations of the other. The conclusion of this interview would be an employment agreement, in which commitments might be made by both parties over and above the legal employment contract itself. Such commitment would motivate the employee, as de Wolff and van den Bosch (1984) observe. Alternatively, no agreement might be reached.

In these ways the interview would gain a new lease of life. Construed as the opportunity for initial meeting and impression-formation, it performs the function of *acquaintance* making. Structured into a job-sample questionnaire, it serves as an *assessment* function for the organization and as a job preview for the applicant. Transformed into a two-sided *negotiation* with four participants, it establishes the roles expected by the organization and accepted by employee. The interview is in these several ways the key to a recruitment policy which reflects the psychological contract between employer and employee. The recruitment policy follows the pattern of subsequent relations between the parties; they start as they mean to continue. Instead of an often alienating experience of being assessed by criteria which are seldom made explicit, the applicant would enter immediately into a mode of contracting which will characterize his or her subsequent employment.

SUMMARY

The interview has been characterized as a social event, when organization and applicant first meet face-to-face. As a consequence of this meeting and of the interpersonal style demonstrated by the participants, they make favourable or unfavourable evaluations of each other. It has been argued that these evaluations should not form the basis of employment decisions as they largely do at present. Rather, they should form the first, acquaintance-making stage of a recruitment process which also involves role negotiation. Thus interview procedures, structured according to whether they serve primarily acquaintance, assessment, or negotiating functions, can act as the principal vehicle for this process of social exchange. Such a social-exchange model of the recruitment process is likely to represent the psychological contract between organization and employee of the future.

FURTHER READING

There are many books on how to conduct interviews. These are prescriptive in nature, and tend to assume that the purposes of the interview are the assessment of the applicant and the imparting of information. They are in general not based on a theoretical account of the interview, nor do they usually refer to the weight of evidence against its use as an assessment device. The best recommendation, therefore, is to read the excellent reviews by N. Schmitt (1976) and R. D. Arvey and J. E. Campion (1982). The examination of evidence on discrimination by R. D. Arvey (1979) is also of key importance. For a superb account of the way forward for selection procedures, see C. J. de Wolff and G. van den Bosch in the *Handbook of Work and Organizational Psychology* (Wiley, 1984).

8

Work-role Transitions: Processes and Outcomes

Nigel Nicholson

Work-role transitions – moves between jobs or major changes in role requirements – are frequent and important events in organizations and in people's lives, but only in recent years have they captured the interest of scholars. In this chapter it will be argued that a more focused attention on the processes and outcomes of transition would enhance our understanding in a number of related areas. Specifically, within the fields of careers psychology, industrial psychology and organizational behaviour, topics of varying relevance to transitions have figured widely, but without any apparent recognition of their common interests. The theme of this chapter is that the study of transitions offers a way forward to achieve greater coherence within and between these fields, because of its promising potential as an area for theory-building, empirical prediction, and practical application.

The structure of this chapter is therefore as follows. Related topics will be briefly reviewed in various fields: career development, work adjustment, organizational socialization and turnover. Then we shall turn to look more directly at transitions: the distinctive processes and outcomes occurring at different stages of the transition cycle.

CAREER DEVELOPMENT

There are four strands to the study of careers which have a bearing upon work-role transitions.

First, originating in differential psychology, is the study of occupational choice. Probably the most influential and widely researched theory within this tradition is that of Holland (1973, 1985), which

160

proposes that people seek out environments congruent with their personalities when they make vocational choices. Matchings are predicted between six types of personality and occupations: Realistic (mechanical and systematic job demands/personal preferences), Investigative (analytical and curious), Artistic (expressive and nonconforming), Social (training and helping), Enterprising (goal-directed and socially manipulative), Conventional (data and information manipulative). The theory could be said to be high on internal validity but low on external validity. A large number of studies have given support to its psychometric model, but the theory's predictions of choice and change in the real world remain in doubt (Super, 1981; Herriot, 1984). Most empirical tests of the theory have been based on student samples and used intentions and preferences rather than actual career decisions and destinations as dependent variables. The few empirical studies that have been based upon actual occupational choice and change have given equivocal support to the theory. For example, some research has suggested that people are more likely to change their work aspirations to fit the jobs they choose than they are to change jobs to fit their aspirations.

Second, from a more developmental tradition, are career-stage theories. Of these, Super's theory (see Super, 1981) has been the most influential, proposing that career development proceeds through stages as individuals seek to 'implement their self-concept'. Early career is characterized by *exploration* as changes and new work experiences are tested. The early–middle period of *establishment* sees continued adjustments and trials. In the later career stage of *maintenance* a more conservative pattern is characteristic, before *decline* into retirement. There is no shortage of anecdotal evidence to show that careers often do follow this kind of sequence, and research does suggest that there are distinctive periods to careers, though not necessarily conforming to the Super typology (Veiga, 1983). More consistent with the theory has been research showing that career choices lead to self-image congruence with organizational as well as occupational types (Tom, 1971). But stage theories do not generate strong theoretical propositions. They offer probabilistic descriptive generalizations rather than specific analytical predictions. Moreover, such schemata can be criticized on two counts: they fail to give an adequate account of how human autonomy and self-consciousness can direct career patterns (Law, 1981), and they do not sufficiently acknowledge the unpredictable way opportunity structures unfold (Rothstein, 1980). From a life-span perspective, Haan (1981) has been similarly critical of the *ad hoc* nature of stage-theory formulations. Reviewing the Berkeley (California) longitudinal studies of personality development, she concluded that more fluid and situationally adaptive concepts of personality fit the available evidence better than stage models.

The third type of theorizing about change within a careers perspective combines the first two, developing typologies of careers at different stages and in specific occupational groups. This is to be welcomed, for if we are to speak meaningfully about adaptation to change, we need to be clear about how it is contextually dependent. There are several interesting empirical studies within this tradition. Bailyn (1980) found professional engineers divisible into distinctive groups according to their status and whether their professional orientation was managerial or technical. Similarly, Rapoport (1970), analysing the values and career patterns of a middle-management sample, found they fell into four categories: metamorphic (ambitious, driving types), incremental (steady climbing), humanistic (interpersonally accommodating), tangential (alienated and diverging). One of the most interesting recent studies of this type has been Rychlak's seven-year longitudinal study of young male managers (1982), extending the research of the classic study by Bray, Campbell and Grant (1974) and illustrating the interdependence of change patterns, context, and individual differences. Rychlak demonstrated that the managers' life-themes changed in salience over time as a function of a range of individual-difference variables. For example, managers who declined in self-confidence over the study period also placed diminishing emphasis on the financial-acquisition life-theme. Rychlak summarizes a large number of complex variations of this kind by means of Bray and colleagues' distinction between 'enfolders', people who cultivate their familiar life-spheres, and 'enlargers', people who actively seek development, adaptation and outward influence. Such typological approaches have the considerable virtue of being empirically grounded and much closer to the realities of organizational life than the more general careers theories we have considered previously. However none of these sheds light directly on the process and outcomes of particular career moves or job changes.

Fourth and finally, careers psychologists are beginning to take a more interactive view of the relationship between work and other areas of life in what has been called a 'life-span, life-space' approach (Super, 1980). Super describes a 'rainbow' model of the life-span to show how a variety of social roles (the colours of the rainbow) are in their different phases at any single point in time; so that one role, say that of parent, may be waning, while others, such as citizen or worker, may be growing. These changes are a function of the individual's varying temporal involvement in, or emotional commitment to, each sphere. Certainly, in recent years there has been growing research interest in the interaction of work and non-work events and experiences (Near, Rice and Hunt, 1980; see also Chapter 12), and major imbalances between these spheres do appear to have a negative impact on career and life satisfaction (Evans and Bartolomé, 1980).

In their review of the field, Sonnenfeld and Kotter (1982) see this kind of life-span approach as representing the 'maturation' of career theory. One can agree with their opinion that it is more dynamic and open-ended than other approaches, but its main use seems likely to be diagnostic and descriptive in counselling settings, rather than offering any distinctive theoretical propositions which might lead towards a causal theory of change reactions. One cause of this limitation, which as we have seen is shared by most career theories, is that life-span approaches are often not contextually embedded. They take entire occupations or careers as their units of analysis, not types of work roles or moves between roles. One can search in vain in the indexes of the major texts on careers we have cited here to find some reference to these variables. So at this point let us turn to literatures where such factors do figure in analyses of change.

ADJUSTMENT TO WORK

Behavioural scientists analysing adjustment have focused on the processes and outcomes of person–job fit and misfit. Some psychologists have approached this by extending the logic of Holland and others' 'matching' theories of occupational choice, to account for what happens to people after they have taken up employment. Lofquist, Dawis and associates from the University of Minnesota (Lofquist and Dawis, 1969; Dawis and Lofquist, 1984), working from a counselling psychology tradition, have been pursuing this theoretical line more consistently and longer than anyone else in the field. Their main argument is this: the degree of congruence between people's needs or abilities and their job characteristics predicts their work satisfaction. Misfitting is predicted to be inversely related to tenure. People are satisfied and stay in jobs which they fit, or they will either change jobs or change their needs and abilities when they have jobs in which they do not fit.

The Minnesota researchers claim extensive support for the theory, but this is almost exclusively from cross-sectional research. They have not studied dynamics of change through longitudinal investigations, though within the turnover literature (see below) there is support for the idea that misfitting and dissatisfied people are more likely to quit their jobs than satisfied workers. This commonsensical discovery does not lead us to any theoretically profound or robust insights in the absence of research into the organizational or individual contingencies that might mediate these adjustments. The Minnesota theory is now attempting to incorporate some more individual-difference factors, but it remains remote from the issues of group and organizational dynamics.

However, the findings of some industrial/organizational psychologists can be related to the predictions of work-adjustment theory. In a large cross-sectional survey, Katz (1978) found that length of time in a job reduces the relationship between job demands and worker satisfaction (i.e. workers progressively accommodate to job conditions), though a more recent study failed to replicate the finding (Kemp and Cook, 1983). Other research has found a U-curve relationship between intrinsic job satisfaction and seniority (Ronen, 1978). Evidently, work satisfaction is not affected in any clear or simple way by the passage of time in a job. None the less, organizational commitment and job involvement have been found to increase with job tenure and seniority in both cross-sectional and longitudinal studies (Rabinowitz and Hall, 1977). However, it has been argued that this may be due to post-decisional rationalization and justification (O'Reilly and Caldwell, 1981), and it is also the case that the self-selection of uncommitted and dissatisfied people out of organizations (by quitting) will have the effect of enhancing cross-sectional relationships between attitudes and tenure. For a more developmental and rigorous analysis of the long-term effects of jobs on people, well-designed longitudinal studies are needed. Because of their high costs in time and resources, these are few and far between, but several such investigations have recently been published, and they all confirm that person–job fit does increase with time.

Three of these studies are of particular importance. Mortimer and Lorence (1979) looked at male college students from shortly before graduation to ten years on, and demonstrated that convergence does take place between work values and job rewards and experiences, through both selection and socialization processes. People gravitate towards jobs which are consistent with their value systems, and people's value systems change over time to become more congruent with the jobs they hold. Brousseau (1983) claims that a similar convergence explains why technical and general oil-company managers in jobs rated high in 'importance' and 'identity' (functional 'wholeness') had increased in their well-being and active orientation to work over the previous six years. But the most ambitious longitudinal research on this theme to date has been conducted at the National Institute of Mental Health, Maryland (Kohn and Schooler, 1983). In a major programme of large-scale cross-sectional and ten-year longitudinal studies, including a number of cross-cultural validation studies, these researchers have used rigorous and sophisticated statistical analyses to demonstrate a consistent and intriguing pattern of reciprocal causal relationships between identity variables and work characteristics. Over time, complex work enhances individuals' intellectual flexibility and self-directedness, while at the same time intellectually flexible and self-directed people tend to move into more complex jobs.

SOCIALIZATION, COMMITMENT AND TURNOVER

Most of the research on work adjustment we have reviewed has been based upon surveys of heterogeneous employee populations and consequently has been silent about specific organizational effects and the outcomes of particular role changes. Research in the field of organization behaviour has been more informative on these issues, portraying psychological commitment as mediating the relationship between organizational socialization and employment stability. Organizational socialization creates commitment, and low commitment is predictive of turnover. We shall look at these linkages in turn.

Socialization can be defined as the process of becoming a member of a society or sub-culture. Through various socializing agencies (significant others, communications media, and structured experiences) one acquires knowledge, attitudes, beliefs, motives and behaviours that facilitate the future performance of social roles. Childhood socialization broadly prepares one for adult life, and more specifically for membership of particular sub-cultures and social strata. Socialization is a life-long process because we have to adapt continually in our adult lives to the distinctive micro-cultures of social institutions, their patterns of shared beliefs, values, mores and customs. Learning and influence-processes induce identity changes that will help members to fit into occupational and organizational cultures. Note that this does not preclude the acquisition of norms and practices which are deviant from the orthodox or dominant values of the institution, as can happen when people are socialized informally by agents from some counter-conforming sub-culture. So it is that, with varying degrees of direction and coherence, occupations and organizations can be viewed as socializing institutions.

There is wide agreement among writers that commitment to or identification with the organization is a principal outcome of the socialization process and that the primary inputs are the growing investments and involvements the individual makes in the life of the organization (Sheldon, 1971). A number of qualitative research studies of particular occupational groups have shown how compelling such socialization activities can be (see Van Maanen, 1976).

From a more psychological perspective, Feldman (1976) has proposed a theory of the various stages and processes of work socialization, though his research with a sample of hospital employees concluded that company socialization programmes often fail to achieve what their agents expect of them but none the less do succeed in creating favourable attitudes among employees. Other studies have shown that the experience of success, particularly early in one's career, is a potent facilitator of commitment and involvement and sets the scene for later career successes; setting in motion what has been called a 'success syndrome' (Hall, 1976). Conversely, it seems that the consequences of frustrated ambitions and failure are low commitment and a shifting of the focus of central life-values away from work into other spheres of life (Faulkner, 1974). However, this linkage should not be taken for granted, for career success, especially in high-flying managerial jobs, may also become increasingly tainted with bitterness at its high costs in personal terms (Korman *et al.*, 1981). The notion of the 'mid-life crisis' has become an over-generalized cliché, but it does express the truth that the linkages between socialization, commitment and success are often fragile in middle and later career stages, when people engage in reassessments of their lives, career goals and values.

If the socialization–commitment linkage represents the way people become bound to their jobs or organizations, the study of turnover has been concerned to show how that bond can be broken. There is a long tradition of turnover research in industrial-organizational psychology. Early studies were absorbed with demonstrating that job dissatisfaction is predictive of turnover. Latterly the notion of commitment has been substituted for satisfaction (Mowday, Porter and Steers, 1982), and theories have begun to take account of the subjective ease and cost of moving (Mobley *et al.*, 1979). These accounts of the linkage between people and jobs are consistent with work-adjustment theory, by concentrating on how person–job misfitting relationships can cause quitting.

But an alternative rationality can be envisaged. Gowler and Legge (1975) have suggested that people can become *too* integrated with their work roles and organizations. Inurement to limited discretion leads to a fusion of expectations and experiences. People become stuck, reluctant to move, underestimating their potential for movement across the organization's boundaries and exaggerating the costs and difficulties. Moreover, as unemployment has risen, low turnover has begun to be seen as a potential impediment to organizational development. In these circumstances one may doubt that turnover is a form of natural selection through which 'misfits' conveniently shed themselves from organizations. Burke and Weir (1982), for example, found that 'locking-in' (employment immobility) was more common among passive personality types high on external locus of control, and was unrelated to work experiences and satisfactions. In a study of nearly 1,000 loan-company staff, Scholl (1983) found that people had subjective timetables for promotion, and as they passed the expected transit time their intent to remain in the organization fell. It then rose again after the expected transit time had passed. He also found that people with high commitment were more likely than less committed workers to seek out job moves that were difficult to implement. There was no parallel effect for easily implemented job moves. These studies demonstrate that the outcomes of high or low commitment vary according to context and are thus a good deal more complex than turnover research has generally suggested.

The ideas and research we have looked at in this section have shown how adjustment is a function of the person's developing relationship with work. We have seen that socialization, investments, experiences of success and failure may bind or break the linkage between individual and organization. Now it is time to look more specifically at the events and experiences at the centre of this linkage: transitions.

TRANSITIONS

The notion of a 'transition cycle' (see Figure 8.1) illustrates how adjustment processes are continual and recursive. Moreover the rate of job change is high and rising. Sell (1983), analysing American census data, noted that occupational relocations had doubled in frequency between the early 1960s and the mid-1970s. Alban-Metcalfe and Nicholson (1984) found that the rising rate of employer-changing recorded by management surveys from the 1950s to the 1970s was

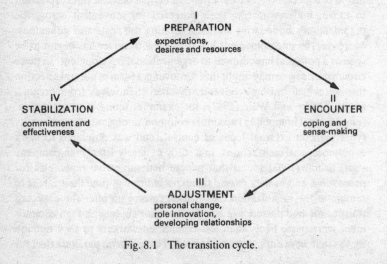

Fig. 8.1   The transition cycle.

continuing to increase into the 1980s, unabated by the impact of recession. In their 1983 survey of 2,300 managers they found that fewer than one in ten middle and senior managers had been with one employer all their careers (compared with one in three in the 1960s). Moreover, apart from employer moves, managers routinely experience many other radical job changes *within* organizations. We shall now look at what research tells us about how people experience the stages of the transition cycle and their personal and organizational consequences. First, we shall look at the preparation and encounter phases (I and II in Figure 8.1) to see what happens at the point of transition, when people cross the boundary between two successive roles. Then we shall look at the aftermath and longer-term adjustments to change.

The Entry Process

People are unequally prepared for the transitions they encounter. In some cases there might seem to be a lifetime of preparation for certain types of occupational role. College students develop occupational plans consistent with their parents' backgrounds (Goodale and Hall, 1976) and working-class school children have been observed to rehearse the values and prevailing norms of the unskilled manual jobs that await them (Willis, 1977). Such 'anticipatory socialization' is a kind of adjustment *before* change to ease adjustment *after* change, and how complete or relevant it is has a bearing on the outcome of transitions. But anticipatory socialization is likely to be more general than specific, yielding general sets of understandings and ways of behaving that are appropriate to a family of occupations, rather than equipping people with the skills, norms and beliefs to fit particular jobs. Indeed, recent research among managers has shown that not only is job change a frequent and recurring event, but it is often also radical and unpredictable (Nicholson *et al.*, 1985). Managers have a less than 50 per cent success rate in predicting their own promotions or employer changes, even looking ahead over so short a period as one year. How can people prepare for a change they do not know is coming? Only in the most general of ways, and hence they cannot make specific preparations which might cushion them against the particular shocks and surprises of entry. Moreover, even when job choices and changes are instrumental towards specified career goals (Vroom, 1966) and anticipatory attitude-changes take place prior to moving jobs (Hall and Schneider, 1973), people are still often unprepared for what they encounter and are forced to make major psychological adjustments after entry (Richards, 1984).

Recruitment and selection procedures play a major part in forming expectations, especially for new entrants to the labour market, whose orientation to prospective employers is typically speculative and ill-informed. Unfortunately, selection interviews are often ritualistic sales pitches, with each party (candidate and employer) striving to make a favourable rather than self-revealing impression on the other (Herriot, 1984; see also Chapter 6). The consequence is often deep disillusionment in the period after entry (Vroom and Deci, 1971). Giving prospective employees realistic and specific previews of the jobs they will perform can reduce this gap between expectation and experience and help to avoid early quitting through disillusionment (Wanous, 1980).

But even with realistic previews some 'reality shock' on entry to a new work-setting is still to be expected. Louis (1980) has provided a thoughtful analysis of experiences in this encounter phase. The newcomer finds *change* from previous roles, *contrast* with prior experience, and *surprise* at disconfirmed expectations or unanticipated novelties. Immediately, sense-making becomes a top priority, but the kinds of attributions newcomers make about their new surroundings are likely to be unsystematic, with plentiful opportunity for interpretive error. Because of the urgency and difficulty of the adaptive challenge of transition, some writers have portrayed it as a stressful life-event eliciting both proactive and defensive coping strategies (Hopson and Adams, 1976; Brett, 1980). Consistent with this view is the fact that new entrants devote more time to seeking out more social supports than do intra-organizational job changers (Feldman and Brett, 1983). However, research also shows that these shock reactions may be very short-lived and rapidly give way to positive outcomes as competence develops (Werbel, 1983).

A variety of formal and informal socialization agents and practices mediate these developments. Drawing upon Van Maanen's research on police organizations and Schein's studies of alumni from the Massachusetts Institute of Technology, Van Maanen and Schein (1979) have provided the most comprehensive analysis yet of organizational socialization strategies, predicting which will lead to (a) 'custodial' responses; conforming to the expectations and acting like a 'caretaker' in the role; (b) 'content innovation': changing the way the role is performed; and (c) 'role innovation': changing the goals and basic objectives of the role. These outcomes are predicted to be related differentially to the following dimensions of organizational socialization: serial–disjunctive (presence or absence of role models); formal–informal (segregated from or integrated with other employees); individual–collective (alone or with other newcomers); fixed–variable (with or without timetables); sequential–random (with or without cumulative stage learning); and investiture–divestiture (building on or supplanting elements of newcomers' former occupational identities). G. R. Jones (1986) has recently tested this model empirically, with generally supportive findings: 'institutionalized' socialization strategies link with custodial responses, and 'individualized' strategies are associated with innovative role-orientations. Jones also found these effects to be mediated by individual differences in self-efficacy, i.e. differences between the two contrasting effects were most pronounced for individuals with low self-efficacy scores.

With the above exception there has been almost no systematic study of formal socialization strategies, though several studies have examined the dynamics of informal socialization. Role-modelling from superiors and mentors has a major influence on work attitudes and values (Weiss, 1978), but groups too can be especially potent influences on adjustment to transition. Moreland and Levine (1983) propose a phase model of how individual–group relations change through transition: an *investigation* phase of mutual exploration; a *socialization* period, involving the complementary processes of assimilation by the individual and accommodation by the group; a *maintenance* phase of role-negotiation over members' contributions and obligations; a *resocialization* phase, when individuals and the group try to encourage further assimilation or accommodation by each other; and a period of *remembrance* after the individual has left the group and memories form additions to the traditions of the group and the history of the individual. This account, like other phase models we have considered, is rather too abstract and over-generalized to offer specific insights into the job-change process, but it proves to be a useful organizing device for Moreland and Levine's comprehensive literature review of individual–group dynamics through transition.

However, in both the theory and research we have been considering in this section, explanatory and predictive potential is limited by lack of attention to two important sets of variables: job characteristics and individual differences. An interactionist perspective is needed (G. R. Jones, 1983). The author (N. Nicholson, 1984) has proposed a theory of work-role transitions to predict how different modes of adjustment (degrees of personal change and role-development) will be brought about by role requirements (discretion and novelty of role-demands), personal dispositions (desire for feedback and desire for control), and induction–socialization mechanisms (extending the Van Maanen and Schein propositions).

Findings from the cross-sectional phase of a British national survey of 2,300 male and female managers have provided some support for the theory's predictions. Need for control and job discretion are associated as predicted with role-development ('role' and 'content innovation' in Van Maanen and Schein's terminology) and need for feedback and job novelty with personal change (Nicholson and West, 1987). However, longitudinal data from a subset of this sample also suggest that personal change may be less an immediate outcome of a single transition than a cumulative consequence of multiple transitions, and that innovation is a general and continual process in many managerial roles, because it draws upon people's accumulated motives and skills from previous multiple transitions. So it seems likely that a fruitful path for future research will be to analyse the characteristics of sequences of role-transitions and how they interact with both stable and changing individual differences. Analytical tools for this purpose have been discussed elsewhere (N. Nicholson, 1987).

A quite different perspective on the entry process is provided by organizational theory and research, concerned with how organizations attempt to manage mobility, career development, and its consequences. There is not space here to do justice to the large and rapidly growing literature in this area, but some contrasting approaches can be mentioned. First, there are studies of role-succession. Research has investigated how rates of managerial succession relate to organizational performance, suggesting that in some circumstances a vicious cycle operates. Poor performance leads to the scapegoating of individual managers, and the subsequent succession of new people to their roles further aggravates performance problems (M. Brown, 1982). Another approach has been to examine how internal transfers are used as a potent mechanism of control (Edstrom and Galbraith, 1977). The calculated presentation of career imperatives and opportunities in this sensitive area is one of the most compelling inducements to conform and perform in organizations (Kanter, 1977). It is becoming increasingly apparent that individual organizations have distinctive 'cultures', whose career development systems and job mobility patterns differ radically in form and function (Kanter, 1984). So we can conclude that the experience of entry is conditioned by the circumstances that give rise to the opportunity to enter the role, and by the organization-specific relationships that exist between performance and career opportunities. An interesting and almost unresearched corollary of this is that job changing itself affects the organizational culture, through its outcomes in experience and behaviour. Some of these outcomes have already been considered. We shall now take stock of the evidence that is currently available.

Adjustment Outcomes

We have seen how successes, failures, shocks, and personal investments give rise to such outcomes as commitment, turnover, deviance, and conformity. Transitions clearly have the potential to transform people's attitudes and behaviours. In the words of Becker and Strauss (1956):

> Stabilities in the organization of behaviour and of self-regard are inextricably dependent upon stabilities in social culture. Likewise, change ('development') is shaped by those patterned transactions which accompany career movement. (p. 263)

Early research on job mobility demonstrated that attitudes change when people switch roles, for example between the role of shop steward, foreman and back again (Lieberman, 1956) and between the worlds of college and business (Schein, 1967; Hinrichs, 1972). Other writers have taken a longer and broader view, proposing that changing jobs is a first step towards the formation of new 'career sub-identities' (Hall, 1976). Research described earlier (Mortimer and Lorence, 1979; Kohn and Schooler, 1983; Brousseau, 1983) confirms that work experiences can be the cause of such identity development. N. Nicholson (1984) has argued that personal change in response to transitions is only one of two major outcome dimensions. The other is that employees can adjust by moulding the environment to suit their capacities and propensities. Both processes, personal change and role-development, have been found to follow job change (Keller and Holland, 1981; Nicholson and West, 1987), and indeed it is common for companies to try to use transfers as a strategy for the development of both their members and their organizations. But if this is the case, it is also true that transitions represent an opportunity that is neglected by many organizations, owing to powerful institutional and psychological barriers (Brett, 1984).

Schein has outlined a series of hypotheses that link socialization strategies and outcomes with different types of intra-organizational job change (Schein, 1971). Transitions within organizations are either hierarchical (between vertical levels), inclusionary (from centre to periphery or vice versa), or functional (across lateral boundaries). He hypothesizes that formal education and training strategies will tend to be invoked for functional transitions, and more informal socialization strategies will apply more to hierarchical and inclusionary moves. He suggests that processes of socialization and personal change occur soon after transition, and that innovation is a later adaptive strategy. A similar proposition is advanced by Katz (1980), though our own research (N. Nicholson and West, 1987) shows that innovation may be a more immediate and salient force in adaptation to jobs than personal change, which may be a longer, slower and more cumulative process.

Brett sees the stresses arising from transitions as potentially counteracting and inhibiting their developmental potential, particularly when they involve geographical relocations, requiring major family adjustments (Brett, 1980). However, Brett's own research, and that of other scholars, shows that the psychological benefits of change generally outweigh the stresses (Brett, 1982), especially when made to favourable locations (Pinder, 1977) or to desirable jobs (Latack, 1984). Indeed, Latack's study of hospital professionals and managers changing jobs suggests that people actively seek out the stress of desirable moves, and those who make major transitions exhibit superior adaptive capabilities to those making minor moves. This is confirmed by our recent research (Nicholson and West, 1987), which shows that the most radical job changes may induce marginally more anxiety prior to change than less

174

radical moves, but bestow far greater subsequent rewards in terms of satisfaction, discretion, and challenge.

To summarize, there are grounds for questioning the generality of stress-coping models of job change, though the account they offer does seem to be relevant to the anxieties of anticipation, to the first short-lived shock reactions at the point of entry, and to problems of family and community adjustment in geographical relocation. Moreover, stress research does have the important feature of alerting our attention to affective reactions to change, and avoiding over-emphasis on cognitive processes and rational outcomes. The role of positive and negative reactions, such as anxiety and frustration, in mediating longer-term adjustments needs to be explored further in empirical research. The literature on job content and redesign is one useful starting point for evaluating these reactions (see Chapters 12 and 13). Indeed the present review suggests there is scope for job redesign research to take greater account of some of the variables we have highlighted: individual differences, career history and career stage, socialization factors and a wider range of adaptive outcomes. Equally, transitions research could, for its part, benefit by drawing upon the job-design literature for more detailed and empirically grounded analyses of job requirements and organizational characteristics.

TRANSITIONS AND PSYCHOLOGY AT WORK

The study of transitions is in its infancy, and we have seen in this chapter that work-role transitions stand as a bridge between highly disparate fields and topics. There are rich opportunities for original research and theory-building to help integrate and advance knowledge in these areas, taking transitions as a primary building block or unit of analysis. The study of transitions also represents a challenge and an opportunity for the psychology of work more generally, in four ways.

First, transitions highlight the importance of individual differences. The varied forms and outcomes of transitions are a product of the interaction between the characteristics of employees and organizational systems. An appreciation of individual identity and organizational cultures therefore is essential.

Second, the study of transitions provides a fresh opportunity to achieve an integrated view of psychology at work across levels of analysis. Transitions stand at the interface between individuals, work groups and organizations, and to understand them fully there is a need to synthesize ideas and data across these levels, in theory-building and research design.

Third, the analysis of transitions challenges the ahistorical assumptions of much occupational psychology. If we are to achieve a better understanding of the dynamics of change, the past history and future goals of individuals and organizations must come to the fore in the analysis of processes and outcomes.

Fourth and finally, these demands and opportunities require an eclectic use of method and theory. The cross-sectional, nomothetic and population sampling methods that predominate in occupational psychology need to be augmented by longitudinal, idiographic and case-study strategies to comprehend the dynamics of transition. Researchers should also be prepared to draw upon theories and concepts from more than one social science field.

In short, the processes and outcomes of change must assume a central role in our conceptions of psychology at work for theory and practice to advance in the future. The study of transitions offers a new way forward to this objective.

SUMMARY

Work-role transitions are frequent and important events in the lives of individuals and organizations, but until recently they have been neglected by scholars. Our current knowledge about their processes and outcomes can be appraised by looking at several related literatures. Within careers psychology, attention has been focused on occupational choice, career stages, occupational orientations, and non-work factors. Elsewhere, behavioural scientists have studied work adjustment by examining the relationships between person–job fit, socialization, commitment and turnover.

Research and theorizing in these areas can be variously criticized for failing to take account of organizational contexts, individual differences and the dynamics of change processes. Research and theory specifically concerned with work-role transitions is a relatively new emphasis, with some important findings and ideas emerging on entry processes and adjustment after transition. There are grounds for optimism that the study of transitions can integrate and advance knowledge across a variety of fields. At the same time it offers a challenge and an opportunity for new ways of thinking about and researching psychology at work.

FURTHER READING

The literature on careers is comprehensively reviewed in two edited collections. D. Brown and L. Brooks' *Career Choice and Development* (Jossey-Bass, 1984) provides a predominantly American overview of theory and practice, while A. G. Watts, D. E. Super and J. M. Kidd's *Career Development in Britain* (Hobsons Press, 1981) gives a more balanced and critically incisive review.

The experience of entering and adjusting to work roles is effectively summarized in J. Van Maanen's chapter in *Handbook of Work, Organization and Society*, edited by R. Dubin (Rand McNally, 1976). E. H. Schein's *Career Dynamics* (Addison-Wesley, 1978) analyses these issues further within an organizational context, and M. Frese's article on 'Occupational socialization and psychological development' (*Journal of Occupational Psychology*, 1982) is a useful review of work adjustment.

N. Nicholson and M. A. West's *Managerial Job Change* (Cambridge University Press, 1987) is the most detailed empirical work published to date on work-role transitions, encompassing the causes, context, processes and outcomes of change. However, it is restricted to a managerial population, though the large proportion of women in the study enables sex differences in career patterns and change reactions to be evaluated.

9

Leadership and Management

David Guest

It is a popular and irresistible assumption that leadership is a key element in success, be it the success of a work group, a sports team, an industrial organization or a country. Successful leaders are the heroes of any age, and the captains of industry, our corporate heroes of today, are no exception. The secret of their success is eagerly sought, and their books, from Sloan's (1964) *My Years With General Motors* to the more recent autobiographies by Michael Edwardes (1983) and Lee Iacocca (1985), are widely read.

Despite the widespread interest in the leaders of industry, over the years psychologists have devoted most of their efforts to the study of supervisors and junior managers. There are some good reasons for this: there are more of them, they are usually more accessible and more easily compared, and their roles can more readily be simulated under controlled conditions. Another important advantage in studying supervisors rather than senior managers is that criteria for successful leadership may be rather more straightforward to identify and measure.

Nevertheless this approach still leaves open the question of what is meant by 'effective' leadership. In comparing the supervisors of more and less successful groups, does one examine their personality, their style of interaction, or some other aspect of their behaviour? Should the focus be on the leader, or on the behaviour, views and reactions of subordinates? Is the conventional formulation, which treats leadership as the independent variable and group performance as the dependent variable, the most appropriate?

Another persisting issue is the origin of leadership. Are effective leaders born or made? This is a key policy concern in organizations, where choices may have to be made about whether to place the emphasis on selection or training. The record of transferring effective leaders from one setting to another has almost as many stories of failure as success, indicating that the environment within which the leader operates is important and that some concept of person–environment fit is required.

Some of the earlier social psychologists, influenced by their own leader, Kurt Lewin, and his experience of the rise of Nazi Germany, were eager to demonstrate the superiority of 'democratic' styles of leadership over a more authoritarian approach. Underlying this is a theme which seldom emerges explicitly in the literature, namely the morality of leadership. Is effective leadership that which gets the best results according to organizational criteria or that which gets the most positive response from subordinates? Predictably, the aim of much research and practice has been to reconcile these two potentially conflicting criteria.

These issues serve to illustrate some of the complexity, the interest and the challenge of studying leadership at work. They also help to explain Bennis's view that 'of all the hazy and confounding areas in social psychology, leadership theory undoubtedly contends for top nomination. Probably more has been written and less is known about leadership than any other topic in the behavioral sciences' (Bennis, 1959, p. 259). More recently, Miner (1975), concerned by the failure to conduct studies which clearly show the impact of leadership compared with other variables, has suggested that the concept of leadership has outlived its usefulness. A more measured analysis from one of the senior figures in the field (J. G. Hunt, 1984) sees the diversity and increasing change in research approaches as an indication of the health of the field.

This chapter first examines the ways in which psychologists have approached the area. Thereafter two themes are developed in more detail; one is the link between leadership and management, the other is leadership in democratic organizations. The final section will consider some new ways of thinking about the subject.

TRADITIONAL PSYCHOLOGICAL PERSPECTIVES ON LEADERSHIP

The Search for Leadership Qualities

Attempts to identify the qualities of successful leaders existed long before the establishment of psychology, and partly because of this they

179

provided the focus for much of the early work by psychologists on leadership. Stogdill (1948) reviewed this early research and concluded that personal qualities are important for the emergence and success of leaders but that their influence is less than popularly thought; further-more, the results, although inconsistent, do seem to confirm that the context is at least as important. Some interpreted this as a rejection of the influence of personal qualities, but a subsequent review of material up to 1970 (Bass, 1981) attempted to correct this impression. Taking the two reviews together, the evidence indicates that leaders tend to be more intelligent, energetic and flexible than group members, and to display greater alertness, originality, personal integrity and self-confidence. The more recent review also emphasizes the tendency for leaders to display higher need for achievement, greater responsibility, task orientation, and goal-directedness. Such summaries are useful, but the amount of variation explained by personal qualities is often small, and the data come from different settings and through a variety of measuring devices.

Although the study of personal qualities now falls outside the main-stream of psychological research on leadership, assessment often plays an important part in the selection of young managers. Follow-ups within organizations (e.g. Campbell *et al.*, 1970) show that factors such as intelligence and need for achievement do seem to predict subsequent managerial success. One of the better predictors of future managerial success is previous success in leadership positions. This' has been incorporated into biographical check-lists which take account, for example, of leadership at school (see Chapter 7).

The problem in the use of personal qualities is not to illustrate their association with leadership behaviour or to show that tests can predict subsequent leadership success. It is to identify which particular qualities matter in which setting or to find a quality which is relevant across settings.

Leadership Style

The failure of studies of traits to produce consistent and useful results and recognition of the limitations of explanations based on one variable led to a shift in emphasis towards the study of leader behaviour.

Building on the work of Lewin, Lippitt and White (1939), Likert and his colleagues at the Michigan University Institute of Social Research developed a long-term programme to examine the impact of 'autocratic' versus 'democratic' styles of leadership. The approach adopted was to compare the styles of leaders of more and less successful groups. Likert (1961) claims that across widely differing contexts the supervisors of successful groups were consistently more democratic and person-centred and exercised general rather than close supervision.

Likert utilized these findings to develop a classification of management styles ranging from System One, an exploitative autocratic style, to System Four, a democratic style. By advocating System Four, and incorporating additional features such as interlocking groups and elements of goal-setting, Likert presented what is probably the most sophisticated outline of a human relations approach to leadership and management. He combined elements of survey feedback training and organizational restructuring to bring about change, and recognizing the time lags involved, claimed that a sizeable organization needed at least five years to move away from System One towards System Four and for the benefits to become apparent.

Several criticisms have been directed at the conceptual and empirical base of those advocating a democratic leadership style. First, the dimension of leadership, utilizing the autocratic–democratic continuum, is unidimensional, and fails in particular to take sufficient account of concern for task accomplishment. Since there is an implication that the autocratic leader is the more task-centred, advocates of the continuum may be setting up a false dichotomy between democratic and task-centred leadership. A second problem is the over-enthusiastic, partly value-based, advocacy of a democratic style of leadership as superior in all circumstances, which leaves protagonists open to criticism when the research results sometimes fail to demonstrate its benefits.

Many of the studies on leadership style are correlational in nature, raising questions about cause and effect. The assumption, which we will examine more closely in a later section, is that leadership style influences group behaviour. However, it is also possible that the causal link may be reversed. Finally there are question-marks against the measures which have been taken of leadership style and group performance. The tendency to move from straightforward measures of performance to indirect measures such as labour turnover and absenteeism, and finally, in Likert's case, to complex accounting principles, illustrates the difficulties of demonstrating clearly the superior impact of democratic leadership on group performance.

While the Michigan University group studied the leaders of more and less effective groups, another research team at Ohio adopted a rather different perspective. They built up a list of descriptions of leadership behaviour, factor-analysed them and produced four dimensions, two of which were dominant. These they labelled 'consideration' and 'initiating structure' (Halpin and Winer, 1957). Consideration measures a leader's concern for the welfare of group members; initiation of structure refers to the extent to which he or she organizes, focuses and directs the group towards task accomplishment. These are descriptive dimensions and the research of this group had a less normative element than the work of Lewin, Likert and others at Michigan. Instead, considerable research was directed towards the development of measures of their dimensions of leadership style. The main measure, the Leader Behaviour Description Questionnaire (LBDQ) (Hemphill, 1950), has been widely used and was adapted by Fleishman (1953) for use with supervisors in industry. Despite its careful development, doubts remain about the psychometric properties of this scale. A review by Schriesheim and Kerr (1974) reports high internal consistency, but claims that evidence on the validity of the scales is hard to find and suggests that the focus on two dimensions restricts the description of leadership behaviour. Furthermore the two dimensions are found to be inter-correlated at about 0·50 (Schriesheim *et al.*, 1976).

The extensive research exploring the impact of these dimensions has been reviewed by Korman (1966) and by Vroom (1976). Generally, high consideration from leaders is associated with high satisfaction among subordinates and lower absence and labour turnover. The correlation between initiating structure and subordinate satisfaction and performance seems to vary according to the context. Once again there are problems arising from failure to take full account of context and from the inability to establish causal relationships from correlational studies.

Building on the assumption that both dimensions are important, Blake and Mouton (1964) developed the 'Managerial Grid' as a sophisticated training package which aims to develop both dimensions. Over the years, the Managerial Grid and its variants have been used for training in many organizations throughout the world.

Contingency Theories

As findings from studies of leadership behaviour accumulated, they highlighted the dangers of advocating one particular style as likely to prove effective in all circumstances and pointed instead to the need to take account of the context within which leadership is exercised. The best-known contingency theory, and an important landmark in leadership work, is that of Fiedler (1967). In effect, Fiedler developed a contingency theory based upon elements of both the trait and behavioural style approaches, which was derived from an impressively large number of studies of leadership in a variety of contexts including sport, the military and industry.

At the heart of Fiedler's theory is the assumption that individuals in leadership positions possess relatively stable personality traits which predispose them towards a leadership style which will be primarily concerned either with the task or with interpersonal relations. He developed a semantic differential measure of an individual's 'Least Preferred Co-worker' (LPC) to assess this disposition. Those who obtained a low LPC score, in other words those who took a very negative view of the person they had least enjoyed working with, were assumed to be more concerned for the task. Those with a high LPC score, and therefore a more benevolent view of their least preferred co-worker, were assumed to be more considerate and more interested in maintaining smooth and harmonious interpersonal relations.

Which of the two styles was likely to be most successful was said to depend on three elements in the environment. These were leader–group-member relations, the task structure and the leader's power position. Ways of measuring each of these were developed, and the resulting scores were presented dichotomously. As Figure 9.1 demonstrates, this results in eight possible combinations. The figure also shows that across the many studies conducted by Fiedler in the inductive development of his theory, reasonably consistent patterns linking leadership style and leadership effectiveness emerged. A low-LPC-scoring, task-centred leader was most effective when conditions were either favourable (Octants 1, 2, 3) or very unfavourable (Octant 8). In the intermediate conditions, a high-LPC-scoring, person-centred leader was most effective.

183

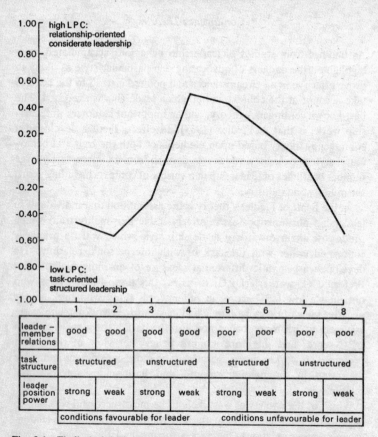

Fig. 9.1 Fiedler's (1967) representation of the relationship between leaders' LPC scores and group effectiveness for eight different classes of context.

Fiedler's contingency theory has proved provocative and controversial and has been extensively tested. There appear to be three important problems with the theory. The greatest amount of critical attention has been directed at the LPC measure. It is presumed to measure a stable personality trait, but there is evidence from some studies that it is not stable over time and that people move from a high to a low LPC score and vice versa (e.g. Stinson and Tracy, 1974). These and other authors (e.g. McMahon, 1972) have questioned the reliability and validity of the measure, and there certainly appears to be a lack of consistent evidence linking a particular LPC score with the expected style of leadership behaviour (Vroom, 1976). Conceptually the approach can also be criticized for its need to dichotomize behaviour as either task- or person-centred. Fiedler (1978) has accepted that an LPC score does not predict behaviour, suggesting instead that situation variables will interact with the LPC score to shape behaviour.

A second set of criticisms concern the contingency variables. There are questions about how they should be measured (McMahon, 1972); how they should combine (Schriesheim and Kerr, 1977); how they should be weighted; and why these dimensions, either individually or when combined into a measure of favourableness to the leader, are the most important contingent variables (Filley *et al.*, 1976).

The third set of criticisms concerns empirical testing of the theory. There are questions about what constitutes an adequate test, and in particular whether it is necessary to test across the eight octants within one study. Because of the problems of studying large numbers of leaders, most investigations have small samples, leading to difficulties with tests of significance. The review by Schriesheim and Hosking (1978) concludes that Fiedler's model has little empirical support. Not surprisingly, Fiedler (1978) has a rather different and altogether more positive interpretation of the evidence.

The more recent utilization of meta-analysis, a statistical device for combining the results of different studies, has only served to fuel the controversy (e.g. Vecchio, 1983). Using meta-analysis, Peters *et al.* (1985) conclude that although the original formulation of the theory is a valid derivation from Fiedler's early studies, subsequent research is less supportive. Like most reviews, they find that in Octant 2 (see Figure 9.1) a high LPC score is more likely to be associated with effectiveness. They also find that additional contingent variables seem necessary to explain some of the results. Finally, but most importantly in the present context, field studies offered less support for the theory than laboratory studies.

In conclusion it would appear that, despite the major contribution made by Fiedler to our thinking about leadership and the undoubted insights to be gained from the adoption of a contingency approach, Fiedler's theory has serious conceptual problems and limited empirical support. Despite the continuing enthusiasm of its advocates and its capacity to evolve, it is ready either for a radical overhaul or to be laid aside.

From a different starting point, and using a very different perspective, Vroom and Yetton (1973) have developed a contingency approach which uses a normative decision-tree to determine the appropriate style of management. They identify five leadership styles along a continuum from autocratic to participative. They list seven questions the manager must ask to diagnose his situation (for example, Is the problem structured?; Is acceptance by subordinates critical to successful implementation?). They also provide seven rules designed to ensure the quality of the decision and its acceptance by subordinates. These rules serve to eliminate certain styles, although it is possible in certain circumstances that a choice of styles remains for the manager to select from. A central assumption is that having identified the most appropriate style, managers will adjust their behaviour to accord with the style.

From a brief description, it can be seen that this model is extremely complex. Indeed most of the initial criticism (e.g. House *et al.*, 1976) made this point, and Field (1979) has tried to produce a simplified version. However, Yetton (1984) has claimed that the capacity to make accurate perceptual judgements is not a problem for the model. Vroom and Jago (1978), in one of the few attempts to test the model empirically, asked managers to recall problems they had tackled successfully and unsuccessfully. It was found that significantly more of those that had been tackled successfully had resulted from behaviour which accorded with the normative prescriptions of the model. However, there are problems of potential bias with this type of self-report data, and the complexity of the propositions has discouraged empirical work.

The main value of Vroom and Yetton's model at present is probably as a training device rather than a testable theory, although one would wish to see more supportive evidence to justify its use in training. The training focuses on the capacity of managers to make accurate diagnoses on the basis of the model and to adjust their behavioural style accordingly. In contrast Fiedler has developed a training package called Leader Match (Fiedler *et al.*, 1976) which also helps leaders to diagnose the environment and then to adjust the environment to fit their style.

Path-goal Theory

Path-goal theory offers a different type of contingency approach by seeking to link leadership to the motivation of subordinates. It still poses the basic contingency question, namely, what kinds of leadership behaviour will result in the best performance among subordinates in a specific situation? Path-goal theory looks for an answer through the supervisor's role in increasing subordinate motivation:

> The motivational functions of the leader consist of increasing the number and kinds of personal pay-offs to subordinates for work-goal attainment and making paths to these pay-offs easier to travel by clarifying the paths, reducing road blocks and pitfalls, and increasing the opportunities for personal satisfaction en route. (House and Mitchell, 1974, p. 85)

Path-goal theory is derived from the expectancy theory of motivation. As the quotation indicates, the supervisor's task is to ensure that effort–performance–reward linkages exist and that subordinate rewards are contingent upon high performance. Four types of leadership style are proposed: supportive (consideration), instrumental (initiating structure), participative and achievement oriented. The two key contingency variables which indicate the appropriate leadership style are subordinate characteristics and the work environment. The key elements in the environment are similar to those identified by Fiedler, namely task, authority and the work group.

Like expectancy theory, this approach contains an attractive rational logic; but it also retains the problems of expectancy theory, such as the inadequacy of rational decision-making as a complete description of reality and the problems of setting up adequate tests. These problems are reflected in much of the research, which has tended to concentrate on task characteristics and to use the Ohio leadership measures. Early studies by House, the main advocate of the theory, provided moderate but not consistent support for a link between leadership style, job performance and satisfaction, using task variables as the moderators (e.g. House and Dessler, 1974). However, subsequent studies (e.g. Downey et al., 1976) have not been encouraging.

Given the failure to find any consistent support for path-goal theory, its status must remain in doubt. It can be argued that it has not yet been fully tested. At the same time it might be claimed that it has not been sufficiently clearly articulated with respect to the range of leadership styles and more particularly the nature of the contingency variables. Its strengths lie in its attempt to integrate and make use of motivation theory and in its switch of emphasis to the subordinate as a key influence on leadership behaviour.

Transactional Systems Approaches

Much of the research described so far is based upon static correlational analysis. Starting from the assumption of leadership as the cause of subordinate performance it typically fails to consider a two-way influence process.

One step in this direction has been taken by Graen with the development of his 'dyad model' of leadership. Rather than treat subordinates as a homogeneous group, this approach examines each supervisor–subordinate dyad individually. It proposes that task interactions, and in particular evolving experience of how subordinates handle discretionary tasks, will lead to a division between an in-group and an out-group. In-group subordinates will have greater access to information, more discretion over their work and more influence over decisions. This influence will evolve from warmer social relationships and the development of trust and therefore greater interdependence. Out-group relationships will be more formal and task-centred. In essence, this means that the leaders will treat subordinates differently according to whether the subordinate is a member of the in-group or out-group. The relationship is a transactional one in that it is shaped by both the supervisor and the subordinate.

The more thorough tests of the model (Dansereau *et al.*, 1975) show a clear relationship between in-group/out-group membership and measures of satisfaction and performance. The approach requires more extensive testing, but, as Yetton (1984) has suggested, it shows promise as a means of explaining contradictory findings from previous research.

More thorough tests of the two-way influence process can be found within a broader systems framework. Conceptually this is an untidy approach in that it hypothesizes that there is a range of interacting causal influences. To reduce it to its simplest level, it suggests that the subordinate will have as much influence on leader behaviour as vice versa. This can only be tested using a longitudinal research design with some manipulation of roles. The few that have been reported lend strong support to the systems perspective. Lowin and Craig (1968) hired forty-eight supervisors for subordinates who had been instructed to perform either well or badly. They found that good subordinate performance led to more considerate supervisory behaviour. Similar findings have been reported by Crowe *et al.* (1972). In a careful study of supervisors in a furniture factory, N. Rosen (1970) switched supervisors at random among the more and less productive groups. The 'leader as cause' hypothesis would suggest that the new group rankings should be a function of the particular leader; the 'group as cause' hypothesis would suggest no change in group performance but some change in leadership style. In the event, the results were mixed, supporting neither of these hypotheses clearly, but indicating that a systems perspective, within which each influences the other, is the most sensible explanation of the outcome. To elaborate this, Rosen used Lewin's (1951) concepts of unfreezing/moving/refreezing, suggesting that the switch of supervisors disturbed the established patterns of behaviour and provided an opportunity for change.

Review

Up to this point we have reviewed the mainstream approaches within industrial psychology to the study of leadership. It is a tradition of growing sophistication, of a move from simplicity to complexity, and it provides an impressive accumulation of thousands of studies.

Certain problems can be discerned. For example, measured leadership variables seldom account for more than a small proportion of the variance in subordinate behaviour. This is theoretically plausible; but the search for statistically significant results has inhibited rigorous analysis of how much influence leadership might be expected to exert under different circumstances. Also, there has been too much dependence on the core variables of leadership behaviour, namely consideration and initiating structure, possibly because of the readily available measures. A third problem has been the reluctance to explore the systems or transactional approach and to develop appropriate field experiments. A further difficulty is that most research has explored the validity of a single theory, with very little testing across theories to explore competing hypotheses. Finally, there has been too much emphasis on leadership at the supervisory level in organizations.

While recognizing these problems, Yetton (1984), in a recent overview of the field, is optimistic about the scope for development. He sees what he terms the four main contingency approaches as complementary, in that Fiedler and path-goal theory look at contingencies across types of role, Vroom and Yetton look across types of problem, and Graen looks across types of subordinate. He sees the prospect of a general theory which integrates these approaches and provides the focus for future research.

The subject of leadership has recently been pushed to the forefront in the wider management literature to a point where it is recognized as a key, if not *the* key, determinant of organizational success. However, much of the emphasis is on 'the art of leadership', and the bulk of the scientific research evidence so painstakingly accumulated by psychologists is largely ignored. In the next section we examine this development.

LEADERSHIP AND MANAGEMENT

An increasingly voiced if not always entirely fair criticism of much psychological study of leadership has been of its inward-looking concern to test and refine narrow elements of theory. Typically, this is accomplished by demonstrating statistically that some facet of leadership influences subordinate outcomes. However, the amount of behaviour explained in this way is often very small, so that in many cases statistical significance appears to replace practical significance (Kerr and Jermier, 1978). For some people this is a case of fiddling while Rome burns, of pursuing matters of minor importance while all around in industry there is a crisis of leadership (Bennis and Nanus, 1985). This crisis is reflected in the failure to compete in terms of productivity growth, of failure to maintain a share of international markets through lack of innovation and drive and of failure to respond to Japanese competition. If this crisis appears to some to be particularly British (Mant, 1983), it is nevertheless in the United States that it has provided the challenge and provoked the main response. From the late 1970s it has resulted in a major growth in the study of leadership at the top of the organization, at what has been termed 'the strategic apex' (Mintzberg, 1983).

In studying managers as leaders, several writers have differentiated the two concepts. Selznick (1957), for example, distinguishes the management role of office holder and institutional decision-maker from institutional leadership which entails the 'institutional embodiment of purpose' and 'the definition of institutional mission and role'. In this, he was essentially utilizing a distinction made earlier by Weber (1947). Zaleznik (1977) distinguishes between the manager, who motivates others and administers resources to achieve organizational goals, and the leader, who motivates people to create and follow new objectives. Thus the leader shapes while the manager implements; the leader opens up new vistas while the manager narrows them down. The leader is said to be emotional and value-laden in approach while the manager is more rational. Bennis and Nanus (1985) summarize this in terms of the distinction between doing the right thing and doing things right.

In making this distinction, Bennis and Nanus, like many other recent writers on this topic, are heavily influenced by the contrast presented by Burns (1978), a political scientist, between transactional and transforming leadership. Transactional leadership involves a form of exchange; compliance results in favourable treatment, for example along the lines of Graen's dyad model. This approach to leadership is essentially concerned with means to achieve ends, and may therefore become concerned with issues such as responsibility, fairness and honouring of agreements, but there is no necessity for shared commitment to exist. Transforming leadership is more concerned with the ends; with the direction the organization should take, its goals and values and with developing commitment and motivation to achieve these goals in the workforce. Burns argues that both forms of leadership are necessary.

The conceptual distinction between management and leadership has some appeal. However, in studying the behaviour of those in positions of power and authority in work settings it may not be very useful. It can be argued that formal authority vests in the manager potential power, while leadership determines how far and in what way the potential will be realized. What is called for is more detailed analysis of managerial roles and behaviour.

Management as Leadership

One of the most thoughtful and thorough analyses of management in recent years has been presented by Mintzberg (1973; 1983). Because too many people write about management and leadership in the absence of any detailed knowledge about what managers actually do, he has conducted research to fill this gap. This has led him to make a number of important observations. For example he finds that management at all levels is extremely complex, often unprogrammed, in the sense that the nature of the decisions to be taken cannot be clearly delineated, and is heavily dependent on possession and use of information, often gleaned verbally and informally. Partly because of the informal, unprogrammed nature of the work, compounded by time pressures derived from inability to communicate the informal information, much of management work is intuitive; too often it is rushed and superficial, and usually it fails to make use of rational 'scientific' techniques.

A further finding from Mintzberg's research and review is the remarkable similarity in managerial work across organizations and across levels. This similarity is reflected in ten roles which Mintzberg claims all managers practise in varying degrees. Three 'interpersonal' roles require the manager to act as figurehead, leader and liaison; three 'informational' roles require the manager to act as monitor, disseminator and spokesman; and four 'decision' roles require the manager to be an entrepreneur, disturbance handler, resource allocator and negotiator. The relative weight given to these roles will depend upon four main factors: environmental variables concerning the industry and organization; the level and function where the job is located; immediate situational demands; and features of the individual, such as personality and preferred style.

Managerial work has also been studied extensively by Stewart (1982), who defines the scope available for exercise of leadership in terms of the demands, constraints and choices facing the manager. Demands include actions that must be undertaken to avoid sanction, constraints set the boundaries on what the manager can do, and choices reflect the area of discretion. In practice, none of these dimensions is likely to be entirely static, and Stewart sees leadership, which she defines as influence, as bearing upon this. Like Mintzberg, Stewart therefore sees leadership as part of the managerial job, although the concept of influence, which may be both vertical and lateral, would appear to embrace some of Mintzberg's dimensions such as 'liaison'.

Studies of Organizational Excellence and Successful Leadership

In recent years, as a growing research effort has been directed towards the analysis of leadership at the senior levels of organizations, concern to derive practical lessons has resulted in an emphasis on leadership in organizations which have been conspicuously successful.

Perhaps the best-known study of organizational success is *In Search of Excellence* (Peters and Waterman, 1982). From a study of sixty-two successful organizations, thirty-three of which were examined closely, eight principles were identified. These included staying close to the customer, autonomy and entrepreneurship, productivity through people and an emphasis on being driven by values. Reflecting on these principles in a subsequent publication (Peters and Austin, 1985) one of the authors identifies leadership and, in particular, transforming leadership as the key factor in organizational success. The same conclusion is reached by Goldsmith and Clutterbuck (1984), who conducted a similar study in the United Kingdom.

In a study of what he described as high-performing systems, Vaill (1984) identified what he terms 'purposing' as the key factor in success. This he defines as 'that continuous stream of actions by an organization's formal leadership which have the effect of inducing clarity, consensus, and commitment regarding the organization's basic purposes' (Vaill, 1984, p. 91). He emphasizes the importance of providing purpose and direction within turbulent environments and describes how the leaders in his sample achieved this by investing their feelings and values as well as a considerable amount of their time in the organization.

There are dangers in attributing too great an influence to organizational leaders when the unit of study is the organization, since organizational performance may be determined by a wide range of factors both inside and outside the organization. However, the same sort of findings emerge when the focus is switched to the leader. Bennis and Nanus (1985) interviewed ninety leaders of successful organizations ranging from industrial companies to concert orchestras and athletics teams. They concluded that these individuals display transforming leadership combined with what they term 'empowerment'. This entails pulling others along with you rather than pushing, cajoling or coercing them; the leader will 'empower others to translate intention into reality and sustain it' (Bennis and Nanus, 1985, p. 80). This type of leader will create a new and compelling vision, develop commitment to it and finally institutionalize it.

Maccoby (1977) identified four types of managerial orientation, one concerned with quality of work and professional expertise, one concerned with the safety of a bureaucratic system, one primarily concerned with company politics and one concerned with winning. Managers with the last orientation are described as 'gamesmen', whose aim is to win, where winning is defined in terms of organizational success attained by providing direction and leading from the front. What he described is close to the concept of transforming leadership.

A key feature of transforming leadership is the capacity to manage change. This has been explored in an influential study by Kanter (1984), who reinforces the emphasis on the capacity of successful leaders to provide value-led direction and to deploy 'empowerment'. However, she argues that this can be spread down the organization through devolution and participation to create a number of entrepreneurial leaders. In this respect she is emphasizing some of the features commonly associated with successful Japanese management, and in particular the use of the 'ringi' method of decision-making. This entails the informal development of ideas for innovation among middle management and those people likely to be involved in implementation. Only after extensive consultation at this level are ideas put down on paper and communicated to senior management (Misumi, 1984). Perhaps surprisingly, the major comparative studies of Japanese attitudes towards managerial style and work-related values (see, for example Haire *et al.*, 1966; Hofstede, 1980) fail to show that the outlook of Japanese managers is distinctly different from that of managers in Western countries. However, when operating in the United Kingdom and employing British workers, through commitment to organizational values and competence in all aspects of performance, Japanese managers appear to demonstrate both transforming leadership and empowerment to good effect (White and Trevor, 1983).

Underlying all these studies of successful leaders is an implication that there has been too much emphasis, in the business schools, among consultants and in industry, on transactional rather than transforming leadership, on managerial techniques and manipulation of subordinates rather than on the generation of commitment. In this context, most of the traditional stream of work on leadership by psychologists, and more especially contingency theory, would fall into the category of being primarily concerned with management technique. The contrast between the two approaches has been highlighted by Miles (1965), drawing on his own research on managerial values to complement the international study by Haire *et al.* (1966). He showed that managers tend to practise on their subordinates what he terms 'human relations': this is transactional leadership involving an exchange and may utilize participation not as an end in itself but as a means to obtain compliance and acceptable performance. In contrast, what these managers want from their own boss is a 'human resource' style, in which participation is used to shape and improve organizational functioning. What is implied is that at each level of management there are problems of lack of trust and lack of confidence in subordinates. This results in too much control and use of technique and too little generation of commitment.

Perhaps predictably, the emphasis on transforming leadership has stimulated a resurgence of interest in the concept of 'charisma'. House (1977) has attempted a more systematic characterization of charisma than previously available. He defines charismatic leaders as those who 'by force of their personal abilities are capable of having a profound and extraordinary effect on followers'. Such leaders usually possess strong moral values combined with high self-confidence and dominance. The impact they have on followers can be described in terms very similar to that of transforming leadership and empowerment. The concept needs refining and measuring; indeed this is equally true for transforming leadership, since charismatic leadership may essentially be an extreme version of this.

In this section, we have reviewed work on managerial leadership, much of it by psychologists who have become impatient with traditional psychological research on leadership. The search for relevance has tended to emphasize the 'art' of leadership and has provided plenty of scope for criticism of the often rather anecdotal and unsystematic quality of the studies. Nevertheless it does clearly point towards a new synthesis around the concept of transforming leadership and empowerment which has struck a chord with a wide audience. An urgent research task and an important challenge for psychologists is to examine these concepts more rigorously. Since they imply commitment from subordinates, one place to start may be the analysis of leadership in democratic settings where individuals can choose the leader they want.

Leadership in Democratic Work Organizations

Most studies of leadership in industry examine individuals who have formal authority within the organizational hierarchy. This means that power is vested in the role and individuals are appointed to these roles by those at more senior levels. Not all leadership roles in industry fall neatly into this category; informal leaders may emerge to give coherence to countervailing forces within the organization. These may be found at managerial levels but are more common at lower levels. Such informal roles can be formalized through election or appointment as a shop steward within a trade union or, where no unions exist, as employee representatives. Because they owe their leadership position to those over whom they have to exercise leadership, it may be expected that their sources of power are rather different from those of most managers.

French and Raven (1960) identified five types of power: legitimate power, deriving from the role; reward power; punishment power; expert power; and referent power. The last of these refers to influence based on liking for or identification with someone. All leaders have some choice over which type of power to utilize, but it seems likely that, whereas legitimate, reward and punishment power may gain compliance, it is expert and referent power that result in commitment. A study by Student (1968), using forty-eight work groups and a variety of performance measures, confirmed through correlational analysis the association between referent and expert power and more positive outcomes.

As an emerging leader, the shop steward is likely to have to emphasize referent and expert power. Once elected, he or she has more scope to exercise legitimate power, but key decisions may still be subject to approval by subordinates. The dilemma of trade-union leaders over whether they should act as representative or delegate has been the subject of extensive debate (e.g. Edelstein and Warner, 1975). However, there are relatively few studies of shop-steward behaviour which specifically address the question of leadership. One of the notable exceptions (Batstone *et al.*, 1977) studied shop stewards in two manufacturing plants. From observation of behaviour and interview and questionnaire data, these investigators classified shop stewards along two dimensions, one concerning pursuit of union principles, the other concerned with whether the steward acted mainly as a representative or delegate. Most stewards fell into one of two groups, labelled 'leaders' and 'populists'.

The leaders, who act as representatives in pursuit of union principles and who are found among the convenors and senior stewards in particular, 'play a major role on the shop-floor in terms of the general re-affirmation of values and their application to major issues' (p. 48). In this respect, leaders among the shop stewards are value-driven, the values reflecting union principles above members' wishes. Implicit in this approach is a belief that individual members' concerns are best met through promoting collective trade-union interests. The populists, in contrast, are superficially more responsive to their members in that they initiate fewer issues themselves, play less of a role in shaping issues from other sources and more readily hand over issues.

How is it that the leader category of shop steward survives, even though they apparently pay less attention to the expressed concerns of those they represent? First and foremost they are successful in decision-making; they also use their ability to identify, shape and direct issues to influence their members; and finally they exert influence through maintenance of ideology. In brief, they are opinion leaders (see also Chapter 10). As a result they possess expert, referent and legitimate power which is reinforced by being part of the key shop-steward network. This network helps to re-affirm power, gives access to information and provides important contacts. Judged by most criteria, these shop stewards are also more successful. For example, they play a greater part in raising wages and maintaining worker control while resorting less frequently to strike activity and disputes procedure.

A rather different form of democratic organization is to be found in workers' cooperatives. These have been the subject of experiment in the United Kingdom and elsewhere over the past ten years (Coates 1976; Bradley and Gelb, 1983), and employee share-ownership and management buy-outs have helped to strengthen this interest. Where the workforce constitutes the dominant group of shareholders, the leadership issues for those in managerial positions are unusual since they are ultimately accountable to their subordinates.

Perhaps the most fully developed example of a workers' cooperative operating within the wider capitalist system is to be found at Mondragon in the Basque region of Spain. The workforce, who must provide a financial stake, elects a managing board which in turn appoints the executive management. A survey of attitudes among cooperative members, compared with a sample of employees in conventional Spanish organizations (Bradley and Gelb, 1981), found that differences between management and workers were perceived to be significantly less in the cooperative than elsewhere. Furthermore, management was perceived as more likely than any other potential interest group, including the workers themselves, to be able to promote the workers' interests. This high trust allowed for vertical control of the sort found in conventional organizations but it was complemented by horizontal controls from colleagues. The shared and mutually reinforcing values meant that managers could do a conventional management job without having to exert constraining controls, and the members of the cooperative retained a sense of being in control.

This ideal for cooperative leadership can be contrasted with the British experience at the three major cooperatives set up by the Labour Government in the 1970s at KME, the Scottish Daily News and Triumph Meriden, all of which eventually collapsed. KME probably provides the extreme example of the problems of leadership (Eccles, 1981). The two trade-union convenors, who had been highly effective in that role, became in effect the management board and, as a result of a failure to appoint competent management, also the executive management. They set out, in the eyes of the workers, with legitimacy and referent power, but they had little expertise. This lack of expertise, combined with a failure to learn and an increasingly isolationist, autocratic stance, meant that they eventually lost their legitimacy and referent power, and the workers became disillusioned with them.

The limited data from democratic organizations indicates that despite important differences in circumstances, the exercise of effective management and day to day leadership may not be so very different from that in successful conventional organizations. Legitimate, referent and expert power mutually reinforce each other, acceptance of leadership being influenced in addition by its demonstrable success.

This leaves one further issue to examine: why do 'followers' apparently seem so willing to allow others to exercise leadership? Indeed, do they perceive the behaviour of those in positions of authority and power as leadership?

Leadership: the View From Below

Why do workers obey their superior? Tannenbaum and colleagues (1974) asked this question in a survey in five countries. In each case the most common reasons cited, from a choice of six, were 'it is my duty' or 'it is necessary if the organization is to function properly'. In other words, legitimacy weighed more heavily than the qualities of the leader or the use of rewards and punishments.

Mintzberg's analysis suggests that this type of survey questioning underestimates the influence of leadership. From his perspective, leadership only exists when it is perceived by others, particularly by subordinates. This opens up the possibility that many acts which are not intended as leadership acts are nevertheless perceived as such.

> Each time a manager encourages or criticizes a subordinate he is acting in his capacity as leader. Most often, he does these things when he is engaged in activities that have other basic purposes – to transmit information or to make strategic decisions. But in virtually everything he does, the manager's actions are screened by subordinates searching for leadership clues. In answering a request for authorization, he may encourage or inhibit a subordinate, and even in his form of greeting, messages (perhaps non-existent ones) may be read by anxious subordinates. (Mintzberg, 1973, p. 61)

Calder (1977) and Pfeffer (1977) have utilized attribution theory to explain the perspective of followers. Starting from the evidence which indicates that at best leadership explains only a small proportion of the variance in subordinate behaviour or organizational outcomes, they pose the question, why do we persist in emphasizing what may sometimes be a redundant concept? They suggest that leadership is a mainly symbolic representation of our desire to believe that individuals have significant effects on outcomes:

> Even if, empirically, leadership has little effect, and even if succession to leadership positions is not predicated on ability or performance, the belief in leadership effects and meritocratic succession provides a simple causal framework and justification for the structure of the social collectivity. (Pfeffer, 1977, p. 108)

This builds on the view that individuals make causal attributions about behaviour to explain success or failure and in so doing reflect a desire to believe that it is possible to influence and control events. This results in a tendency for observers to attribute motives, emotions and intentions to individuals and to ignore or underplay the influence of factors outside the control of the individual such as luck, market forces or the behaviour of other people. A belief in the influence of leadership is one manifestation of this and helps to explain the persistence of our belief about its impact on subordinate behaviour, despite the limited empirical evidence to support this. It also helps to explain why the type of 'innocent' communication by a superior, cited by Mintzberg, can be interpreted as a manifestation of leadership control.

Pfeffer (1977, 1981) argues that the symbolic role of leadership is reinforced by personnel systems of careful selection and training for management positions. These raise expectations about the importance of the personal qualities, knowledge and skills, which popularly constitute 'leadership', in the performance of management roles. As a result, leadership is frequently assigned or attributed to those who are placed in positions of authority.

This use of leadership to explain group behaviour, even where it may not be a valid explanation, is illustrated in another approach which has developed out of attribution theory, known as 'implicit leadership theory'. One research focus has demonstrated how perceptions of a leader's behaviour contribute substantially to interpretations of group performance (Phillips and Lord, 1981). In other words, successful group performance is widely attributed to the leader's qualities, including high scores on the dimensions of consideration and initiating structure, rather than to other factors.

Attribution theory provides a valuable new perspective on leadership. By adopting the viewpoint of the follower, the function of leadership can be seen in a very different light. However, there are still limits to the theory's ability to provide coherent predictions for those interested in improving leadership effectiveness, and it is not always easy to develop from it anything other than rather general prescriptions.

SUMMARY

This chapter has drawn out three central points. The first is that the psychological study of leadership, which has accumulated a mass of results and which has come to be dominated by variants of the contingency paradigm, provides an impression of progress which has more form than substance. For some years it has not significantly improved our understanding of leadership, and in its practical application it has not proved particularly useful. The second point is that one source of greater understanding is a shift in focus towards a more interdisciplinary perspective. The benefits of such a shift can be seen in the lessons to be learned from the study of leadership in other contexts and from other disciplinary perspectives; and in the multidisciplinary approach to the study of management. Here the work of Mintzberg and Burns, neither of whom are psychologists, has provided a crucial contribution.

Finally, within psychology we can see a paradigm shift, reflected in the application of attribution theory and the analysis of symbolic leadership. The insights which can be derived from this perspective, with its shift in emphasis from leader to follower and its application to a range of contexts including those where more democratic forms of work organization exist, provide perhaps the best prospect for further progress.

FURTHER READING

A good introduction to the conventional approaches to leadership in work settings can be found in A. Bryman's *Leadership and Organizations* (Routledge and Kegan Paul, 1986). Anyone wanting a thorough review of available research is referred to B. Bass's updating of the mammoth *Stogdill's Handbook of Leadership* (Free Press, 1981). For an excellent analysis of management and its relation to leadership, H. Mintzberg's *The Nature of Managerial Work* (Prentice-Hall, 1973) has yet to be bettered. A recent set of papers by psychologists is to be found in *Leaders and Managers*, edited by J. G. Hunt *et al.* (Pergamon, 1984). A more personalized view can be obtained in autobiographies such as M. Edwardes' *Back from the Brink* (Collins, 1983). A useful and stimulating range of perspectives on leadership can be found in B. Kellerman (ed.), *Leadership: Multidisciplinary Perspectives* (Prentice-Hall, 1984). For an enjoyable but thorough psychological study of leadership, with particular emphasis on personality and the consequences of poor selection and training, try N. F. Dixon's *On the Psychology of Military Incompetence* (Cape, 1976).

10

Bargaining and Industrial Relations

Geoffrey Stephenson and Peter Allen

In this chapter we review some of the attempts of psychologists to examine the setting and the processes of industrial relations. This term refers to those activities by which employees, or more usually their representatives, come to fix the conditions of their work. We concentrate on the more enduring aspects of industrial relations, starting with a discussion of the notion of an industrial relations system, widely defined to include the contribution of influences normally the territory of sociology, economics or history. We focus, however, on the social psychological treatment of the subject and begin by an examination of the ways in which psychological factors come to play a part. Noting the importance of analysis at the group and intergroup levels, we examine ideas of group processes, and then we develop the notion of industrial relations climate. In the final section we review the findings of research into bargaining.

THE COMPLEXITY OF INDUSTRIAL RELATIONS SYSTEMS

Cultural Variation

The typical industrial relations systems in different countries vary independently of the more obvious economic constraints (Kassalow, 1980), and vastly different patterns of organization and practice occur with a variety of outcomes in terms of production and strife. For example, comparisons between Britain and Germany reveal differences not only in the degree of regulation originating outside the workplace, with German regulation operating more at regional level (Marsh *et al.*, 1981), but even in the workplace the realm of activity covered by lay officers of the trade unions is significantly different (Ebsworth, 1980). For example, in Germany lay officers tend to represent the union to both workers and management; in Britain the shop steward is largely an elected representative of a particular group.

With such differences it is not difficult to see why cross-national generalization might be problematic, especially when, in addition to different organization and practice, there may be other cultural and historical factors operating. Union–management relations in the USA, for example, have always been associated with a considerably higher level of strikes than in Europe (Edwards, 1981). Furthermore, industrial relations take place in the context of historical change, embracing both local events and legislation, and large-scale economic changes such as recession. The latter might especially be thought likely to affect the pattern of industrial relations, though it may be difficult to detect in exactly what ways (International Labour Office, 1984).

How can psychology begin to unravel the common threads in these situations? Comparing situations with as many similarities as possible may be a first step, but, as Warner and Sorge (1980) argue, '. . . factories in different countries . . . [we would add 'or even in the same country'] . . . can be perfectly alike from the point of view of products, technology, size and the task environment and yet bring forth distinctly dissimilar forms of organization and industrial relations.' Pure cultural and historically specific forces appear to be at work, contributing to particular industrial relations patterns, which may, in turn, affect production in otherwise identical industrial circumstances. (A comparison between UK and Swedish companies is given by Pratten, 1976.)

This diversity across and within countries has had at least three effects on research methodology in the field of industrial relations. It has led, for example, to the frequent use of the case study, with its concentration on specific details in particular settings. Investigators seeking to go beyond such particulars have most often confined themselves to the study of formal institutions (e.g. Clegg, 1979), an approach which binds the subject closely to history. In consequence industrial relations outcomes have often been explained in terms of historical processes, such as tradition formation and the notion of custom and practice (see, for example, Eldridge, 1968). Diversity and historical change have also been tackled by using surveys, either culture-bound (e.g. Gennard,

1985) or comparative (e.g. Kerr and Siegel, 1954). These may aim to identify common trends or merely to bring the subject matter up to date for description and comparison.

Application of Systems Theories

Such high degrees of complexity have often been successfully approached through application of control and information theories. Concepts of systems analysis were first applied to industrial relations by Dunlop (1958). His formulation, viewing an industrial relations system as a producer of rules, can be seen as within the tradition of institutional analysis. More recently, however, organization theorists have used the systems approach to account for the intra-organizational distribution of decision-making power (Abell, 1975). In doing so, there is explicit recognition that a functioning organization cannot be properly understood when attention is limited to the formal rules and published structure of authority. Psychologists have drawn attention to the additional contribution of informal behaviour (Williams and Guest, 1969) and have emphasized the 'dynamic' aspects of the industrial relations system within the organization (Blain and Gennard, 1970).

These arguments have been usefully summarized by K. F. Walker (1979), who interprets the output of rules from an industrial relations system as 'regularities in the interaction of workers and managers in the production system, which correspond to a given "price" that governs the exchange between them'. Such a rule, for example, could be the understanding by management that an increase in production may have to be 'bought' with a particular level of overtime pay. Figure 10.1 shows the general structure of an industrial relations system and its relationship with the wider environmental systems with which it interacts.

Direct inputs to the system may originate in the wider environment, for example following a change in the law, but the environment also acts indirectly by its effects on actors and their *immediate* environment; the effects of inflation for example. *Actors* originate inputs as goals, values and capacities. Following the distinction introduced by Fox (1971), goals may be of two types: substantive, such as a desire for changes in wages, or procedural, such as the desire for a better grievance

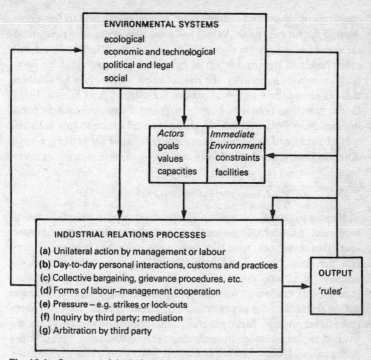

Fig. 10.1   Structure of the industrial relations system. (After Walker, 1979.)

procedure. The outputs of the system match these sorts of input. As the feedback loops in Figure 10.1 show, the 'rules' produced by the system may have consequences (a) for the wider environment, for example when a pay settlement helps establish a norm; (b) for the actors in their immediate environment, for example by a pay settlement; or (c) for the industrial relations processes, for example a new grievance procedure.

Two points need to be noted about these processes. The first is that they are not necessarily independent of one another. The second, and more important, is that the 'normal' intra-organizational operation of such processes can break down, leading to fresh input from environmental systems. An example of this might be where a strike is the subject of novel legal action. Otherwise routine (or customary) conduct can in other words become unstable, taking on a life of its own. The precise character of inputs and outputs is of interest in relation to this point. Among the former, goals, values and capacities are clearly psychological variables and, in the operation of any process, they combine with other inputs in the production of behaviour. The potential for instability, however, means that the pursuit of ends may often be a discontinuous rather than a gradual process (cf. Stagner and Rosen, 1956). Goals, values and capacities can be changed dramatically within social interaction, for example when a strike is called in connection with one sort of event and evolves to represent a demand for settling a quite different issue (e.g. Marsh, 1967).

Group and Intergroup Phenomena

Reference to 'goals', 'values' and 'capacities' implies an individualistic focus, but in industrial relations it is most often collectivities, or representatives therefrom, who take part in the industrial relations system, and the goals, values and capacities in question are usually some function of groups within the organization. They may derive from processes of consensus formation and leadership style, for example within sections of the organization (cf. Batstone *et al.* 1977, on shop-steward leadership). More generally, intergroup processes may assume overriding importance in moulding the motivations, perceptions and processes that parallel individual goals, values and capacities. Individualistic psychological approaches are inadequate for tackling these phenomena; a properly constituted social psychology is required.

When there is an incompatibility of goals between any set of groups, then intergroup processes may be set in train, which in turn may act to constrain or induce variations in goals and values. Social psychological theories which address such processes may thus help illuminate the operation of industrial relations. It is the *relationship between goals*, for example, that is central to the intergroup theory of Sherif (1966). Three types of relationships between groups can be classified with respect to goals. No necessary interactions are anticipated where groups have completely *independent* goals; but where groups are competing over some resource, there are *opposing* goals; and where cooperation is necessary it is clear that the groups may have shared *superordinate* goals. In the competitive situation, group members come to share favourable stereotypes of their own group and unfavourable stereotypes of the opposing group. They judge their group performance more favourably than that of the opposition and bring about changes within their group structure which contribute to the chances for success in the intergroup dispute.

However, it is not only goals which are important. Merely being a member of a particular group may be sufficient to induce intergroup discrimination. Random assignment to arbitrary groups has been shown to result in favourable in-group, as well as unfavourable out-group bias, as individuals appear to strive for positive social identity (Tajfel *et al.*, 1971; Turner, 1975). Of course, many groups with overlapping membership exist in the industrial context – differential union membership, occupational (trade) differences, departmental and working groups – and intergroup discrimination may be widespread, especially when gains can be made at the expense of other groups rather than solely at the expense of management. R. Brown (1978) provides an excellent example of the complexity inherent in a factory where groups are concerned over wage differentials. Applying a social psychological interpretation, Brown shows that competitive social comparison processes between particular groups of employees may come to dominate the negotiating stance of representatives from different groups, who nevertheless know that in order to confront *management* they should establish an agreed position.

This brings us to a further important factor operating within the industrial relations system; the products of intergroup communication are available for actors to perceive as social objects in their own right. The organizational pattern of attitudes, at any one time, is therefore not the mere reflection of immediate concerns. Potentially at least it also represents a tradition of interpretation, which people may refer to in structuring their present perceptions. This tradition will be based partly on knowledge of past events and partly on beliefs about the opposition that can be inferred from both past actions and present behaviour. Clack (1967) provides an example of the first kind from the car industry, where workers 'knew' that industrial action got results; and Purcell (1979) shows how mutual management/worker perceptions may develop, through discussions of attitudes associated with greater trust based on effective cooperation in the past. Deteriorating patterns are also documented, however (e.g. Deutsch, 1973).

Characterizing the Context: Industrial Relations Climate

There is an extensive literature within organization theory that addresses the concept of organizational climate. In a synthesis of previous definitions Pritchard and Karasick (1975) offer the following:

> [climate is] . . . a relatively enduring quality of an organization's internal environment distinguishing it from other organizations; (a) which results from the behaviour and policies of members of the organization, especially the management; (b) which is perceived by members of the organization; (c) which serves as a basis for interpreting the situation; and (d) which acts as a source of pressure for directing activity . . .

Although subsequent research has tended to extend the concept to include subsystem climate as well as that pertaining to an entire organization (Field and Abelson, 1982), the usefulness of the general notion in the present setting is plain (see, for example, N. Nicholson's (1979) application to a local level climate within a steelworks).

In an analysis of the causation of strikes, Kelly and Nicholson (1980) elaborate the notion of industrial relations climate to include:

1. Frames of reference; people's basic value orientations.

2. Intergroup perceptions, as discussed above.

3. Perceptions of the climate itself.

4. The general effect from the economic environment.

They develop a model, based on that originally proposed by Pondy (1967), which links industrial relations climate and organizational structure via strike processes to final output. Following the arguments summarized above, the model includes a feedback link from activities back into subsequent climate.

The Importance of Mutual Intergroup Perceptions: the Concept of Intergroup Understanding

Within the above classification, psychologists are likely to make their major contribution to the perception categories, but research has not often gone beyond the description of basic differences of opinion between workforce and management (Rim and Mannheim, 1964; Glendon *et al.*, 1975). Walker (1959; 1962) took such work a stage further with research in Australia, in which he elicited not only the attitudes of union and management representatives but also their perceptions of each other's views as well. He found that both groups perceived more conflict than actually existed in the groups surveyed. Walker, however, aggregated individual responses and compared union and management views overall. A more detailed approach was adopted in a British study of twenty-four firms in four different industries (Stephenson *et al.*, 1983).

Respondents in that study completed an attitude instrument twice, once for their own views and once for what they thought would be the response of a typical member of the opposing group; either a manager or a worker. Analysis of intergroup attitudes and perceptions revealed significant variation between firms, which was linked to general structural characteristics such as organization size (Allen and Stephenson, 1983; Allen, 1983). While the attitudes of workers and managers were typically different, the sorts of bias in their estimates of one another were very similar and were related in turn to factors such as size.

One effective way to characterize these findings relies on comparing the attitudes *attributed* to the opposition, and the mean of the opposition's *expressed* attitudes, for each group. Examination of the resultant mismatches, or errors, shows that within a firm both workers *and* management make the same form of error: they *both* view the other side as consistently more (or less) favourable to their own side. Given that in some cases the parties make little or no error, Allen and Stephenson term this characteristic of the firm 'Inter-Group Understanding'. It is convenient to identify three basic types of Inter-Group Understanding: *Group Assimilation*, where both parties wrongly attribute opponents' attitudes closer to their own interest; *Group Differentiation*, where both parties conventionally stereotype the opposition in negative terms; and *Realistic*, where both parties have a fairly accurate grasp of the opposition's views.

The character of Inter-Group Understanding within a company appears to be a key variable in industrial relations. In any structured conflict, it is necessary for each party to have some way of estimating what the opposition will *do*. We could expect therefore that parties would view one another's attitudes as consistent with the behaviour that has been witnessed in the past. In fact, as Allen and Stephenson show, both parties are frequently wrong in their assumptions about the other side's attitudes. Furthermore, both parties make the same form of distortion, within a particular firm, either seeing the opposition as closer to or further from their own interests. This mutual misperception seems to be one important component of a company's industrial relations climate.

The practical significance of these different atmospheres of misperception is revealed in a further study, in which Allen and Stephenson (1984) traced the long-term effect of Inter-Group Understanding on subsequent industrial behaviour. At least three years after attitudes were measured, recorded instances of behaviour were collected from the firms of the original survey. Actions initiated on both sides, for example disciplinary dismissals as well as strikes, were combined into a single index of friction, which was found to be correlated with the previously measured climate of Inter-Group Understanding. Higher overall frequencies of action were found to be associated with greater Group Differentiation at the earlier measurement, while Group Assimilation appeared to suppress the subsequent incidence of friction. There is thus evidence for the long-term survival of an industrial relations climate, at least the Inter-Group Understanding aspects of it, and for the generality and impact of such climates.

In order to understand the formation and functioning of industrial relations climates, research into general comparative effects, such as those we have discussed, is very valuable. However, most negotiators must operate within individual firms. Dimensions of climate must therefore be measured at this level to be of practical use. Furthermore, those engaged in negotiations are subject to processes and effects quite apart from the industrial relations climate. We now examine how psychology can illuminate these bargaining and negotiating processes.

THE SOCIAL PSYCHOLOGY OF BARGAINING

Negotiating in Different Climates

There have been no systematic comparisons of the quality of bargaining in different industrial relations climates, and we can only surmise what would be the effects of a prevailing climate of, say, 'assimilation' or 'differentiation' on the outcomes of negotiations. We can, however, usefully explore the issue by reflecting on the tasks faced by representatives of groups when they negotiate in different circumstances. First, however, let us examine the broad theory of negotiating behaviour as it has been elucidated over the years by social psychologists working within the experimental tradition.

Bargaining as Dispute Over Limited Resources

Pruitt (1981) provides the most comprehensive survey of social psychological work on bargaining and negotiation, and his book represents a classic summary of the assumptions which have guided two or three decades' experimental study. Broadly it is assumed that a 'general theory of negotiation' may be elaborated, which will account for the processes observed in, for example, children's squabbling over toys as well as international argument on arms limitation. Negotiation begins when 'parties first verbalize contradictory demands and then move towards agreement by a process of concession-making or search for new alternatives' (p. 1). Parties have conflicting goals and objectives (a particular wage increase, an increase in holidays, a longer tea break on the union side; alternative, and conflicting, proposals by management) which centre on maximizing one's own side's profit. On any issue, there is presumed to be a fixed sum available, such that one side's gain is the other side's loss. Targets are set by each side, and 'resistance points', beyond which no further concessions will be made, are covertly established. If a 'positive settlement range' exists (i.e. resistance points overlap, so that, for example, management is eventually prepared to give more than the union finds minimally acceptable), then a compromise may more readily be achieved than when resistance points do not overlap and a 'negative settlement range' prevails (cf. Walton and McKersie, 1965).

Although preferences, targets and resistance points are assumed to remain constant over time, actors have three broad choices: to maintain demand, to concede, or to 'coordinate' their demands in a mutually profitable way. Typically, it is found that, unless constrained by instructions to do otherwise, experimental subjects will act in the way we are accustomed to think of industrial bargaining. They take a 'distributive' approach, single-mindedly defending their side's claim, exaggerating and disguising the truth of their position, attacking the basis of their opponent's claim, and conceding only reluctantly, if at all, after prolonged wrangling. In such circumstances the 'integrative' potential of bargaining is overlooked.

The concept of integrative bargaining, in which the essential interests of both parties are served, was developed at length by Walton and McKersie (1965) and has formed the basis of an extensive programme of research by Pruitt and his colleagues. The distributive 'win–lose' orientation leads to the neglect of integrative options, and available alternatives that offer the highest *joint* benefit are not utilized or even considered by the contestants. (This happened, for example, in the study by R. Brown (1978), quoted earlier, in which different union representatives preferred to emphasize relativities between themselves to the detriment of both joint gain and maximization of own profit.) Pruitt lists a number of integrative strategies, principally, (i) cutting the other's costs, which may enhance the other's benefit while not materially affecting one's own; (ii) compensation, in which the other side is indemnified in some way for losses incurred; (iii) logrolling, in which concessions are exchanged on different items, to the overall advantage of each party; and (iv) bridging, in which a new option is introduced which goes a long way towards satisfying the demands of both parties.

Pruitt's research focuses on the means whereby the exploration of integrative potential can be facilitated. Essentially, this requires each side to be prepared to give information about the priorities and 'real needs' which underlie their demands. However, such information can readily be exploited by a manipulative opponent, so negotiators are reluctant to divulge such material. A critical factor is the extent to which the parties trust one another not to take advantage of information they receive, other than for purposes of exploiting mutually advantageous options. Such trust is engendered by superordinate goals, to which reference has already been made. For example, in one study of buyer–seller transactions, subjects who were told to act as if they were members of the same organization discovered integrative, more profitable options to a greater extent than those who acted as members of different organizations (Schulz and Pruitt, 1978).

Even more compelling results were obtained in studies of accountability to constituents, a factor first studied indirectly by Druckman and

Zechmeister (1970). In Pruitt's studies (Pruitt *et al.*, 1978; Carnevale *et al.*, 1981), accountability was manipulated in two ways: by having a confederate subject to whom the subject had to report back, or by building into the background information a hypothetical principal (e.g. a managing director of the company for a management representative). In both instances, under conditions of low accountability there was more exchange of information about priorities and more integrative solutions were achieved than when the negotiators' accountability to others was strongly emphasized.

In conditions of low accountability, or where superordinate goals are salient, the negotiators are more likely to coordinate their behaviour, and hence to achieve integrative solutions. The concept of 'coordinative behaviour' embraces the cooperative exchange of concessions, as well as the exchange of information, which may lead to the achievement of integrative solutions. A review of relevant studies has led Pruitt and his colleagues to formulate the 'goal-expectation hypothesis', which states that 'for most forms of coordinative behaviour to be enacted, it is necessary for there to be both a goal of achieving coordination and some degree of trust in the other party's readiness for coordination' (Pruitt, 1981, p. 227). Magenau and Pruitt (1979) suggest that coordinative behaviour will be most evident when the 'motive to maintain demand' (MD) and the 'motive to reach agreement' (MA) are in balance and when trust in the other's cooperative intention is high. If MD predominates and trust is low, then competitive, distributive tactics will prevail; whereas if MA predominates and trust is low, concession-making will be elicited. This model is presented in Figure 10.2.

The three differently shaded areas represent the three alternative strategies, concession-making, distributive behaviour and coordinative behaviour. The vertical axis portrays the Motive continuum (from predominantly MD to predominantly MA) and the horizontal axis the Trust variable. How strongly a bargainer wishes to maintain demand will depend on how ambitious the demand is, the perceived importance of projecting an image of strength, the degree of publicly expressed commitment to the claim, and so on. The value of obtaining agreement, and hence the strength of MA, may be affected by the personal relationship between the bargainers (cf. Morley and Stephenson, 1977) and by the costs of failure to agree. These costs may be exceptionally high for both sides, for instance when a strike has been called or is

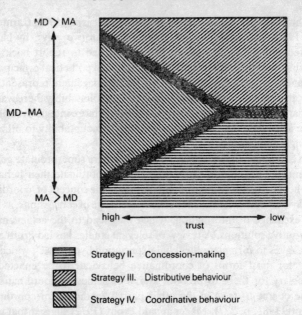

Strategy II. Concession-making

Strategy III. Distributive behaviour

Strategy IV. Coordinative behaviour

Fig. 10.2   Choice of strategy as a function of motive to maintain demand (MD), motive to reach agreement (MA), and trust in the other's cooperative intentions. (From Magenau and Pruitt, 1979.)

imminent. In such cases the time constraint on negotiators is especially salient, and the motive to reach agreement may be keenly felt.

The Bargaining Process

Pruitt's analysis rests heavily on that tradition which views negotiation as a purely strategic interaction, in which the central task is to maximize one's own gain. What the model lacks is any indication of how issues are constructed by negotiators, of the key decisions which must be taken, and of the points at which individual social and persuasive skills may be expected to influence the outcome.

Figure 10.3 is a greatly simplified version of Snyder and Diesing's (1977) model of negotiation, in which we have distinguished between

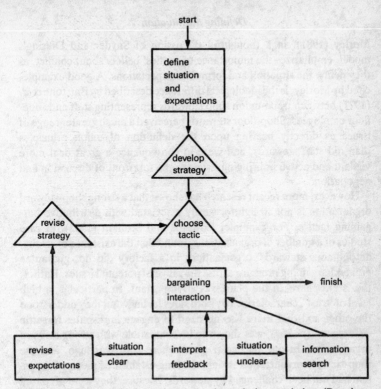

Fig. 10.3 Strategic and information-processing tasks in negotiation. (Based on Snyder and Diesing, 1977.)

the strategic tasks and those which concern information and evaluation. It is the latter (developing a strategy, choosing a tactic and revising the strategy) with which most social psychological research on bargaining has been concerned, the results of which have been portrayed in Magenau and Pruitt's model. The squares convey those information-processing activities which lead to the definition of goals, evaluation of progress, revision of goals and evaluation of outcome. Let us now consider the principal factors affecting the way information-processing is carried out during negotiations in organizational settings.

Defining the Situation

Morley (1981), in a thoughtful discussion of Snyder and Diesing's model, emphasizes the importance of parties' beliefs about conflict, as they define the situation and formulate expectations. A good example, cited by Morley, is the ideological difference described by Batstone *et al.* (1977) between trade-union shop stewards representing staff and shop-floor employees. Shop-floor stewards perceived a much greater range of issues as directly bearing upon the definition of union principles than did staff stewards, and were in consequence a great deal more vigilant and active in bringing issues to the forefront of discussion and negotiation.

However, more recent research has shown that a strong shop-steward organization is not straightforwardly associated with distributive bargaining tactics. For example, Edwards and Scullion (1982), in case studies of a number of organizations, found that the existence of strong, autonomous stewards' organizations in a factory did not guarantee greater bargaining pressure across the range of potential issues. Rather, the 'atmosphere' in the plant was all-important. In particular, a high level of 'trust', characterized by both sides feeling 'that they understood the other and that there was no need to engage in disputes to settle differences' (p. 264), was shown to be compatible with strong steward organization. In one particular plant where trust was high, and the shop-steward organization strong, the long-established piece-work system had not been challenged by stewards, because 'they were prepared to work within the system and to be, as managers often stressed, "responsible"' (p. 265).

Intergroup attitudes and expectations affect the range of issues over which bargaining occurs, and undoubtedly determine what is expected from negotiations. Intergroup differentiation (perceiving the other side as more ideologically opposed to one's own views than in reality they are) may well lead to an exaggerated statement and justification of position, which, according to Allen and Stephenson's (1983) results, will be reciprocated in antagonistic form by the other side.

Interpretation and Revision of Expectations

Interpretation of what happens in the interactions between the parties will be influenced by their conception of the other's motives and expectations. The experience of negotiation may, indeed, confirm worst fears and lead to a sharpening and tightening of demands. On the other hand, coordinative behaviour and integrative agreements may be promoted by information-processing strategies elicited by the process of bargaining itself, as Figure 10.3 indicates. Information search is prompted when the implications of behaviour in the negotiations are unclear in some respect. One may question the opponent or initiate searches for relevant information elsewhere, such that new possibilities emerge which may be seen to justify a change in expectations. This process will occur, however, only in those bargainers who are open to the influence of new information they obtain during the course of negotiation. Such openness cannot be guaranteed, and, as Pruitt's model indicates, is critically dependent on a degree of trust in the relationship between the bargainers.

Stages in Negotiation

Neither side is initially inclined to make concessions, so the early stages of negotiations are characteristically competitive in tone. In terms of Magenau and Pruitt's model (see Figure 10.2), they are located firmly in the distributive region. A number of writers have suggested that negotiations move through distinct stages or phases (e.g. Warr, 1973) and even that these stages are necessary if negotiations are to be successfully concluded (Douglas, 1962; Morley and Stephenson, 1977). Magenau and Pruitt's model indicates that a critical time will be reached when, following a period of distributive behaviour, the motive to reach agreement increases in strength but not to the extent that concession-making seems appropriate. At that point, should trust in the other's good faith be sufficiently high, negotiators may coordinate their moves. Douglas talked of movement from 'establishing' to 'reconnoitring' the bargaining range, Warr of 'accepting a common goal', and Morley and Stephenson of the transition from 'distributive' to 'integrative' bargaining. In the industrial relations literature, a final decision-making stage is discerned in which the tentatively agreed proposals are tested for their acceptability to constituents.

These stages bear some resemblance to Bales and Strodtbeck's (1950) three stages of problem solving (orientation, evaluation, and control). Some observers (Landsberger, 1955a, 1955b; Warr, 1973) have drawn attention to this parallel, and Warr in particular has attempted to adapt the problem-solving approach to the stages of negotiation. He stresses the overriding problem that agreement has to be reached somehow and that negotiations also involve each side in intra-organizational bargaining. Hence it is important that we understand the process of negotiation within groups as well as between groups if we are to understand fully the processes of negotiation. However, there is a danger that application of a problem-solving model may lead us to overlook essential differences between problem solving and negotiation. These stem from the fact that conflict between groups is the basis for negotiation, so that negotiators come together initially not as interchangeable discussants but antagonists. Morley and Stephenson (1977), Stephenson *et al.* (1977) and Stephenson (1978) have produced evidence to show that the 'role identifiability' of negotiators is especially high in the early stages of negotiation. In this first stage negotiators are typically not only forcefully stating their own case but attacking their opponent's position, and it is quite easy when reading an unlabelled transcript of a negotiation to tell which side (management or union) any given speaker comes from. In later stages the degree to which reference is made to the parties decreases, and along with it the role identifiability of the negotiators, because negotiators increasingly talk about the issues in a non-partisan way.

Fells (1985) has significantly advanced our understanding of phases in negotiations by elaborating the concept of 'deadlock' in negotiations. He distinguishes three points during negotiation at which deadlocks of different kinds may occur. The first he calls 'Process Deadlock', and this

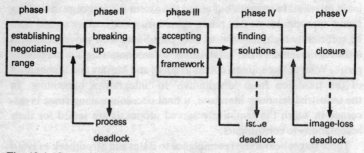

Fig. 10.4 Stages in the industrial relations negotiation process. (After Fells, 1985.)

occurs when negotiators fail to advance committed positions which establish a 'positive settlement range' as defined earlier. 'Issue Deadlock' occurs when attempts to find acceptable solutions or compromises consistently fail. Finally, an 'Image Loss Deadlock' occurs when an agreement is envisaged which includes the need for one to make seemingly unjustifiable concessions. Fells' account of the phases in negotiation is shown in Figure 10.4. This indicates that, although the transition from one phase to another may be smooth and uninterrupted, when deadlocks occur the current phase must be re-entered before progress can be made.

Like previous stage models, this one has a prescriptive element: acting appropriately within each phase is presumed to facilitate transition from one phase to the next. As with all such models, the evidence for it is based on the analysis of a limited number of case studies, but also, in Fells' case, on experience of conciliation within the framework of British industrial relations. One interesting observation made by Fells is the importance of the 'key negotiators' in the phase of Finding Solutions; those who lead negotiating teams find it necessary to meet away from the negotiating table, both with their own group and privately with one another, in the interests of breaking the Issue Deadlock which may occur during this stage. Principal negotiators, in other words, have a leadership role, a topic which we shall now consider in more depth.

Leadership and Negotiation

Leadership has commonly been studied as a feature of role relationships within groups, although the existence of groups within larger social systems implies that defining relationships between members of own and other groups is an integral part of the leader's role. This point has been taken up by Morley and Hosking (1984), who emphasize the pervasiveness of bargaining and negotiation processes within organizations. They write as follows:

> Organizations, then, are systems of bargaining and influence, containing different social groups. Groups may be regarded as sets of people who share a social identity because they belong to the same social category. They may also consist of people orga-

nized into more or less stable relationships based on considerations of role and considerations of status. Leaders play a key role in establishing group norms and in regulating competition within and between groups. In many respects leaders act as *negotiators*. Much of their time is spent building close relationships within and between groups. These help them to define problems and to generate commitment to solutions which are proposed. (p. 76)

This view of negotiation as a component of leadership (see also Chapter 9) reinforces the importance of the information-processing tasks featured in Figure 10.3. To be able to represent one's group effectively in negotiation requires more than the ability to outwit one's opponent strategically; it requires having knowledge of the values and interests of one's own and other group members, which will facilitate the construction of imaginative agreements designed both to satisfy own group requirements, and to be effective within the organization.

'Building close relationships' seems, in this respect, to be a particularly important part of the process. This serves two major functions. In the first place, an extensive network of social relationships, both within and between groups, provides a rich source of information about what is *really* going on. This serves to inhibit stereotyped thinking, and to promote the formulation of new proposals which meet group and organizational needs. Equally important it creates the means whereby progress through the stages of negotiation (Figure 10.4) may be effected. As Batstone *et al.* (1977) put it, 'the basic opposition of interests which exists within negotiation is mediated by personal relationships which facilitate the constructive resolution of problems' (p. 169). It is important to emphasize this point because social psychological approaches to intergroup relations, such as social identity theory (Tajfel) and realistic conflict theory (Sherif), commonly emphasize the *opposition* between interpersonal and intergroup behaviour. Studies of relationships between groups in organizations, and in particular of relationships between key negotiators, suggest on the contrary that strong interpersonal bonds develop, necessarily, in circumstances of greatest intergroup differentiation (Stephenson, 1981, p. 187).

The various phase models of negotiation suggest that high intergroup differentiation at an early stage is a prerequisite of successful negotiation, and different investigators have provided evidence for this (e.g. Douglas, 1962; Walton and McKersie, 1965; Stephenson, 1981). In the absence of interpersonal understanding between the respective sides, management of the transitions between stages would, indeed, be problematic.

SUMMARY

This chapter has reviewed the contributions of psychologists to some key features of industrial relations. Despite wide cultural variations, an open systems approach may be used to highlight the role of psychological and social psychological factors in determining the 'rules' which govern the exchange between management and workers. Intergroup relations over time establish an industrial relations climate, a key feature of which is the degree to which members of an organization have a realistic appreciation of the attitudes of opposing groups ('Intergroup Understanding'). Where 'Intergroup Differentiation' prevails, conflict is more likely to occur.

Psychologists have examined bargaining and negotiations extensively in the laboratory and, to a lesser extent, in industrial and other naturalistic settings. Results of their observations suggest that the degree to which bargainers will attempt to coordinate their activities and achieve outcomes which are optimally profitable to both sides depends on the degree of trust which exists in their relationship and the existence of a suitable balance between the motive to maintain group demands and the need to reach agreement. The ways in which expectations are formulated before negotiation and revised during negotiation play a vital role and are strongly influenced by intergroup climate and understanding. Negotiations are seen to progress through a series of stages, in which interpersonal relationships between the bargainers assume increasing importance with time, especially in bypassing or overcoming potential deadlocks and successive stages. Negotiation is discussed finally as a component of leadership within organizations.

FURTHER READING

A useful summary of the range of contributions by psychologists to the field of industrial relations is provided by J. Hartley in her chapter in

Social Psychology and Organizational Behaviour, edited by M. M. Gruneberg and T. D. Wall (Wiley, 1984). Several of the topics discussed in the present chapter are treated in more detail in *Industrial Relations: A Social Psychological Approach*, edited by G. M. Stephenson and C. J. Brotherton (Wiley, 1979). I. E. Morley provides a readable account of the processes of negotiation and bargaining in his chapter for the volume *Social Skills and Work*, edited by M. Argyle (Methuen, 1981). Another useful source is *Negotiation Behavior*, by D. G. Pruitt (Academic Press, 1981).

11

Women and Employment

Marilyn Davidson

The purpose of this chapter is to examine the changing position of women at work and to highlight some of the major problem areas. The central issues arise from the fact that marriage and motherhood have a substantial influence on women's job prospects, and that women's employment is mostly concentrated in a limited number of industrial sectors and certain low-status, low-pay job categories. The effects of legislation on women's rights in the workforce and the barriers to women's advancement will be considered, as will those additional stressors often experienced by working women, particularly if married with a family.

On a more optimistic note, the chapter will review likely future trends of women's employment and the positive strategies being initiated through legislative pressure, changing work patterns, new technology, organizations, unions and women themselves. Firstly, let us examine the position of women at work, by looking into the changes in work patterns over the years.

CHANGES IN WOMEN'S WORK PATTERNS

Since the 1960s, there has been a large increase in the number of women entering paid employment throughout Western Europe, Australasia and the USA (Davidson and Cooper, 1983a; Larwood and Gutek, 1984). In the USA, for example, in 1950 women constituted 30 per cent of the labour force and this had increased to 43 per cent by 1980, with 51 per cent of American women over the age of 16 being engaged in part-time or full-time employment. Interestingly, these same years saw a steady decline in men's participation in the workforce, from a high 87 per cent in 1951 to 77 per cent in 1980 (US Department of Labor, 1980).

Similar trends have occurred in the United Kingdom, with the female labour force having increased by 43 per cent over the last twenty-five years, whereas the male labour force has increased at a rate of only 3 per cent. By 1985, the economic activity rate for British women was 66 per cent, and women made up 38 per cent of the labour force (*Social Trends*, 1987). Moreover, one of the significant changes in the female labour force has been the influx of married working women. Twenty-five years ago, only a quarter of working women in the UK were married, but by the early 1980s more than three fifths of married women under 60 years of age went out to work (Equal Opportunities Commission, 1985).

Throughout the rest of Western Europe, women make up between a quarter and a third of the workforce, with Finland having the highest percentage of any Western country with nearly half of the labour force being female (Davidson and Cooper, 1984a). Similar patterns emerge in Australia and New Zealand, where women account for 37 per cent and 38 per cent of the workforce respectively. In 1901, 31 per cent of all Australian women over the age of 15 were in paid employment (compared to 32 per cent of their British counterparts) and this figure had climbed to over 44 per cent in 1978, 62 per cent of whom were married. In New Zealand, an even higher 47 per cent of all women aged 15 and over are in paid employment (New Zealand Department of Statistics, 1981; Australian Bureau of Statistics, 1984).

The Changing Family

This significant rise in the level of economic activity among women throughout the past two decades has its roots in a number of developments. These include the changing role of women in society, influenced by the Women's Movement, the expansion of service industries, the increase in part-time employment, the changing nature of the family; and women now marrying earlier, having fewer children, living longer and divorcing more frequently. The United Kingdom, for example, is following the American divorce trends with one in three marriages now ending in divorce. Consequently, more and more people are living in one-parent families with dependent children (predominantly headed by women): 14 per cent in 1985, compared with 2·5 per cent in 1961 (*Social*

Trends, 1987). In the USA, 15 per cent of households were headed by women in 1979 (Larwood and Gutek, 1984). The necessity for many of these women to work because of financial pressures is obvious.

Part-time Work

During the 1970s there was also a swing from employment in traditional industries such as manufacturing towards the service sector, an area of employment which is traditionally female and one which offers plenty of part-time employment. In fact, over 1·5 million part-time jobs were created in Britain between the mid-1960s up until the end of the 1970s. Between 1971 and 1981, while the number of full-time workers declined, the number of part-time jobs rose from 15 per cent to 20 per cent of total employment. What is significant is that by 1984, 24 per cent of British married women worked part-time, compared to 2 per cent of men. Throughout the European Community, women occupy 90 per cent of Europe's part-time jobs, and the figures in Australia and New Zealand are 77 per cent and 80 per cent respectively (New Zealand Department of Statistics, 1981; Australian Bureau of Statistics, 1984; *Social Trends*, 1987).

Life-stages clearly have a much greater influence on women's working lives than on men's. Married women with or without children are more likely to work part-time than full-time, and the lowest proportion of working women are those with a youngest child under 5 years (J. Martin and C. Roberts, 1984). While it is still common for women to work full-time until the birth of their first child (the highest proportion of working women in Britain is found among childless women under 30), a high majority return to part-time rather than full-time work after having children (*Social Trends*, 1987). In Europe, the highest percentages of women returners are in the UK, Denmark, France and Germany (50–75 per cent) and the lowest in Belgium, Italy, Ireland, Luxembourg and the Netherlands. Moreover, the higher proportion of women returning to work in the UK and Denmark is undoubtedly due to the fact that more part-time working opportunities are offered in these countries (Davidson and Cooper, 1983a). An interesting new trend is that British women are now returning to work after having a baby at a quicker rate than any of their European counterparts (Davidson, 1985).

While the majority of women's full-time jobs are concentrated in the clerical and secretarial areas, women in part-time jobs dominate the other personal services (Lockwood and Knowles, 1984). A large-scale survey by Elias and Main (1982) revealed some interesting information concerning female part-timers in Britain. Firstly, two out of five part-time female workers were in low-status, low-skilled occupations, which rarely lead to promotion or more responsible positions. Examples of these include jobs such as waitresses, cleaners and catering assistants. Secondly, women returning to work as part-timers are often subject to skill-downgrading, with one fifth of women having belonged to a more highly skilled occupation group when working full-time ten years earlier. Furthermore, the Elias and Main (1982) study revealed that, compared with two out of every five women and almost one half of men who are full-time employees, only one woman part-timer in five belonged to a union. With union representation being associated with better pay, job benefits and opportunities, this under-representation of women in unions acts as a major disadvantage for women workers.

Unemployment

Women have also been hit very hard by the recession and associated high unemployment levels (see Chapter 16). In Britain between 1976 and 1984, male unemployment increased by 1·1 million, and female employment by 0·6 million, with a continued decline in female full-time employment (Equal Opportunities Commission, 1985). Throughout Europe women constitute 41 per cent of Europe's unemployed, which means there are more women out of work than men in proportion to their share of the total workforce (Commission of the European Communities, 1984a).

Sex Segregation of Jobs

Throughout the West there is still job segregation based on gender, the arbitrary division between 'men's jobs' and 'women's jobs' which is so often taken for granted (Hankim, 1979). In all the EEC countries, over 50 per cent of women are employed in the service sector, which includes trade, education, retail, health care and clerical duties. Approximately

20 to 25 per cent of women workers are employed in the textile and food industries, and a large number in the chemical and electronics sectors. In comparison, men are employed in a wider range of occupations and a wider range of industries (Davidson and Cooper, 1983a).

Figure 11.1 shows the high concentration of female workers in Great Britain in a limited number of occupations, particularly those dominated by part-timers, for example hairdressing, cleaning, catering and other personal service occupations. Of all full-time women workers, 42 per cent are employed in clerical and related occupations and 19 per cent in professional and related occupations in health, education and welfare.

In Australia, the picture is very similar, with 6 per cent of female employees concentrated in three major occupational groups: clerical, sales and services. Moreover, of the 19 per cent of female employees in professional and technical occupations, 34 per cent were nurses and 38 per cent were teachers (Australian Bureau of Statistics, 1984). Even in the USA, with the strongest legislation affecting the employment of women, approximately 75 per cent of all employed women belong to only five occupational groups, which include secretary/clerical, nursing, household worker, service employee and elementary school teacher (Terborg, 1985).

Women's advance into what have been traditionally men's jobs is still very limited. In their examination of the US Department of Labor statistics for 1980, Larwood and Gutek (1984) calculated that between 1950 and 1979 women carpenters increased from 0·4 per cent to 1·3 per cent; women engineers from 1·2 per cent to 2·9 per cent; women protective service workers from 2 per cent to 9 per cent; and women bus drivers from 1 per cent to 8 per cent. On the other hand, there has been a larger growth in the proportion of women entering many of the formerly male-dominated professional jobs. During the past fifteen years, the percentage of American female economists, architects and lawyers has more than doubled. Today, 31 per cent of American managers and administrators are women, followed by the UK with over 20 per cent, Australia with 14 per cent and New Zealand with only 8 per cent (US Department of Labor, 1980; New Zealand Department of Statistics, 1981; Department of Employment, 1984). Nevertheless, the occupations in which women are most likely to be managers are still the

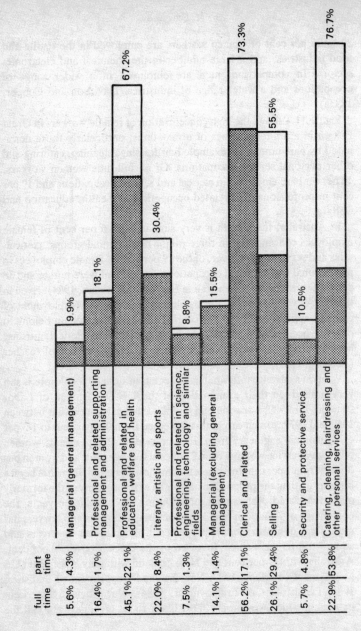

	full time	part time
Managerial (general management)	5.6%	4.3%
Professional and related supporting management and administration	16.4%	1.7%
Professional and related in education welfare and health	45.1%	22.1%
Literary, artistic and sports	22.0%	8.4%
Professional and related in science, engineering, technology and similar fields	7.5%	1.3%
Managerial (excluding general management)	14.1%	1.4%
Clerical and related	56.2%	17.1%
Selling	26.1%	29.4%
Security and protective service	5.7%	4.8%
Catering, cleaning, hairdressing and other personal services	22.9%	53.8%

Bar chart totals: 9.9%, 18.1%, 67.2%, 30.4%, 8.8%, 15.5%, 73.3%, 55.5%, 10.5%, 76.7%

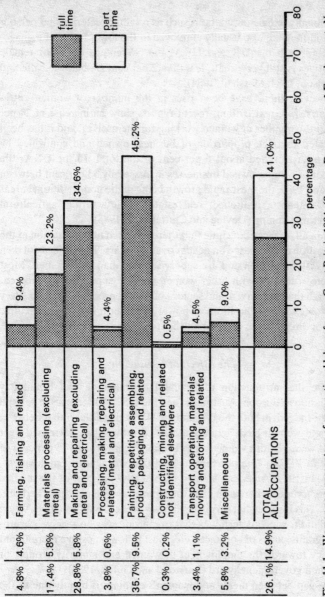

		full time	part time
Farming, fishing and related		4.8%	4.6%
Materials processing (excluding metal)		17.4%	5.8%
Making and repairing (excluding metal and electrical)		28.8%	5.8%
Processing, making, repairing and related (metal and electrical)		3.8%	0.6%
Painting, repetitive assembling, product packaging and related		35.7%	9.5%
Constructing, mining and related not identified elsewhere		0.3%	0.2%
Transport operating, materials moving and storing and related		3.4%	1.1%
Miscellaneous		5.8%	3.2%
TOTAL ALL OCCUPATIONS		26.1%	14.9%

Fig. 11.1 Women as a percentage of occupational labour forces, Great Britain 1984. (Source: Department of Employment, *New Earnings Survey 1984.* Part E, table 138.)

traditionally female occupations such as retailing, catering and personnel, and they are also usually employed in the lower levels of management. In both the UK and USA, the percentage of senior female executives is still very small, less than 2 per cent (Alban-Metcalfe and Nicholson, 1984; Marshall, 1984).

However, there have been rises in the number of women entrepreneurs. In Great Britain, recent reports show an increase of 24 per cent in the number of women working for themselves, and it has been estimated that the proportion of business owned and controlled by women has reached about 6 per cent of the total. In the USA, the number of women-owned businesses increased by 33 per cent between 1977 and 1980, the most rapid growth being in the non-traditional areas such as finance, insurance, real estate, manufacturing, agricultural services and mining (Devine and Clutterbuck, 1985).

All in all, one can conclude that there has been little reduction in the segregation of jobs based on gender over the years. The majority of men work with other men and are supervised and managed by men. Most women work only with other women and are supervised by women, although their employers and senior bosses will probably be male. Very few women occupy positions of power, whether it be senior executive posts or directorships on company boards.

The Effects of Legislation

Despite the introduction of Sexual Discrimination and Equal Pay Legislation in Europe, Australasia and the USA, differences in pay still persist. Indeed, in both the UK and the USA, pay differentials between men and women have actually increased rather than decreased over recent years. British women's pay dropped from around 75 per cent of men's in 1977 to 73·5 per cent in 1984 (Department of Employment, 1984). In 1979, American women earned 58·9 per cent of the median income for men whereas in 1939 the figure was 60·8 per cent (Terborg, 1985). This is somewhat surprising in view of the US Affirmative Action Legislation, which determines that organizations who receive government grants, loans or contracts, etc. must follow a positive recruitment strategy towards the employment of women and minority groups, or lose their government award (Larwood and Gutek, 1984).

The gap between men's and women's earnings is mainly due to the majority of women working in lower-echelon 'women-only' jobs and to the limited number of female employees being covered by job evaluation schemes (only 25 per cent in Britain) (*Social Trends*, 1985). Also, it has been found that, even though women earn less than their male counterparts, it is the men who express more dissatisfaction with their pay (Davidson and Cooper, 1983b; 1986).

Legislation has sometimes incorporated provisions entitling working women to take a specified period of maternity leave with some pay. The length of leave and restrictions regarding the eligibility vary from country to country. Only a few countries offer any kind of paternity leave and these include France, Italy and Sweden (Davidson and Cooper, 1983a).

Finally, the law still sanctions unequal treatment in one major area: pensions and retirement. In Britain, men qualify for a state pension at 65, whereas women qualify at 60. However, recent research has shown that sick pay, paid holidays and access to occupational pension schemes are determined far more by whether or not one works full-time, regardless of sex (Equal Opportunities Commission, 1985). In the UK, among women who worked part-time, 69 per cent had no access to a pension scheme, with an additional 14 per cent having access but deciding not to join (Ritchie and Barrowclough, 1983). Interestingly, studies have also found that many men would ideally prefer to retire earlier than they are being allowed to at the moment (McGoldrick, 1985).

BARRIERS TO WOMEN'S ADVANCEMENT

Besides weak legislation, barriers to women's advancement stem from numerous sources, including sex stereotyping from an early age and the substantial influence of the pattern of women's working lives. These are compounded by barriers within organizations related to organizational structure and climate, prejudice and discrimination, and attitudinal barriers from both men and women themselves. These in turn subject women to additional stressors in the workplace, which are also enhanced by home/work conflicts.

Sex Stereotyping and the Education System

Sex stereotyping begins at birth. According to J. Nicholson (1984), a random sample of adults react differently to an infant depending on whether it is dressed in a blue or pink bonnet. Males are commonly characterized as being strong, logical, assertive, scientific, unemotional and aggressive. Conversely, women are often described as weak, passive, anxious, caring, timid and so on (Gettys and Cann, 1981). This kind of stereotyping is reinforced even in co-educational school environments. In mixed classes, boys dominate both physically and verbally, and teachers of both sexes have been shown frequently to encourage girls to keep their comments short, in case the boys start to get restless and misbehave (Mahoney, 1985). Indeed, Mahoney recommends that mixed schools should introduce segregated classes for girls and 'consciousness-raising' groups for both sexes.

There is still a marked stereotyped division between the courses taken by males and females within both academic and vocational subjects. This split in the school curriculum occurs with girls opting for domestic and craft studies at the beginning of secondary school and opting out of technical and science subjects from about the age of 14 (Commission of the European Communities, 1984a). Certainly, job segregation often has its roots in the education system, with females still being found mainly in the arts and males in the science subjects, both at school and university.

Even so, in Britain there has been a gradual increase in female entry to higher education. Women constituted 41 per cent of university undergraduates in 1983–4 and 32 per cent of postgraduates. Although the majority of women still study education or arts subjects (including languages), more women are studying engineering and technology (from 4 per cent in 1975 to 10 per cent in 1984) and over 33 per cent of science undergraduates and 45 per cent of social administration and business studies students are female (Equal Opportunities Commission, 1985). While local government and the other public authorities are the major destinations for female graduates, women graduate entrants to industry and commerce have almost doubled over the last ten years to one in four (Davidson, 1985).

Patterns of Women's Working Lives

Once established in the workforce, another barrier which has been linked to women's predominance in low-status, low-pay jobs is the fact that, unlike men, the majority of women have discontinuous work patterns, as they withdraw from the labour market to care for young children. Even so, recent British statistics show that the average break from the workforce for all women is only about five years, which accounts for around 13 per cent of the time between the ages of 20 and 59. Thus the working lives of mothers are reduced, but not dramatically curtailed (Joshi, 1984). This break has been shown to be even shorter for professional working women (Davidson and Cooper, 1984b; 1985; P. Long, 1984; J. Martin and C. Roberts, 1984). In fact, professional women such as managers are far less likely to be married compared to their male counterparts.

Women also report that their career-related dilemma concerning whether to start a family is a major stressor in their lives (Davidson and Cooper, 1983b). Many say they would benefit greatly from job-break schemes, as well as more flexible working arrangements such as part-time work, flexi-time, job sharing, job splitting, etc. (Povall, 1983; P. Long, 1984; Davidson, 1985). More and more organizations are now introducing maternity break schemes for their female employees, and the economic losses as well as the losses in terms of talent when women are not encouraged to return to work after childbearing are now beginning to be acknowledged.

Women are unfairly penalized by the majority of employers for taking a break from employment. Povall (1983) makes the point that unlike the maternity break, breaks initiated by employers (e.g. study leave, transfer to other jobs etc.) are accepted as being inevitable, essential or for the greater good. Indeed, Davidson (1985) emphasizes that the important skills required for the low-status, unpaid job of 'house-wife' are grossly undervalued and should be acknowledged. In the role of 'household executive', women acquire important business skills such as planning, budgeting, contracting, organizing, and supervising; all of which are valuable assets transferable to the world of paid employment.

It is also often assumed that women are not as mobile as men. However, much of the British and American research evidence refutes this assumption (e.g. US Department of Labor, 1980; Davidson and Cooper, 1983b). Interestingly, Alban-Metcalfe and Nicholson's (1984) study of British managers found that professional and managerial women were slightly more mobile than men, changing employers on average 3·6 times compared to 3·4 changes for male managers. However, the researchers reported that many of the women referred to job changes which had been imposed on them because their male partners had to move location for career reasons. (Unlike the majority of married male managers, the majority of married women managers were in dual career partnerships.)

Finally, it is also a myth that working women, particularly working mothers, are a liability as far as high absenteeism from work is concerned. The average for full-time women workers is ten days compared to nine for men. Women tend to take time off more often, but for shorter periods. The best absence records are for part-timers, who of course are predominantly female (Equal Opportunities Commission, 1984).

Barriers Within Organizations

Barriers within organizations hampering women's development in the workplace fall into two broad categories, namely structural and attitudinal. Structural barriers include personnel policies, procedures and practices. Attitudinal barriers, on the other hand, relate to women's attitudes and attitudes towards working women generally, particularly those held by employers.

Structural Barriers

Although the majority of clearly discriminatory practices within personnel policies and practices have been eliminated, owing largely to antidiscrimination legislation, many forms of indirect discrimination still persist. Examples of indirect discrimination against women (which are illegal in Britain) include job vacancies only open to candidates of certain age groups (which may exclude older women re-entering the labour market), certain height requirements, specific qualifications and job experience, and so on (Elias and Main, 1982; Povall, 1984).

Discriminatory personnel practices have also been found to persist within recruitment, promotion appraisal systems and training opportunities. These particularly affect women in non-traditionally female jobs (Terborg and Shingledecker, 1983; Davidson and Cooper, 1983b, 1984b). Recent reports have revealed that British women workers receive fewer training opportunities than male workers, and employers are often reluctant to retrain women re-entering the workforce after a break, even though they may have many years of working life in front of them (Elias and Main, 1982). Women working full-time receive less training than male full-time workers, and female part-timers fare even worse than full-time workers. In fact, the women who are most likely to have training opportunities are those full-time non-manual women who work where both men and women do the same work (J. Martin and C. Roberts, 1984).

Women's Attitudes

Undoubtedly, women's attitudes and behaviour also have a bearing on their position within the workforce. Particularly important are their attitudes towards work, job segregation and promotion.

Reasons for Working. Whether working full- or part-time, the majority of women work not only for financial rewards but also because they enjoy their job. Almost two thirds of a sample of European working women (only slightly fewer than among working men) maintained they would continue working even if they had enough money to live comfortably without a job, and only 6 per cent of British working women surveyed wished they did not work (Commission of the European Communities, 1984; J. Martin and C. Roberts, 1984). In the Department of Employment survey which included a sample of 5,500 British women, over half of the women (52 per cent) stated most often that they worked because they enjoyed working, followed by 'financial reasons' (47 per cent), 'for the company of other people' (44 per cent), and 'to earn money of my own' (37 per cent) (J. Martin and C. Roberts, 1984).

Job Satisfaction. In terms of job satisfaction, women who said they were working for money to provide basic essentials were the least satisfied, and those who worked because they enjoyed it were the most satisfied (J. Martin and C. Roberts, 1984). Furthermore, large-scale US studies have found no differences in job satisfaction between the sexes when job-content variables are controlled (e.g. F. J. Smith *et al.*, 1977; Weaver, 1980). Terborg (1985) suggests that this is possibly due to the fact that many women (particularly those working in all-female environments) are unaware of the extent to which they are discriminated against.

Job Segregation. The British Department of Employment survey also investigated the attitudes of both men and women towards their segregation in the workforce. Not surprisingly, women working in higher occupational levels were least likely to class their work as 'women's work', whereas women working in all-female environments (particularly part-timers) were most likely to think of their jobs as 'women's work'. It is important to note that this study highlighted that working in all-male environments also influences men's attitudes towards women as workers. A higher proportion of men (60 per cent) saw their work as 'men's work', compared to 40 per cent of women who viewed their work as 'women's work' (J. Martin and C. Roberts, 1984).

Ambitions. There is also little evidence to suggest that working women are any less ambitious about promotion and attaining leadership positions. Almost half of all the employees surveyed by Martin and Roberts said they would like to be considered for promotion and, of these, 32 per cent were in jobs which were viewed as having no promotion prospects. In an Australian survey of workers in New South Wales, 67 per cent of women, compared with 77 per cent of men, said that promotion was important to them. But the majority of these women did not believe that they would be promoted (New South Wales Anti-Discrimination Board, 1978).

While women in higher occupational groups are most likely to desire promotion and also enjoy promotional opportunities, the Department of Employment survey revealed that a high proportion of women clerical workers (39 per cent) who desired promotion also asserted that they had no promotional prospects. In fact, women working in clerical and secretarial jobs have been found to be particularly vulnerable as far as frustrated career development is concerned (Brief *et al.*, 1981; Silverstone and Towler, 1983).

Lastly, it has been suggested that a major problem for women professionals' career advancement is women's fear of responsibility and leadership positions, the 'fear of success syndrome' (e.g. Horner, 1970). However, several recent studies have reported no differences between males and females on achievement motivation, aspirations towards promotion and motivation to manage (Blackstone and Weinreich-Haste, 1980; Moore and Rickel, 1980; Davidson and Cooper, 1983b).

Moreover, in a British survey, women managers viewed themselves as more sociable, intellectual and slightly more ambitious than did the men (Alban-Metcalfe and Nicholson, 1984).

Attitudes Towards Working Women

Prejudiced attitudes towards working women are associated with beliefs such as 'a woman's place is in the home', women are suited only for certain types of jobs, and women do not make as good leadership or management material as men. It is heartening to note that a recent survey comparing the attitudes of over 9,000 men and women in EEC countries in 1975 with their attitudes in 1983 showed shrinking discriminatory attitudes in relation to women's rights to work and women working in non-traditional roles. The majority of both men and women maintained they would trust a woman just as much as a man in the role of bus driver, member of parliament, surgeon, gynaecologist or lawyer (Commission of the European Communities, 1984b). Nevertheless, discriminatory attitudes towards women still persist. For instance, studies have shown that compared to their male counterparts women managers are more likely to say that prejudice against them as a group has affected their promotional prospects (Henning and Jardim, 1979; Davidson, 1985). Women have also quoted examples of less qualified and less experienced male colleagues achieving considerably faster promotion; having a female boss does not always prevent this (Alban-Metcalfe and Nicholson, 1984). A study by A. Hunt (1975) discovered that managers in Britain thought that all the qualities needed for managerial jobs were more likely to be found in men than in women. A follow-up study five years later revealed that although attitudes had become slightly more favourable, women were still regarded as inferior (A. Hunt, 1981). More recent research still indicates that many interviewers continue to assume that the managerial qualities they are seeking are more likely to be found in a man than a woman (Rothwell, 1984).

Even so, numerous cross-cultural studies have failed to confirm these suspicions and few differences have been found in relation to the managerial style and performance of men and women (e.g. Bartol, 1978; Ferber et al., 1979; Tkach, 1980). Where differences in leadership style do exist, they usually relate to women managers' greater concern for relationships, interpersonal skills which have been identified by researchers as a widely neglected managerial asset (Marshall, 1984).

Encouraging evidence is now being presented by American researchers that the increase in the number of females in senior positions is itself having an important influence on changes in attitude. For example, a study investigating the responses of male and female managers found a direct relationship between having been supervised by a woman and positive attitudes towards women as managers (Ezell *et al.*, 1981). These authors suggested that being in direct contact with a woman as a superior may dispel traditional female stereotypes, such as women not being as career-orientated as men.

Stress at Work

Certain female-dominated jobs such as secretary, waitress and clinical technician have been isolated as being particularly stressful (Terborg, 1985). As the topic of jobs and mental health is treated as a whole in Chapter 12, we shall concentrate on those additional pressures faced by working women which are gender-related. In particular, it is women working in non-traditional jobs, whether blue or white collar, who have been found to suffer most from discriminatory attitudes and behaviour at work.

Sexual Harassment. Sexual harassment of a verbal or physical nature is a potential problem for the majority of working women, and victims of sexual harassment have complained of depression, chronic fatigue, nervousness and feelings of victimization (US Department of Labor, 1978; Read, 1982). An American survey found that about 15 per cent of men in employment and 42 per cent of women had experienced some form of sexual harassment in the office. The researchers concluded that sexual misconduct was a substantial problem which can affect the self-confidence, morale and efficiency of many workers, particularly women. In Britain, one survey revealed that more than one in ten working women had felt that a man had been taking advantage of his position at work to make persistent sexual advances (National Council for Civil Liberties, 1982). Furthermore, women in professional and management positions are in no way immune; in a random sample of British female managers, 52 per cent had at some time experienced sexual harassment at work (Davidson and Cooper, 1983b).

Although research shows that all women are at risk regardless of their appearance or age, certain groups of women appear to be particularly vulnerable victims of sexual harassment. These include women working in masculine sex-typed jobs, women in non-senior positions, and divorced and separated women (US Department of Labor, 1978; National Council for Civil Liberties, 1982).

In the USA, sexual harassment is now treated seriously, having become an economic issue whereby damages have been awarded against companies sanctioning the behaviour of harassers (Terborg, 1985). Conversely, in Britain it has been difficult to get employers or the media to treat the issue seriously. Gradually though, sexual harassment is becoming a trade-union issue and the Trades Union Congress has issued guidelines on how to deal with the problem, as have Britain's largest white collar union, the National Association of Local Government Officers (NALGO) (Davidson, 1985).

Token Women. When women comprise less than 15 per cent of a total category in an organization, they can be labelled 'tokens', which means that they tend to be viewed as symbols of their group rather than as individuals (Stead, 1978). Women working in traditionally male jobs have been shown to have higher self-esteem than homemakers of similar educational status. Nevertheless, as a minority group subjected to male-dominated policy making, research indicates that women are subjected to a greater number of work-related pressures than their male counterparts (Nelson and Quick, 1985). For example, women managers have been found to have more psychosomatic ill-health symptoms than men. The specific problems and pressures which have been observed in female managers include: strains of coping with prejudice and sex stereotyping; overt and indirect discrimination from fellow employees, employers and the organizational structure and climate; lack of role models; feelings of isolation; and burdens of coping with the role of the 'token woman' (Davidson and Cooper, 1984b).

Home/Work Conflicts

Besides being subjected to additional pressures at work, the majority of working women, especially those with children, are far more easily affected by the burdens and pressures of their home and childcare duties than are most employed men. Indeed, working women who appear most vulnerable to stress-related maladies (including coronary heart disease) are those who have acquired a dual role in which they combine paid work and the unpaid domestic work of the family (Haynes and Feinleib, 1980; Cooper and Davidson, 1981; Nelson and Quick, 1985; Glowinkowski and Cooper, 1985).

The main forms of inter-role conflict for many working women revolve around guilt feelings, lack of domestic social support from partners, and inadequate childcare facilities. Thus, in families where both partners work full-time, a major source of stress is the fact that the number of demands on the partner (particularly a female) often exceeds the time and energy to deal with them (e.g. Hall and Hall, 1980; Sekaran, 1985, 1986).

Guilt Feelings. It was the child psychologist John Bowlby who played a large part in stirring up guilt feelings in working mothers by his post-war studies on the effects of maternal deprivation and the perils of being separated from one's mother when young. His influence has been long-lasting, even though much of his early research has been in-validated by subsequent studies (Rutter, 1972). A recent large-scale American study, for example, reported that there was no conclusive evidence to suggest that the mother's employment *per se* (by single mothers or mothers in two-parent families) has consistent, direct effects, either positive or negative, on children's development and educational outcomes (US National Academy of Sciences, 1983).

Inadequate Childcare Facilities and Lack of Support from Partners. British studies have repeatedly shown that many women who want to work are either unable to do so, or restricted to part-time hours, because of the severe shortage of childcare facilities (Lockwood and Knowles, 1984; *Social Trends*, 1985). While higher-income families can afford the luxuries of nannies and au pairs, the majority of working women with young children have to rely on family-based childcare, frequently fathers or grandmothers (J. Martin and C. Roberts, 1984). Another reason why employed women suffer more than non-employed women, and in some respects more than their male colleagues, is the expectation that they ought to fulfil the roles of both homeworker and worker simultaneously, without much support from their partners (Nelson and Quick, 1985; Davidson and Cooper, 1985). Over half (54 per cent) of British wives employed full-time said they did all or most of the housework, while 77 per cent of wives working part-time said this. Of the 20 per cent of women who were dissatisfied with the amount of help they received from their husbands, a greater proportion were working wives (J. Martin and C. Roberts, 1984). Although husbands of working wives are likely to help more with childcare duties and with housework, men tend to carry out the more creative and non-routine tasks, such as cooking, home improvements, shopping, playing with children or taking them out (Oakley, 1981; J. Martin and C. Roberts, 1984). Consequently, job segregation based on gender still persists even in the home environment.

FUTURE TRENDS AND PROSPECTS

With the advent of changing employment patterns and new technology, what does the future hold for working women? What are the changes necessary in order to improve women's position in the workforce?

According to projected trends in employment for the UK over the period 1982 to 1990, women are expected to take two thirds of the net increase in jobs, with their part-time employment projected to increase by 7 per cent and full-time by 1 per cent. Increases in women's employment are anticipated mainly in the areas of part-time jobs classed as miscellaneous and professional services, with distribution being the only major area of projected job loss for women (Institute for Employment Research, 1983).

It has also been suggested that large numbers of people might soon be working remote from their employing organizations and be home-based. Estimates of the number of Americans who will be using home offices by the end of the century range as high as 20 million, and British Telecom's long-range planners have identified twenty-four occupational groups, including over 13 million workers, which contain potential for home-based jobs (Huws, 1984; Upton, 1984). Working from home with new technology is already on the increase, particularly by women who have young children at home. Less than a third of homeworkers in England and Wales are carrying out manufacturing work, and the

241

majority of new technology homeworkers are either applying computer programming skills or working for companies in the computing field (Upton, 1984). However, women homeworkers have a history of earning less than the going rate and being exploited generally, and there is concern that this new group may suffer a similar fate (Huws, 1984).

The Impact of New Technology

The impact of new technology on women's employment is a relatively new topic of research. But fears are already being voiced that the new job opportunities will appear at higher levels of the hierarchy and hence be predominantly accessible to men rather than women. For example, Huggett *et al.* (1985) argue that, owing to greater technological knowledge and training, the new job opportunities are being appropriated by men.

Certainly, unless there are radical changes, these jobs in new technology are in danger of becoming 'masculinized' and contributing to yet another facet of gender segregation in the workforce. In the early days of women's involvement with the computing industry for instance, women were allowed to play a very significant role as programmers and program researchers/developers, when software was considered much less important than the hardware controlled by male engineers. However, after the importance of programming became recognized, the proportion of women involved dropped sharply (Simons, 1981). Similar changes are being forecast when the devalued job of 'secretary' is renamed 'information assistant', thus becoming more attractive to men (Softly, 1985).

It has also been suggested that, in certain female occupations such as office workers, the spread of microelectronic technology will cause considerable job losses for women. Softly (1985) refers to a report by the International Federation of Commercial, Clerical and Technical Employees, which estimated that technical change in offices will lead to the displacement of 20 to 25 per cent of clerical staff in Western Europe – about 5 million people.

One factor which will help the position of women in future new-technology jobs is the predicted shortage of employees in the electronics industry. This has been recently acknowledged by a British Government study carried out by the Information Technology Skills Shortages

Committee. This report advocated that information technology companies can no longer afford to ignore the intellectual resources offered
by females, and recommended that teachers and employers had to make
positive efforts to encourage girls and women to train in computer and
technical skills (Department of Trade and Industry, 1985).

Recommendations for the Future

In addition to all the moral arguments, it is in the long-term economic
interest of governments and work organizations to better accommodate
the needs of the increasing numbers of women at work, particularly the
married ones. There are several strategies available to help alleviate
some of the burdens of working women. These include:

- flexible working arrangements, such as flexi-time, job sharing,
  job splitting, working from home, shortened working week, and
  part-time work (Lockwood and Knowles, 1984);
- better maternity and paternity leave, increased childcare facilities, and parental leave when children are sick (Cooper and
  Davidson, 1981);
- stronger union support, with union officials taking active steps
  in promoting equal opportunities for women at work, as well
  as unions encouraging women to stand for office (J. Martin
  and C. Roberts, 1984). Furthermore, unions ought to consider
  seriously an affirmative action policy regarding the proportion
  of appointed female union officials.

The long-term solution for the elimination of job segregation and
inequalities in the workplace for women also depends on changes in sex
stereotyped attitudes from parents, teachers, and males and females
generally. At school, guidance and counselling should be provided for
girls at the pre-option stage. At work, organizations should actively
encourage women to participate in non-traditional training schemes,
especially in the areas of science and new technology. Also, courses
should be introduced which specifically aim to cater for the needs of
women, for example in the areas of assertion and confidence-building.

Organizations should also introduce job/career break schemes for employees wishing to leave the workforce for a period while childrearing. Furthermore, refresher courses should be provided for those wishing to return to the workforce in order to enable future returners to keep abreast with current developments and skills and regain confidence. These retraining schemes might best be done by professional associations or by work organizations providing up-dating courses for ex-employees who have temporarily left employment to raise a family.

In the final analysis, if the position of women at work is to improve, there is a need for stronger legislative programmes to force equal opportunities. Britain and European countries should follow the example of Australia, which has adopted and adapted the US approach of Affirmative Action Legislation. In Australia, all private-sector organizations employing over 100 people, and all universities and colleges of advanced education, are legally obliged to adopt Affirmative Action Programmes in order to ensure equal employment opportunities for women and men (Australian Government, 1984). An Affirmative Action Resource Unit has been set up which assists organizations to design their Affirmative Action Programmes and helps them overcome any problems that arise.

The elements that are common to all Australian Affirmative Action Programmes include:

- commitment of senior management to the implementation of the programme;
- consultation with trade unions and employees;
- analysis of the position of women within the organization;
- a review of all employment policies and practices;
- development of programmes to remedy discriminatory practices and to encourage women to apply for a wider range of jobs within the organization;
- setting realistic goals and targets;
- monitoring the progress and success of the programme.

Until legislative changes occur in Britain and other countries, organizations themselves should develop their own equal opportunities guidelines and Positive Action Programmes. A number of companies now employ an Equal Opportunities Manager to carry out positive action, which involves the evaluation and reassessment of job opportunities, creating new career structures enabling movement into formerly unavailable positions and occupations, ensuring special training (including on-the-job training denied in the past), and the building up of equal opportunity awareness and skills training for employees of both sexes (Robarts *et al.*, 1981).

SUMMARY

The material presented in this chapter clearly illustrates that on the whole, women at work in Western countries do not enjoy the same job conditions, pay, status and career opportunities as their male counterparts. Despite the increasing numbers of women entering employment, the majority of women are concentrated in a limited number of occupations, particularly those dominated by part-time workers. Women's advance into what have been traditionally men's jobs (especially the higher status professions) is still very small.

This situation is due to a number of different reasons: sex stereotyping; job segregation based on gender; deficiencies in education, vocational guidance and training; poor union support; weak legislation; home/work conflicts and stressors; discriminatory practices within organizations; and prejudiced attitudes and behaviour towards working women. If the position of working women is to improve, constructive strategies must be introduced in terms of educational, organizational and union policies, as well as through legislation, including Affirmative Action.

FURTHER READING

The position of women at work in a representative cross-section of developed countries in the West is examined in *Working Women – An International Survey* edited by M. J. Davidson and C. L. Cooper (Wiley, 1984). The Department of Employment's report *Women and Employment – A Life Time Perspective* by J. Martin and C. Roberts (HMSO, 1984) provides one of the most recent and comprehensive surveys of working women in Britain. Other useful bulletins of British statistics and research include *The Annual Report* by the Equal Opportunities Commission and the regular reports published by both the E O C and the Manpower Services Commission. In addition, there is a new series of books edited by L. Larwood, A. A. Stramberg and B. A. Gutek entitled *Women and Work – An Annual Review* (Sage, 1985, 1987).

12

Job Characteristics and Mental Health

Peter Warr

It has long been recognized that jobs can strongly influence health in its physical forms. Working in dangerous conditions increases the probability of sudden injury, long hours of continuous hard labour may lead to gradual physical deterioration, and extended exposure to dust, fumes or other toxic substances can give rise to specific physiological impairments. The parallel effects of job conditions upon mental health have been examined only in recent decades, but important causal associations have already been established.

This chapter will review some of the principal issues in this field. Several overlapping research approaches will first be identified, for example in terms of the carry-over of feelings from job to home and in terms of research into 'occupational stress'. These will then be brought together within a classification of job characteristics, summarizing previous investigations under nine broad headings. Finally, practical implications will be considered, examining ways in which employee mental health might be enhanced.

It is extremely difficult to provide a detailed and all-embracing definition of 'health', whether physical or mental. In part this is because the concept is to a considerable degree value-laden, being a reflection of what is considered appropriate and desirable by members of a society. However, there is widespread agreement that a primary indicator of good or poor mental health is the level and quality of a person's 'affective well-being'. We are here concerned with feelings of happiness, satisfaction, high self-esteem, interest in the environment and other positive emotions; or with anxiety, tension, depression, apathy, sense of hopelessness, and generalized feelings of distress. Statements about affective well-being often refer to physiological as well as psychological processes, with, for example, anxiety being displayed in bodily tenseness, sweating, gastric disturbance or sleeping problems.

However, mental health extends beyond affective well-being into aspects of a person's behaviour during interaction with task or social environments. We need also to consider people's ability to respond to and cope with problems in daily living, their tendency to seek out challenge and variety, and their functioning as autonomous, self-regulating individuals (e.g. Jahoda, 1958; Warr, 1987). These components of mental health are more difficult to measure than affective well-being, and they will receive relatively less attention in this short chapter.

An important distinction is between 'context-free' mental health and that which is 'job-related'. The former covers well-being and behaviour in one's life-space generally, whereas the latter is restricted to the job environment. In examining job-related mental health we might consider well-being in terms of, for example, job satisfaction, job-related anxiety or job-related depression. The sections which follow will examine the impact of job characteristics upon both these forms of mental health.

FOUR RESEARCH PERSPECTIVES

It is often the case that a single set of topics can be viewed from several different perspectives, each associated with a particular framework of concepts and empirical procedures. In the area of this chapter, four overlapping perspectives may be identified.

Work and non-work

The first perspective is an approach which asks about the links between two separate domains of life, job and non-job environments. Many authors have analysed possible forms of interaction between these settings (see, for instance, the review by Kabanoff, 1980), sometimes drawing a contrast between 'spill-over' and 'compensation' hypotheses.

The former (also referred to as the 'generalization' or the 'carry-over' hypothesis) predicts that job conditions and attitudes carry over to affect behaviours and experiences in other aspects of life; positive correlations between job and non-job factors are thus expected. The compensation

248

hypothesis predicts negative associations, as people seek out non-job activities and experiences which make up for the deficits or excessive demands in their paid work.

Within this general perspective, two research designs may be illustrated. First, there have been many studies concerned with quantitative indices of affective well-being. These have examined the association between people's job attitudes and their well-being outside employment. As would be expected from the spill-over hypothesis, correlations between job satisfaction and both life satisfaction and relative absence of psychiatric symptoms are strongly positive (e.g. Kornhauser, 1965; Rice, 1984).

The direction of causality underlying this pattern is unlikely to be simply from work to non-work. However, additional evidence comes from research comparing husbands' job-related affective well-being with wives' descriptions of at-home behaviour and experience. S. E. Jackson and Maslach (1982) observed that the level of husbands' job-related emotional exhaustion was significantly associated with wives reporting that their husband comes home tense, unhappy, tired, and upset, and that he has difficulty sleeping at night. Husbands' job-related emotional exhaustion was also significantly correlated with wives reporting a low quality of family life.

A second type of study has examined, through detailed observation and interview, the impact of husbands' jobs on family interactions. For example, Piotrkowski (1978) studied working-class and lower middle-class American families, identifying three forms of spill-over between an employed husband's job and family life at home. First was 'positive carry-over', when a husband enjoyed his job and experienced feelings of self-enhancement from successes during the working day. Such a husband came home cheerful and was described as both 'emotionally available' and 'interpersonally available' to other family members. He laughed and joked, initiated warm and interested interactions, and responded positively to his wife and children.

Somewhat more common was 'negative carry-over', where low affective well-being at work was brought into the family system, displacing the potential for positive family interactions and requiring family members to expend their personal resources to help the husband manage his feelings of strain. In these cases, a job contained negative features, and the impact of these reduced the worker's emotional and interpersonal availability at home. Irritability, non-responsiveness and disengagement were visible, and family members had to work hard to sustain the husband's and their own affective well-being.

The third type of spill-over described by Piotrkowski was 'energy deficit'. This was widely observed in terms of a husband's personal depletion and lack of energy after time spent on his job. These effects sometimes derived from physical tiredness but they also arose from extended low psychological arousal in boring work. Husbands described how as a result of their jobs they felt 'slowed down', 'beat', 'lifeless', 'lazy', 'worn down', 'dead', and 'disconnected from life'. This relationship between work and home was distinguished from negative carry-over, above, in that feelings about work were not brought directly into the family system. However, the effects, in terms of reduced emotional and interpersonal availability, were often very similar. Piotrkowski points out that negative consequences of this kind are likely to be particularly harmful at certain stages in a family life-cycle, especially when young children place considerable demands upon psychological resources.

Occupational Stress

A second broad perspective has viewed jobs as sources of 'stress'. This term is difficult to define precisely, and it is used in many different ways in the literature. Reference is sometimes made to features of the environment (for example, 'this level of noise is stressful') and sometimes to the individual ('I am feeling very stressed today'). However, there appears to be a growing tendency to describe noxious environmental features as 'stressors' and a person's reaction to these as 'strain', retaining 'stress' as a generic label to refer to the topic area as a whole. It is also becoming conventional to distinguish between 'physical' stressors (such as noise, heat or vibration) and those which are 'psychosocial' (job demands, interpersonal problems, etc.).

Three overlapping approaches to occupational stress may be identified, concerned primarily with people's responses ('strain'), environmental features ('stressors'), or the interaction between stressors and responses (through continuing processes of appraisal and coping).

From the first standpoint, we are interested in the nature and measurement of psychological and bodily conditions which might occur in response to stressors. There is general agreement that feelings of distress, anxiety and tension should be included as aspects of 'strain', and these have been widely studied. For example, occupational researchers have often measured the degree to which jobs are reported as causing feelings of nervousness and worry, perhaps associated with sleeplessness. Job-related 'burnout' has been examined, including within this emotional exhaustion arising from work, especially in jobs which require the sustained provision of support and help to other people (e.g. Maslach and Jackson, 1981). Strain has also been assessed in physiological terms, for example through measures of heart-rate or excretion of adrenalin.

However, the concept has sometimes been stretched rather more widely. It has been measured through feelings of low job satisfaction, and has even been taken to include obesity (e.g. Caplan *et al.*, 1975). Definitions tend to err on the side of over-inclusiveness. For example, Caplan and colleagues opt for an account in terms of 'any deviation from normal responses'. With such an extended scope, the word can be in danger of losing its meaning.

A second approach within this research tradition has focused upon jobs as stressors. Two types of study have been undertaken. In the first, comparisons are made between occupations (defined in terms of job titles) to learn which are more stressful than others. For example, in an investigation of twenty-three different occupations, assemblers and machine tenders were found to show particularly high levels of job-related anxiety, depression and somatic complaints, whereas low scores were found among physicians and university professors (Caplan *et al.*, 1975). Working within a single industry, Johansson *et al.* (1978) studied two groups of jobs in Swedish sawmills. One set of workers comprised sawyers, edgers and graders in a mechanized plant; these were compared with a control group of repairmen and maintenance workers in the same plant. Of particular interest were differences between the two groups in feelings of irritation and being rushed. Significantly lower well-being in the former group was accompanied by differences in adrenalin levels, with a build-up during the working day in the more stressed group. A differential ability to relax after work was also observed, with the stressed group requiring up to two hours' recovery time after leaving their jobs.

The other approach to jobs as stressors is to identify separate features in the environment which may give rise to strain. For example, Cooper and Marshall (1976) draw attention to time pressures, role ambiguity, role conflict, uncertainty at organizational boundaries, overpromotion and underpromotion, lack of job security, poor relations with boss, subordinates or colleagues, difficulties in delegating responsibility, limited participation in decision-making, restrictions on budgets, office politics, and several other features. It then becomes possible to examine individual jobs in these terms to identify employees likely to be 'at risk'.

The third approach to stress brings together the other two, combining the separate accounts of strain in the person and stressors in the environment. This approach emphasizes that stress should be viewed in relational terms, as a process of interaction between the environment and the person. For example, Lazarus and Folkman (1984) point out that strain arises only in circumstances where an environmental feature is actively appraised as threatening; and that people differ widely in their appraisals. Furthermore, processes across time should be studied, examining both stressors and people's coping responses. Appraisal and coping themselves come to influence the nature of demands imposed by an environment, and thereby affect the level of strain.

This approach gives rise to research designs which are more oriented than the previous two to individual differences and to qualitative accounts of extended processes. It has less often been adopted in occupational research, although the central importance of appraisal has been widely accepted. This is often summarized in terms of a distinction between 'objective' and 'subjective' stressors. The latter are as perceived by the individual person, not necessarily in agreement with assessments made by other people or with measurements in more 'objective' terms.

As a result, job stressors are widely indexed through reports made by individual job-holders. This procedure generates a separate score for each employee, with the expectation that different values can be obtained even from people working in the same job. It has the advantage of capturing something of the appraisal process, but does give rise to the possibility that correlations between reported stressors and reported strain will be artificially inflated. This might come about, for example, because of a tendency for people to distort their responses in the direction of overall internal consistency.

Viewing the field of occupational stress as a whole, we should note the difficulty of deciding at what level a given feature should be defined as 'stressful', enough to create 'strain', either for an individual person or for employees in general. This problem is compounded by the fact that features which are stressors at high levels can often provide an attractive challenge in moderate amounts. Furthermore, brief and intermittent episodes of experienced strain are not necessarily harmful, often being essential within sequences of activity which yield goal-attainment and enhanced mental health. A further limitation of an exclusive focus upon 'stress' is that by definition it prevents investigation of the positive aspects of jobs.

Job Characteristics and Satisfaction

The third broad perspective covers several elements embraced by occupational stress research, but has concentrated upon a slightly different range of job attributes and employee responses.

Feelings about jobs have been extensively measured in terms of 'job satisfaction', either through overall assessments (viewing one's job as a whole) or through sub-scales to tap specific satisfactions. In the latter case, discrete scores may be derived to measure satisfaction with separate features, such as pay, supervision, promotion prospects, or the kind of work which is undertaken (e.g. J. D. Cook *et al.*, 1981).

A distinction is often drawn between 'intrinsic' and 'extrinsic' job satisfaction. The first of these covers satisfaction with aspects inherent in the conduct of the job itself: freedom to choose how to undertake the work, amount of responsibility, skill requirements, variety, etc. Extrinsic job satisfaction concerns aspects of a job which form the background to the task itself: pay, working conditions, hours of work, industrial relations procedures, job security, etc. Intrinsic and extrinsic satisfaction scores (sometimes described as 'content' and 'context' satisfaction respectively) tend to be positively intercorrelated, but their conceptual separation has been emphasized by many investigators.

For example, Maslow (e.g. 1973) distinguished between 'higher-order' and 'lower-order' needs. The former were said to include desires for enhanced self-respect and self-actualization, whereas the latter were described as physiological and safety needs. Maslow claimed that lower-order needs were largely met in most employment settings, but that deficiencies were widespread in respect of self-respect and self-actualization. He saw the need to improve the content of jobs, their 'intrinsic' aspect in the terms outlined above.

This conclusion was also reached by Herzberg (e.g. 1966). His 'two-factor theory' suggested that the determinants of job satisfaction were qualitatively different from the determinants of job dissatisfaction. In the latter case, dissatisfaction was thought to be attributable only to inadequate work conditions, supervision, administrative procedures, etc. (the 'extrinsic' factors above), with variations in 'intrinsic' job features being irrelevant. On the other hand, feelings of satisfaction were said to be associated only with variations in intrinsic job factors, with extrinsic features making no contribution to these particular responses. Such a sharp separation has not been confirmed in later research. Both sets of factors are now usually considered to influence satisfaction as well as dissatisfaction, which are themselves viewed as opposite poles of a single continuum.

This general perspective, emphasizing the importance of intrinsic job features, has been associated with empirical inquiries based upon standardized measurement of intrinsic content. Most influential within this tradition has been the Job Characteristics Model of Hackman and Oldham (e.g. 1975, 1980), with its accompanying measurement tool, the Job Diagnostic Survey.

The model and the survey embrace five 'core job dimensions'. These are as follows: skill variety (the number of different activities which the job requires), task identity (the degree to which a 'whole' and identifiable piece of work is involved), task significance (the job's impact on the lives of others), autonomy (the degree of freedom and independence possessed by an employee), and feedback (the extent to which the job provides clear information about one's performance).

High scores on these five dimensions (usually measured through employee self-reports) have been found to be significantly correlated with both intrinsic and extrinsic satisfaction. However, the model's prediction that elevated values would be associated with high work quality and quantity have less often been borne out (e.g. Hackman and Oldham, 1980; Kelly, 1982).

This overall perspective and its empirical procedures have generated a substantial bank of information about job content and the correlates of job satisfaction. The perspective has also been important in its contribution to studies of 'job redesign' (procedures to change the content of jobs), usually in respect of one or more of the five core dimensions. (These interventions will be summarized later.) However, from the standpoint of this chapter it is limited in its narrow concentration on feelings defined in terms of job satisfaction; these are only one small part of the broader concept of mental health.

Socio-technical Systems Theory

A fourth perspective differs from the others in giving more emphasis to the fact that work organizations are human and technical systems operating within a wider environment; the other three traditions have taken a primarily individualistic stance at the level of a single job.

An important concept here is that of a 'socio-technical system' (e.g. Trist *et al.*, 1963). Any working organization may be viewed as a combination of technological elements (the formal task, the physical conditions, layout of work, equipment available, and so on) and social networks among those who perform the work. The technology and the social system are primarily linked to each other through the allocation of tasks to work roles. They are in mutual interaction, and to some extent each determines the other. In understanding the organization, we have to think not only in technical, material and financial terms but also in terms of the motives, values, expectations and norms of the people within it. Just as an organization cannot aim entirely to maximize member satisfaction, so must it avoid attempting only to maximize technical efficiency.

This argument leads to the central concept of 'joint optimization': when the attainment of a goal depends upon both the social system and the technical system, it is necessary to seek to optimize the two systems in interdependence with each other. In many cases the explicit goal will be to increase performance, but in the present setting the implication is that enhancement of employee mental health also depends upon joint consideration and modification of the two systems in interaction.

Despite the obvious plausibility of this view, socio-technical systems theory has served more as a general framework of values to guide thinking and research than as a source of concrete predictions or specific issues for examination. This is because socio-technical changes require simultaneous alteration to a wide range of factors: job content, group composition, type of equipment, spatial layout, work schedules, payment systems, supervisory relationships, and possibly exchanges with the environment outside the organization. The perspective is important because of its comprehensiveness, and, in the setting of this chapter, because suggestions about joint optimization have included themes similar to those already introduced. For example, it is recommended that employees should perform a variety of tasks, that work-groups should take responsibility for a whole set of activities, and that individuals should be involved in decisions about their work and about their interaction with other people (e.g. Thorsrud, 1972).

Overview

These four perspectives share an interest in the subject-matter of this chapter, but they also differ among themselves. As noted above, the first three tend to take an individualistic focus, whereas the last one is explicitly concerned with organizations as complex systems.

Another difference may be identified, through the distinction made earlier between mental health which is 'job-related' and that which is 'context-free'. The former is restricted to a person's job setting, whereas context-free mental health extends to feelings and processes in a life-space more generally. In studying the impact of jobs on mental health we are concerned with health in both these forms. Research within the third perspective described here (job characteristics and satisfaction) has almost entirely been restricted to job-related responses. The same is true, but to a lesser extent, of the second perspective (occupational stress); and, as pointed out above, the focus there is especially upon negative reactions to jobs. The first perspective (work and non-work) has examined both job-related and context-free mental health, but has paid relatively less attention to the job conditions which give rise to variation in them. The final approach (socio-technical systems theory) is apparently silent in respect of this distinction, with greater attention instead being paid to systemic properties rather than to individual reactions.

NINE PRINCIPAL JOB FEATURES

Bringing together findings from all four research traditions, this section will consider nine principal aspects of jobs which have been shown to influence job-related and context-free mental health. The nine-feature framework has been developed as applicable to any environment, not merely to jobs, and it recognizes that a given feature can both promote and impair mental health, depending upon its level and duration (Warr, 1987). In thinking about jobs, in making comparisons between them, and in considering movements from one to another, we should bear in mind all of these nine factors.

The account here will be in general terms, with a limited number of illustrative studies cited under each of the nine headings. More concrete examples in particular job settings will be presented in the following two chapters. Chapter 13 will examine the characteristics of new-technology jobs, and Chapter 14 will describe environments at specific locations within five defined types of organization.

Opportunity For Control

The first feature to be considered is the degree to which a work environment permits an individual to control activities and events. Related terms in the literature include autonomy, discretion, influence, power, participation in decision-making, and decision latitude. There is now considerable evidence that this factor has substantial and wide-ranging consequences for mental health; very low levels of personal control in a job are psychologically harmful, and, at least up to moderate amounts, greater control is associated with better mental health.

This is particularly clear in respect of 'intrinsic' control, using this term as before to refer to control over the content of one's job. For example, scores on the 'autonomy' scale of the Job Diagnostic Survey (see above) are consistently found to be positively associated with job-related mental health of many kinds (overall and specific job satisfactions, job-related exhaustion, etc.). Cross-sectional correlations have been supported by longitudinal research, where changes in opportunity for intrinsic control are followed by predicted shifts in job-related mental health (e.g. Hackman *et al.*, 1978).

A similar pattern has been observed for mental health that is context-free. Generalized anxiety, depression, exhaustion and psychosomatic symptoms are greater among employees with limited opportunity for intrinsic job control than for those with moderate levels of control; and life satisfaction and self-esteem are lower (e.g. Payne and Fletcher,

1983). Furthermore, changes in level of control are followed by shifts in context-free mental health (Parkes, 1981).

Opportunity For Skill Use

A second job characteristic known to be associated with mental health is the degree to which a worker has the opportunity to use or extend his or her skills. This relationship was clearly demonstrated in Kornhauser's (1965) study of American car workers, where context-free mental health was assessed through an interview covering freedom from anxiety, high self-esteem, freedom from hostility, sociability, life satisfaction, and personal morale. Workers reporting no opportunity to use their abilities in their job were substantially impaired in these terms; they also exhibited significantly lower job satisfaction.

These findings have been replicated in samples of many kinds in several parts of the world. Furthermore, multivariate investigations have indicated that this job feature retains its importance after statistically controlling for the influence of other variables (e.g. O'Brien, 1983).

Goals and Task Demands

Workers are required to accept certain goals, often imposed as task demands arising from the definition of their job. Aspects of goals and demands have been widely studied, and influences upon both context-free and job-related mental health have been identified.

Most research has concerned 'intrinsic' demands, those inherent in the work itself. 'Extrinsic' demands derive from the setting of a job, having to fit paid work into one's domestic and leisure life. Investigations in the two areas may be considered in turn.

Intrinsic Job Demands. The general thrust of research into intrinsic workload is a demonstration that moderate levels of externally generated goals are of considerable psychological importance. An extreme example of low demand was illustrated during the 1950s in laboratory investigations of 'sensory deprivation'. Subjects who were required to spend their time lying unoccupied in a soundproof room soon developed hallucinations, delusions and anxiety symptoms. Less extreme forms of low workload have been found in laboratory research to give rise to physiological changes (for instance, in adrenal hormone secretion and in cortical activity) as well as to motivational decrements (e.g. Frankenhaeuser and Johansson, 1981). Within job settings, extremely low demands are exhibited through low opportunity for control and skill use, factors shown above to impair mental health in both job-related and context-free forms.

Turning to particularly high levels of work demand, it is not surprising that research has found significant associations with low job satisfaction, job-related anxiety and job-related exhaustion; workload which becomes 'overload' is naturally stressful. Of greater importance, and to be expected from the studies of work and non-work summarized earlier, are consistent effects on context-free mental health. These have been recorded for life satisfaction, psychosomatic symptoms, generalized anxiety, exhaustion and depression (e.g. Karasek, 1979; Billings and Moos, 1982; Payne and Fletcher, 1983).

Coronary heart disease has also been found to be more prevalent among high-workload employees. In a Swedish national survey, Karasek *et al.* (1981) used a self-report index of signs and symptoms of coronary illness, finding a significant cross-sectional association with high job demands. Furthermore, reported level of job demands was predictive of the incidence of signs and symptoms in the subsequent six years.

This study also examined the combined effect of job demands and opportunity for control (the first factor described above). It was apparent that employees with job features adverse in both these respects were particularly likely to exhibit signs and symptoms of coronary heart disease. A similar pattern has been described by Karasek (1979) in respect of both job satisfaction and context-free mental health. Although there has been some disagreement about the precise manner in which job features combine to influence mental health, it seems most likely that the effect is approximately linear, with characteristics combining additively with equal weight. However, research into this question has been very limited, and it remains possible that different modes of combination occur in respect of different variables (Warr, 1987).

Task Identity and Traction. In addition to goal difficulty, reflected in workload demands as examined above, it is also important to consider the structure of an interconnected set of goals. For example, work activities differ in the degree to which they form a coherent, organized whole. Some tasks are linked together in ways which tend to give rise to goal attainment smoothly as a result of the structure of the activities themselves, whereas others are fragmented and unstructured. This feature has been tapped through measures of 'task identity' (as in the Job Diagnostic Survey described above), and both cross-sectional and longitudinal studies point to the psychological importance of this characteristic.

A related notion has been referred to as 'traction'. Baldamus (1961) described this as a feeling of being pulled along by a particular activity, and he saw it as a pleasant experience even within jobs which were, in general, unsatisfactory. He pointed out that traction was similar to the 'rhythm', 'swing' or 'pull' of a job, and noted that jobs can vary in the degree to which they possess this attribute.

Time Demands. Finally under this heading we should note that studies have also examined extrinsic demands in terms of conflicting time requirements: jobs vary in terms of how difficult they are to fit within time demands from family and leisure commitments.

In part this is a question of *amount* of time required by a job, with conflicts between demands being particularly severe for married women in full-time employment (see Chapter 11). In addition, however, the *pattern* of time demands is important, reflected in varying commitments to the workplace associated with differing shift systems (see Chapter 2).

Variety

The importance of moderate levels of variety was established during the 1920s by the Industrial Fatigue Research Board. Observation of British workers before and after the introduction of greater variety into their jobs made it clear that highly repetitive work gave rise to low satisfaction.

Subsequent research has confirmed this link with job-related well-being and extended its findings to include context-free variables. For example, Johanson *et al.* (1978) reported that low levels of variety (assessed by independent observers) were associated with workers' reports of more irritation and less calmness. Excretion of catecholamines (adrenalin and noradrenalin) was also greater in low-variety jobs.

Environmental Clarity

This fifth section will examine a range of perceived features associated with employees' ability to understand their environment and to predict what will happen. Low levels of clarity, or high uncertainty, are generally found to be detrimental, especially over long periods of time. Three types of clarity may be mentioned.

Information About the Results of Behaviour. Feedback about the consequences of action is essential for mental health in several ways. For example, it is a minimum requirement for the establishment and maintenance of personal control and for the development and utilization of skills.

In job settings, the level of task feedback has consistently been found to be associated with higher job-related and context-free mental health (e.g. Brousseau, 1978). Learning promptly about outcomes is also important for the generation of pleasant feelings of traction (see above). This factor is increasingly important in work requiring interaction with computer systems. Clear information is needed about the state of the system after one's most recent input, but long feedback delays can occur intermittently, perhaps at unpredictable intervals, giving rise to increased feelings of tension.

Information About the Future. A second aspect of environmental clarity is the degree to which it is possible to forecast what is likely to happen, irrespective of one's own behaviour. The importance of this has been documented in many occupational investigations. For example, Caplan *et al.* (1975) developed a measure of 'job future ambiguity', covering a worker's degree of uncertainty about future career developments. Low clarity of this kind was found to be significantly associated with high levels of job dissatisfaction, job-related depression, and job-related anxiety.

Information About Required Behaviour. Another strand of research has examined the degree to which an employee knows what is required and

261

which behaviours will be rewarded or punished. Kahn *et al.* (1964) introduced this in terms of 'role ambiguity', showing that high ambiguity is associated with lower job-related mental health. This finding has been extensively replicated (e.g. Jackson and Schuler, 1985) and extended into context-free measures of anxiety and depression (e.g. Billings and Moos, 1982).

Availability of Money

A positive relationship between standard of living and mental health has been recorded in many national populations. In part this is a reflection of very low incomes during unemployment being associated with low mental health among unemployed people, but within samples of paid workers the same pattern is presumably also to be expected.

Few studies have addressed this question directly. Some research has found, unsurprisingly, that people with higher incomes are more satisfied with their pay; and others have obtained similar results in respect of perceived fairness, relative to one's own and others' responsibility, skill level, etc.

In view of the central importance of money to meet the needs of oneself and one's family, it seems very probable that incomes judged to be inadequate will be associated with mental health impairments of the kinds illustrated previously. This possibility appears not to have been tested directly among employed samples, so that retention of this sixth job feature as a determinant of mental health should remain more speculative than is the case for the other eight attributes. In general, it is to be expected that variations at lower levels (extending into poverty) will have greater impact than at higher income levels.

Physical Security

Environments in general need to protect people against physical threat and to provide an adequate level of security. In job environments, this feature concerns physical working conditions rather than those variables which were earlier described as 'psychosocial'.

Poor working conditions (bad light, dangerous equipment, excessive heat, and so on) are naturally expected to give rise to negative job-related feelings. In addition, context-free mental health may be affected in two ways. Firstly through the carry-over of feelings from work to non-work described earlier in the chapter, and secondly through a job-induced deterioration in physical health having its own effect upon mental condition. For example, workers with chronic back complaints arising from continuous heavy lifting, or those recovering from crushed limbs after an industrial accident, are expected to show poorer context-free mental health than those whose physical health is unimpaired (e.g. Hendrie, 1981).

However, the possible impact of poor working conditions on mental health has rarely been studied. Information is accumulating about performance effects or reported discomfort in a job setting (e.g. Kantowitz and Sorkin, 1983), but there remains a need to examine the consequences in terms of context-free mental health.

Opportunity for Interpersonal Contact

Rather more research within the domain of this chapter has been addressed to the eighth feature. It is obvious that several aspects of interpersonal contact are essential for good mental health, and these general associations are expected to be present within job settings.

Reported friendship opportunities at work are significantly positively correlated with job-related mental health (e.g. Oldham and Brass, 1979). Support received from one's co-workers and boss is found to contribute significantly to a range of context-free variables, such as low anxiety, depression and somatic symptoms, and high self-esteem and subjective competence (e.g. Billings and Moos, 1982). Different forms of social support will be discussed in Chapter 14.

Another set of studies has examined aspects of privacy and personal territory. Privacy regulation occurs in all social settings, as people establish boundaries around themselves or their group (e.g. Altman, 1975), and similar processes are expected to occur in work environments. For example, employees might seek to avoid continuously high levels of contact with others, and workplace layouts might be designed with this in mind.

Oldham and Brass (1979) studied a move from separate conventional offices into a single large open-plan environment. The latter had no interior walls and no partitions or cabinets more than three feet high. The move gave rise to a significant decrease in job-related well-being, as well as a decline in reported ability to concentrate, reduced sense of task identity, and reduced feedback from supervisors. Reported friendship opportunities were also found to have declined significantly. Lacking their own private space, employees were concerned that they could not have separate discussions with colleagues without being overheard.

Valued Social Position

Finally, research has considered some ways through which the esteem attached to a person's job can contribute to his or her broader well-being. There is some general agreement about the prestige ranking of jobs, and it is expected that people whose occupational roles are accorded very little social value will tend to experience dissatisfaction with their position.

Several investigations have taken measures of perceived social value from job-holders themselves, consistently finding a significant association with job-related well-being (e.g. Hackman and Oldham, 1975). It seems probable that this relationship will be particularly marked for jobs perceived to have low rather than high social merit, but that comparative possibility appears not to have been studied directly.

Overview

This section has classified a range of different investigations under nine broad headings. These seem to represent principal environmental sources of variation in mental health, and all nine should be considered in assessing the impact of a job or a possible transition between jobs. Although the nine features have been treated singly, they are of course to some extent covariant (e.g. J. D. Cook *et al.*, 1981; Roberts and Glick, 1981). Investigations taking broader measures of job content (for example, combining several intrinsic aspects into an overall assessment of job 'complexity') have consistently yielded results similar to those described above (e.g. Kohn and Schooler, 1983; Wall and Clegg, 1981).

Because individual jobs can be measured in these several ways, and because scores on the different dimensions may be intercorrelated, there is always a danger that a significant finding in respect of one job factor may in practice represent the causal influence of a related but unmeasured variable. There is thus a strong need for multivariate research, examining several job features simultaneously, and investigating the statistical contribution to mental health of certain factors in the context of others. Some studies of this kind have been cited above, but more are needed.

There is also a need for systematic research into individual differences in this area. It is clear that people are differentially affected by particular job features (with, for example, some more able than others to tolerate high task demands), but empirical progress to specify these differences has been slow. This is largely because it is not usually possible to measure aspects of individuals which might modify their response to job characteristics independently of their exposure to those characteristics.

For example, we might expect that some people are consistently more anxious and nervous than others, irrespective of their current situation (e.g. Depue and Monroe, 1986; Watson and Clark, 1984). This aspect of 'baseline mental health' will presumably modify a job's impact upon their current mental health, when they are exposed to that job. To learn about this, we ideally have to measure baseline mental health prior to entry into the job, since measures taken after entry will be contaminated by the influence of job features themselves. Such a research design is in practical terms extremely difficult.

A second problem is that, in order to identify personal factors which modify the impact of jobs, we need to be able to control the nature of jobs in the research comparison. For example, if we wish to examine differences in job-related mental health between men and women, we must study samples of each sex who are employed in equivalent jobs. This is difficult, since women tend to be located in different employment roles from men (see Chapter 11). That means that, if we found sex differences in employees' mental health without controlling for occupational role, we could not be sure whether those arose from differences between the two sexes or from differences between their jobs.

There are of course ways around this difficulty, through careful selection of samples and through appropriate statistical analyses, but research to date has often been rather unsophisticated. Some progress has been made in studies of individual differences in values and motives. Here the research design has usually involved collection of data from individuals in similar jobs, examining simultaneously job content, employee mental health, and a potentially relevant motivational variable. One of these may be illustrated here.

Much attention has been directed to the notion of 'growth-need strength'. This refers to the strength of a person's desire to obtain 'growth' satisfaction from his or her work. The latter is viewed in terms of the 'higher-order' needs described by Maslow (see above), and growth-need strength is typically measured through items which tap a person's liking for work which presents challenges and which permits independence, creativity and personal development. Given that people differ in respect of this relatively stable motivational factor, we might expect that it would influence the way they react to certain job characteristics, those which are 'intrinsic' in the sense described above.

Broadly speaking, that appears to be the case. For example, opportunity for control in a job (the first of the nine features introduced here) is found to be more important for employees of high growth-need strength than for those of lower growth-need strength (e.g. Loher *et al.*, 1985; Spector, 1985; Warr, 1987). However, the impact of individual-difference measures of this kind has so far not been found to be large, and there is a need for more concentrated research in the area.

PRACTICAL IMPLICATIONS

A large number of other fascinating research questions remain to be answered, for example about the detailed impact of specific combinations of job features. But the knowledge acquired so far makes it clear that practical steps should now be taken in many work organizations, directed at mental health problems in particular groups. A proportion of jobs (probably a minority) are likely to be harmful in the nine terms described here, and attention should be focused upon these, seeking to reduce their negative impact upon mental health.

There are three kinds of reason for instituting change. First is the moral argument. Given that there are significant causal effects of these job factors on mental health, outside as well as inside the workplace, we have a moral responsibility to act upon that knowledge. Second is the practical argument, that better employee mental health is associated with better work performance (e.g. Iaffaldano and Muchinsky, 1985; Jamal, 1985). Such an association is no doubt circular in causal terms, as job conditions affect mental health, and level of mental health itself influences task demands and perceptions of stressors.

A third reason for advocating change is rather different. Research designs have very often been cross-sectional, assessing both job conditions and mental health at one point in time. There is now an urgent need to carry out longitudinal studies, monitoring across periods of time the psychological consequences of changes at the workplace (e.g. Wall and Clegg, 1981). Such intervention studies can both contribute to greater understanding and also provide benefits to employees within the organization in question.

How should organizations set about identifying and improving harmful job conditions? In general terms there is a requirement for management and trade unions to formulate a long-term strategy in the area of this chapter. In doing this, conflicts between the mental health needs of employees and the productivity requirements of management will inevitably become clear. Progress will therefore not always be easy. However, given that only a minority of jobs within an organization are likely to be problematic in terms of mental health, energy can be directed to reforming this limited number. Another approach is to recognize the special problems of working with new technology, and to tackle these systematically in the light of suggestions in Chapters 4 and 13.

Interventions to improve employee mental health can be of two kinds, either directed primarily at changing the organization or job, or aimed to assist individual people without directly modifying their environment. Issues at both levels are covered in Chapter 15, but some additional themes may be briefly mentioned here.

Attempts to change the nature of jobs can be viewed as exercises in 'job redesign'. Design specifications may be created and applied (for example, in terms of the nine features described above), in order to build jobs in a systematic manner, rather than letting them develop haphazardly in the absence of an overall plan.

Early approaches to redesign of this kind were sometimes referred to as 'job enrichment', a term closely associated with Herzberg's two-factor theory (e.g. 1966; see above), with 'enrichment' aiming to enhance the intrinsic content of work. Employees in very simple jobs may be given additional tasks to perform, particularly ones which involve greater responsibility and require more skilled work. Another procedure is in terms of 'job rotation', where employees change jobs with others in the same wage grade, either within a period of work or between periods. This increases variety, but is unlikely to be of great advantage if rotation is between jobs which are all equally poor; there needs also to be some increment in the other characteristics identified here.

These approaches to job redesign have recently been assimilated into more comprehensive frameworks, often emphasizing the interdependence between tasks undertaken by different employees and groups of employees. It is now seen as desirable to examine and if necessary change the content of jobs undertaken by groups of employees as well as by single individuals (e.g. Wall *et al.*, 1986). Groups are increasingly permitted to work in a semi-autonomous manner, planning and controlling their own activities and solving problems relatively independently of their supervisor. The need to treat extrinsic as well as intrinsic features has also become accepted. For example, redesigning jobs to increase opportunity for control or opportunity for skill use requires consideration of wage levels, since the new tasks may have shifted their location in a job evaluation framework. Financial savings may of course be expected elsewhere, and many instances of job redesign have occurred within pay and productivity agreements (e.g. Kelly, 1982).

Further details of redesign procedures are included in the chapter which follows. Employee mental health may also be addressed through counselling or psychotherapeutic assistance, without directly confronting the nature of work tasks undertaken. For example, some organizations have introduced 'stress management' programmes, providing training which aims to help employees to relax and cope better with job stressors (e.g. West *et al.*, 1984). Psychotherapy from clinical psychologists or psychiatrists is increasingly available to clients with job-related problems (e.g. Firth and Shapiro, 1986) and offers considerable potential in this area. In general, a closer integration of the work of clinical and occupational psychologists is much to be encouraged.

SUMMARY

This chapter opened by describing and comparing four overlapping perspectives: work and non-work, occupational stress, job characteristics and satisfaction, and socio-technical systems theory. A distinction was drawn between 'job-related' and 'context-free' mental health, and the need to consider both of these was emphasized.

Aspects of jobs which can enhance or impair mental health were then presented under nine headings: opportunity for control, opportunity for skill use, goals and task demands, variety, environmental clarity, availability of money, physical security, opportunity for interpersonal contact, and valued social position. Illustrative research studies were cited in each case, and the importance of multivariate research and studies of individual variation was underlined.

Finally, practical implications were considered. Within organizations, management and trade unions should formulate a long-term strategy and seek to redesign jobs identified as particularly harmful. Assistance may also be considered at the level of individual counselling or psychotherapy.

FURTHER READING

The material in this chapter is treated in greater depth in P. B. Warr, *Work, Unemployment, and Mental Health* (Oxford University Press, 1987). Issues excluded here for lack of space but examined in that book include the meanings of 'mental health', probable non-linear relationships between job features and mental health, and a detailed consideration of individual differences.

Current Concerns in Occupational Stress, edited by C. L. Cooper and R. L. Payne (Wiley, 1980), covers many central themes, as does the chapter by Winnubst (1984). Reviews of research into job characteristics and job satisfaction have been presented by Loher *et al.* (1985) and Spector (1985). Chapter 16 of the present book extends the nine-factor account introduced here to a consideration of the environment of people who are unemployed.

13

New Technology and Job Design

Toby D. Wall

The term 'new technology' or 'information technology' applies to recent developments in the use of computers to support and control information and mechanical systems. As will be discussed later, its novelty lies not so much in the use of computers for these purposes, but more in the economic viability and increased range of application brought about by advances in microelectronics, particularly through development of the powerful, robust yet low-cost silicon chip. This technical advance has resulted in today's £500 micro-computer having all the information-processing and control capacity that only a few years ago would have required a mainframe computer costing over £50,000. Applications range from small home computer and games systems, through computer-controlled machinery such as robots, to large networked systems which can integrate and process information from numerous and remote sources, as used for example by large retailers and banks.

At present the penetration of new technology into work organizations is uneven and in general not high. Word processors and other 'desk top' systems are widely used across all sectors to support administrative and clerical work. Most large banks, building societies and retailers have developed their existing computer systems by linking them to electronic cash dispensers and tills which automate data entry. These allow almost instantaneous recording, updating and integration of information obtained from numerous outlets. In manufacturing, however, diffusion has been slower. For example, it has been estimated that there are only two robots per thousand workers in Sweden, 1·46 in Japan, 0·43 in the USA and 0·32 in the UK (Attenborough, 1984). Similarly, 'computer numerically controlled' machine tools account for less than 5 per cent of the machine tool population in Britain (Metal Working Production, 1983). Large-scale applications involving computer integration of groups of machine tools, robots and so on into a 'Flexible Manufacturing

System' are rare. Bessant and Haywood (1985) suggest there are only 150–200 such systems worldwide. In short, new technology has not yet become the primary means of production in the vast majority of organizations (Burnes and Fitter, 1987).

Nevertheless, it is clear that the adoption of new technology is accelerating. Child (1984a) reports market growth rates estimated at 34 per cent per year for new office technology, 51 per cent for industrial robots, and 23 per cent for computer-aided manufacturing equipment. Charlish (1985) estimates a growth in the market for Computer Aided Design and Computer Aided Manufacturing (CAD/CAM) systems of 30 per cent a year. Governments worldwide have actively promoted development in this area. In Britain, for example, 1982 was designated 'Information Technology Year', and various long-term initiatives have been taken to encourage the use and development of new technology. Among these is continuing support for the development of information technology following the recommendations of the Alvey Committee (Department of Trade and Industry, 1982). The European Strategic Programme for Research and Development into Information Technology (ESPRIT), funded by the European Commission, has parallel objectives.

Most large organizations now have some experience of new technology and many have appointed specialists to advise on how to exploit the opportunities it offers. Above all, the reducing cost and the increasing range of application of computer technology suggest it will become an integral part of working life (Sharlt *et al.*, 1986). It is this potential that has led many to regard new technology as heralding 'The Second Industrial Revolution' (Halton, 1985) and to refer to the 'Microelectronics Revolution' or the 'Information Technology Revolution' (Forester, 1985).

The prospect of a technology with such wide-ranging socio-economic implications appropriately attracts the attention of concerned people from all walks of life. It raises questions of how best it can be exploited, and what dangers are inherent in its use. By analysing the properties of the new technology and examining early applications, commentators and researchers are beginning to identify important social issues and effects. Those looking at new technology from a human factors or ergonomic perspective focus on the design of software and hardware to promote more effective interfaces with the operator (see Chapter 4).

Others have considered the following points: the new kinds of skills required, and the implications of this for training, education and manpower planning generally; effects on unemployment; implications for management practice and organizational design; influence upon patterns of work (including the possibility of increased homeworking); health and safety aspects; industrial relations issues; and the question of protecting personal privacy (e.g. Marstrand, 1984; Wall *et al.*, 1987).

Central among these issues are the implications of new technology for the nature of operators' jobs and their well-being at work. It is to this question the present chapter is addressed. To provide a theoretical and substantive context, a brief review will be made of trends and developments in the wider field of job design. This will build on some of the ideas and evidence introduced in the preceding chapter. It will be followed by a description of the nature of new technology and a review of the current argument that its application, especially in manufacturing, will lead to simplified, boring jobs on the shop-floor. Investigations of early applications of new technology will then be considered from this standpoint. Finally, the chapter will conclude by outlining the research and practical implications of the material reviewed.

EXISTING TRENDS IN JOB DESIGN

Many jobs, particularly those of blue-collar employees in manufacturing industries, are narrow and specialized. The range of operations performed by the individual is closely prescribed and allows little discretion. The prime example of this is the assembly line, where people can be found carrying out merely a single operation on a small part of the total product, at a pace predetermined by a conveyor belt, and with little or no discretion over how they perform their work. Cycle times of such jobs can be as low as two or three seconds.

The financial argument for requiring such simplified jobs is straightforward. If the making of a complex product is divided into a series of simple tasks, then less skilled labour needs to be recruited, training times are short, errors are less likely and thus the unit cost of production is reduced. The formulation of this strategy is usually traced back to Adam Smith (1776) and Charles Babbage (1835), whose approach centred on this idea of the 'division of labour'. Taylor (1911) extended the argument by proposing that one should not only subdivide work into small discrete jobs, but also clearly separate the management and supervision from the job's execution. Thus control and responsibility were to be taken out of the hands of the operator. Taylor's development of 'scientific management' showed how this could be put into effect (e.g. Kelly, 1982).

The degree to which these ideas were absorbed into subsequent job design practice has been examined by several researchers. As early as 1955, Davis, Canter and Hoffman obtained information on criteria used by those in organizations responsible for designing jobs. Of a list of fifteen items, the following were rated most important: minimizing the time required to perform an operation; obtaining the highest quality; and minimizing skill requirements. More recent studies by Hedberg and Mumford (1975) and Taylor (1979) obtain parallel results. Few would deny that during this century a process of work simplification has affected a wide range of lower-level jobs and is embedded in current practice (e.g. Braverman, 1974; Kelly, 1982; L. Klein, 1976). Most would agree this has played an important part in raising the material standard of living in the industrialized world; but the emphasis on material gain has overshadowed the question of psychological cost and constrained a search for alternatives.

As the trend towards work simplification developed, so too did research into its human consequences. Some of the earliest investigations were undertaken in the 1920s by the Industrial Fatigue Research Board (later known as the Industrial Health Research Board, supported by the British Medical Research Council). These involved intensive study of such repetitive jobs as pharmaceutical-product packing, bicycle-chain assembly and tobacco weighing. The findings are summarized in the Board's Eleventh Annual Report (1931) as follows: 'boredom has become ˙ncreasingly prominent as a factor in the industrial life of the worker and its effects are no less important than those of fatigue' (p. 30). One of the principal causes was identified as 'semi-automatic operations which prevent freedom of thought but are insufficient to keep the mind fully occupied' (p. 36).

This focus on repetition and pacing has continued to the present, through the work of Fraser (1947), Walker and Guest (1952), Kornhauser (1965), Caplan *et al.* (1975), Cox *et al.* (1982) and Broadbent (1985). In general, it is clear that jobs simplified in this way are associated with less positive work attitudes and in some circumstances with poorer mental health. Only a minority of employees, however, are engaged on such jobs, and repetition and pacing are only part of the outcome of job simplification. Thus research into job design more generally has adopted a broader approach to the characterization and measurement of job characteristics, and placed greater emphasis on another aspect of simplification, the question of the degree to which jobs allow employees autonomy, responsibility and control over their work activities (see 'opportunity for control' and 'intrinsic job demands', two of the nine principal job features introduced in the preceding chapter). In so doing investigators have been able to encompass a wider range of jobs.

An example of this more general approach is research into the Job Characteristics Model, proposed by Hackman and Oldham (1976). Drawing on earlier work by Turner and Lawrence (1965) and Hackman and Lawler (1971), this specifies five features of jobs salient to both attitudes and behaviour. These are skill variety, task identity, task significance, autonomy and task feedback (see Chapter 12). Jobs with higher levels of these characteristics are predicted to promote work motivation, work performance and job satisfaction, and to reduce labour turnover and absenteeism. Among the job characteristics, autonomy is ascribed particular importance.

Over the last decade the Job Characteristics Model has served as the most popular basis for empirical research, and has given rise to a substantial body of evidence. Much of this is cross-sectional in nature, and consistently confirms that employees' perceptions of the five job characteristics are positively related to their job satisfaction and re-ported motivation (e.g. Brief and Aldag, 1975; Hackman and Oldham, 1976; Wall *et al.*, 1978). Roberts and Glick (1981) offer a critique of this area and point out that, because job characteristics have so often been measured by self-report methods, the consistent findings could reflect that perceptions rather than actual job properties account for the relationships obtained. But the force of this argument is somewhat reduced by findings showing that perceptual measures provide useful information about actual jobs (Algera, 1983; Griffin, 1983; Schneider, 1985).

Overall, although there are aspects of the Job Characteristics Model which have attracted justifiable criticism, the central propositions concerning the relationship between job properties and psychological reactions are well supported. Recently the model has been adapted and extended to encompass the design of jobs for work groups (Hackman, 1983). Here it merges with the socio-technical approach to work design (see Chapter 12), from which the idea of 'autonomous work groups' has evolved. As in the job characteristics approach, this emphasizes the psychological importance of variety, work identity and significance, feedback, and above all, autonomy (Gulowsen, 1972; Rousseau, 1977).

The cross-sectional studies introduced so far are based on traditional technology, but are significant in that they identify properties of general psychological importance relevant to the design of new-technology work. The research has shown that simplified jobs are clearly associated with feelings of boredom and dissatisfaction, and that they may contribute to mental ill-health more broadly. This suggests that jobs deliberately redesigned to provide more variety and autonomy would be beneficial. Studies which set out to introduce those characteristics support that view.

An example is the field experiment reported by Kemp *et al.* (1983) in a food-manufacturing company. The traditional design of jobs allowed individuals little control over their work, and most decisions were taken by supervisors. The new method of autonomous group-working involved teams of eight to twelve employees, all of whom were required to carry out each of the eight tasks within the production process. Team members were collectively responsible for: allocating jobs among themselves; reaching production targets and quality and hygiene standards; recording production data; solving local production problems; ordering and collecting raw materials; delivering finished goods to stores; training new recruits; and in other ways managing their day to day work activities. They also participated in the selection of new team members. The degree of self-management was such that no supervisors existed. Teams reported directly to first-line management.

The research design involved a comparison after six months between the attitudes and behaviours of experimental employees and those in three comparison groups. This was followed up over a further two years, during which autonomous work groups were introduced into one of the comparison groups (Wall *et al.*, 1986). It was found that experimental employees clearly saw themselves as having enhanced levels of work autonomy and were much more satisfied with their jobs, both in the short and the longer term. Productivity was improved, not because employees each produced more under autonomous work groups, but because they could match the output of those under conventional work designs without the need for the company to employ supervisors.

A number of other studies of the psychological effects of redesigning jobs to provide greater employee autonomy have been reported. These show positive but nevertheless diverse outcomes. Locke *et al.* (1976), for instance, found increases in productivity following job enrichment among clerical employees, but no attitudinal effects; Orpen (1979), also with clerical workers, reported positive effects on job satisfaction, motivation, absenteeism and labour turnover, but not on performance; Wall and Clegg (1981) recorded both attitudinal and performance effects in a manufacturing setting; and Champoux (1978), Hackman, *et al.* (1978), and Trist *et al.* (1977), reported attitudinal and other benefits.

Taken as a whole, the evidence from change studies of job redesign is neither unproblematic nor definitive. Performance effects without corresponding attitudinal ones, and vice versa, point to theoretical deficiencies and suggest there may be factors which inhibit or promote particular outcomes. These may include differences in technology, supervisory and management practices, operator characteristics, and so on, which remain generally unspecified in contemporary theory. Methodological considerations also cloud the issue. For example, only a small proportion of investigations are based on strong research designs; it seems likely that failures are under-represented in the literature; the vast majority of studies examine consequences only in the short term, a few weeks to six months; and it is often difficult to ascribe the improvements recorded solely to job redesign itself, as opposed to the various associated changes (e.g. in management practice or payment systems) which the redesign may have necessitated (Wall and Martin, 1987).

From a scientific perspective the above criticisms are troublesome, as they make clear that neither existing theory nor the supporting evidence is entirely satisfactory. From a practical standpoint, however, the picture is more encouraging. Here the finer detail of theory and particular lines of cause and effect are of less immediate concern. The practical issue is more general: is job redesign a viable proposition of likely value in work situations? The large majority of reported attempts involving the enhancement of employee autonomy, control and responsibility have resulted in attitudinal, performance or other benefits. This is not to say that such change in jobs is always easy to introduce. Clearly it can conflict with many existing organizational factors. For example, giving shop-floor workers more autonomy can detract from the conventional role of supervisors (e.g. Lawler *et al.*, 1973; Cordery and Wall, 1985), require changes in information systems (Clegg and Fitter, 1978), challenge demarcation lines between different groups of employees, require technological change, or challenge management or trade-union values. All these are considerations which may prevent the occurrence of such change or undermine its potential effects. The evidence does show, however, that these impediments can in many instances be overcome. Moreover, where job changes are required for other reasons, as when new technology is to be introduced, a particularly clear opportunity becomes available for the deliberate design of more psychologically rewarding jobs.

THE NATURE OF NEW TECHNOLOGY

Before considering the implications for new technology of the job design research summarized above, it is necessary to consider the technology itself in a little more detail.

The term 'new technology' is used to describe technology of which microelectronic information processing forms an integral part. The microprocessing element provides a powerful and cheap means for storing, retrieving and manipulating information, and for using these data to control associated equipment and machinery. As a consequence 'new technology' encompasses a wide variety of applications. However, two main forms may be distinguished. In the first, the emphasis is on the information processing rather than the control capacity of the microprocessor. Examples are office technologies for word-processing and electronic filing, which rely mainly on the storage and retrieval of information. An extension of this is where the technology is also used to manipulate or transform information, as in the case of computer-aided design, statistical analysis, accounting, and various expert systems. A further example is that of the 'Electronic Point of Sale' technology now commonly seen in supermarkets. This makes use of a sensor device to read bar codings on products for sale. The information thus obtained at the checkout point is used automatically to access information on prices and to derive total costs to the purchaser, which are displayed on an electronic till. The same information is used for stock control, for example to re-order for particular outlets and to monitor rates of sale for different products. In this first group of new technologies the information processing is the primary component, and associated equipment such as sensors, keyboards, visual display units, tills and printers are merely mechanisms for capturing or outputting the information handled. These new technologies operate primarily on the information itself.

In the second group of new technologies, the focus is on applications of microprocessor technology for the control of machinery. Here the information storage and retrieval capabilities are used to control equipment which physically transforms other materials. The computing element is proportionately much smaller and the associated machinery much more important. Such new technologies take a wide variety of forms. One example is the 'computer numerically controlled' machine tool now commonly found in precision engineering. This machine is like its manual predecessor, the machine tool, in that it mills, grinds or drills metals. The new element, however, is that these operations, rather than being directed by a human operator, are controlled by a program fed into its microprocessor. The program makes the machine carry out an entire sequence of operations without the need for operator intervention. Another example is the robot, which can be used to pick and place objects, spray paint or carry out a range of other functions, in a sequence and in particular positions predetermined by its program.

The particularly important feature of these new technologies is that, unlike their custom-made predecessors, each can be used for a wide range of different products, simply by loading different programs. Also important is that they can be combined, through shared information processing, into a more comprehensive production system. Thus metal can be passed from one computer numerically controlled machine to another, to complete the different operations required entirely through the use of robots or conveyors, with the whole sequence under the control of information processing technology. Such computer integrated systems are often referred to as 'Flexible Manufacturing Systems', and it is the possibility of such integration on an even larger scale that has given rise to the vision of the fully automated factory of the future. For the present, however, where new technology is implemented, stand-alone computerized machines or relatively small systems are the rule, since the development of large integrated systems is at an early stage and the cost still very high.

It can be seen from these examples that generally the former group of new technologies covers office systems, whereas the second group encompasses manufacturing or production systems. In principle there is little new in either of these types of application. Since the 1950s, computers have been employed to process information and indeed to control production. One example comes from within process industries, such as chemical plants and oil refineries, where mainframe computers have been used to monitor and control entire multi-million pound plants. Sensors, recording temperature, material flow, and so on, feed information back to the computer which either advises operators, or directly adjusts heating systems and valves, to balance the process. In practice, however, there is a particularly important ingredient which is novel to the application of information technology. The development of the silicon microchip has radically affected the nature of the hardware available. It is now cheap, compact, robust and very fast in operation. Whereas computer technology was previously an economic proposition only for large centralized office and production systems (as in banking and the process industry), the falling cost, reduced size and increased tolerance of a wide variety of physical environments have opened up a multitude of additional applications. Associated with these have been developments in telecommunications and in software. It is these practical and economic properties, brought about by the development of the silicon chip, which account for the use of the term 'new' and have made computer power applicable on such a wide scale in work settings. It is with these newer applications we are here concerned.

NEW TECHNOLOGY AND WORK SIMPLIFICATION

As Child (1984) states, an important aspect of new technology is that it 'substitutes for or complements people's mental and clerical capabilities, in contrast to mechanical technology which substitutes for people's physical capabilities' (p. 245).

To many people the potential of new technology to displace the 'mental' component of jobs is its most critical feature. This encompasses the exercising of judgement and discretion, and hence responsibility, so central to the quality of work. They foresee a situation in which operators are increasingly made subordinate to technology, perhaps merely loading and unloading machines, with no control over work itself. It is predicted by these observers that the new technology will dictate the pace of work, the process of production and so on, as predetermined by its program. The person, if not altogether displaced, is expected to become merely an aid to the technology, performing only those tasks which the system is unable to carry out for itself, or those which it is uneconomic to automate. In terms of job design, this is thought likely to lead to further simplification and de-skilling of jobs.

The argument that new technology will become a force to further the simplification of jobs is based jointly on the assumption that the historical trend towards simplification will persist, an analysis of how the technology itself could in principle be used for this purpose, and upon selected case material where simplification did in practice occur. The argument has been applied to work of many kinds and at different levels within organizations. It has been most clearly articulated, however, in relation to manufacturing technology and particularly with regard to computer numerically controlled (CNC) machine tools as introduced in precision engineering companies. These are currently the most prevalent form of new manufacturing technology. The argument will therefore be considered in respect of them.

Shaiken (1979, 1980) vividly describes the nature of work in precision engineering, and the effects of CNC machine tools on shop-floor jobs. In this industry, work is characterized by the production of small batches of metal components often machined to very fine tolerances. Traditionally, these parts are made by skilled machinists on general-purpose machine tools which cut, grind, drill, turn and in other ways shape metals. The machinist translates information from a drawing into a finished part. The skill required to do this has been learned over several years. The operator has to select the right cutting edge and speed for a given metal to achieve the end product. The machine tool is controlled by turning wheels or cranks to bring the cutting edge on to the metal at exactly the right place and to the specified depth. Designers will often consult the machinist to find out which designs can be made. The skilled machinist, therefore, is the information processor between design and product, and is very much in control of the physical production process. It is a job high on variety and over which he or she has almost complete operational control.

The introduction of a CNC machine tool can fundamentally change this job. In this new technology the machine element is essentially the same as previously, but now its operation is under the control of a microprocessor. Decisions on how to machine a given part are pre-recorded and embedded into a program. This defines precisely both the location of cuts to be made to the metal, and the cutting tool required. Some machines can also be programmed to load appropriate tools from a rack at different stages in the cutting cycle. The program needs 'proving out' on its first run to make sure that it is accurate. Once this has been achieved, however, the knowledge required to make the part has been permanently captured in the program.

The production advantages of such technology can be substantial. A part once made can be exactly reproduced as many times as required, without the variability inherent in human performance. Information can be stored and retrieved at will for repeat orders. Each machine can be rapidly changed from one part to another, simply by calling up alternative programs. In some cases CNC machine tools can be programmed to make parts which human operators could not. From the point of view of the machinist's job, however, the effect can be fundamental and harmful. His or her role can be reduced essentially to one of loading and unloading the machine, and occasionally making necessary adjustments should the unexpected occur.

Several other forms of new manufacturing technology show similar features, allowing previously skilled work to be absorbed into a program and potentially leaving the human operator with the ancillary preparatory, monitoring and unloading tasks. Robots, for example, are used in modern car plants for a variety of purposes such as spot welding and paint spraying. These often include a facility to be programmed by copying a human operator. A skilled paint-spray operator, for instance, can guide a robot arm through the physical movements necessary to complete a given product, and this is recorded on its program. The whole sequence can then be reproduced on demand.

It is clear from the above instances that new technology has important implications for the design of jobs. In particular it provides an opportunity to simplify the kinds of jobs which hitherto, because of the skill and wide range of products involved, were protected from the de-skilling effects of conventional technology. To argue, however, that because new manufacturing technology can simplify jobs it necessarily will have this effect is not a tenable position. This form of 'technological determinism' uses the false logic of equating a person's job merely with the operation of technology. That is a possible but not a necessary practice. Jobs can be and often are wider than the tasks immediately required by a given technology. In the case of CNC machine tools replacing conventional machinery, for example, there is evidence that although jobs are changed by its introduction, this does not always result in simplification. Operators can in these circumstances be asked to develop different skills and take on additional responsibilities. It is also the case that in some jobs new technology can be used to eliminate the most undesirable elements, such as repetitive movements or handling dangerous materials. The fact that such options exist is well documented in the literature and will be considered shortly. For the moment the simplification argument will be pursued further.

Most proponents of the view that new technology will simplify jobs clearly recognize that the nature of the technology itself is only one factor to be taken into account. Their argument rests also on the assumption that management will use the opportunity such technology offers to create more simplified work. This is the essence of the arguments put forward by Braverman (1974), Cooley (1984) and Shaiken (1980). Braverman bases his analysis on a Marxist interpretation of the labour process. He suggests that the 'laws' of capitalist exploitation lead to reduced autonomy for lower-level employees through skill reduction and increasing management control over the production process. In support of this view he points to the influence of Scientific Management over jobs associated with conventional technologies. Since we have witnessed a trend towards work simplification since the turn of the century, he predicts that managements will continue to pursue this using the opportunities offered by new technology. Cooley takes a similar line. He analyses the job implications of both CNC technology and Computer Aided Design (CAD) systems. With regard to the latter, even as used by architects and engineers, he argues that CAD 'tends to deskill the designer, subordinate the designer to the machine and give rise to alienation' (p. 201). Cooley argues more generally: 'it is possible to so design systems as to enhance human beings rather than to diminish them and subordinate them to the machine.' But he goes on to say: 'it is my view that systems of this kind, however desirable they may be, will not be developed and widely applied since they challenge the power structure in society. Those who have power . . . are concerned with extending their power and gaining control over human beings rather than with liberating them' (p. 204). Thus the prediction is one of new technology de-skilling jobs as a result of management choice.

INVESTIGATIONS OF THE USE OF NEW TECHNOLOGY

Proponents of the work-simplification perspective have thus based their argument largely on an historical analysis of trends in managerial use of power and an assessment of the potential of new technology for allowing further simplification of jobs. Though they have introduced descriptions of selected forms of new technology to illustrate their view, they have not systematically investigated the issue empirically. Yet the validity of their position depends on demonstrating that in practice new technology generally results in simplified jobs. Let us now turn to evidence bearing on that point.

With the application of new technology still in its early stages, research on its implications for job design is also necessarily in its infancy and consists almost exclusively of exploratory case studies. One instructive investigation of this nature is reported by Buchanan and Boddy (1983), who examined the effects of new technology on the job characteristics and job attitudes of biscuit-making operators. Their focus was on two jobs: that of doughmen, who made the basic mix for the biscuits; and ovensmen, who baked them.

For doughmen, the job prior to the use of new technology involved considerable responsibility. As time-served master bakers they had a team of workers who brought ingredients from the stores. They supervised the mixing in large open vats, using their experience of sound, colour and touch to adjust the mix to produce the desired results. In short, they were skilled craftsmen in charge of others and were held personally responsible for their part of the production.

The new technology which was introduced revolved around 'recipe desks' in a central control room. Here recipes were stored on programs which activated controls to deliver the flour, water and sugar to the mixing machines. Each program also stopped the mixing cycle at appropriate intervals to allow small amounts of additional ingredients to be added (e.g. colouring and flavouring) and controlled the time, speed and temperature of the process. The doughman's job was now very different. At the start of each shift he checked on the recipe program and ensured the additional ingredients were available. He then: called up the program to the mixing machine; added the extra ingredients when the computer stopped the mix; passed a sample of the product to the ovensman for testing; and emptied the finished mix into a hopper for further processing (stamping out shapes, cooking and packing).

The mixing vessel was enclosed and the operator could no longer see, feel or hear the mix. If the equipment failed it was repaired by others. The doughman's job was retitled 'mixer operator' and classed as semi-skilled. The new technology had reduced the skill, responsibility and status of his work. The result was higher output and a reduced number of bad mixes. But these benefits were obtained at some cost. As some managers observed: 'It has made it a very boring job'; 'operators don't appreciate as fully as before the consequences of what they do'; 'it affects our ability to get foremen and managers from the operators' (p. 114). The doughmen themselves expressed similar views.

Before the introduction of new technology, ovensmen (the second group of employees to be considered) were responsible for baking biscuits and ensuring these were of the correct bulk, weight, moisture content and colour. This was a complicated skill because adjusting for one aspect (e.g. longer cooking or higher temperatures) could affect the others. Moreover, the required adjustments were not predictable, as mixes had different properties due to variations in their ingredients. Some flours, for example, absorbed more moisture than others. Maintaining the weight of biscuits within fine tolerances was an important production goal. Traditionally, information on this was fed back to the ovensman from the later packing stage where the biscuits were weighed manually. However, the new technology involved a computer-controlled checkweigher which fed results back to the ovensman much more quickly on a video screen in his work area. When this showed something was amiss, it remained his responsibility to adjust the baking process to ensure biscuits returned to within the right tolerances. In this case the new technology was seen as having enhanced the operator's job. A supervisor remarked that 'the feedback . . . makes operators more aware of passing problems down the line' (p. 115); and an ovensman felt that the technology had increased the interest and challenge in the job, as it provided a goal he could affect.

In this study, new technology clearly had different effects on the design of the two jobs and upon attitudes in the two cases. This was partly a function of the technology itself. But in part it was also a consequence of how jobs were designed around the technology. Wall *et al.* (1987) reach equivalent conclusions on the basis of a comparative study of job properties associated with the operation of alternative forms of new technology used in the assembly of computer boards.

Another study demonstrating divergent effects of new technology on operator jobs is reported by Clegg *et al.* (1984). They compared the use of CNC machine tools in two British engineering companies making components for aerospace customers. In one company the operator's job had been simplified much in the way that Braverman (1974) and Shaiken (1980) describe. A programming department was responsible for creating and proving out the programs which controlled the machine tools. Specialist tool and machine setters prepared the equipment. The previously skilled job of the operator was thus reduced to that of monitoring the machine and calling up help should something go amiss (e.g. breakage of a tool). In the other company responsibilities were allocated rather differently. As before, specialists produced the basic CNC programs. However, the CNC operators themselves proved out and edited the new tapes. They also undertook the bulk of their own tool setting and always set up their own machines. The operators reported that although they no longer needed some of the old physical skills, they still used all the basic engineering knowledge required to operate manual machines. Thus they had to read technical drawings and use their experience of cutting properties and speeds for different metals. In addition, however, they had acquired a range of new computing skills, so as to edit programs. They felt very positively about their new jobs.

Sorge *et al.* (1983) (see also I. Nicholas *et al.*, 1983) found similar contrasts in job design associated with CNC machine-tool use in a comparison of West German and British organizations. They found that in Germany more control was typically given to operators than in Britain, and they ascribed this to different 'work cultures' and traditions. They also showed how batch-size had different job-design implications. Where production consisted of small batches of complex components, one was more likely to find operators skilled in all aspects of CNC use. The authors argue that there are good economic reasons for this. Short runs and complex parts are most likely to encounter production problems requiring human intervention, even with the most advanced technology. If operators have the skill and are permitted to deal with these as they arise, disruption to production is minimized. However, larger runs and less complex parts encounter fewer problems. Here, centralized expertise, supporting less skilled operators, is sufficient to handle operational problems, and can be more cost-effective. Blumberg and Gerwin (1984), from an analysis of five case studies, and Cummings and Blumberg (1987) similarly argue that more complex manufacturing processes, because they involve greater uncertainties, encourage a move towards more skilled specifications for operators' jobs.

Several other studies, though not focused on job design, touch on the job and organizational implications of new technology. These cover such diverse applications and environments as: new mining automation (Burns *et al.*, 1983; B. Wilkinson, 1983); management information and office systems (Child, 1984b; Earl, 1984; Long, 1984; Mansfield, 1984); manufacturing systems (Goodman and Argote, 1984; Rosenbrock, 1983; Scarborough and Moran, 1985; Staehle, 1984; Wall *et al.*, 1984); process control systems (Butera, 1984; Ekkers, 1984); retail systems (Sawyers, 1984); printing technologies (Smith and Quinlan, 1983); and service industry (e.g. hospitals and banking) applications (Child *et al.*, 1984).

From the evidence available to date, the argument that new technology will foster the development of more simplified shop-floor jobs appears itself too simple. Certainly, examples of such a process have been documented and it could perhaps become the dominant trend. It is thus a justifiable fear, but not an established fact. The cited instances of equivalent new technology being associated with both simplified and enriched jobs make it clear that alternatives are available and that new technology can be used in different ways. Various factors affect the direction taken. Existing values concerning job design, be these explicit or implicit, must certainly have a strong influence. But so too do the logistics of production, prevailing trade-union positions, and skills available in the internal and external labour markets. As B. Jones concludes (1982): 'there are grounds for rejecting a unilateral motivation and capacity to deskill on the part of capitalist management' (p. 179); the extent to which simplification occurs will 'vary in accordance with differences in, and interrelationships between, trade union positions, product markets and pre-existing systems of management control' (p. 182).

It must be emphasized, however, that existing findings concerning the job design implications of new technology should be regarded as tentative, as they arise largely from atheoretical and opportunist exploratory studies of technology which in itself and its application is at a very early stage of development. One implication of this is that researchers should observe further technological progress and monitor its effects more systematically. That would indeed be helpful. However, a more exciting proposition is to take a proactive role. Existing principles of job design offer clear guidelines for the development and implementation of new technology; at the same time, the use of this technology shows up some of the limitations of current job design theory and practice and suggests directions for improvement. This relationship between the two areas of inquiry is considered next by way of a conclusion to the chapter.

CONCLUSIONS

Job design theory, even at its current stage of development, has an important contribution to make to the development of new technology. At present, most new technology is created, selected and implemented without explicit consideration of its job content implications. Typically, the process is dominated by technical specialists, whose objective is to automate as much of the work as possible. The human tasks can thus turn out to be those miscellaneous elements which it proved impossible or uneconomic to allocate to the machine. Increasingly, practitioners are recognizing that this strategy may be suboptimal, for it can lead to demotivating job requirements upon which the operation of the technology nevertheless crucially depends. They are consequently looking for a framework to handle the human side of such technological change at the stage of design and implementation. Job design theory offers one useful perspective.

The problem is how to put job design theory to work in this field. One approach is to include job design principles in the design of new technology itself. The work on 'human-centred systems' described by Rosenbrock (1983, 1985) and Corbett (1985) is a pioneering example of this, and it offers the prospect of new technologies allowing a greater range of possible job designs. Another strategy is to include 'human-centred criteria' in the choice and implementation of new technology. For many organizations this is the more practical alternative, as they purchase and adapt 'off the shelf' systems rather than design their own. And, as discussed earlier, the majority of new technology applications can be used in ways compatible with good as well as bad job design.

Here the involvement of personnel specialists, psychologists, social scientists, trade-union representatives, operators and other relevant employees in the implementation process would broaden the range of alternatives considered and encourage more creative experimentation (Clegg and Kemp, 1986). It seems likely that the door is now open for such an approach. Many organizations are in the early stages of using or planning new technology, which they see as necessary for economic survival and commercial development. Against this background, attitudes towards change are becoming more flexible, and people are willing to countenance issues which before were not open to discussion. In short there is a greater readiness to experiment with both technology and jobs.

A final point concerns the contribution which research into new technology may make to the development of job design theory and practice. Two major areas of weakness in existing job design approaches have already come to light. The first concerns the range of job characteristics covered. Most forms of new technology, if the employee is to be given responsibility for its operation, require that the individual has a clear conceptual grasp of how it works (including programming aspects). In other words, one important aspect is the requirement for abstract thought. This dimension is ignored by existing theory based on traditional technology. Second, as new technologies develop towards more integrated systems, whether these be Flexible Manufacturing Systems or general office systems, it becomes increasingly clear how operator jobs interrelate with a variety of other organizational factors, such as production planning methods, information systems, stock control, supervisory and management practices and structures, and specialist support functions. More than ever, the operator needs to understand how his decisions and actions are affected by, and will affect, the work of others using the system. These contextual factors affect the nature of jobs, and need to be taken into account both in designing jobs and assessing their effects. Again, they are not adequately covered by current approaches to job design. Such interrelationships are not unique to jobs associated with new technology. Rather, research into new technology serves to emphasize existing theoretical limitations and to stimulate the development of job design theory and practice more generally.

SUMMARY

This chapter began by considering the diffusion of new technology into work organizations and the many social and psychological issues to which this gives rise. Among these, the implications of new technology for the design of operator jobs and people's well-being at work was taken as a primary focus.

To set the scene, some central findings from studies of the effects of job characteristics on work attitudes and performance were introduced. These suggest that repetitive jobs requiring the exercise of little or no discretion on the part of the job holder have undesirable human consequences, and that designing jobs to enhance autonomy and control can be of value. The nature of new technology and its forms of application were then described.

Against this background, examination was made of the argument that the implementation of new technology will encourage the development of simplified jobs, in which control is removed from the operator. Research studies were introduced which showed how this could happen. At the same time they demonstrated that simplification is not a necessary consequence, and that the nature of jobs related to new technology is affected by a range of factors.

The chapter concluded by suggesting how job design principles could usefully be applied to enhance the design and implementation of new technology, and that job design theory and practice would benefit by its application in this area.

FURTHER READING

An authoritative and wide ranging account of new technology is provided in T. Forester (ed.), *The Information Technology Revolution* (Blackwell, 1985). This covers: the history of 'the computer revolution'; the use of new technology in the home, school, factory and office; and its impact on unemployment, the quality of work and industrial relations. *The Degradation of Work?*, edited by S. Wood (Hutchinson, 1982), focuses on the job design area, from a labour process perspective. Psychological and organizational aspects of manufacturing applications of new technology (including implementation, job design, selection and training, organizational design and industrial relations issues) are considered in T. D. Wall, C. W. Clegg and N. J. Kemp (eds.), *The Human Side of Advanced Manufacturing Technology* (Wiley, 1987). A useful annotated bibliography, *The Social and Economic Impact of New Technology 1978–1984*, covering the political, social, economic, industrial, administrative and industrial relations aspects of new technology, is provided by L. Grayson (Technical Communications, 1984).

14

Organizations as Psychological Environments

Roy Payne

The purpose of this chapter is to locate workers in the context of the organization as a whole. As Kahn *et al.* (1964) say: 'Organizations are reducible to individual human acts; yet they are lawful and in part understandable only at the level of collective behavior.' This chapter offers a typology of organizations, and indicates some of the forces that incline organizations to adopt particular patterns of organizing. A framework for examining roles is used to analyse how jobs differ at different locations in organizational structures and how those differences in roles affect satisfaction, stress and achievement.

TYPES OF ORGANIZATIONS

There are several typologies of organizations, the earliest of which were developed in the 1950s. The best known are those by Thompson and Tuden (1959), Blau and Scott (1963) and Etzioni (1961). All of these contain less than five types, and 'business' organizations in contrast to religious or military organizations are classified as a single type. It does not require much thought to appreciate the very different environments created in car manufacturing, steel-making, coal-mining, retailing or the commercial theatre, and thus to recognize the limitations of these early typologies. The 1960s gave rise to major research efforts to provide empirically based classifications of organizations, allowing much more sophisticated differentiation between business, commercial and service organizations, which in the earlier typologies were classified as a single type.

One of the most influential of these studies is that of Woodward

(1965), who classified manufacturing organizations according to the nature of their production technology; commercial and service organizations were excluded. Woodward created a dimension of production complexity which could be divided into three broad categories. The simplest mode of production was called Unit Production, because goods were made one by one (e.g. hand-made pottery, trains, and ships). The next broad grouping Woodward named Mass Production, where goods were produced in batches (e.g. cars, crockery, television sets). The final grouping covered the production of petro-chemicals, steel etc., which are made continuously, and was named Process Production. Woodward was able to show that different production technologies were associated with different sorts of organizational structures. Mass production companies tended to have more first-line supervisors, and the number of levels of authority in the organization tended to increase as the complexity of the production process increased. This study promoted the idea that technology was a major determinant of organizational structures and processes; the arguments for and against this can be found excellently argued in Gerwin (1981).

Two other contemporaries of Woodward also made an enduring impact on the field of organizational theory. They wrote a book called *The Management of Innovation* (Burns and Stalker, 1961). The modern electronics industry was in its infancy, and in studying twenty different firms, one of which was in electronics, Burns and Stalker observed how very different it was from the other organizations. They attributed this to the rapidly changing environment of electronics both in terms of technological change and market change. Survival in electronics involved regular adjustment to sometimes dramatic alterations, and this required a flexibility of the organization which more stable industries did not need. Burns and Stalker argued from this that organizations could be described as lying along a dimension, the extreme ends of which they named as 'mechanistic' and 'organismic'. These are described below in more detail.

Mechanistic	*Organismic*
1. Great division of labour and specialist tasks.	The person with the specialist knowledge goes where he or she is needed.

2.	Clear hierarchy of authority.	Authority vested in the people who can deal with the problem whoever they are.
3.	Precise definition of job duties, rules, etc.	Continual re-definition of individuals' jobs as the situation requires.
4.	Centralization of information and decision taking.	Information and knowledge may be located anywhere in the organizational network.
5.	Preponderance of vertical communication.	Preponderance of horizontal communication.

The mechanistic organization is closely similar to that described by the sociologist Weber (1947) as the 'ideal bureaucracy'. What is important about Burns and Stalker's contribution is their discovery of organic structures and the idea that, as environments get more complex and unstable, the organization needs to develop a structure capable of absorbing the uncertainty created: it needs to become more organic.

Both these studies had much influence on researchers in the United States and the United Kingdom. In the U K what came to be known as the Aston Studies (from the University of Aston) were started in the mid-sixties. These have been described in a series of books which have involved studies in communist Poland and capitalist Hong Kong and many countries in between (Pugh and Hickson, 1976; Pugh and Hinings, 1976; Pugh and Payne, 1977; Hickson and McMillan, 1981). What is distinctive about this work is that the investigators designed psychometrically sound measures of a wide range of aspects of organization structure *and* of the organization's technology and environment. These latter measures they called contextual, and examples of both are described below:

Context	*Structure*
Origin and history – whether an organization was privately or publicly founded, and the	*Specialization* – the degree to which an organization's activities are divided into

kinds of changes of ownership, location, etc. it has experienced.

Ownership and control – the kind of ownership (e.g. public or private) and its concentration in a few hands or dispersion into many.

Size – number of employees, net assets, market position, etc.

Charter – the nature and range of goods and services.

Technology – the degree of integration achieved in an organization's work processes.

specialized roles.

Standardization – the degree to which an organization lays down standard rules and procedures.

Formalization – the degree to which instructions, procedures etc. are written down.

Centralization – the degree to which the authority to take certain decisions is located at the top of the management hierarchy.

Configuration – the 'shape' of the organization's role structure, e.g. whether the managerial chain of command is long or short, or whether the organization has a large percentage of 'support' personnel.

The Aston group's research strategy was to predict structure from context, and then to relate different structures to measures of performance for organizations in different contexts. Little good research exists on the relationship between structure and performance, and what does has not provided strong evidence for the size and nature of the relationship between them. Relationships between structure and context, however, have been fruitful both empirically and theoretically. Essentially, the Aston studies have led to these conclusions:

1. Organizations control people and events by the use of rules and procedures (i.e. bureaucracy) or by decentralizing authority to

individuals (often specialists or managers and supervisors). There is little correlation between these two aspects of structure, so some organizations use mixtures of both.

2.   As organizations become larger, they get more specialists and they also rely more on rules, regulations and procedures for controlling what takes place (i.e. they become more bureaucratic).

3.   If an organization is heavily dependent on other organizations (e.g. it is owned by them, or it is part of local or central government) then this tends to centralize authority at the top of the subsidiary organization.

4.   The type of production technology affects the structure of the organization independently of the size of the organization. Its effect on the structure of rules and supervision tends to be greater at the bottom of the organization than among senior and middle management. The more complex the technology, the more specialists, rules and procedures are employed as control devices.

5.   Measures of structure are sophisticated enough to distinguish among organizations which have similar functions (e.g. schools or hospitals), and they can be used to create empirical taxonomies of organizations.

   Mintzberg has produced an excellent synthesis of the literature on organizational structures, and from it he has developed a typology which will be used as the basis for this chapter.

MINTZBERG'S CONCEPTS FOR ANALYSING ORGANIZATIONS

The Five Basic Parts

Mintzberg has written an abbreviated version of his original (1979) book in *Structure in Fives* (1983). The reason for the title will become clear. Mintzberg divides an organization into five basic parts. At the top is the

Strategic Apex, where policies are decided, plans made to execute them, resources allocated and orders given to ensure their execution. Below the apex is the *Middle Line* of employees, who are responsible for carrying out the orders and making sure the policies are pursued. To do the actual work itself (whether it is producing goods or providing a service) there is the *Operating Core*. In an organization like a university this is the staff of lecturers; in a hospital it is the doctors and the nurses. In other words, the operating core can consist of highly qualified individuals, though in many manufacturing organizations the role is filled by blue-collar workers, skilled and less skilled.

This central part of the structure is assisted by two other groups. Firstly, what Mintzberg calls the *Technostructure*. Individuals in the Techno-structure are analysts or technical advisors. They plan and design work, they select and train people to do the work, they decide strategies for controlling how work is done, but they do not directly produce the main output or service. A major role they have is to create standardization of products and processes and thus improve efficiency. Included here are staff within departments of personnel, work study or systems analysis. The second group to assist the main workflow is the *Support Structure*. These individuals and groups service the organization's needs by look-ing after buildings, keeping accounts, paying bills and wages, providing meals, distributing mail, etc.

Coordination Mechanisms

The task for the managers of an organization is to coordinate these five different parts so that they function as a purposeful whole. This is achieved in a number of ways; Mintzberg suggests five. The first is *Mutual Adjustment*. This relies on people communicating regularly, so that they can adjust to each other and changing circumstances. Much depends on trust and personal competence and commitment. Managers of a more autocratic bent, however, might prefer to use another method of coordination. They might like to keep a close eye on people, issuing instructions and monitoring their actions to see that the instructions have been carried out. Mintzberg identifies this as *Direct Supervision*.

If neither of these options is preferred or adequate, then the manager has to create some measure of control by standardizing one or more parts of people's work performance. There are three basic ways of standardizing. Firstly, one can *Standardize the Input* of personnel to the system. That is, the manager can select people who are trained to produce a standard performance. The training which professionals receive makes them responsible for achieving a 'professional standard'. If the task is too simple to demand the use of highly trained professionals, then the next option is to *Standardize the Work Processes*. That is, systems are carefully designed, rules provided about how to make the system work, and procedures are built in to monitor the quantity and quality of work achieved. The mass production process is based on this coordination mechanism.

If it is not possible to standardize either the input or the work process, then the organizational designer is left with *Standardizing the Output*. Those in the strategic apex produce clear and precise specifications for the quantity, quality and delivery of a product or service. Put simply, standardization of input controls *who* does things, standardization of work processes controls *how* things are done, and standardization of output controls *what* gets done. The social mechanisms for controlling *when* things are done and the *quality* of performance vary in these three. For organizations employing standardization of input, control of timing and performance is largely dependent on trust. Standardization of work processes depends on good design, and standardization of output relies on specification of standards and deadlines, and the sanctions associated with failure to meet them.

Mintzberg uses these five basic parts and five coordinating mechanisms to create a typology of organizations. There are five types. His ideas about the structuring of organizations are summarized in Figure 14.1, where the shapes at each of the five points indicate the relative importance of the five basic parts in each organizational type. Thus the Simple Structure has a largish strategic apex, no specialized support or technostructure at all, but a very thin middle line and a relatively large operating core. The Professional Bureaucracy has a tiny technostructure, large support structure, small middle line, very large operating core and relatively small strategic apex. In the Machine Bureaucracy the sizes of each of the five parts are relatively balanced.

Figure 14.1 also gives examples of the kinds of organizations that make up each type. Organizations using Simple Structure tend to be new, small and entrepreneurial; frequently governed by the owner (often also the founder) and not infrequently managed in a relatively

297

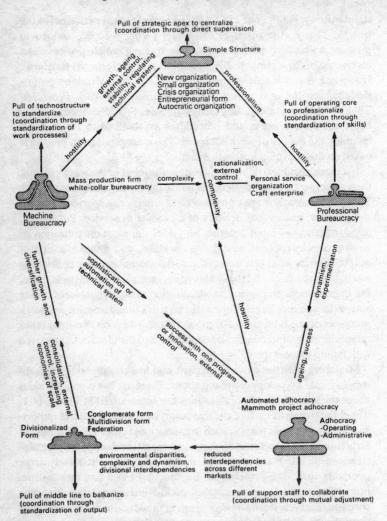

Pull of strategic apex to centralize
(coordination through direct supervision)

Simple Structure

growth, ageing
external control,
stability, regulating
technical system

professionalism

New organization
Small organization
Crisis organization
Entrepreneurial form
Autocratic organization

Pull of technostructure
to standardize
(coordination through
standardization of
work processes)

hostility

Pull of operating core
to professionalize
(coordination through
standardization of skills)

hostility

Mass production firm
white-collar bureaucracy

complexity

rationalization,
external
control

complexity

Personal service
organization
Craft enterprise

Machine
Bureaucracy

Professional
Bureaucracy

further growth and
diversification

sophistication or
automation of
technical system

dynamism,
experimentation

hostility

ageing, success

success with one program
or innovation, external
control

consolidation, external
control, increasing
economies of scale

Conglomerate form
Multidivision form
Federation

Automated adhocracy
Mammoth project adhocracy

Divisionalized
Form

Adhocracy
-Operating
-Administrative

environmental disparities,
complexity and dynamism,
divisional interdependencies

reduced
interdependencies
across different
markets

Pull of middle line to balkanize
(coordination through
standardization of output)

Pull of support staff to collaborate
(coordination through mutual adjustment)

Fig. 14.1   Mintzberg's pentagon typology of organizations. (From H. Mintzberg (1979), *The Structure of Organizations*. Reprinted by permission of Prentice-Hall Inc., Englewood Cliffs, New Jersey.)

autocratic manner. An Adhocracy is often new too, for they arise in fast-changing technologies such as computer companies. They also arise in large organizations, where they spring up as separate 'think tanks', examining where the company ought to be the decade after next. Dealing with rapid change and containing experts who are often from a range of disciplines requires them to put much effort into communication of a free-wheeling, informal kind, so their main coordination mechanism is mutual adjustment. The difficulties this presents and the lack of knowledge about how best to facilitate this sort of interdisciplinary cooperation are described by Epton *et al.* (1983). The epitome of the notion of an *industrial* organization is found in the Machine Bureaucracy, with its formally defined hierarchies and high use of specialists, combined with regulations, rules and procedures for controlling people and activities. Large, white-collar organizations, such as those in government, insurance and banking, also have this sort of structure.

In the Divisionalized Form, since the specialization comes from producing just a few standard products under the direction of the conglomerate or the directors of the multi-divisional company, the middle line and the operating core predominate, with small technostructure and support staff to provide basic needs and expert advice. While there may still be many regulations in the divisions of large companies, much control comes from the large numbers of managers and supervisors in the middle line.

The arrows in Figure 14.1 indicate the power struggles that occur within organizations, as members of the different structural types struggle to adjust to environments which are frequently changing. Take a small manufacturing organization using Simple Structure. As it grows it needs larger manufacturing facilities, and to design and service them it may employ technocrats who begin to exercise their power and influence on how the organization is run. This threatens the power of the strategic apex. If the organization's structure moves towards becoming a Machine Bureaucracy, then the occupants of the strategic apex will have to decentralize some of their power. If they do not, they lose the advantages of standardization of products and economies of scale.

The major conflict within a Machine Bureaucracy is between the technostructure and the middle line. If particular products become very successful, then the middle-line employees increase their power by turning the product(s) into a division. So the Machine Bureaucracy is threatened by the diversification and growth achieved by its own success, while the Divisionalized Form is always open to the threat of becoming over-specialized, out of date and defunct. The Divisional Form comes under pressure from 'bright boys' at head office, encouraging it to maintain flexibility in response to changing environments, but the Divisionalized Form's very success is built on keeping internal change at bay to optimize the benefits of specialization and standardization.

Although Figure 14.1 indicates the pulls among each of the five structural types, it is important to recognize that these pulls also exist within single organizations. By their very nature, organizations exist to do something which cannot be done by individuals on their own. This leads to the creation of a range of jobs and duties, and inevitably some jobs are more central to the task than others. Organizational theorists have more and more recognized the wide variety of ways in which politics and power distort the organizational designs that top decision-makers have created (e.g. Pettigrew, 1973; Pfeffer, 1981b). Thus in Figure 14.1 Mintzberg has conveyed the effects of markets, technologies and growth (size) on organizations, as well as the conflicts which arise within them from the occupants of the five basic parts (the strategic apex, etc.).

So far I have described a typology of organizations to illustrate the wide variety of organizations that exist. It must be recognized that the types in Figure 14.1 are ideal types. Most organizations are hybrids of more than one type, partly because this resolves some of the conflicts between the different parts of the organization, and partly because organizations are continually forced to adjust to the changing technical, commercial and political world that surrounds them. Thus, there are many more kinds of organizations than five. In thinking of the psychological implications of organizations, however, even five creates more complexity than can be fully dealt with in this short chapter.

To reduce the size of the problem I shall concentrate on a tiny sample of the potentially huge population of job environments. Figure 14.2 uses the five main types and each of the five basic parts to create a matrix of possible job environments. Clearly, organizations do not have a single internal environment. For example, the tasks and resources of people in the strategic apex differ from those in the operating core. Figure 14.2 indicates that there are twenty-five potential environments in these five

300

| ORGANIZ- | | BASIC PARTS | | | |
ATIONAL TYPE	strategic apex	middle line	operating core	support structure	techno- structure
simple structure	*				
machine bureaucracy					*
professional bureaucracy				*	
divisionalized form			*		
adhocracy		*			

Fig. 14.2 A matrix of possible job environments. Those indicated by an asterisk are examined in the text.

types of organizations. Since this is too many to deal with, we shall concentrate on those indicated by an asterisk. Examples from all five types and all five parts will thus be considered. In describing the kinds of environments each creates, I will refer to some of the literature which supports the suggestions made. My aim is to provide a framework for analysing how organizations create different psychological environments and some evidence supporting the claims the framework leads to.

SOME CONCEPTS FOR UNDERSTANDING THE PSYCHOLOGICAL ENVIRONMENT

The term 'psychological environment' is taken to refer to the effect an organization has on a person working in it. In considering psychological environments I will concentrate on their implications for achievement, affective satisfaction, and psychological strain.

The first thing that is likely to make an impact upon a person starting a new job is the *physical environment*: architecture, equipment, noise, lighting, decoration, use of plants, etc. While this will have an important effect on experience and behaviour, the physical environment varies enormously even within organizations of the same structural type. I will not, therefore, consider its effects, but direct the interested reader to Oldham and Rotchford (1983).

At least two concepts are necessary to understand the effects of jobs on experience. They are *role structure* and *role demands*. Role structure parallels the use of structure at the organizational level. It refers to the degree to which a job role is specified, and the degree to which the role-holder is given discretion about what, when and how he or she does the job. Roles can be very clearly defined with detailed written instructions, or they can be left unspecified and ambiguous. There is a considerable literature about role clarity, role ambiguity and role conflict which shows they are correlated with each other. The conclusion drawn is that clear jobs create less ambiguity and lead to less conflict among the role-holders of associated jobs. A meta-analysis of results relating these role variables to measures of job satisfaction shows that both role conflict and role ambiguity relate to lower satisfaction and more signs of psychological and physical illness (C. D. Fisher and Gitelson, 1983; see also Chapter 12).

The second element of role structure is discretion. While high discretion tends to be associated with more loosely defined jobs, such as those given to senior managers, the two role attributes are by no means the same. Some jobs can be clearly laid down, but leave the person discretion within the boundaries specified. Others may require even a manager to check with a senior before taking any decision that is not strictly routine. The balance between the degree of clarity in the role and the amount of discretion allocated to it is important, for between them they determine the degree of *control* the person has over his or her environment. Control is becoming a central concept in the stress literature, where lack of it seems to increase people's perceptions of stress which leads them to experience emotional strain (e.g. S. Fisher, 1984; Folkman, 1984). This theme has been developed further in Chapters 12 and 13.

Another potential stress at work arises from the *role demands*. This refers to what the person is required to do, and particularly to the quantity and quality of work to be done. Jobs which simultaneously demand high quantity and high quality can be particularly stressful. Such a situation can, of course, be very challenging and exciting, so it all depends on the strength of the demands. Too little demand leads to boredom, just enough to excitement, and too much to breakdown (McGrath, 1976).

Karasek (1979) showed that the most stressful, least satisfying jobs are those that have high demands combined with low discretion. Unskilled and semi-skilled blue-collar workers occur more frequently in this 'strained' quadrant, whereas managerial, technical and professional workers are more likely to be in 'active' jobs, with high levels of both discretion and demand (Kauppinen-Toropainen *et al.*, 1983).

One of the environmental factors which can modify the effects of job conditions of high demand and low discretion is the social 'climate' that exists among people doing the job. The concept of climate had an active research life in the 1960s and 1970s (Payne and Pugh, 1976; Jones and James, 1979), when it focused on *organizational* climate. It can, however, refer to the group climate, or the individual job climate. At the individual level the social relationships surrounding a person (climate) have been shown to have important consequences for mental health and even physical well-being. This literature is known by the title *social support*, and recent reviews can be found in Kessler *et al.* (1985) and Payne and Jones (1987). J. House (1981) argues that social support occurs in four different forms. Firstly, there is *emotional* support, where one person provides comfort and emotional security to another. Next there is *instrumental* support, where the stressed person gets direct help with things like money or practical assistance. Thirdly, House identifies *informational* support, where the support-provider gives information which can help the person to solve their problem (e.g. how to get a job, find a therapist, learn a relaxation technique). Finally, there is *appraisal* support, which is information about a person's decisions and actions in facing their situation. It is evaluative and helps a person to avoid self-delusion and/or making the same mistakes repeatedly. Receiving positive appraisals also encourages people to believe in themselves when they do begin to overcome a problem.

Having established some working concepts, we can now return to each of the five situations defined by Figure 14.2 and ask how particular kinds of organizations are likely to affect demands, discretion and social support for employees in different parts of the organization.

THE PSYCHOLOGICAL ENVIRONMENT IN THE STRATEGIC APEX IN A SIMPLE STRUCTURE

As indicated in Figure 14.2, organizations adopting a Simple Structure tend to be new, small and entrepreneurial. The functions of the strategic apex within such a structure are, therefore, likely to be carried out by a single person, probably the founder and owner of the company. The small size facilitates communication among the workforce, but also means the owner can closely supervise what is going on. The kind of environment created will depend much on the personality and leadership style of the owner, but successful entrepreneurs tend to be risk-takers and very hard workers whose behaviour is often characterized by hostility and aggressiveness. They do not understand workers who adopt a nine-to-five attitude to work, and thus can be difficult bosses (Kets de Vries, 1977).

While the owner has very high levels of discretion to decide what the company will make or sell, and how it will be made and managed, he or she has much less control over the customers, suppliers or banks which create the environment in which the organization operates. The role structure, therefore, is ambiguous and often full of conflict between the different demands made by groups in the environment. The role demands are almost certain to be strong in terms of quantity of work required, and, if the business is to grow rather than just survive, then many aspects of the role will require high-quality performance too. Since the owner is a generalist, often handling several specialist tasks such as marketing, design, production control and accounting, this makes it a most difficult job to do well.

Such stresses can be moderated by high levels of social support. However, many owners of small firms will not find this within the organization, and may depend on their spouse and family to provide it. Being the owner, with a large stake in the success of the company, and possibly trying to optimize the use of human resources in the early years of a company's development, often creates distance between them and the rest of the workforce. They have to keep an image of being tough and in control of problems, and this does not make it easy for such a person to receive emotional support from the workforce, or for them to provide it for the workforce.

Many small organizations have workforces that are willing to work overtime, and in this sense provide good instrumental support to the owner. Getting instrumental support from other companies such as consultants, banks, venture-capital companies and so on is often much more difficult, as the owner is often short of the resources and/or expertise which make this accessible.

As for appraisal support this again is difficult for the workforce to provide: telling the owner he or she is doing it wrong is not easy. Similarly, other organizations such as suppliers and customers are capable of benefiting from the entrepreneur's mistakes, so they are not necessarily objective with their appraisals.

All in all these jobs can provide a demanding and potentially stressful environment. What they offer in compensation, and this is the life-blood of the entrepreneur, is great satisfaction if a high level of achievement is obtained.

THE PSYCHOLOGICAL ENVIRONMENT IN THE TECHNOSTRUCTURE OF A MACHINE BUREAUCRACY

The typical Machine Bureaucracy is an old organization which has a large workforce. There is much horizontal and vertical differentiation resulting in many different levels and many departments and sections in each of them. They usually survive well if the environment remains stable and achieve economies of scale by standardizing products, and the processes by which employees, machines and materials are controlled. There is top-down decision-making, and formal rather than informal communication is encouraged. The managers and professionals in the technostructure design and maintain the procedures and practices which drive this system.

A group of specialists at the heart of such a 'technocracy' are those concerned with systems analysis and work study. Their role structure is usually quite clear: to define effective systems and procedures for getting work done. As trained specialists they will have reasonable discretion over how they go about this task. They will have much less discretion, however, over what jobs and systems they are to design. This will be determined ultimately by the strategic apex, but suggestions for change often come into conflict with the wishes of the middle managers and the workers. Thus the daily tasks of the technostructure are clear, but their inter-team connections are ambiguous and conflictual.

Role demands vary. A reasonable standard of quality is always expected, but the quantity of work tends to vary over time. It may be intense for months, as new systems are designed and installed, but it may then be quite comfortable and fairly routine.

Role supports tend to be supplied from within the specialism. Since they all tend to be from similar professional backgrounds, informational and instrumental support can often be quite good. However, the formality of Machine Bureaucracies is not the best place to foster intimate emotional support. Indeed, some large organizations have actually formalized their emotional support by employing full-time counsellors, occupational health specialists or welfare specialists to provide this sort of help. Appraisal also is often turned into a bureaucratic, formal procedure in these kinds of companies and is sometimes linked to pay and rewards. This has the effect of making appraisal a very controversial subject (Landy and Farr, 1983). Getting informal feedback on performance is made very difficult in such a climate.

In summary, the technocrat in a Machine Bureaucracy is likely to have a fairly predictable and moderately satisfying life. There may be short periods of stress, but there are opportunities to practise professional skills.

THE PSYCHOLOGICAL ENVIRONMENT IN THE SUPPORT STRUCTURE OF A PROFESSIONAL BUREAUCRACY

A university, polytechnic or hospital is a good example of a Professional Bureaucracy. They have many specialist departments and relatively few rules and regulations relating to work performance of the professional staff, though their moderate size can create bureaucratic controls in the administrative parts of the organization. Power is decentralized both horizontally and vertically, and the professionals in the operating core are the key personnel of the organization, since the organization achieves its goals through their professional skills and values (helping the patient or student in a professional relationship).

The support staff in such an organization are often professionals themselves (staff development specialists, research clinicians, etc.), but in the Professional Bureaucracy they are very much the servants of the members of the operating core. They therefore have influence rather than power. In terms of the concepts we are employing, their role is at first glance well structured. They have to be experts in their field and provide the service to the operating core. In fact, being in a professional environment, the support staff's clients (the professionals in the operating core) expect the support staff to educate them about the services they can provide. How they go about this educational/marketing process is not at all clearly specified, so they have clarity about their own knowledge but not about the ends or goals they are expected to achieve.

Role demands tend to be more about quality than quantity, for that is consistent with the professional values (Katz and Kahn, 1978). Since the professionals in the operating core often see support staff as peripheral to the main task, these support personnel have to work very hard to convince those in the operating core of the quality and value of their services.

Given their relatively low power and status in a Professional Bureaucracy, support personnel are largely dependent on themselves for providing social support. Other members of the organization expect the support professionals to be well informed, so informational support has to be worked for rather than readily received. Instrumental support too is also rarely forthcoming, because it may draw resources from the operating core itself: support staff may be seen as an expensive administrative 'overhead'. Most professional training involves values concerned with providing a service to the client. The underlying value of giving support to people is, therefore, widespread in professional organizations. As Gowler and Parry (1979) point out, however, this value also conflicts with the value of achieving professional standards in doing one's job: the professional should not be seen to be weak or unsure. The offering of emotional support to another can, therefore, be seen as an insult to the latter's professionalism.

As for appraisal, professionals are expected to set their own standards based on those inculcated in their professional education and training.

The challenge to support personnel in Professional Bureaucracies is considerable. If they succeed in persuading their colleagues to use their knowledge and skills, they can achieve much satisfaction and personal development. If they do not, there is no evidence from mortality and absence statistics that professionals suffer dangerous levels of stress (Fletcher and Payne, 1980), but these particular ones may experience considerable frustration.

THE PSYCHOLOGICAL ENVIRONMENT IN THE OPERATING CORE OF THE DIVISIONALIZED FORM

The key part of the Divisionalized Form is the middle line, but I have chosen to focus on the operating core because that specific structure creates what we typically think of as factory work. The Divisionalized Form tends to occur in old, stable industries where the market is well known and the divisions have been created to focus on specific products and markets. In achieving economies of scale, such organizations frequently produce large workforces, where the concentration of personnel, both workforce and its controlling management, is in the operating core. The organizational structure within a division is often like a machine bureaucracy, with standard operating procedures which are formalized into rule books and manuals. Because they are usually long-established they are often also highly unionized, thus tending to formalize relationships between management and workers. Because they are part of larger groups, the management of a division will often have to refer industrial-relations issues to headquarters staff, which is indicative of the lower levels of discretion found at all levels in the Divisionalized Form.

The role structure of jobs in the operating core is usually clear and unambiguous, for the jobs are often simple and have short cycle times. The production technology may be such that both quantity and quality of role demands are determined by the machinery rather than the operator. This is not to say the jobs are not demanding. They are often physically demanding, requiring the maintenance of uncomfortable physical postures for extended periods. They may also be mentally demanding, either because they are totally boring, or because they are very repetitive but still require constant attention. They also permit the worker very little discretion, even to the point where he or she may have to ask a supervisor for permission to go to the toilet. Because stopping the production process is likely to be very expensive, operators may also be closely supervised and somewhat harassed by first-line supervision.

In a comparison of twenty-three different occupations, Caplan *et al.* (1975) found workers in these repetitive machine-minding jobs had worse mental and physical health and were much less satisfied than professional workers, even though some of the professional groups worked many more hours (40 versus 55 hours per week). It is these sorts of jobs that often create the strained conditions described by Karasek (1979) in terms of high demand and low discretion.

The evidence from the Caplan study and others is that these groups of workers also have low social support. The noise and physical layout of such plants often hinders interpersonal communication. The simplicity and fractionated nature of the tasks mean that individuals are given information only about their part of the process and often lack a wider understanding of what is taking place. Instrumental support also tends to be focused on what needs to be done to keep production going. The communication barriers and narrow focus inhibit the development of emotional relationships. In many factories friendships can only develop round the lunch break or the trade-union meeting. Traditional work communities such as mining, steel-making and ship-building often overcame these difficulties by creating community solidarity outside the work organization itself. However, modern urban populations travel to work over much greater distances, and this community support is, therefore, much less readily available. These points were well made in the 1960s, in a book *The Affluent Worker* (Goldthorpe *et al.*, 1968). The title indicates the reward that can come from work in the operating core of a divisionalized firm: to compensate for the strain such jobs entail and the lack of personal achievement they provide for most workers, the jobs are often well paid.

THE PSYCHOLOGICAL ENVIRONMENT IN THE MIDDLE LINE OF AN ADHOCRACY

Adhocracies spring up in new technologies and the fast developing markets they create. They are by definition young, staffed by well-educated professionals even in the operating core, and usually small in size. The boundaries between the middle line, the operating core and the support structure are in fact very blurred. Power comes from knowledge and expertise rather than location in the structure. There are few formal communication channels, and people go where they need to get information and resources to get 'their' job done. Informal communication is significant in all parts of the organization. In its early days Apple Computers held beer parties every Friday afternoon, attempting to make sure everyone stayed in touch with everyone else.

The role structure of a manager in the middle line in most organizations is to create stability, and this must be part of the job even in an Adhocracy, but uncertainty and change make it a difficult task. The role is very unclear, full of ambiguities and fraught with conflicts from customers, colleagues and advisers from the support structure. Since the allocation of authority in Adhocracies is not formally controlled, the manager appears to have high discretion. Indeed, he or she has, except that other colleagues may interfere with the operation of that discretion if they feel, or can prove, that the decisions being recommended have costs for design, production or customer satisfaction. Decision-making influence is repeatedly up for negotiation: it is the most politicized of the five structures. In terms of role demands, innovation and quality are what is expected. People may or may not work hard at producing these, but many work very hard indeed. Hard work alone, however, will not make for success in Adhocracies: their success depends on creativity and innovation.

The success criteria indicate the sort of support that might be expected in an Adhocracy. The whole system is set to reward innovation and creativity. Rigidity and an inability to produce the goods when they are required will just as rapidly receive criticism. So appraisal is only too readily available, but it tends to be informal and not necessarily carried out with skill or sympathy.

Information abounds in Adhocracies, but the user needs to ask for it and also has to ask if it is the information he or she wants. These organizations are full of people with idiosyncratic solutions to problems, and information is easily offered. However, the sheer volume and variety of information presents the user with the challenge of choice. Information also tends to be task-based rather than social-process based. These organizations are driven by technological developments, and interpersonal skills do not usually play a large part in job specifications. For this reason Adhocracies often appoint specialist project managers, whose role it is to create coordination among the varied experts. In describing work in the Moon Project at NASA, Sayles and

Chandler (1971) describe their role: 'The project manager must constantly seek to penetrate the organizations upon which he is dependent but which he does not directly supervise . . . *Time* is of the essence and constant *monitoring* is the rule. *Knowing whom to contact, when and how is crucial'* (p. 212).

While Adhocracies are emotional places, being full of drama and joy, despair and elation, they are not noted for a high level of emotional support. They are competitive places where empathy may be common and sympathy rare. Equally common may be the provision of good instrumental support. These organizations often function in environments where the job has to be done regardless of cost. Like everything else in an Adhocracy, however, this can change quickly. Yesterday's front-runner can easily become tomorrow's also-ran.

For people with creative ability and a high tolerance for ambiguity who wish to be at the forefront of their field or profession, the Adhocratic structure provides a stimulating environment. The achievements and the satisfaction they bring, including financial rewards, may be sought at the cost of some strain, but rewards frequently outweigh the costs. For the 'organization man' the Adhocracy would be a nightmare.

CULTURAL DIFFERENCES

The research data and the concepts so far used have been drawn largely from the United States and the United Kingdom. The last decade, however, has seen a growing interest in cultural differences in organizational structure and behaviour. An excellent summary of this literature has been presented by Pugh (1985). This discusses the notion that organizations even in different countries are becoming more and more alike owing to the pressures of increasing size, changing technology and political and market forces. There is evidence that as organizations grow they become more bureaucratic, even in a worker-owning state like Communist Yugoslavia (Tannenbaum *et al.*, 1974). Pugh quotes similar trends for other countries.

On the other hand, even in large Japanese companies there are far fewer rules, regulations and specifications about who does what. This is because Japan does not attempt to educate specialists as such. People are trained to do a range of jobs. Since pay is based on seniority rather than the work done, employees are willing to learn new jobs whenever this is required. Japan also tends towards single-union plants, so if a plant fails the union fails. As up to 50 per cent of earnings can be paid in bonus, a Japanese company can cut costs but not make people redundant by simply cutting the annual bonus. This protects both worker and organization: this added security alters the psychological contract between organization and employee, regardless of the organizational structure employed.

Even within Europe, Maurice (1979) found that French organizations of the same size, using the same technology as German organizations, had more organizational levels and greater pay differentials. Maurice attributes this to the more élitist French education system.

Finally, we should note that organizations not only vary across cultures, they produce their own internal cultures. This is an area of research that has developed rapidly in recent years, and its insights into organizational life have been well illustrated by Morgan (1986).

SUMMARY

This chapter shows how organizational structures develop as a result of decisions about how to respond to pressures and opportunities in the environment, and political pressures from powerful sub-groups within the organizational system itself. The social complexity this produces means that even within an organization there are a range of psychological environments created by differences in function and location in the structure. Five of these were illustrated to show how differences in job demands, job discretion and social support lead to differences in achievement, job satisfaction and psychological strain. Finally, it was noted that cultural factors also play their part in shaping the organization as a psychological environment.

FURTHER READING

Apart from Mintzberg's books mentioned in the text, the development of organization theory is concisely presented by J. Child in *Organizations: a Guide to Problems and Practice* (Harper and Row, 1984). The essential ideas of the major thinkers about the subject of organizing work can be found in *Writers on Organizations* by D. S. Pugh and colleagues (Penguin, 1983). A textbook which takes a more psychological orientation is F. J. Landy's *Psychology of Work Behavior* (Dorsey, 1985): it covers a wide range of subjects of a psychological nature, but says less about how they might apply to organizations with different characteristics. K. Weick's book *The Social Psychology of Organizing* (Addison-Wesley, 1979) presents an idiosyncratic but stimulating perspective on social processes in organizations.

15

Change in Organizations

Stephen Fineman and Iain Mangham

Work organizations, such as factories, offices, workshops, schools and universities, often convey an impression of order and regularity. Indeed, the essence of 'organization' is the achievement of a certain stability over time; a similar range of faces, tasks and routines. For people inside organizations, stability can lend a reassuring predictability to their work. For some, though, such predictability is just what is wrong: a lack of new ideas, old-fashioned work practices, unquestioned ways of management.

Thus, people at work vary considerably in their desire for change and how much energy they will commit to achieving it. Executive efforts to change others' working practices for 'sound economic' reasons, or in order to 'increase efficiency', can be met with responses varying from enthusiasm to vigorous resistance. Consideration of change, therefore, firmly focuses our attention on the social organization of work. This chapter will examine ways by which we can view, create, and evaluate change.

WHY CHANGE?

The demand for organizational change may arise for a number of reasons. Today, it is common to express a need for change in order for a company to survive. The logic of commercial enterprises (competition, profit, growth) presses directors and managers to seek cheaper, more efficient, means of production and administration. Here, the apparent goals of changes are strictly economic: to ensure that the business survives to provide a sufficient return of income to its investors.

314

Non-commercial organizations, such as police and social work departments, the civil service, schools and other publicly funded bodies, may need to look for ways of providing their services on less money. Like private industry, they can be vulnerable to economic recession and government ideology. Changes in attitudes and work practices may be necessary in order to meet new stringencies.

The forces for change in these circumstances emanate from the broader environment: the social, political and market context in which the organizations are located. Yet change can be more locally inspired. A new managing director or supervisor may wish to improve the organization of work, expand a department, reduce waste, lift morale, reduce absenteeism, or expunge inefficiency. Alternatively, a shop-floor committee or union representative may argue for safer equipment, shorter working hours, higher production quotas, or non-redundancy agreements. This can press management into negotiation towards agreeing new practices.

Our initial appreciation of change should, therefore, consider three aspects:

1. The *initiating circumstances* of change: its social and political context; what is wanted by whom.

2. The *manifest* goals of change: for example, improved working conditions, more pay, greater efficiency, a restructuring of the organization, new attitudes.

3. The *latent* goals of change. Some social analysts (e.g. Argyris and Schon, 1974; Silverman, 1970) draw our attention to the importance of considering what we would term the hidden agenda, or symbolic significance, of change. For example, a managing director may declare his or her desire to make the organization more efficient by replacing key personnel and changing the shape of the enterprise. But the undeclared end can be to demonstrate the wielding of personal power. This type of behaviour is often the image portrayed of big-corporation, Dallas-type, politics (see also Iacocca, 1985). The principles, however, seem far more generalizable (Mintzberg, 1985; Pfeffer, 1981b). Many of us will disguise our personal desires in the more 'acceptable' logic and language of organizational efficiency and effectiveness.

MODELS FOR CHANGE

How change occurs, or is brought about, is intimately connected to the way an organization is seen to operate and how decision-making is expected to take place. The literature provides us with a number of contrasting perspectives. In this chapter we will consider four: the structural, human resources, political, and symbolic approaches.

The Structural Approach

This perspective has its origins in a number of writers. It is related to the philosophical comments of people such as Herbert Spencer (1873), who held that the 'superior' (who were to become known as 'managers') were to lead those less gifted – the 'workers'. However, its major source lies in the thoughts of Frederick 'Speedy' Taylor (1911), the father of scientific management. His ideas on the breaking down of tasks and the role of management in planning the execution of them were filled out by others such as Henri Fayol, Luther Gulick and Lyndell Urwick (1943). This stream of thought was also connected to the views of Max Weber (1947) on bureaucracy, and others who followed his thinking, notably Peter Blau (1955) and Charles Perrow (1972).

The structural approach is based upon a number of characteristic assumptions:

1. Organizations exist to accomplish purposes or goals.

2. For any organization there is an appropriate structure for the realization of its purposes or goals; this possibility has been explored in Chapter 14.

3. Tasks must be highly differentiated.

4. Supervision must be effected through a clear chain of command and through the application of impersonal rules.

5. Only those at the top have the capacity and opportunity to direct the enterprise.

For those of this persuasion it seems obvious that any problems may be resolved by redesigning the structure to fit better with the purposes of the enterprise. Such people tend to be concerned with goals, roles, relationships and formal ways of controlling and coordinating activities. Work-study experts help to specify the most efficient cycle of operation for a task. Personnel managers will develop comprehensive job description and methods of individual assessment, and systems engineers will design optimum ways of establishing and linking the mechanisms of production and information flow.

The vast majority of change efforts have reflected this kind of philosophy. A study by Miles (1975), for example, of 1000 managers indicated the distrust they had in their subordinates' capacity for self-direction and control; their preference was clearly for a fairly authoritarian style of management, at least where methods and control of work were concerned. This orientation is summarized rather pithily by Herman-Taylor (1985):

> The guiding belief here is that if you can explain clearly to a subordinate what you want him or her to do, and you can devise a suitable system for measuring his or her performance and then reward or punish him or her accordingly, the desired result, in terms of strategy execution, will be achieved. (p. 390)

Expressed in this way, change from a structural perspective closely resembles features of behaviourism, or stimulus–response psychology (e.g. Skinner, 1971). Indeed, it is hard to find an organization which does not use rewards and punishments in *some* form to encourage development or change, or to maintain regularity and order. The most obvious examples are the formal reward systems, such as piece-work, prizes for salesmen, and salary increments for good performance. These are deliberately manipulated rewards. Likewise, the withholding of benefits, delaying someone's promotion, demoting, or threatening dismissal, are devices of 'negative reinforcement'.

Behaviourism has been used more literally, and self-consciously, to induce change in organizations. For example, Luthans *et al.* (1983) describe attempts to improve the quality and quantity of performance in a large production organization. One hundred and thirty-five production supervisors received special training which enabled them (a) to identify measurable employee behaviours that contributed to more effective performance, (b) to chart the frequency of the occurrence of the behaviours, and then (c) to provide specific attention and recognition to employees, encouraging the appropriate behaviours and performance. Through such Skinnerian reinforcement, the authors claim to have achieved marked increases in performance quality and quantity over a range of different products.

Employee productivity is only one area where 'organizational behaviour modification' has taken place. Applications have been reported on problems of absenteeism and tardiness, safety and accident prevention, and sales performance. Organizations have ranged from restaurants and retail stores to airlines and telephone companies. All have developed systematic programmes to reinforce and extinguish specific behaviours, in order to achieve desired outcomes (Frederiksen, 1982; Luthans and Kreitner, 1985).

There is persuasive evidence that change can be brought about in this manner, and such methods appear quite consistent with a structural approach. A key debate, however, is whether the ends justify the means: whether such psychological pragmatism is ethically defensible (see Rogers and Skinner, 1956; Gregory, 1971; Salaman and Thomson, 1980).

The Human Resources Approach

After the Second World War social scientists began to respond to what they considered the dehumanizing and dysfunctional consequences of structural approaches to organizations. The sociologist Robert Merton (1957) spoke of the 'bureaucratic personality', noting the petty bureaucrat who was preoccupied with rules and forms as ends in themselves. C. Wright Mills (1951) developed the theme of 'alienation' in this context, considering the big organization which spawns paper-processors who are divorced from any resultant product and who also become divorced from themselves.

Evidence of the unresponsiveness of the bureaucratic organization to human needs was emerging from other work. The results of the Hawthorne Studies carried out in the late 1920s were taken to illustrate the importance of social factors and informal groups on satisfaction and performance at work (Roethlisberger and Dickson, 1939). Lewin (1951) extended these findings into a 'field theory' of human functioning which stressed the centrality of people's perceptions of their environment and in particular the nature of the social group which affected these perceptions and the values it supported.

The view that jobs are something to do with the quality of people's lives, and are not just a means of material production, is the bench-mark of humanistic writers, who essentially define the human resource approach. Workers' feelings and social settings are seen as the key to the process of organization. Consequently, it is argued that management practices and organizational structures should provide opportunities for individuals to fully realize their potential for psychological growth, and to participate in a range of important work affairs (Maslow, 1943; McGregor, 1960; Argyris 1962, 1964; Likert, 1961).

To summarize the major assumptions of the human resource approach for change:

Individuals have needs which they seek to satisfy in organizations: they do not exist in order to serve the purposes of organizations.

The relationship between individuals and organizations is symbiotic; they need each other. Organizations need energy, talent, skill, endeavour, enthusiasm; and people need careers, money and the opportunity for self-actualization. When the fit is good, both prosper.

Democratic leadership is the most effective means of managing so as to realize the optimum fit.

Openness and participation are the most effective means of demonstrating democratic leadership.

Early applications of human resource principles to change in work settings focused on participative approaches. In 1948, for example, Coch and French conducted a field experiment comparing four different ways in which work groups could manage change. A garment factory was changing its product and packaging, which necessitated new work methods and posed a threat to incentive earnings. In two groups of operators everyone participated in a discussion about the need to change and what had to be done. A third group appointed representatives to act on their behalf. A final group, acting as a control, had a meeting where the change details were simply announced to them. Subsequently this group showed a considerable drop in output, was aggressive towards management, had high labour turnover, and was eventually disbanded. By way of contrast, the fully participating groups took only four days to reach their pre-change levels of production and eventually settled at a 14 per cent increase on this. The group which nominated a representative took fourteen days to reach its pre-change level, and remained at that level.

This investigation was followed by a number of field experiments and correlational studies, some of which indicate the benefits of a participative approach, while others reveal no such advantage (e.g. French *et al.*, 1960; Fleishman, 1965; Juralewicz, 1974). The complexity of both studying and evaluating participation is revealed in more critical reviews (Warr and Wall, 1975; Bate and Mangham, 1981; Bartlem and Locke, 1981). Among the questions arising are: who judges the 'benefits' of participation, and by what criteria?; what types of change are facilitated by participative methods?; what are the cultural and situational circumstances which lend themselves to participation?; can some processes of participation end up looking like, and feeling like, processes of mechanistic control?

Participation has become a cornerstone of human resource approaches to organizational change. It is also a significant strand of a far broader, humanistically based, orientation to change called *Organization Development* (OD). This is a term which describes the application of behavioural science knowledge to the planned development of organizational strategies, structures and processes. In its purest form OD applies to an entire organizational system, such as a whole company, a complete department, or a working group. It recognizes the interdependency of the parts of an organization and aims at both the creation and reinforcement of change for increased effectiveness.

Through formal and informal networks, including specialist publications, OD has become an international phenomenon. Its roots, though, are firmly American and can be found in the 'laboratory training' movement, the development of survey research and feedback, and in the work of Kurt Lewin. It is helpful to examine this background a little more closely, as it expresses the philosophy and techniques of today's OD.

Laboratory training involves a small group of strangers learning from their own interactions and evolving group dynamics to achieve changes in behaviour 'back-home'. Initial attempts with the technique (in the late 1940s) by Kurt Lewin and his team at the National Training Laboratories led them to conclude that training groups (abbreviated to 'T-groups') were a rich and powerful medium for learning and change. Their efforts came to be adopted and developed for use in a wide range of organizations.

A typical T-group programme might consist of five or six long meetings of a group of ten to fifteen strangers. If several people from the same organization attend, then they are usually assigned to different groups. Unlike traditional group or committee meetings, the T-group has no specific agenda. At the beginning of a training session, a trainer, who sits in, announces that his or her role is to serve as a resource to the group. Then, after a brief introduction, there is a lapse into silence. Given the vacuum in leadership the group has to work out what to do next and how to organize itself.

What happens then is very much a matter of the 'here-and-now'. Group members will try out different roles and various ways of influencing others in attempting to come to grips with the procedure, or lack of procedure. Many attempts can fail. One person may try very hard to direct others towards his way of thinking. Others rebuff him; they tell him to stop trying to take over things. He eventually backs off and starts reading a book as if sulking. Is this indicative of his typical response to frustration?

The trainer's job is to help participants gain insight into their own and others' feelings and behaviours in a supportive climate. He or she encourages individuals to examine immediately the impact of their behaviours, and to understand what is going on in the group.

What changes, if any, do T-groups bring about in work attitudes and behaviour? Because of the intensity of the event, it is perhaps not surprising that there have been accounts of individuals emerging over-anxious and disturbed from T-groups, so there is an indication that they can have their dangers (Cooper and Mangham, 1971). However, a more dominant picture is one of increased flexibility in role behaviour; more openness, receptivity, and awareness; more open communication with better listening skills, and less dependence on others (Dunnette *et al.*, 1968; P. Smith, 1980). Yet such conclusions have been criticized for being based upon reports which lack scientific rigour (Campbell and Dunnette, 1968; Campbell *et al.*, 1970).

It does appear that T-groups can influence what people feel and do, and therefore contribute to change. How *general* this effect is across different people and different work situations is hard to judge. Furthermore, the expressed values of openness and trust which underpin T-groups are, self-evidently, normative. They reflect a humanistic view of interaction and organizing. If the back-home situation operates instead by, say, mechanistic principles, the transfer of learning from the laboratory training can be difficult, leading to anti-climax and possibly stress. For these reasons it is important that T-group experiences are part of the training for all members of a working unit, and are tied in with an appropriately supportive culture back at work. Indeed, T-group effects on 'hard' indices, such as productivity and absenteeism, are most noticeable when the groups are specifically structured to be relevant to these outcomes (J. Nicholas, 1982).

The second major source of influence on OD practice is *survey research and feedback*. This is probably the widest-used OD method for encouraging change on an organization-wide basis. The guiding philosophy behind the survey approach is, like T-groups, concerned with confronting individuals with aspects of themselves as an essential precursor to change. It reflects a three-stage model of the change process outlined by Lewin (1951):

1. *Unfreezing.* A procedure to unlock or disengage organizational members from their conventional organizational practices; to draw attention to and examine the differences between what people do and believe now, and what they would like to be and do.

2. *Moving.* The development of new values, attitudes and behaviours through changes in organizational structures and processes.

3. *Refreezing.* The new state of the person or organization is stabilized. Norms of work, and organizational policies, are developed accordingly.

This framework has been developed and refined over the years but remains at the heart of many 'orthodox' OD programmes. It was implicit in a 1948 study described by Mann (1961). Researchers conducted a systematic, company-wide attitude survey of management and workers at the Detroit Edison Company. They then fed back their findings through an 'interlocking chain of conferences'. This started with top management and then moved to task groups (comprising supervisors and their immediate subordinates) throughout the organization. It was the researchers' intuitive belief that this process itself encouraged change. Two years later they were to be more specific in their conclusions following a repeat survey in the same company. In a natural experiment, they compared changes in departments which received feedback with those that did not. They reported more significant, positive changes among those who had received feedback. In Lewinian terms, the survey had started the unfreezing process, and the feedback had set the scene for shifts in attitudes and behaviour, which in turn were consolidated (refrozen) in the norms of new work practices.

A British application of survey feedback in a change programme by Warr *et al.* (1978) illustrates some of the nuances, and problems, of the approach. A questionnaire opinion survey of all members of four departments of a steel works was introduced as part of an ongoing programme of change aimed at improving the climate of employee relations. The questionnaire items were drawn from an extensive list of problems and issues already identified by representative 'project groups' of workers and managers. The questionnaire provided an opportunity to contact all of the employees, approximately 1000 of them, for their views on what needed changing, and to feed back the results in order to determine possible actions.

Questions of general, and departmental, concern were contained in a specially produced project newspaper. They were framed as simple statements to be endorsed, disagreed with, doubted, or found non-applicable. Typical items were: 'Shop floor workers in my department are good at making complaints, but not so good at making positive suggestions'; 'Managers in this works are changed around too often for them to be able to do a good job.'

The results were presented in another edition of the newspaper, giving readers an overview of opinions in the works as well as departmental trends. A separate, job-by-job, breakdown was available on request, but few took up the offer. A special Project Steering Committee of management, workers and the researchers considered the survey findings separately. From this it was decided to change a number of industrial relations procedures, which was encouraging. But when the works manager was presented with the survey results (and the opinions from project groups) he evaded most specific actions, suggesting that 'Things here are not as bad as in some other works that I know'. The project groups themselves were asked to incorporate the survey feedback into their own, more localized, discussions about possible changes, but they were found to focus upon current practical difficulties rather than systematically examining results fed back from the earlier survey.

This case illustrates that the practicalities of survey feedback can be more problematic than the simple elegance of the model suggests. It appears to be of crucial importance that the medium is suitable for those involved. If 'the lads don't like filling in bits of paper' (a sentiment expressed by some shop stewards in the study), then responses immediately begin to lack validity. Management, likewise, can pay lip service to the questionnaire process, but reveal their true feeling when confronted with their responsibility for taking action. The momentum of an organization-wide change project is very likely to carry along individuals of varying degrees of interest and commitment, some of whom can be essential to the success or failure of the project. When challenged, these people can readily deny the worth of the questionnaire items, or denigrate the 'accuracy' of the statistics, influencing their colleagues and subordinates in an adverse manner.

In sum, to be successful, a survey feedback programme must pay particular attention to: the nature and structure of the organization involved; the contract with participants and their understanding of the action implications of their involvement; the presentation of the survey and the way feedback is organized; and mechanisms to develop and monitor change following feedback. (See Bowers, 1973; S. M. Klein *et al.*, 1971; Mohrman *et al.*, 1977.)

T-groups and survey feedback indicate something of the range of interventions associated with O D. As the movement has developed, a variety of techniques have evolved which have both extended and developed this range, some aimed at individual change, others concerned with group and intergroup matters, and still others focused on the organization as a whole: its strategy, reward system, technology, and skills of its members. Much of the theory behind such applications derives, as we have indicated, from human resource assumptions of organization. More recently, however, developments in OD have acknowledged that a comprehensive approach to developing an organization should include an examination of the goals and structures of that enterprise, alongside the more traditional, person-centred OD analysis. We have also witnessed a growing awareness of political and symbolic activity as being a legitimate part of OD (e.g. Mintzberg, 1985), approaches that we will discuss shortly.

Individual interventions are aimed at bringing about personal changes in skills, attitudes or behaviours which will influence (and be influenced by) organizational relationships. Much of this work rests upon psychotherapeutic theories of counselling. For example, a 'gestalt' consultant will press for deeper exploration of individual and interpersonal problems than one concerned with quickly locating objective solutions to difficulties. The gestalt worker will encourage clients to fully air their passions and to express how anxious, aggressive or powerless they might feel. It is an approach which attempts to capitalize and build upon the disturbance it creates in seeking longer-term change and client understandings (Harman, 1974; Herman, 1972). Sometimes counselling is directed towards change in a particular problem area, such as personal stress. Utilizing both theoretical knowledge about the aetiology of stress, and principles of counselling, the interventionist works with a client to produce changes which will directly affect the management or alleviation of stress (K. Davis and Newstrom, 1985; Fineman, 1983a, 1985).

Transactional analysis is an interpersonal diagnostic tool, used for assessing the many transactions and 'games' that occur between people; it was pioneered by the psychiatrist Eric Berne (1964). In organizational settings it has been used to help people to become more sensitive to the nature of their interactions with others, such as colleagues or customers, and to be aware of more effective behaviours. The language of transactional analysis contains notions of 'ego states' – Parent, Adult and Child. According to Berne, psychological difficulties occur when one or more of these states unduly dominates, or disturbs a 'healthy balance'. It is argued that in everyday organizational life we can all profit from a better understanding of how the three ego states are being used in a given situation. Problems are most likely to arise in crossed transactions, such as when an employer gives an Adult direction to an employee, but the Child in the employee responds as though dealing with a Parent (see Rush and McGrath, 1973).

One widely employed individualistic OD technique is that of Life-Career Planning. Firmly based on humanistic principles, Life-Career Planning meets the desires of organizational members to achieve their potential by helping them to examine their life goals and plans. Lippitt (1970) argues that, among other things, such activity demonstrates the care and social responsibility of the organization, while more effectively releasing the potential of the individual on behalf of the organization.

Typically, Life-Career Planning takes place in a structured workshop. Participants are given a number of self-reflective questions or activities; they then discuss their responses in a supportive group. For example, there is a 'Who am I?' exercise where that question is answered in ten different ways on separate sheets of paper. Another device is the composition of a 'life inventory', a record of all that a person has done and would like to do. It is expressed in terms ranging from 'peak' experiences to 'values to be realized'. All this material contributes to the setting of life objectives: helping the individual to reflect on what he or she wants out of life and work, and what career steps and development might assist in reaching one's objectives.

There are a number of OD *group interventions* which aim to assist groups to change and become more effective. *Process consultation* and *team building* are major approaches.

A process consultant does not offer expert help to a group, as a doctor to a patient. Rather, the process consultant observes group members in action and helps them to diagnose the nature and extent of their own problems and to work together by learning to solve those problems. The precise nature of change is ultimately determined by the client (in this case the group). Group members are encouraged to admit to or accept responsibility for personal ideas and feelings; to be open to others' feelings; and to suggest new ideas and thoughts for the rest of the group to consider (Schein, 1969; M. Foster, 1972). Through techniques of observation and feedback, the process consultant will assist the group in examining itself and certain of its activities, such as patterns of decision-making and styles of interaction.

Process consultation seems to have been fairly successful in achieving a greater feeling of group effectiveness within organizations, mutual influence, and well-being among group members (Kaplan, 1979;

Lippitt, 1969; Argyris, 1965). Its effect on 'harder' indices of perform-ance, such as production quantity and quality, and financial profit, has been more difficult to determine.

Team building helps work groups to improve the way that they accomplish their tasks and the quality of their interpersonal and problem-solving skills. It addresses a range of difficulties that perma-nent or temporary teams may encounter, but which they find difficult or impossible to rectify by themselves, such as apathy, their lack of interest in their work, hostility and conflicts, low productivity, complaints from others, lack of innovation, and confusion about aims and purpose. Clearly, teams with such problems may impair the operation of the organization as a whole.

In practice, most team building includes some process consultation; but the consultant in a team-building assignment is likely to look beyond just the internal workings of the group. He or she may offer some predetermined solutions, as well as focusing attention on the position and context of the group within the organization as a whole.

Typically, team building begins diagnostically, by identifying the issues that team members view as important. The aim at this stage is to produce an agenda for action: identifying problems, rather than solving them. This may occur by bringing the total group together for discus-sion, with everyone presenting ideas to the whole group. Alternatively the group may break up into sub-groups or pairs who report back to the entire group. Another approach is for the consultant to conduct indi-vidual interviews with group members and report his or her findings at the meeting.

What actions are required, and by whom, are derived from this work. Within a meeting the team manager may be charged with coordinating new initiatives directed, for example, towards objective setting and staff development. Specific skill-requirements may be identified for particu-lar individuals, and appropriate training resources be made available. Some members may agree to work separately on clarifying their roles. Often such actions are reviewed and, if necessary, modified or renego-tiated at a subsequent team-building meeting. Indeed, the essential elements of the process may continue for some months in regular review and check-up meetings with the consultant. Such continuity can be important to reduce fade-out in beneficial effects.

Finally within this summary of OD approaches, we must consider *organizational interventions.* Survey feedback, mentioned earlier, is an example of an intervention aimed at changing an entire organization. It is now not uncommon to combine survey feedback with individual and group interventions in order to tackle organization-wide problems. This orientation tends to reflect a contingency approach to organization, that managerial practices should vary according to the situation. In other words, there is no 'one best' form of organization or style of management; it all depends on the nature of the task, the types of people involved and the culture of the enterprise. While much of the humanistic roots of OD still pervade, contingency interventions may encompass a range of directions and 'solutions' to match the complexity of the organization. It contrasts distinctly with strictly normative interventions, which advocate an ideal type of management and process of change (e.g. Likert, 1967; Blake and Mouton, 1964).

Achieving change throughout a complete organization is often the aspiration of a new director or owner of an enterprise. Our newspapers inform us of 'shake ups', new strategic plans, advanced technology and computerization as changes instigated from the top of an organization which can affect all workers. But we also read of the industrial relations disputes which are associated with such moves. Such events point to the difficulties of achieving smooth organizational change from a uni-directional thrust. Some OD professionals argue that a programme directed to broad changes must incorporate a range of interventions. Kilmann (1984), for example, suggests that an integrated and continuing programme of change is essential in order to address the complexities of organizational life. A 'quick fix' may work for a machine, but not for an organization. Kilman describes the development and practice of five 'tracks' of intervention which, he claims, when applied together can bring about effective change. He details a series of action steps to be conducted by managers and consultants. Firstly, the culture of the organization is explored with the aim of developing a new culture sufficiently open to handle the other change efforts. Secondly, management skills are refined to enhance complex problem solving and self-questioning. The third track is team building, helping work groups to make use of the new culture and revised assumptions about business practice. All this prepares teams to address their own strategy and structure, out of which the fifth track develops: designing an appropriate reward system.

Interventions aimed at comprehensive change tend to recognize, as has Kilmann, a need to examine strategic and structural features of the organization along with job roles and individual skills (Lippitt *et al.*, 1985; Pennings, 1985). They regard all facets of organizational life as relevant to the change process: individuals, groups, tasks, goals and economic and strategic plans.

The Political Approach

'Politics' in organizational life refers to the way in which people influence other people and events, often outside of the normal, 'rational' channels. It focuses attention on people's personal desires and needs as prime motivators of behaviour, but directed towards ends which can appear at odds with the stated goals of the organization. Politics, in these terms, is neither necessarily good nor bad. They reflect the intuitive, and the planned, behaviour of people for whom the more conventional avenues of communication and persuasion may prove to be ineffective in achieving the sorts of changes and directions they desire. Political behaviour, then, may constitute the life-blood of an organization. But it might also create a milieu of secrecy, confusion and conflict.

Some will argue that political behaviour is inevitable whatever the shape or structure of the organization. This is the third approach to be examined here. It has four main elements:

1.   Organizations are coalitions composed of a number of individuals and/or interest groups.

2.   Individuals and groups differ in their values, needs, goals and aspirations and are predisposed to struggle to have their values, needs, goals and aspirations prevail.

3.   Power and conflict are thus endemic to organizations.

4.   Organizational goals and decisions result from this process.

The University of Bath, in which we both work, may be defined as a loose collection of individuals and interest groups, or 'coalitions' (Cyert and March, 1963), each of whom wishes to have a say in the running of the institution. We severally seek to exercise influence by participating in a process of decision-making, which includes spelling out our interests (initially at least to ourselves), struggling to have them translated into institutional policy through various committees and hierarchies, and participating in attempts to reconcile our interests with, say, those of other Schools, in order that the University can determine, and implement, its policy. The political approach emphasizes that individuals have different goals and resources and that each member attempts to bargain or create coalitions in order to influence the overall direction of the enterprise. All order is negotiated and negotiable (Strauss, 1978; Mangham, 1986a).

From this perspective, change is endemic to the system. The literature on bargaining is clearly pertinent to this approach (Walton and McKersie, 1965; Rubin and Brown, 1975; Schelling, 1960) as is the burgeoning material on power in organizations (Bacharach and Lawler, 1980; Pfeffer, 1981b; Mintzberg, 1985; Mangham, 1979); see also Chapters 9 and 10. Change occurs when one individual or group wins and others lose. However, such a state of affairs, and any agreement about goals and purposes as then exists, will be but temporary, to be replaced tomorrow, next week or next month by another individual's or group's goals and objectives. In many circumstances, however, the balance of power is such that remarkably little change of consequence occurs; powerful people may, in their own interests, cooperate to maintain the status quo.

Seen from this perspective, significant change can only be brought about by the use of power, either by enforcing one's wishes from above or mobilizing support from below. Books such as that by Sir Michael Edwardes (1983) purport to outline some mix of the two; but his decision to replace key managers in British Leyland, to subject others to psychological tests, to restructure the company, and to confront the unions, is a clear example of the top-down, power-orientated approach to change. Lee Iacocca's (1985) biography charts similar territory in the Chrysler Corporation, with the hero (himself) firing virtually all of the Vice-Presidents on his accession to the most senior post in the corporation.

The material on the development of trade-union activities is a good guide to the mobilizing of support for bottom-up change (Poole, 1974; Mulder, 1971; Hyman, 1972; Daniel, 1973; Batstone *et al.*, 1977). For example, Batstone, Boraston and Frenkel (1977) provide a fascinating account of the day-to-day tactics of shop stewards as they struggle to define, raise and resolve issues. The authors' contention that the notion of 'us' versus 'them' is simplistic and that it is not always clear whose interests are being pursued by union officials should surprise none of us, but it serves to highlight the rather simplistic concepts of power used in many studies of bottom-up change.

The Symbolic Approach

The fourth approach is more recent than any of the other three, and depicts a world that is much less rational and purposive. People either do not have or do not know their goals; they are considered unlikely to determine their action through rational choice which is then followed by systematic execution. The symbolic approach holds that:

1. Events in an organization are often uncertain and ambiguous: it is often difficult to know what has happened, let alone what may happen next.

2. This uncertainty and ambiguity render planning and control difficult, if not impossible.

3. In these circumstances social actors create symbols and meaning to reduce the uncertainty and ambiguity.

4. Such symbols and meanings are a matter of interpretation.

The symbolic approach appears to advance the notion that individuals and groups within organizations devote considerable amounts of time to developing myths, metaphors, rituals and ceremonies, in order to render their existence less confusing. Essentially, it is suggested that an organization's stories, anecdotes, jokes, decorations and buildings all reflect, in one coded form or another, the significance and meaning of that enterprise to its actors. What organizational life means to an individual, and how relationships function, is mirrored in the verbal, action and material symbols of that culture (Dandridge *et al.*, 1980; Hofstede, 1986; Morgan, 1986).

331

The tales people tell, the 'lore' which is passed on to new members, are all part of the process of creating meaning. So, for example, the novice may be told that 'people don't ask questions around here', backed up with the story of the dire consequences which befell Jim Smith who did not heed this advice. The same person may soon pick up the view that the organization is making 'Mickey Mouse' products, and the managing director has failed miserably in his industrial relations management. All this tells the novice what is appropriate to believe.

From this perspective, leaders principally provide a series of symbols, rituals and ceremonies around which others can cluster. *The I C L Way*, *The Shell Philosophy* and *The I B M Approach* are company-produced booklets which describe, in fairly 'glossy' terms, the way the organizations are supposed to operate. They may or may not reflect actual practices within those particular companies, but what they do is focus attention and inculcate a sense of corporate identity and direction that, hitherto, employees may have found lacking. Peters and Waterman (1982), Deal and Kennedy (1982), Schein (1985) and many others emphasize the point that 'strong' cultures (which are marked by shared symbols, rituals and myths) 'produce results'.

The implications of the symbolic approach for organizational change depend almost entirely upon the strength of particular cultures (Marshall and McLean, 1985; Foster, 1962; Martin and Siehl, 1981). Companies which have evolved strong beliefs, ideologies, symbols, rituals, ceremonies, myths and the like will be highly resistant to change. Uncertainty and ambiguity, it is argued, are much reduced by the elaboration and inculcation of appropriate symbolic activities; they provide meaning, stability and direction in an otherwise confusing world (Brunson, 1985). On the other hand, they preclude the evaluation of alternatives and change. They so fuse the individual with the setting and the system as to make it extremely difficult for individuals to see different ways of operating, either alternative attitudes or behaviours (Mangham, 1979; Fineman, 1983b).

There is a problem even in those organizations where change can be brought about. By definition they are likely to be those where a relatively weak culture or ideology exists since, as we have indicated, a strong one resists change. Given a situation of a weak culture, top management can effect change through the use of consultants. Once this has been done, and revised practices have become institutionalized, the organization can then become too rigid for necessary future changes (Lorange and Vancil, 1977; Meyer and Rowan, 1977). Mangham (1986b), in a passage reviewing the difficulties of effecting change from the symbolic perspective, stresses the role of the leader in so managing a company that it is at once both stable and innovative. A strong consensus and identity of interests ensures that smooth and relatively predictable interaction and action can occur; but they may forfeit the opportunity for innovation to arise. Too little consensus is equally likely to threaten the survival of the company, since nothing can be jointly determined and order itself will collapse.

It will be clear from what we have written that there is no shortage of comment upon change and its implementation. Nor is there a dearth of material purporting to evaluate it, some of which we have mentioned. There is even a book on failures in organizational development and change (Mirvis and Berg, 1977). It is plain, however, that what change is and how it can be brought about are intimately connected with how we believe order is sustained. And here we have a variety of perspectives to consider and refine, to reject or accept.

SUMMARY

In this chapter we have looked at the ways in which change in organizations is initiated and managed. Our examination has focused upon two traditional perspectives, the structural approach and the human relations orientation, and two more recent perspectives, the political and the symbolic. Each leads to rather different conclusions about the nature of order in organizational life and, consequently, change. Techniques which claim to bring about change have been examined, particularly those which are concerned with Organization Development, an area which is prominent in the change literature. If we are to provide realistic and helpful advice on change, then our theories must continue to reflect the experienced realities of organizational members. Change, in essence, is a very human concern.

FURTHER READING

Useful general texts on organizational change are E. F. Huse and T. C. Cummings, *Organizational Development and Change* (West, 1985), and *Organizational Strategy and Change* by J. M. Pennings (Jossey-Bass, 1985). An excellent set of readings which examine in depth some of the theoretical and practical issues in change is P. S. Goodman's *Change in Organizations* (Jossey-Bass, 1982). More directly concerned with practice and application is *Implementing Organizational Change* by G. L. Lippitt, P. Langseth and J. Mossop (Jossey-Bass, 1985); also, R. Kilmann's *Beyond the Quick Fix* (Jossey-Bass, 1984).

Two classic texts are still worthy of recommendation: M. Beer, *Organizational Change and Development* (Goodyear, 1980), and W. G. Bennis, K. D. Benne and R. Chin, *The Planning of Change* (Holt, Rinehart and Winston, 1976). A recent, comprehensive examination of issues in evaluation of change is to be found in *Evaluating Planned Organizational Change* by K. Legge (Academic Press, 1984). Reports focused on Organization Development are provided in journal articles by Alderfer (1977) and Friedlander and Brown (1974), and in a more recent book, *Organization Development in Transition*, by A. McLean, D. Sims, I. L. Mangham and D. Tuffield (Wiley, 1982).

16

Workers Without a Job

Peter Warr

Previous chapters have explored the applications of psychology in work settings, focusing upon people in their jobs. This final chapter will examine the position of those members of the labour force who are currently unemployed. The consequences of unemployment for their psychological and physical health will be reviewed, and some effects upon family life will be considered.

The study of unemployment is important in its own right, but in the setting of this book it has an additional interest. Examining what happens to people who lack paid work may help us better to understand the meaning and impact of having a job itself. This possibility will be explored here through an application of the conceptual framework set out in Chapter 12. The environmental factors which were there said to give rise to high or low mental health in a job will be proposed to operate in a similar manner during unemployment. Jobs and joblessness will thus be interpreted through the same perspective.

First, a point of definition. People said to be of 'working age' (between approximately 16 and 65 in most countries) may occupy one of three positions in relation to the labour market. Most are in paid jobs, which usually means working for someone else, although a minority of the employed population are 'self-employed' (about 10 per cent in the United Kingdom).

A second group includes people who are 'unemployed'. Official definitions of this status vary slightly from country to country, but usually include the notion that a person must be looking for a job as well as lacking one. The third group may be referred to as 'non-employed', containing working-age adults who have no job and are not seeking one. Among these are people who are voluntarily caring for their children, or who for other reasons do not wish to take up paid employment.

335

Distinguishing between membership of the latter two categories is occasionally difficult, especially in view of the fact that people are widely ambivalent in their feelings about paid work: most adults want to be active in an employed role, but they also desire to relax and to be free from work demands. Furthermore, views of oneself as 'wanting a job' can sometimes vary according to the availability of paid work in the neighbourhood. For example, some married women may see themselves as 'non-employed' when jobs are very scarce, but enter the labour market as initially 'unemployed' (wanting a job) when opportunities are perceived to be available.

However, in many other cases a person can without equivocation be described as unemployed: he or she clearly wants a job but cannot find one. Official figures suggest that more than 10 per cent of many Western countries' labour forces are unemployed in this sense. For several sub-groups the rate is appreciably higher. Teenage workers, those who are older, unskilled, or previously employed in declining manufacturing industries are particularly likely to be without jobs, as are members of ethnic minorities and disabled people.

THE CONSEQUENCES OF BEING UNEMPLOYED

Much research into the impact of unemployment has been cross-sectional, comparing a group of people who at the time are unemployed with similar people who are in paid work. Such comparisons regularly show that employed people are on average psychologically more healthy than those who are unemployed. For example, Hepworth (1980) obtained from employed and unemployed British men responses to the General Health Questionnaire measure of general distress (Goldberg, 1972). This contains items about feelings of anxiety, depression, worthlessness, hopelessness, lack of confidence, and loss of sleep through worry. Distress scores for the employed group were generally low relative to published norms, but the mean value for unemployed respondents was almost six times greater.

In principle, such a difference could arise from prior personal characteristics rather than from the effect of being unemployed: the unemployed people might have had poorer mental health even when they were in a job. That seems extremely improbable in times of high unemployment, when large numbers of people are made redundant by the closure of a factory or by wide-ranging cutbacks.

Furthermore, longitudinal studies indicate that the differences are at least in part caused by changes in employment status. For example, significant deterioration in affective well-being after job loss has been reported by Cohn (1978) and Cobb and Kasl (1977), and significant improvements after re-entry into employment have been described by P. R. Jackson *et al.* (1983) and Warr and Jackson (1985). Several other investigations have shown that teenagers moving from school into unemployment are likely to experience a significant drop in well-being, whereas those entering paid work tend to exhibit improvement (e.g. Banks and Jackson, 1982; Feather and O'Brien, 1986).

Some other studies have obtained an overall indication of the personal impact of unemployment by asking unemployed people whether their health has changed at all since job loss. Research has shown that between 20 and 30 per cent of unemployed men are likely to report a deterioration in their health since job loss (Warr, 1987). In respect of psychological health, changes are typically described in terms of increased anxiety, depression, insomnia, irritability, lack of confidence, listlessness, and general nervousness. In addition, unemployed people may describe a worsening in psychosomatic conditions such as dermatitis, eczema, headaches, high blood-pressure, and ulcers.

However, it is important to note that around 10 per cent of men in these studies report an improvement in their health since becoming unemployed. In some cases this is in respect of physical illnesses which had been exacerbated by working conditions (bronchitis, back problems, and so on), but it is also found that a small number report improved psychological health, usually because they are now free from negative aspects of their jobs. Health improvements are particularly likely to be reported by those who have only recently become unemployed.

What about those illnesses which are primarily physical with no psychological causes, or at least with very little psychological input? Bronchitis, the cancers, or pneumonia might be taken as an example of such primarily physical illnesses. If unemployment is to bring about illness of that kind, the causal mechanisms are presumably different from those yielding poor mental health. Most probable is an increase in poverty, leading to deficiencies in food intake, heating, clothing or sanitation, or some other harmful change in lifestyle. More extended time-lags are also to be expected, with these forms of physical ill-health developing over longer periods.

It is known from cross-sectional studies that in general unemployed people have poorer physical health than those who are in jobs. However, it is not possible from the cross-sectional results to distinguish between physical ill-health leading to unemployment and unemployment causing ill-health.

A longitudinal inquiry has been described by Moser *et al.* (1984). These authors analysed mortality data for the years 1971 to 1981 with regard to individual characteristics previously recorded in the 1971 England and Wales census. Among males aged 15 to 64 the standardized mortality ratio in the subsequent period was considerably greater for people who had been unemployed and seeking work on the date of the 1971 census than for those in jobs on that date. Analyses showed that some but not all of this difference in subsequent mortality could be accounted for by differences in age and social class, factors which were found to be associated with both mortality and unemployment rates. However, after controlling for those two variables, unemployed men remained significantly more likely to die in the course of the following decade; the differential probability was particularly marked for death by suicide or lung cancer.

In respect of this last finding, a risk factor prior to 1971 must probably be invoked, since lung cancer develops slowly over a number of years. However, it is interesting that research by other investigators has suggested that unemployment may be accompanied by an increase in smoking, at least among working-class men (D. G. Cook *et al.*, 1982; Bradshaw *et al.*, 1983; Warr and Payne, 1983; Warr, 1984).

Investigations into alcohol consumption have yielded varying results, but the overall pattern seems to be one of no change or reduced consumption after job loss, probably as a result of increased financial constraints. It is possible that unemployment is associated with a 'polarized' pattern of alcohol consumption. Heavy drinkers, or those people who already have serious drinking problems, may consume increased amounts of alcohol when faced with the difficulties of unemployment, whereas moderate or light drinkers may reduce consumption as part of a general cutback in non-essential expenditure. For example, surveys of the British male population have suggested that, although there is a higher proportion of 'heavy' drinkers among the unemployed than the employed, there are also relatively more unemployed people who abstain or are only 'occasional' drinkers.

Another question is whether suicide is significantly associated with being unemployed. Cross-sectional studies indicate that people committing suicide are disproportionately likely to be out of work, but it is apparent that over time the same personal and environmental factors may have operated to yield both unemployment and suicide. Aggregate time-series investigations in the United States (looking at national data over a number of years) have found a positive association across time between suicide frequency and high unemployment rates, but the evidence from European studies is more conflicting (Platt, 1984).

A possible explanation for the lack of an aggregate positive correlation over recent years in the United Kingdom was considered by Kreitman and Platt (1984). They noted that during the 1960s the carbon monoxide content of domestic gas was gradually removed from different parts of the country, so that household gas was decreasingly available as a poison for would-be suicides. Associated with this change, overall suicide rates showed a decline over the period, whereas unemployment was gradually rising. The correlation between the two variables was thus negative, rather than positive as found in the United States. However, examination of suicides by all other methods in the same period (excluding deaths by carbon monoxide poisoning) revealed a strong positive correlation with the national unemployment rate.

Research has also examined parasuicide ('attempted suicide' or 'deliberate self-harm') as a function of unemployment. Individual-level studies again reveal a particularly high probability of parasuicide among the unemployed, especially among those without a job for more than a year (Platt and Kreitman, 1985). However, interviews with people who have survived parasuicide rarely point to unemployment as a major precipitating factor. Some form of interpersonal relationship problem is most often seen as the main proximal cause. Nevertheless, unemployment might exacerbate relationship difficulties, and Platt and Kreitman conclude that their findings are compatible with the hypothesis that unemployment is a cause of parasuicide.

Finally, it should be noted that a husband's unemployment is clearly liable to cause increased strain within the family (e.g. Thomas *et al.*,

1980; Madge, 1983; Fagin and Little, 1984). Relationship problems arising from financial difficulties during unemployment have been particularly emphasized in many studies (e.g. Liker and Elder, 1983; Binns and Mars, 1984). However, it is difficult at present to be specific about how widespread or damaging are these problems; large-scale studies of random samples have yet to be carried out.

The covariation between divorce and unemployment rates has been investigated by South (1985), in an aggregate time-series analysis of data from the United States between 1948 and 1979. After controlling for other variables, such as changes in age distribution, a significant positive contribution was recorded over time from unemployment level to the frequency of divorce in the following year: divorce rate was found to increase in periods of economic recession and to fall (or rise more slowly) during economic expansion. As with all other aggregate time-series analyses, these findings should not be extrapolated to the level of individuals. They describe overall trends, at the level of an entire nation, and do not demonstrate that individual persons are more likely to become divorced after losing their job.

In general, however, the findings presented in this section leave no doubt that unemployment has substantial harmful effects upon many individuals and their families. Furthermore, the consequences are likely in practice to be more serious than is revealed in most survey investigations. Survey researchers typically have difficulty in obtaining access to unemployed people, with large numbers of those approached preferring not to be interviewed. It is not known whether unemployed people who decline to take part differ substantially from those who do, but it seems very likely that non-respondents will in general be of poorer mental health. Average findings from published surveys are thus likely to underestimate the destructive impact of unemployment.

EXPLAINING THE CONSEQUENCES OF UNEMPLOYMENT

In seeking to understand the processes which give rise to the outcomes described above, we need to look at changes in lifestyle, environmental pressures and supports, and the specific events and daily hassles which accompany unemployment. In terms of a process over time, 'unemployment' should be seen to cover both the transition out of a job (or from school, in the case of teenagers) and also the extended period of joblessness which may follow.

Within this short chapter, attention will mainly be focused upon general models of the unemployed person's environment. These can provide a framework for considering particular individuals or categories of people. Later in the chapter the position of several specific unemployed groups will be discussed.

Jahoda's Latent Functions Model

An important contribution to explaining the generally negative impact of unemployment has been the 'latent functions' model of Jahoda (e.g. 1982). She construes the psychological value of paid work in terms of its manifest and latent functions, and argues that unemployment is harmful in that it reduces the availability of these features.

Earning one's living is accepted as the manifest function of paid work, and five latent consequences are suggested: employment imposes a time structure on the waking day; it brings about regularly shared experiences and contacts with people outside the family; a job links one with goals and purposes beyond one's own; it also defines aspects of personal status and identity; and paid employment enforces its own activity.

Jahoda argues that the negative psychological effects of unemployment arise from the fact that people are deprived of these benefits, which are themselves inherent in an employment relationship. Although other roles may contain one or more of the functions, paid work is unique in the overall combination which it provides.

This suggestion is persuasive, and Jahoda's model has guided much research and reflection. However, the emphasis has tended to be on the 'latent' functions rather than upon that which is 'manifest'. As a result, loss of income has sometimes been viewed as being relatively unimportant. As will be described later, financial problems are in fact usually central to the harmful impact of unemployment. The model's concentration on the five latent functions is also limiting, in that other sources of problems and threats (for example, uncertainty about the future) tend to be underemphasized.

A Nine-factor Framework

It would therefore be helpful to think in terms of a wider set of environmental factors. Within Chapter 12, a nine-component account of job characteristics was introduced. This was in fact developed in order to encompass both employment and unemployment (Warr, 1987), and we can now examine the environment of unemployed people in the same terms.

If the negative consequences of unemployment arise from deficiencies in respect of the nine factors, we would expect two sets of findings. First, the environments of employed and unemployed people should be observed to differ significantly in respect of each feature. Second, within the population of unemployed people themselves there should be a significant association between the level of a factor and the level of mental health.

Some research evidence of these two kinds is available, and will be illustrated shortly. However, there have been relatively few studies which seek to identify specific causal factors during unemployment, so that relevant findings are scarce. Furthermore, it is clear that combinations of factors (rather than individual items on their own) lie behind any response to complex environments. The practical and conceptual difficulties in studying particular configurations are substantial, in all other areas as well as in this particular field.

OPPORTUNITY FOR CONTROL   In general, unemployed people have less chance than those in jobs to decide and act in their chosen ways. This is the first factor to be considered. Lack of success in job-seeking, inability to influence employers, lack of money, and increased dependence upon welfare bureaucracies all contribute to a reduction in people's ability to control what happens to them.

Opportunity to influence the environment is widely found to be important in relation to well-being and sense of personal competence (e.g. Seligman, 1975; Langer, 1983). A chronic lack of control can generate feelings of helplessness and hopelessness which are central to the syndrome of depression. Conversely, a sense of personal worth often depends upon feeling that one is to some extent responsible for what happens and for what is achieved.

The contribution of this feature to low mental health during unemployment appears obvious. Perhaps for that reason empirical research has not systematically examined differences between levels and types of control opportunity in the situations of employed and unemployed people. Detailed inquiries into the nature of changes in opportunity for control as people move into unemployment would be very worthwhile.

OPPORTUNITY FOR SKILL USE   This second feature is also likely to be reduced during unemployment. Its importance in jobs has been stressed in Chapter 12, where significant correlations with mental health were reported.

Restrictions during unemployment are of two kinds: those which prevent people from using skills which they already possess, and those which prevent the acquisition of new skills. Specifically occupational skills are by definition unused during unemployment, although there are of course opportunities to use certain abilities in domestic, hobby or repair work. A small number of unemployed people may sustain or develop their skills by providing help to neighbours and friends, for example through household electrical and plumbing work, or through administrative and managerial work in clubs or societies. However, there is no doubt that unemployed people in general are likely to have only restricted opportunity for using and developing their skills. Individual differences in personal motivation are of course important here, and these will be considered later.

GOALS AND TASK DEMANDS   A related change brought about by unemployment is a reduction in externally generated goals. Fewer demands are made, objectives are reduced, and purposeful behaviour is less encouraged by the environment. Routines and cycles of behaviour are less often set in motion, and opportunities for 'traction' (see Chapter 12) may be limited. With fewer goals, one can less look forward to their successful attainment, so that a person's experience may come to lack positive tone as well as being homogeneous in its limited challenge.

There are also important consequences of reduced goals upon a person's sense and use of time. An absence of demands can produce an excess of time and remove the need to choose between activities or allocate fixed amounts of time to individual tasks. Since external demands are often linked to particular points (such as mealtimes or the start of a working day), a general reduction in demands is sometimes accompanied by a loss of temporal differentiation. Time-markers which break up the day or week and indicate one's position in it are no longer as frequent or as urgent. There is thus likely to be a prolonged sense of waiting, for the next time-marker, or (rarely) for something unexpected to occur.

Research has frequently confirmed that unemployed people have difficulty filling their days, with long periods spent without activity, merely sitting around, sleeping, or watching television (e.g. Fagin and Little, 1984; Kilpatrick and Trew, 1985). The degree to which unemployed people report an increase in such inactivity is significantly associated with low affective well-being (e.g. Warr and Payne, 1983; Warr, 1984), as is their reported difficulty in filling the time (e.g. Hepworth, 1980; Feather and Bond, 1983).

As with other features considered here, the causal processes linking the environment and the person are presumably cyclical. Loss of a job may lead to a reduction in externally generated goals, which itself gives rise to impairments in mental health. The latter changes (increased anxiety, depression, listlessness, etc.) are expected in their turn to lower the probability that a person will recognize or create the environmental conditions required to restore mental health to its former level.

VARIETY   Unemployment is likely also to reduce the level of variety in a person's life. This is associated with changes in externally generated goals, being partly a question of less often having to leave the house, and also arising from a loss of contrast between job and non-job activities. Homogeneity of experience is increased through the reductions in activity which follow an unemployed person's drop in income. Furthermore, those domestic and other demands which do impinge on the individual are likely to be similar and unchanging from day to day, with standard routines and an absence of novelty.

Differences between the amount of variety in unemployed teenagers' lives have been studied by Warr *et al.* (1985). They observed that lower levels of reported variety were significantly correlated with high anxiety, depression and general distress. Furthermore, variety retained its independent contribution to those forms of low well-being after statistical controls had been introduced for a range of labour-market attitudes and job-seeking behaviours.

ENVIRONMENTAL CLARITY   The fifth feature is also likely to be diminished during unemployment. Information about the consequences of behaviour and information about the future are both reduced. Such information is important because it permits appropriate decisions and actions, allows planning within predictable time schedules, and reduces the anxiety which is typically generated by uncertainty.

The unemployed person's environment is unclear in all these respects. He or she is likely to be unsure what behaviours or attributes would lead to the offer of a job (or even an interview for a job), and planning for the future is difficult in view of uncertainty about one's occupational or financial position in the months to come. In the study by Payne *et al.* (1984) of British men unemployed for between six and eleven months, some 60 per cent reported that they were troubled by 'not knowing what is going to happen to me in the future'.

AVAILABILITY OF MONEY   Studies of unemployed people consistently indicate that shortage of money is viewed as the greatest source of personal and family problems (e.g. D. J. Smith, 1980). Poverty bears down not only upon basic needs for food and physical protection, but also prevents activity and reduces one's sense of personal control.

The extent to which income is reduced after unemployment naturally varies between individuals, within and between countries. In the United Kingdom, welfare benefits are paid according to a number of criteria of need, size of family for example. Studies to identify the extent of financial deterioration after job loss suggest that unemployed people receive on average between 45 and 60 per cent of their employed income (e.g. D. J. Smith, 1980; Davies *et al.*, 1982). This proportion does of course depend upon the level of a person's income while in a job, and for many unemployed people (previously in unskilled work) income was already low. The joint presence of previously low wages and benefits paid for high family needs does however make it possible for a small number of unemployed people (perhaps 3 to 5 per cent) to earn slightly more than they did in their last job.

A substantially impaired standard of living means that many unemployed people have to borrow money to meet pressing needs. In a sample of British working-class men unemployed between six and eleven months, 55 per cent had needed to borrow money since becoming unemployed (Payne *et al.*, 1984). In Brinkmann's (1984) German sample, the figure was 23 per cent after eighteen months of unemployment, and two thirds of the Australian sample studied by Finlay-Jones and Eckhardt (1984) were in debt after an average of ten months without a job. White (1985) has shown that debts during unemployment are particularly common among married men with dependent children.

The cost of maintaining and repaying debts is typically greater for unemployed people than for people whose living standard is higher. For example, interest rates payable to money-lenders, pawnbrokers and through trading vouchers are substantially greater than rates on money borrowed by more 'credit-worthy' applicants through banks and other sources. Instances of unemployed people's hardship cited by D. J. Smith (1980) include inability to keep up repayments (about half the sample) and having one's fuel supply cut off because of debt (8 per cent). In addition, shortage of money during unemployment is associated with reduced social contact, and people may incur additional expenditure through the very fact that they are unemployed. For example, additional home heating and lighting may be required, and job-seeking activities depend upon money for postage, travel and effective self-presentation at interviews.

Given the extensiveness of these difficulties, it is not surprising that financial anxiety is typically high during unemployment, and that low levels of well-being are significantly associated with worries about money and being in debt. P. R. Jackson and Warr (1984) measured availability of money through separate indices of income change since job loss and number of dependants, finding that both these factors made independent contributions to the level of distress, after controlling for age, length of unemployment and attitudes to job-seeking. In a follow-up study of this sample, absence of someone to turn to for financial help was found to be significantly predictive of greater deterioration in affective well-being over nine months of unemployment (Warr and Jackson, 1985).

PHYSICAL SECURITY   The seventh feature is closely associated with the availability of money. Environments need to protect a person against physical threat and to provide an adequate level of warmth and space for food preparation, relaxation and sleeping. There appears to be a general need for some personal and private territory, the presence of which can contribute to a stable self-concept and raised well-being.

Physical security is also reflected in an expected permanence, in that occupants can look forward to their continued presence or can predict moving to other adequate settings.

This aspect of the environment is clearly likely to be affected by unemployment. Reduced income can give rise to loss of adequate accommodation, or to the chronic threat that this will happen. Individuals may become homeless, and families can be forced into run-down, unsanitary and overcrowded conditions. Alternatively, an unemployed person and his or her family might remain housed as before, but be unable to afford essential repairs or to pay for fuel for heating and lighting.

OPPORTUNITY FOR INTERPERSONAL CONTACT   Interaction with others is essential for reducing feelings of loneliness, for providing emotional support, and for helping individuals to attain goals which cannot readily be achieved alone. We should thus expect that opportunity for interpersonal contact is an important contributor to levels of mental health during unemployment. This should be observed both in terms of an impact in general (reduced opportunity for interpersonal contact after job loss on average causing a reduction in mental health) and in terms of differences between individual unemployed people (those with less opportunity should show worse mental health than those with more opportunity).

In respect of the first comparison (employed versus unemployed), several investigations have suggested that certain forms of social contact are likely to increase rather than decrease after job loss. These include time spent with friends and family members, at least by married men (e.g. Fröhlich, 1983; Warr and Payne, 1983; Warr, 1984). However, older women whose husbands have jobs are more likely to report a reduction in interpersonal contact after losing their job, often spending their days alone at home (R. Martin and Wallace, 1985).

In addition to studying the *amount* of interpersonal contact, we must also consider its diversity, an aspect of the fourth environmental feature in the present model. Unemployed people may have more social contact but with fewer people. Separate types of social encounter should also be examined. For example, we might investigate changes of four principal kinds: contact with work colleagues, entertainment in social settings, contact with family members, and casual meetings which 'pass the time of day' with friends and neighbours. It seems likely that the first two of these will in general decline in quantity after loss of a job, whereas the other two are likely to increase.

What of the second comparison, between people all of whom are unemployed but who differ in their amount of social contact? Results here consistently indicate that affective well-being is positively associated with greater interpersonal contact (e.g. Warr, 1984; Kilpatrick and Trew, 1985; Warr *et al.*, 1985). Other studies have examined reported quality of interaction (rather than merely its quantity), sometimes under the label of 'social support'. There are some suggestions that greater support is correlated with better mental health (e.g. Gore, 1978; Kilpatrick and Trew, 1985), but the evidence for this very plausible association is at present still somewhat indirect (Warr, 1987).

VALUED SOCIAL POSITION   Holding a position within a social structure which carries some esteem is also likely to be important to mental health. Many different types of role can be significant in this regard, but there is no doubt that in most societies being employed rather than unemployed is a central source of public and private esteem.

On becoming unemployed a person loses a socially approved role and the positive self-evaluations which go with it. The new position is widely felt to be one of lower prestige, deviant, second-rate, or not providing full membership of society. Even when welfare benefits remove the worst financial hardship, there may be shame attached to receipt of funds from public sources and a seeming failure to provide for one's family.

In introducing a book of interviews with people in jobs, Terkel (1972) draws attention to this extract from a Labor Day speech by American President Nixon: 'The "work ethic" holds that labor is good in itself; that a man or woman becomes a better person by virtue of the act of working.' Such a normative framework is widely held in most Western societies, often being traceable back to seventeenth-century ascetic Protestantism. It underlies the loss of public esteem which often follows unemployment. Unemployed people appear to be widely aware of their stigmatized position, and they wish to escape from it.

OVERVIEW   The model in terms of unemployment causing decrements in nine environmental features can be seen to receive support in several ways. However, as is the case with all broad-ranging perspectives on complex social processes, it would be unrealistic to expect complete and incontrovertible empirical evidence. As a first step, we might look for support in terms of significant correlations between identified environmental features and certain psychological indices. Such evidence is gradually becoming available, as summarized above.

However, the pattern of causal influence is likely to be cyclical, with environmental changes and psychological changes augmenting or inhibiting each other in multiple ways. Detailed studies of processes through time are now required to elucidate these types of mutual determination.

INDIVIDUAL DIFFERENCES

It has been emphasized throughout the chapter that the impact of unemployment varies substantially between people. As illustrated above, these differences can be viewed as arising largely from variations in personal and family circumstances. However, an individual-difference perspective may also be adopted, seeking to identify relatively stable personal characteristics which can mediate the effects of being unemployed.

Three types of enduring attribute will be considered here: emotional stability, proactivity, and employment commitment. Then some differences between particular groups of unemployed people will be summarized, in comparisons between men and women, teenage and middle-aged men, and those people who have been unemployed for long versus short periods.

Enduring Personal Attributes

It is widely assumed that some individuals are more vulnerable than others, reacting with greater distress to unemployment because of enduring high levels of anxiety or emotional instability. Few studies have examined this question, but one that has is the longitudinal investigation of income loss during the 1930s which was reported by Liker and Elder (1983). Their inquiry extended beyond merely unemployment (with some people remaining in jobs but at lower rates of pay), but certain findings are of direct relevance here. Interviewer ratings of instability and tenseness were made in 1930 and also between 1933 and 1935. It was found that men initially defined as relatively unstable became still less stable as a result of economic stress, whereas no significant change occurred among the more stable members of the sample.

A different type of personal characteristic which might affect the influence of unemployment is concerned with continuing levels of activity. Some people exhibit a stronger preference than others for purposive activity, associated with the establishment of personal goals, the search for stimulating environments, and the perception of opportunities which are unrecognized by others. It might be expected that 'proactive' individuals of that kind would be harmed less by unemployment, since they would create for themselves environments which are relatively rich in terms of most of the nine features in the present model.

Fryer and Payne (1984) have illustrated how people who exhibit this enduring characteristic can locate themselves during unemployment in settings which contain high levels of opportunity for control and for skill use, externally generated goals, variety, opportunity for interpersonal contact, and a valued social position. Their sample contained unemployed men and women who adopted roles in community, religious or political organizations which permitted them to be active and personally satisfied despite the absence of payment for their work. Mental health was not formally measured during this study, but appears from the researchers' account to have been high. The sample had exhibited stable levels of proactivity over many preceding years; they brought to their unemployment a value system which strongly determined its impact.

A similar relationship, but in the reverse direction, has been found in respect of 'employment commitment', the tendency in general to value paid work rather than to prefer a non-employed role. This aspect of the work ethic has frequently been shown to mediate the impact of being without a job. Consistent with an account in terms of frustrated motivation to obtain paid work, unemployed people with higher employment commitment exhibit significantly poorer mental health than those with lower commitment to the labour market (e.g. Warr, 1978; Warr and Jackson, 1985).

Placing together these three patterns of individual difference, it can be seen how certain individuals might cope less well with unemployment than others. People who are particularly at risk are those with a chronic high level of anxiety or emotional instability, who lack a proactive orientation, or who exhibit employment commitment to a marked degree.

Differences Between Groups

What about sex differences? Is there any evidence, or reason to expect, that unemployment would particularly harm men more than women, or women more than men? Certainly not, if attention is restricted to men and women who are formally defined as unemployed through their registration with official agencies. For such people, the impact of unemployment on affective well-being is equally negative, and associations between well-being during unemployment and the environmental features examined earlier are in general equally strong for the two sexes (e.g. Banks and Jackson, 1982; Finlay-Jones and Eckhardt, 1984).

However, many investigators have failed to distinguish in their samples between women who are 'unemployed' and those who are 'non-employed' in terms of the definitions at the beginning of this chapter. There is some overlap between these categories and marital status, and it is helpful to consider separately research into women who are married and studies of those who are single, divorced or separated. Examining thirty-eight previous investigations, Warr and Parry (1982) recorded that for married women in general there was no significant difference in affective well-being between those with and those without paid employment; subsequent investigations have generally supported that conclusion. However, for unmarried women, who are usually in effect principal wage-earners and often registered as unemployed, paid work was found to be significantly beneficial.

Within those two groups of women, we may consider possible differences associated with the nine environmental features examined above. For women who are married, the necessary comparison is between their domestic role alone (unemployed or non-employed) and an aggregation of both a domestic role and a job role (employed). The variety of possible combinations of features in the two sets of environments is clearly very great, some implying potential gains from a job and others predicting psychological harm. The net result of a comparison between

351

environments naturally depends in each case upon the quality of both a woman's home environment and her job environment.

In many cases, married women who take a paid job are likely to gain in terms of features such as variety, availability of money, and opportunity for interpersonal contact. Greater variability is expected in respect of goals and task demands. As described in Chapter 12, environments which generate very few goals are liable to impair mental health. Married women whose domestic environments are of this kind might be thought likely to gain from paid employment, since this carries with it specific goals and goal-oriented activities. In contrast, married women whose home environments are already very demanding are likely to suffer from the addition of job-related goals.

Similar analyses of the position of other groups of unemployed people may be made in terms of these nine factors. For example, comparisons may be made between middle-aged men and their teenage counterparts. It is widely found that the impact of unemployment on mental health is more severe for the former group (e.g. Eisenberg and Lazarsfeld, 1938; Warr and Jackson, 1984, 1985). It seems likely that middle-aged men, especially those with families to support, suffer particularly in terms of the features here identified as availability of money, environmental clarity and valued social position. For example, in respect of the second of these, middle-aged men's uncertainty about the future is compounded by the fact that their unemployment generates uncertainty which also extends into the lives of all family members: plans can less easily be made and the future is less clearly predictable. In addition, they are at that stage of the life-cycle which is often accompanied by insecurity and self-questioning, irrespective of employment status.

The position of unemployed teenagers is somewhat different. As a group, they show significantly less impairment in well-being than do middle-aged people, and this may be interpreted principally in terms of four environmental features from those described above: availability of money, physical security, opportunity for interpersonal contact, and valued social position. In each case, the environments of unemployed teenagers are likely to be less problematic than those of middle-aged people.

For example, the income differential between having a job and being unemployed may be relatively small, especially for those teenagers with few qualifications. Money and material assistance are often provided by parents, and financial requirements are generally less than for older groups. Associated with that, physical security is often unchanged by the transition from school into unemployment, as many teenagers continue to live within their family's accommodation.

They may also have relatively good opportunities for interpersonal contact, as they carry forward from school a network of friends and established patterns of leisure activities. In the male samples studied by Fröhlich (1983) and Warr (1984), teenagers reported particularly large increases in social interaction following loss of their job.

Although unemployed teenagers also experience the lack of a valued social position which is common during unemployment at all ages, they may see themselves as members of that large group of unemployed youth who are at the mercy of bad economic conditions. With unemployment so widespread among teenagers in recent years, personal responsibility and social stigma are liable to be less strongly felt. Non-employment roles may be adopted which provide their own source of esteem, for example as an active member of a music group or youth club, or through providing care for younger siblings or for invalid parents.

Despite these potentially ameliorating conditions, there is no doubt that unemployment has a strongly negative impact upon teenagers' mental health (e.g. Banks and Jackson, 1982; P. R. Jackson *et al.*, 1983; Winefield and Tiggemann, 1985). Furthermore, this harmful effect may be expected to become still more severe two or three years after leaving school, as teenagers move into the adult labour market and into adult relationships independent of their parents.

Finally, let us consider the position of people who have been unemployed for a considerable length of time. There has been a steady increase in the size of this group. For example, 40 per cent of officially counted unemployed people in Britain in 1986 had been continuously out of paid work for more than a year, some 1·3 million from a total of more than three million; almost 25 per cent (750,000 people) had been continuously unemployed for more than two years.

Research has indicated that the impact of job loss on mental health is typically rapid, so that affective well-being is significantly impaired at an early stage of unemployment. Further deterioration is observed in the period after job loss, until a plateau of particularly poor mental health is reached after three to six months. This pattern is most clear for middle-aged men (e.g. Jackson and Warr, 1984; Warr and Jackson, 1985).

The early decline in mental health seems likely to arise from rapid decrements in most of the features described in this chapter. Initial days of unemployment may be experienced as something of a relief from previous uncertainty, providing an opportunity to carry out activities long promised but not taken up; and money may at first be relatively plentiful. However, availability of money is in many cases likely to decline quickly, and, as jobs become perceived as unattainable, there is often a growing concern about loss of important skills. Inability to predict and plan may become worrying, and social contact through entertainment requiring money is likely to show a steady decrease. Furthermore, it may become increasingly clear that one is going to remain in this stigmatized social position for a long period.

The observed stabilization at a low level of mental health after three to six months (rather than a continuing decline) seems likely to be attributable mainly to a change in environmental clarity. The initial period of unemployment often contains much uncertainty, as a person strives to deal with the complexities of official benefit procedures, learns about job-seeking practices, takes up new patterns of interaction with family members, assesses him or herself in relation to personal values, and experiences unusual pressures from other people.

However, these high levels of uncertainty are likely gradually to decline, as an unemployed person finds that previously new situations have become familiar and the frequency of novel threatening events has diminished. Associated with that, daily and weekly routines become established, expenditure limits become clarified, and behaviour may be shaped to avoid threats from new situations or other people. For example, job-seeking is likely to decline as people accept that the probability of success is low. At the same time, unemployed people may take up additional role activities, and may, in a small number of cases, locate additional sources of income, perhaps outside the formal economy.

In general, however, the changes which accompany long-term unemployment seem most appropriately viewed as passive and restricted forms of coping. Overall levels of mental health among the long-term unemployed are exceptionally low, and their environments in terms of the nine features examined here remain chronically impoverished.

354

Good and Bad Jobs and Good and Bad Unemployment

The thrust of this section has been that, although unemployment is in general harmful to individuals and their families, there are wide variations between people. In terms of its impact upon mental health, unemployment is undoubtedly 'bad' in overall terms; however, it can sometimes be relatively 'good' for a limited number of persons. Consider a 55-year-old unemployed man, whose previous job was highly stressful, who now has a regular income (from an occupational pension or elsewhere), and who is active in managerial roles in several clubs and societies. The environment of this person, in terms of the nine factors introduced earlier, is likely to be one which enhances mental health, perhaps beyond the level attained in previous employment.

We may thus think of the circumstances of unemployed people as ranging from psychologically 'bad' (the most common case) through to those which are reasonably 'good'. Jobs may also be construed along that dimension: from those which are psychologically 'good' (the typical situation) through to others which are psychologically 'bad'. Variations between the goodness of jobs, in terms of the nine principal factors, have been considered in Chapter 12.

This type of thinking is important in order to avoid the mistaken assertion that all jobs are always better than unemployment. In fact, both roles vary in their costs and benefits, and employment as well as unemployment can be psychologically harmful. In any one case the impact of the transition from paid work to unemployment will be a function of changes which occur in the nine primary environmental features. In most cases these shifts will impair mental health, but the transition can sometimes be neutral or even beneficial in its effect.

We have seen in earlier chapters that jobs can be redesigned, to make them 'better' in their content. If unemployment remains at its current high level, society will have to take more urgent steps to restructure the jobless role, seeking to ensure that it shifts from 'bad' to 'relatively good' in the terms illustrated here.

SUMMARY

This chapter has described significant negative consequences of unemployment, exhibited in raised distress, anxiety, depression, psychosomatic symptoms, and family strain. Possible causal associations with physical ill-health and suicide have also been considered.

Differences between individuals in their response to unemployment have been emphasized. These arise both from variations in environmental conditions and also from differences in enduring personal characteristics. Important factors have been classified in the same nine terms as adopted in Chapter 12, providing a single overall account of the impact on mental health of both jobs and joblessness. Enduring differences between individuals have been illustrated in terms of specific personality and value orientations, and through comparisons between groups of men and women, young and middle-aged samples, and between those who have been out of work for varying durations.

FURTHER READING

The points covered in this chapter have been developed in greater detail in P. B. Warr, *Work, Unemployment, and Mental Health* (Oxford University Press, 1987). Other recent reviews are by D. M. Fryer and R. L. Payne (1986) and by D. Dooley and R. A. Catalano (1986).

A readable account of unemployment and family processes has been provided by L. Fagin and M. Little in *The Forsaken Families* (Penguin, 1984). Discussions of possible societal responses to changing patterns of employment and unemployment include *The Future of Work* by C. Handy (Blackwell, 1984) and *A Job to Live* by S. Williams (Penguin, 1985).

References

Abell, P. (1975). *Bargaining and Influence Systems*. London: Heinemann.

Adams, J., Folkard, S., and Young, M. (1986). Coping strategies used by nurses on night duty. *Ergonomics*, 29, 185–96.

Akerstedt, T. (1985). Adjustment of physiological circadian rhythms and the sleep–wake cycle to shiftwork. In S. Folkard and T. H. Monk (eds.), *Hours of Work*. Chichester: Wiley.

Alban-Metcalfe, B. M., and Nicholson, N. (1984). *The Career Development of British Managers*. London: British Institute of Management.

Alderfer, C. P. (1977). Organization development. *Annual Review of Psychology*, 28, 197–223.

Alderfer, C. P., and McCord, C. G. (1970). Personal and situational factors in the recruitment interview. *Journal of Applied Psychology*, 54, 377–85.

Algera, J. A. (1983). 'Objective' and perceived task characteristics as a determinant of reactions by task performers. *Journal of Occupational Psychology*, 56, 95–107.

Algera, J. A., Jansen, P. G. W., Roe, R. A., and Vijn, P. (1984). Validity generalization: some critical remarks on the Schmidt-Hunter procedure. *Journal of Occupational Psychology*, 57, 197–210.

Allen, P. T. (1983). Understanding in industry: who gets it right? *Employee Relations*, 5, 13–16.

Allen, P. T., and Stephenson, G. M. (1983). Inter-group understanding and size of organization. *British Journal of Industrial Relations*, 21, 312–29.

Allen, P. T., and Stephenson, G. M. (1984). The relationship of inter-group understanding and inter-party friction in industry. *British Journal of Industrial Relations*, 23, 203–13.

Altman, I. (1975). *The Environment and Social Behavior*. Monterey, Calif.: Brooks Cole.

Anastasi, A. (1976). *Psychological Testing*. New York: Collins-MacMillan.

Anderson, J. R. (1982). Acquisition of cognitive skill. *Psychological Review*, 89, 369–406.

Anderson, J. R. (1985). *Cognitive Psychology and its Implications*. (2nd ed.) San Francisco, Calif.: Freeman.

Anderson, J. R., and Bower, C. H. (1973). *Human Associative Memory*. Washington D C: Winston.

Annett, J. (1969). *Feedback and Human Behaviour.* Harmondsworth: Penguin.

Annett, J., and Sparrow, J. (1985). Transfer of training: a review of research and practical implications. *Programmed Learning and Educational Technology*, 22, 116–24.

Annett, J., Duncan, K. D., Stammers, R. B., and Gray, M. J. (1971). *Task Analysis.* Training Information Paper No. 6. London: HMSO.

Argyle, M. (1983). *The Psychology of Interpersonal Behaviour.* (4th ed.) Harmondsworth: Penguin.

Argyris, C. (1962). *Interpersonal Competence and Organizational Effectiveness.* Homewood, Ill.: Irwin.

Argyris, C. (1964). *Integrating the Individual and the Organization.* New York: Wiley.

Argyris, C. (1965). *Organization and Innovation.* Homewood, Ill.: Irwin.

Argyris, C., and Schon, D. A. (1974). *Theory in Practice: Increasing Professional Effectiveness.* San Francisco, Calif.: Jossey-Bass.

Arvey, R. D. (1979). Unfair discrimination in the employment interview: legal and psychological aspects. *Psychological Bulletin*, 86, 736–65.

Arvey, R. D., and Campion, J. E. (1982). The employment interview: a summary and review of recent literature. *Personnel Psychology*, 35, 281–322.

Aschoff, J., and Wever, R. A. (1962). Spontanperiodik des Menschen bei Ausschluss aller Zeitgeber. *Naturwissenschaften*, 49, 337–42.

Attenborough, N. G. (1984). Employment and Technical Change: The Case of Micro-Electronic Based Production Technologies in UK Manufacturing Industry. Working Paper 74, Government Economic Service. London: Department of Trade and Industry.

Australian Bureau of Statistics (1984). *The Labour Force Australia: November and December, 1983.* Canberra: Australian Government Publishing Service.

Australian Government (1984). *Affirmative Action for Women.* Canberra: Australian Government Publishing Service.

Babbage, C. (1835). *On the Economy of Machinery and Manufacturers.* London: Charles Knight.

Bacharach, S. B., and Lawler, E. J. (1980). *Power and Politics in Organizations.* San Francisco, Calif.: Jossey-Bass.

Baddeley, A. D. (1986). *Working Memory.* Oxford: Oxford University Press.

Baddeley, A. D., and Lieberman, K. (1980). Spatial working memory. In R. S. Nickerson (ed.), *Attention and Performance VIII.* Hillsdale, NJ: Lawrence Erlbaum.

Baddeley, A. D., Thomson, N., and Buchanan, M. (1975). Word length and the structure of short-term memory. *Journal of Verbal Learning and Verbal Behavior*, 14, 575–89.

Bailyn, L. (1980). *Living With Technology: Issues at Mid-Career*. Cambridge, Mass.: MIT Press.

Baker, M. A., Holding, D. H., and Loeb, M. (1984). Noise, sex and time of day effects in a mathematics task. *Ergonomics*, 27, 67–80.

Baldamus, W. (1961). *Efficiency and Effort: An Analysis of Industrial Administration*. London: Tavistock Publications.

Bales, R. F., and Strodtbeck, F. L. (1950). *Interaction Process Analysis: A Method for the Study of Small Groups*. London: Addison-Wesley.

Banks, M. H., and Jackson, P. R. (1982). Unemployment and risk of minor psychiatric disorder in young people: cross-sectional and longitudinal evidence. *Psychological Medicine*, 12, 789–98.

Barnard, P., Hammond, N., Morton, J., and Long, J. (1981). Consistency and compatibility in human–computer dialogue. *International Journal of Man–Machine Studies*, 15, 87–134.

Baron, R. A. (1983). Sweet smell of success? The impact of pleasant artificial scents on evaluations of job applicants. *Journal of Applied Psychology*, 68, 709–13.

Bartlem, C. S., and Locke, E. A. (1981). The Coch and French study: a critique and re-interpretation. *Human Relations*, 34, 555–66.

Bartlett, F. C. (1932). *Remembering*. Cambridge: Cambridge University Press.

Bartlett, F. C. (1949). What is industrial psychology? *Occupational Psychology*, 23, 212–18.

Bartol, K. M. (1978). The sex structuring of organizations: a search for possible causes. *Academy of Management Review*, 3, 805–15.

Bass, B. (1981). *Stogdill's Handbook of Leadership*. New York: Free Press.

Bate, S. P., and Mangham, I. L. (1981). *Exploring Participation*. Chichester: Wiley.

Batstone, E., Boraston, I., and Frenkel, S. (1977). *Shop Stewards in Action*. Oxford: Blackwell.

Beatty, J. (1982). Task-evoked pupillary responses, processing load, and the structure of processing resources. *Psychological Bulletin*, 91, 276–92.

Becker, H., and Strauss, A. L. (1956). Careers, personality and adult socialization. *American Journal of Sociology*, 62, 253–63.

Beech, G. (1983). *Computer-Based Learning*. Wilmslow, Cheshire: Sigma Technical Press.

Beer, M. (1980). *Organizational Change and Development*. Santa Monica, Calif.: Goodyear.

Beggs, W. D. A., and Howarth, C. I. (1970). Movement control in a repetitive motor task. *Nature*, 225, 752–3.

Beggs, W. D. A., and Howarth, C. I. (1972). The movement of the hand towards a target. *Quarterly Journal of Experimental Psychology*, 24, 448–53.

Bennis, W. G. (1959). Leadership theory and administrative behavior: the problem of authority. *Administrative Science Quarterly*, 4, 259–69.

Bennis, W. G., Benne, K. D., and Chin, R. (1976). *The Planning of Change*. New York: Holt, Rinehart and Winston.

Bennis, W., and Nanus, G. (1985). *Leaders*. New York: Harper and Row.

Berne, E. (1964). *Games People Play*. New York: Grove Press.

Bernstein, V., Hakel, M. D., and Harlan, A. (1975). The college student as interviewer: a threat to generalizability. *Journal of Applied Psychology*, 60, 266–8.

Berry, D. C., and Broadbent, D. E. (1984). On the relationship between task performance and associated verbalizable knowledge. *Quarterly Journal of Experimental Psychology*, 36A, 209–31.

Bessant, J., and Haywood, W. (1985). *The Introduction of Flexible Manufacturing Systems as an Example of Computer Integrated Manufacturing*. Final report, Innovation Research Group, Department of Business Management, Brighton Polytechnic, UK.

Billings, A. G., and Moos, R. H. (1982). Work stress and the stress-buffering roles of work and family resources. *Journal of Occupational Behaviour*, 3, 215–32.

Binet, A., and Simon, Th. A. (1905). Méthodes nouvelles pour le diagnostic du niveau intellectuel des anormaux. *L'Année Psychologie*, 11, 191–336.

Binns, D., and Mars, G. (1984). Family, community and unemployment: a study in change. *Sociological Review*, 32, 662–95.

Bjerner, B., and Swensson, A. (1953). Shiftwork and rhythm. *Acta Medica Scandinavica*, (Supplement 278), 102–7.

Blackstone, T., and Weinreich-Haste, H. (1980). Why are there so few women scientists and engineers? *New Society*, 51, 383–5.

Blain, A. N. J., and Gennard, J. (1970). Industrial relations theory: a critical review. *British Journal of Industrial Relations*, 8, 389–407.

Blake, M. J. F. (1971). Temperament and time of day. In W. P. Colquhoun (ed.), *Biological Rhythms and Human Performance*. London: Academic Press.

Blake, R. R., and Mouton, J. S. (1964). *The Managerial Grid*. Houston, Texas: Gulf.

Blau, P. (1955). *The Dynamics of Bureaucracy.* Chicago, Ill.: University of Chicago Press.

Blau, P. M., and Scott, W. R. (1963). *Formal Organizations: a Comparative Approach.* London: Routledge and Kegan Paul.

Blumberg, M., and Gerwin, D. (1984). Coping with advanced manufacturing technology. *Journal of Occupational Behaviour*, 5, 113–30.

Bobko, P., Karren, R., and Parkington, G. J. (1983). Estimation of standard deviations in utility analyses: an empirical test. *Journal of Applied Psychology*, 68, 170–76.

Boden, M. (1977). *Artificial Intelligence and Natural Man.* Hassocks: Harvester Press.

Bower, G. H., and Springston, F. (1970). Pauses as recoding points in letter series. *Journal of Experimental Psychology*, 83, 421–30.

Bowers, D. (1973). OD techniques and their results in 23 organizations: the Michigan ICL study. *Journal of Applied Behavioral Science*, 9, 21–43.

Bradley, K., and Gelb, A. (1981). Motivation and control in the Mondragon experiment. *British Journal of Industrial Relations*, 19, 211–31.

Bradley, K., and Gelb, A. (1983). *Worker Capitalism: the New Industrial Relations.* London: Heinemann.

Bradshaw, J., Cooke, K., and Godfrey, C. (1983). The impact of unemployment on the living standards of families. *Journal of Social Policy*, 12, 433–52.

Braverman, H. (1974). *Labor and Monopoly Capital.* New York: Monthly Review Press.

Bray, D. W., Campbell, R. J., and Grant, D. L. (1974). *Formative Years in Business.* New York: Wiley.

Brett, J. M. (1980). The effect of job transfer on employees and their families. In C. L. Cooper and R. Payne (eds.), *Current Concerns in Occupational Stress.* Chichester: Wiley.

Brett, J. M. (1982). Job transfer and well-being. *Journal of Applied Psychology*, 67, 450–63.

Brett, J. M. (1984). Job transitions and personal and role development. In K. Rowland and J. Ferris (eds.), *Research in Personnel and Human Resource Management*, vol. 2. Greenwich, Conn.: JAI Press.

Brief, A. P., and Aldag, R. J. (1975). Employee reactions to job characteristics: A constructive replication. *Journal of Applied Psychology*, 60, 182–6.

Brief, A. P., Schuler, R. S., and Van Sell, M. (1981). *Managing Job Stress.* Boston, Mass.: Little Brown.

Brinkmann, C. (1984). Financial, psychosocial and health problems associated with unemployment. In G. Fragniere (ed.), *The Future of Work*. Assen: Van Gorcum.

Broadbent, D. E. (1958). *Perception and Communication*. New York: Pergamon.

Broadbent, D. E. (1970). Sir Frederic Bartlett: an appreciation. *Bulletin of the British Psychological Society*, 23, 1–3.

Broadbent, D. E. (1979). Is a fatigue test now possible? *Ergonomics*, 22, 1277–90.

Broadbent, D. E. (1982). Task combination and selective intake of information. *Acta Psychologica*, 50, 253–90.

Broadbent, D. E. (1985). The clinical impact of job design. *British Journal of Clinical Psychology*, 24, 33–44.

Broadbent, D. E., and Gregory, M. (1965). On the interaction of S-R compatibility with other variables affecting reaction time. *British Journal of Psychology*, 56, 61–7.

Broadbent, D. E., Fitzgerald, P. F., and Broadbent, M. H. P. (1986). Implicit and explicit knowledge in the control of complex systems. *British Journal of Psychology*, 77, 33–50.

Brousseau, K. R. (1978). Personality and job experience. *Organizational Behavior and Human Performance*, 22, 235–52.

Brousseau, K. R. (1983). Toward a dynamic model of job-personal relationships: findings, research questions, and implications for work system design. *Academy of Management Review*, 8, 33–45.

Brown, D., and Brooks, L. (eds.) (1984). *Career Choice and Development*. San Francisco, Calif.: Jossey-Bass.

Brown, M. (1982). Administrative succession and organizational performance: the succession effect. *Administrative Science Quarterly*, 27, 1–16.

Brown, R. (1978). Divided we fall: an analysis of relations between sections of a factory. In H. Tajfel (ed.), *Differentiation between Social Groups*. London: Academic Press.

Browne, R. C. (1949). The day and night performance of teleprinter switch board operators. *Occupational Psychology*, 23, 121–6.

Brunson, N. (1985). *The Irrational Organization*. Chichester: Wiley.

Bryman, A. (1986). *Leadership and Organizations*. London: Routledge and Kegan Paul.

Buchanan, B. G., and Shortliffe, E. H. (eds.) (1984). *Rule-based Expert Systems: The MYCIN Experiments of the Heuristic Programming Project*. Reading, Mass.: Addison-Wesley.

Buchanan, D. A., and Boddy, D. (1983). Advanced technology and the quality of working life: the effects of computerized controls on biscuit-making operators. *Journal of Occupational Psychology*, 56, 109–19.

Buckley, P., and Long, J. (1985a). Identifying usability variables for teleshopping. In D. Oborne (ed.), *Contemporary Ergonomics 1985*. London: Taylor and Francis.

Buckley, P., and Long, J. (1985b). Effects of system and knowledge variables on a task component of 'Teleshopping'. In P. Johnson and S. Cook (eds.), *People and Computers: Designing the Interface*. Cambridge: Cambridge University Press.

Burke, M. J. (1984). Validity generalization: a review and critique of the correlation model. *Personnel Psychology*, 37, 93–115.

Burke, R. J., and Weir, T. (1982). Occupational locking-in: some empirical findings. *Journal of Social Psychology*, 118, 177–85.

Burnes, B., and Fitter, M. (1987). Control of manufacturing systems: supervision without supervisors? In T. D. Wall, C. W. Clegg and N. J. Kemp (eds.), *The Human Side of New Manufacturing Technology*. Chichester: Wiley.

Burns, A., Feickert, D., Newby, M., and Winterton, J. (1983). The miners and new technology. *Industrial Relations Journal*, 14(4), 7–20.

Burns, J. M. (1978). *Leadership*. New York: Harper and Row.

Burns, T., and Stalker, G. M. (1961). *The Management of Innovation*. London: Tavistock.

Buros, O. K. (1938, 1941, 1953, 1956, 1969, 1972, 1978). *The Mental Measurement Yearbook*. Highland Park, NJ: Gryphon Press.

Burt, C. (1949). The structure of the mind. *British Journal of Educational Psychology*, 19, 100–111.

Butera, F. (1984). Automation, industrial development and industrial work in Italy. In F. Butera and J. E. Thurman (eds.), *Automation and Work Design*. Amsterdam: North-Holland.

Buzzard, R. B. (1971). Sir Frederic Bartlett, 1886–1969. *Occupational Psychology*, 45, 1–11.

Byrne, D. (1969). Attitudes and attraction. In L. Berkowitz (ed.), *Advances in Experimental Social Psychology*, vol. 4. New York: Academic Press.

Calder, B. J. (1977). An attribution theory of leadership. In B. M. Staw and G. R. Salancik (eds.), *New Directions in Organizational Behavior*. Chicago, Ill.: St Clair Press.

Campbell, J. P. (1976). Psychometric theory. In M. D. Dunnette (ed.), *Handbook of Industrial and Organizational Psychology*. Chicago, Ill.: Rand McNally.

Campbell, J. P., and Dunnette, M. D. (1968). Effectiveness of T-group experiences in managerial training and development. *Psychological Bulletin*, 70, 73–103.

Campbell, J. P., Dunnette, M.D., Lawler, E. E., and Weick, K. E. (1970).

Managerial Behavior, Performance and Effectiveness. New York: McGraw-Hill.

Caplan, R. D., Cobb, S., French, J. R. P., Jr, Van Harrison, R., and Pinneau, S. R., Jr (1975). *Job Demands and Worker Health*. Washington DC: National Institute of Occupational Safety and Health.

Card, S., Moran, T., and Newell, A. (1983). *The Psychology of Human–Computer Interaction*. Hillsdale, NJ: Erlbaum.

Carnevale, P. J. D., Pruitt, D. G., and Seilheimer, S. (1981). Looking and competing: accountability and visual access in integrative bargaining. *Journal of Personality and Social Psychology*, 40, 111–20.

Carter, R. C., and Cahill, M. C. (1979). Regression models of search time for color-coded information displays. *Human Factors*, 21, 293–302.

Champoux, J. E. (1978). A serendipitous field experiment in job design. *Journal of Vocational Behavior*, 12, 364–70.

Charlish, G. (1985). Competitiveness with computers: computer-aided design. *Financial Times*, 27th February.

Child, J. (1984a). *Organizations: A Guide to Problems and Practice*. London: Harper and Row.

Child, J. (1984b). New technology and developments in management organization. *Omega: International Journal of Management Science*, 12, 211–23.

Child, J., Loveridge, R., Harvey, J., and Spencer, A. (1984). Microelectronics and the quality of employment services. In P. Morstrand (ed.), *New Technology and the Future of Work and Skills*. London: Pinter.

Clack, G. (1967). *Industrial Relations in a British Car Factory*. Cambridge: Cambridge University Press Occasional Papers.

Clancey, W. J., and Shortliffe, E. H. (eds.) (1984). *Readings in Medical Artificial Intelligence: the First Decade*. Reading, Mass.: Addison-Wesley.

Clark, H., and Clark, E. (1976). *Psychology and Language: an Introduction to Psycholinguistics*. New York: Harcourt, Brace and Jovanovich.

Clegg, C. W., and Fitter, M. J. (1978). Information systems: the Achilles' heel of job redesign? *Personnel Review*, 7, 5–11.

Clegg, C. W., and Kemp, N. J. (1986). Information technology: personnel where are you? *Personnel Review*, 15, 8–15.

Clegg, C. W., Kemp, N. J., and Wall, T. D. (1984). New technology: choice, control and skills. In G. C. van de Veer, M. J. Tauber, T. R. G. Green and P. Gorny (eds.), *Readings on Cognitive Ergonomics: Mind and Computers*. Berlin: Springer.

Clegg, H. (1979). *The Changing System of Industrial Relations in Great Britain*. Oxford: Blackwell.

Cloudsley-Thompson, J. L. (1980). *Biological Clocks: Their Functions in Nature*. London: Weidenfeld and Nicolson.

Coates, K. (ed.) (1976). *The New Worker Cooperatives*. Nottingham: Spokesman Books.

Cobb, S., and Kasl, S. V. (1977). *Termination: the Consequences of Job Loss*. Cincinnati, Ohio: US Department of Health, Education and Welfare.

Coch, L., and French, J. R. P. (1948). Overcoming resistance to change. *Human Relations*, 1, 512–32.

Cohn, R. M. (1978). The effect of employment status change on self-attitudes. *Social Psychology*, 41, 81–93.

Colquhoun, W. P. (1971). Circadian variation in mental efficiency. In W. P. Colquhoun (ed.), *Biological Rhythms and Human Performance*. London: Academic Press.

Colquhoun, W. P., Blake, M. J. F., and Edwards, R. S. (1968). Experimental studies of shift work. II: Stabilized 8-hour shift system. *Ergonomics*, 11, 527–46.

Commission of the European Communities (1984a). *Equal Opportunities for Women*. Brussels.

Commission of the European Communities (1984b). *Women and Men of Europe in 1983*. Brussels.

Conrad, R. (1960). Letter-sorting machines – paced, 'lagged', or unpaced? *Ergonomics*, 3, 149–57.

Conrad, R. (1962). The location of figures in alpha-numeric codes. *Ergonomics*, 5, 403–6.

Conrad, R. (1964). Information, acoustic confusion, and memory span. *British Journal of Psychology*, 55, 429–32.

Conrad, R. (1970). Sir Frederic Bartlett, 1886–1969: a personal homage. *Ergonomics*, 13, 159–61.

Constantin, S. W. (1976). An investigation of information favorability in the employment interview. *Journal of Applied Psychology*, 61, 743–9.

Cook, D. G., Cummins, R. O., Bartley, M. J., and Shaper, A. G. (1982). Health of unemployed middle-aged men in Great Britain. *The Lancet*, June 5, 1290–94.

Cook, J. D., Hepworth, S. J., Wall, T. D., and Warr, P. B. (1981). *The Experience of Work*. London: Academic Press.

Cooley, M. (1984). Problems of automation. In T. Lupton (ed.), *Proceedings of the First International Conference on Human Factors in Manufacturing*. Amsterdam: North-Holland.

Coombs, R. (1978). Labour and monopoly capital. *New Left Review*, 107, 79–96.

Cooper, C. L., and Davidson, M. J. (1981). The pressures on working women: what can be done? *Bulletin of the British Psychological Society*, 34, 357–60.

Cooper, C. L., and Mangham, I. L. (1971). *T-groups – a Survey of Research*. Chichester: Wiley.

Cooper, C. L., and Marshall, J. (1976). Occupational sources of stress: a review of the literature relating to coronary heart disease and mental ill-health. *Journal of Occupational Psychology*, 49, 11–28.

Cooper, C. L., and Payne, R. L. (eds.) (1980). *Current Concerns in Occupational Stress*. Chichester: Wiley.

Corbett, J. M. (1985). Prospective work design for a human-centred CNC lathe. *Behaviour and Information Technology*, 4, 201–14.

Cordery, J. L., and Wall, T. D. (1985). Work design and supervisory practices: a model. *Human Relations*, 38, 425–41.

Cox, T. (1978). *Stress*. London: Macmillan.

Cox, T., Thirlaway, M., and Cox, S. (1982). Repetitive work, well-being and arousal. In R. Murison (ed.), *Biological and Psychological Basis of Psychosomatic Disease*. Oxford: Pergamon.

Cronbach, L. J. (1984). *Essentials of Psychological Testing*. (4th ed.) New York: Harper and Row.

Cronbach, L. J., and Gleser, G. C. (1965). *Psychological Tests and Personnel Decisions*. (2nd ed.) Urbana, Ill.: University of Illinois Press.

Crowe, B. J., Bochner, S., and Clark, A. W. (1972). The effects of subordinates' behaviour on managerial style. *Human Relations*, 25, 215–37.

Cummings, T. G., and Blumberg, M. (1987). Advanced manufacturing technology and work design. In T. D. Wall, C. W. Clegg and N. J. Kemp (eds.), *The Human Side of Advanced Manufacturing Technology*. Chichester: Wiley.

Cummings, T. G., and Molloy, E. S. (1977). *Improving Productivity and the Quality of Working Life*. New York: Praeger.

Cyert, R. M., and March, J. G. (1963). *A Behavioral Theory of the Firm*. Englewood Cliffs, NJ: Prentice-Hall.

Czeisler, C. A., Weitzman, E. D., Moore-Ede, M. C., Zimmerman, J. C., and Knauer, R. S. (1980). Human sleep: its duration and organization depend on its circadian phase. *Science*, 210, 1264–7.

Czeisler, C. A., Moore-Ede, M. C., and Coleman, R. M. (1982). Rotating shift work schedules that disrupt sleep are improved by applying circadian principles. *Science*, 217, 460–63.

Dalessio, A., and Imada, A. S. (1984). Relationships between interview selection decisions and perceptions of applicant similarity to an ideal employee and self: a field study. *Human Relations*, 37, 67–80.

Dandridge, T. C., Mitroff, I., and Joyce, W. F. (1980). Organizational symbolism: a topic to expand organizational analysis. *Academy of Management Review*, 5, 77–82.

Daniel, W. W. (1973). Understanding employee bargaining behaviour in its context: illustrations from productivity bargaining. In J. Child (ed.), *Man and Organization*. London: Allen and Unwin.

Dansereau, F., Graen, G., and Haga, W. J. (1975). A vertical dyad linkage approach to leadership within formal organizations: a longitudinal investigation of the role making process. *Organizational Behavior and Human Performance*, 13, 46–78.

Davidson, M. J. (1985). *Reach For the Top: a Women's Guide to Success in Business and Management*. London: Piatkus.

Davidson, M. J., and Cooper, C. L. (1983a). Working women in the European Community. *Long Range Planning*, 16 (4), 49–54.

Davidson, M. J., and Cooper, C. L. (1983b). *Stress and the Woman Manager*. London: Martin Robertson.

Davidson, M. J., and Cooper, C. L. (eds.) (1984a). *Working Women – An International Survey*. Chichester: Wiley.

Davidson, M. J., and Cooper, C. L. (1984b). Occupational stress in female managers: a comparative study. *Journal of Management Studies*, 21, 185–205.

Davidson, M. J., and Cooper, C. L. (1985). Women managers: work, stress and marriage. *International Journal of Social Economics*, 12, 17–24.

Davidson, M. J., and Cooper, C. L. (1986). Executive women under pressure. *International Review of Applied Psychology*, 35, 301–26.

Davies, R., Hamill, L., Moylan, S., and Smee, C. H. (1982). Incomes in and out of work. *Employment Gazette*, 90, 237–43.

Davis, K., and Newstom, J. (1985). *Human Behavior at Work: Organizational Behavior*. New York: McGraw-Hill.

Davis, L. E., Canter, R. R., and Hoffman, J. (1955). Current job design criteria. *Journal of Industrial Engineering*, 6, 5–11.

Dawis, R. V., and Lofquist, L. H. (1984). *A Psychological Theory of Work Adjustment*. Minneapolis: University of Minnesota Press.

de Wolff, C. J., and Bosch, G. van den (1984). Personnel selection. In P. J. D. Drenth, H. Thierry, P. J. Willems, and C. J. de Wolff (eds.), *Handbook of Work and Organizational Psychology*, Vol. 1. Chichester: Wiley.

Deal, T. E., and Kennedy, A. A. (1982). *Corporate Cultures*. Reading, Mass.: Addison-Wesley.

Department of Employment (1984). *New Earnings Survey*. London: HMSO.

Department of Trade and Industry (1982). *A Programme for Advanced Information Technology: the Report of the Alvey Committee*. London: HMSO.

Department of Trade and Industry (1985). *Signposts for the Future*. London: HMSO.

Depue, R. A., and Monroe, S. M. (1986). Conceptualization and measurement of human disorder in life stress research: the problem of chronic disturbance. *Psychological Bulletin*, 99, 36–51.

Deutsch, M. (1973). *The Resolution of Conflict: Constructive and Destructive Processes*. New Haven: Yale University Press.

Devine, M., and Clutterbuck, D. (1985). The rise of the entrepreneuse. *Management Today*, Jan., 63–107.

Dipboye, R. L., and Wiley, J. W. (1977). Reactions of college recruiters to interviewee sex and self-presentation style. *Journal of Vocational Behavior*, 10, 1–12.

Dixon, N. F. (1976). *On the Psychology of Military Incompetence*. London: Cape.

Dooley, D., and Catalano, R. A. (1986). Do economic variables generate psychological problems? In A. J. MacFadyen and H. W. MacFadyen (eds.), *Economic Psychology*. Amsterdam: North-Holland.

Douglas, A. (1962). *Industrial Peacemaking*. New York: Columbia University Press.

Downey, H. K., Sheridan, J. E., and Slocum, J. W. (1976). The path-goal theory of leadership: a longitudinal analysis. *Organizational Behavior and Human Performance*, 16, 156–76.

Drenth, P. J. D. (1976). *Inleiding in de Testtheorie*. Deventer: Van Loghum Slaterus.

Drenth, P. J. D., Flier, H. van der, and Omari, I. M. (1983). Educational selection in Tanzania. *Evaluation in Education*, 7, 93–217.

Dreyfus, H. L. (1979). *What Computers Can't Do*. (2nd ed.) New York: Harper and Row.

Druckman, D., and Zechmeister, K. (1970). Conflict of interest and value dissensus. *Human Relations*, 23, 431–8.

Duda, R. O., and Shortliffe, E. H. (1983). Expert systems research. *Science*, 220, 261–8.

Duncan, J. (1983). Perceptual selection based on alphanumeric class: evidence from partial reports. *Perception and Psychophysics*, 33, 533–47.

Duncan, K. D. (1981). Training for fault diagnosis in industrial process plant. In J. Rasmussen and W. B. Rouse (eds.), *Human Detection and Diagnosis of System Failures*. New York: Plenum.

Dunlop, J. (1958). *Industrial Relations Systems*. New York: Holt, Rinehart and Winston.

Dunnette, M. D. (1963a). A note on the criterion. *Journal of Applied Psychology*, 47, 251–4.

Dunnette, M. D. (1963b). A modified model for test validation and selection research. *Journal of Applied Psychology*, 47, 317–23.

Dunnette, M. D. (1966). *Personnel Selection and Placement*. Belmont, Calif.: Wadsworth.

Dunnette, M. D. (1972). *Validity Study Results for Jobs Relevant to the Petroleum Refining Industry*. Washington DC: American Petroleum Institute.

Dunnette, M., Campbell, J., and Argyris, C. (1968). A symposium: laboratory training. *Industrial Relations*, 8, 1–45.

Earl, M. (1984). Emerging trends in managing new information technologies. In N. Piercy (ed.), *The Management Implications of New Information Technology*. London: Croom Helm.

Ebsworth, D. (1980). Lay officers in the German chemical workers' union: a case study. *Industrial Relations Journal*, 11(4), 63–70.

Eccles, T. (1981). *Under New Management*. London: Pan.

Edelstein, J. D., and Warner, M. (1975). *Comparative Union Democracy: Organization and Opposition in British and American Unions*. London: Allen and Unwin.

Edstrom, A., and Galbraith, J. R. (1977). Transfer of managers as a co-ordination and control strategy in multinational reorganizations. *Administrative Science Quarterly*, 22, 248–63.

Edwardes, M. (1983). *Back from the Brink*. London: Collins.

Edwards, P. K. (1981). *Strikes in the United States 1881–1974*. Oxford: Blackwell.

Edwards, P. K., and Scullion, H. (1982). *The Social Organization of Industrial Conflict*. Oxford: Blackwell.

Ehret, C. F., Groh, K. R., and Meinert, J. C. (1978). Circadian dyschronism and chronotypic ecophilia as factors in ageing and longevity. *Advances in Experimental and Medical Biology*, 108, 185–213.

Eisenberg, P., and Lazarsfeld, P. F. (1938). The psychological effects of unemployment. *Psychological Bulletin*, 35, 358–90.

Ekkers, C. L. (1984). Job design and automation in the Netherlands. In F. Butera and J. E. Thurman (eds.), *Automation and Work Design*. Amsterdam: North-Holland.

Eldridge, J. E. T. (1968). *Industrial Disputes*. London: Routledge and Kegan Paul.

Elias, P., and Main, B. (1982). *Women's Working Lives*. Warwick: University of Warwick Institute for Employment Research.

Epton, S. R., Payne, R. L., and Pearson, A. W. (1983). *Managing Interdisciplinary Research*. Chichester: Wiley.

Equal Opportunities Commission (1984). *The Fact About Women is . . .* Manchester: EOC.

Equal Opportunities Commission (1985). *Ninth Annual Report 1984*. London: HMSO.

Etzioni, A. (1961). *A Comparative Analysis of Complex Organizations*. New York: Free Press.

Evans, P., and Bartolomé, F. (1980). *Must Success Cost So Much?* London: Grant McIntyre.

Eysenck, M. W. (1982). *Attention and Arousal: Cognition and Performance*. Berlin: Springer.

Eysenck, M. W., and Folkard, S. (1980). Personality, time of day, and caffeine: some theoretical and conceptual problems in Revelle *et al. Journal of Experimental Psychology: General*, 109, 32–41.

Ezell, H. F., Odewahn, C. A., and Sherman, J. D. (1981). The effects of having been supervised by a woman on perceptions of female managerial competence. *Personnel Psychology*, 34, 291–9.

Fagin, L., and Little, M. (1984). *The Forsaken Families: the Effects of Unemployment on Family Life*. Harmondsworth: Penguin.

Faulkner, R. R. (1974). Coming of age in organizations: a comparative study of career contingencies and adult socialization. *Sociology of Work and Occupations*, 1, 131–73.

Feather, N. T., and Bond, M. J. (1983). Time structure and purposeful activity among employed and unemployed university graduates. *Journal of Occupational Psychology*, 56, 241–54.

Feather, N. T., and O'Brien, G. E. (1986). A longitudinal study of the effects of employment and unemployment on school-leavers. *Journal of Occupational Psychology*, 59, 121–44.

Feigenbaum, E. A., Barr, A., and Cohen, P. (eds.) (1981, 1982). *The Handbook of Artificial Intelligence* (3 volumes). London: Pitman.

Feldman, D. C. (1976). A contingency theory of socialization. *Administrative Science Quarterly*, 21, 433–52.

Feldman, D. C., and Brett, J. M. (1983). Coping with new jobs: a comparative study of new hires and job changers. *Academy of Management Journal*, 26, 258–72.

Fells, R. E. (1985). *The Industrial Relations Negotiations Process*. Discussion Paper 5. Department of Industrial Relations, University of Western Australia.

Ferber, F., Huber, J., and Spitze, G. (1979). Preferences for men as bosses and professionals. *Social Forces*, 58, 19–23.

Fiedler, F. E. (1967). *A Theory of Leadership Effectiveness*. New York: McGraw-Hill.

Fiedler, F. E. (1978). The contingency model and the dynamics of the leadership process. In L. Berkowitz (ed.), *Advances in Experimental Social Psychology*, Vol. 11. New York: Academic Press.

Fiedler, F. E., Chemers, M. M., and Mahar, L. (1976). *Improving Leadership Effectiveness: the Leader Match Concept*. New York: Wiley.

Field, R. H. G. (1979). A critique of the Vroom–Yetton contingency model of leadership behavior. *Academy of Management Review*, 4, 249–57.

Field, R. H. G., and Abelson, M. A. (1982). Climate: a reconceptualization and proposed model. *Human Relations*, 35, 181–201.

Filley, A. C., House, R. J., and Kerr, S. (1976). *Managerial Process and Organizational Behavior*. Glenview, Ill.: Scott Foresman.

Fineman, S. (1983a). *White Collar Unemployment: Impact and Stress*. Chichester: Wiley.

Fineman, S. (1983b). Work meanings, non-work and the taken-for-granted. *Journal of Management Studies*, 20, 143–57.

Fineman, S. (1985). *Social Work Stress and Intervention*. Aldershot: Gower.

Finlay-Jones, R. A., and Eckhardt, B. (1984). A social and psychiatric survey of unemployment among young people. *Australian and New Zealand Journal of Psychiatry*, 18, 135–43.

Firth, J., and Shapiro, D. A. (1986). An evaluation of psychotherapy for job-related distress. *Journal of Occupational Psychology*, 59, 111–19.

Fischer, G. H. (1974). *Einführung in die Theorie Psychologischer Tests*. Bern: Huber.

Fisher, C. D., and Gitelson, R. (1983). A meta-analysis of the correlates of role conflict and ambiguity. *Journal of Applied Psychology*, 68, 320–33.

Fisher, C. D., Ilgen, D. R., and Hoyer, W. D. (1979). Source credibility, information favorability, and job offer acceptance. *Academy of Management Journal*, 22, 94–103.

Fisher, S. (1984). *Stress and the Perception of Control*. London: Erlbaum.

Fitts, P. M. (1962). Factors in complex skill training. In R. Glaser (ed.), *Training Research and Education*. Pittsburgh: University of Pittsburgh Press. Republished, 1965, New York: Wiley.

Fitts, P. M., and Seeger, C. M. (1953). S–R compatibility: spatial characteristics of stimulus and response codes. *Journal of Experimental Psychology*, 46, 199–210.

Fleishman, E. A. (1953). The measurement of leadership attitudes in industry. *Journal of Applied Psychology*, 37, 153–8.

Fleishman, E. A. (1954). Dimensional analysis of psychomotor abilities. *Journal of Experimental Psychology*, 48, 437–54.

Fleishman, E. A. (1965). Attitude versus skill factors in work group productivity. *Personnel Psychology*, 18, 253–66.

Fleishman, E. A., and Quiantance, M. K. (1984). *Taxonomies of Human Performance*. New York: Academic Press.

Fletcher, B. (C.), and Payne, R. L. (1980). Stress and work: a review and theoretical framework, Part I. *Personnel Review*, 9(1), 19–29.

Fletcher, C. (1981). Candidates' beliefs and self-presentation strategies in selection interviews. *Personnel Review*, 10, 14–17.

Flier, H. van der, and Drenth, P. J. D. (1980). Fair selection and comparability of test scores. In L. J. Th. v. d. Kamp, W. F. Langerak and D. N. M. de Gruijter (eds.), *Psychometrics for Educational Debates*. Chichester: Wiley.

Folkard, S. (1983). Diurnal variation. In G. R. J. Hockey (ed.), *Stress and Fatigue in Human Performance*. Chichester: Wiley.

Folkard, S., and Monk, T. H. (1979). Shiftwork and performance. *Human Factors*, 21, 483–92.

Folkard, S., and Monk, T. H. (1980). Circadian rhythms in human memory. *British Journal of Psychology*, 71, 295–307.

Folkard, S., and Monk, T. H. (1985a). Circadian performance rhythms. In S. Folkard and T. H. Monk (eds.), *Hours of Work*. Chichester: Wiley.

Folkard, S., and Monk, T. H. (eds.) (1985b). *Hours of Work: Temporal Factors in Work Scheduling*. Chichester: Wiley.

Folkard, S., Monk, T. H., Bradbury, R., and Rosenthall, J. (1977). Time of day effects in school children's immediate and delayed recall of meaningful material. *British Journal of Psychology*, 68, 45–60.

Folkard, S., Monk, T. H., and Lobban, M. C. (1978). Short- and long-term adjustment of circadian rhythms in 'permanent' night nurses. *Ergonomics*, 21, 785–99.

Folkard, S., Wever, R. A., and Wildgruber, C. M. (1983). Multioscillatory control of circadian rhythms in human performance. *Nature*, 305, 223–6.

Folkard, S., Condon, R., and Herbert, M. (1984). Night shift paralysis. *Experientia*, 40, 510–12.

Folkard, S., Hume, S. I., Minors, D. S., Waterhouse, J. M., and Watson, F. L. (1985a). Independence of the circadian rhythm in alertness from the sleep/wake cycle. *Nature*, 313, 678–9.

Folkard, S., Minors, D. S., and Waterhouse, J. M. (1985b). Chronobiology and shift work: current issues and trends. *Chronobiologia*, 12, 31–54.

Folkard, S., Marks, M. N., and Froberg, J. E. (in press). Towards a causal nexus of human psychophysiological variables based on their circadian rhythmicity. *Revija za Psihologiju.*

Folkman, S. (1984). Personal control and stress and coping processes: a theoretical analysis. *Journal of Personality and Social Psychology*, 46, 839–52.

Forbes, R. J. and Jackson, P. R. (1980). Non-verbal behaviour and the outcome of selection interviews. *Journal of Occupational Psychology*, 53, 65–72.

Forester, T. (ed.) (1985). *The Information Technology Revolution: the Complete Guide.* Oxford: Blackwell.

Forsythe, S., Drake, M. F., and Cox, C. E. (1985). Influence of applicant's dress on interviewer's selection decisions. *Journal of Applied Psychology*, 70, 374–8.

Foster, G. M. (1962). *Traditional Cultures and the Impact of Technological Change.* New York: Harper.

Foster, M. (1972). Introduction to the theory and practice of action research in work organizations. *Human Relations*, 25, 529–56.

Fox, A. (1971). *A Sociology of Work and Industry.* London: Macmillan.

Frankenhaeuser, M., and Johansson, G. (1981). On the psychophysiological consequences of understimulation and overstimulation. In L. Levi (ed.), *Society, Stress and Disease*, Vol. 4. Oxford: Oxford University Press.

Fraser, R. (1947). *The Incidence of Neurosis Among Factory Workers.* (Report No. 90, Industrial Health Research Board.) London: HMSO.

Frederiksen, L. W. (ed.) (1982). *Handbook of Organizational Behavior Management.* New York: Wiley.

French, J. R. P., Jr, and Raven, B. H. (1960). The bases of social power. In D. Cartwright and A. Zander (eds.), *Group Dynamics: Research and Theory.* (2nd ed.) New York: Row, Peterson.

French, J. R. P., Israel, J., and As, D. (1960). An experiment on participation in a Norwegian factory. *Human Relations*, 13, 3–19.

Frese, M. (1982). Occupational socialization and psychological development: an underemphasized research perspective in industrial psychology. *Journal of Occupational Psychology*, 55, 209–24.

Frese, M. and Sabini, J. (eds.) (1985). *Goal-Directed Behavior.* Hillsdale, NJ: Erlbaum.

Friedlander, F., and Brown, L. D. (1974). Organization development. *Annual Review of Psychology*, 25, 313–41.

Fröhlich, D. (1983). *The Use of Time During Unemployment.* Assen: Van Gorcum.

Fryer, D. M., and Payne, R. L. (1984). Proactivity in unemployment: findings and implications. *Leisure Studies*, 3, 273–95.

Fryer, D. M., and Payne, R. L. (1986). Being unemployed: a review of the literature on the psychological experience of unemployment. In C. L. Cooper and I. Robertson (eds.), *Review of Industrial and Organizational Psychology*. Chichester: Wiley.

Gagne, R. M. (1977). *The Conditions of Learning*. (3rd ed.) New York: Holt, Rinehart and Winston.

Gagne, R. M., and Briggs, L. J. (1974). *Principles of Instructional Design*. New York: Holt, Rinehart and Winston.

Gallistel, C. R. (1980). *The Organization of Action*. Hillsdale, NJ: Erlbaum.

Garraty, J. A. (1978). *Unemployment in History*. New York: Harper and Row.

Gates, A. I. (1916). Variations in efficiency during the day, together with practise effects, sex differences, and correlations. *University of California Publications in Psychology*, 2, 1–156.

Gennard, J. (1985). What's new in industrial relations? *Personnel Management*, 37, 19–21.

Gerwin, D. (1981). Relationship between structure and technology. In P. C. Nystrom and W. H. Starbuck (eds.), *Handbook of Organizational Design: volume 2*. Oxford: Oxford University Press.

Gettys, L. D., and Cann, A. (1981). Children's perceptions of occupation sex stereotypes. *Sex Roles*, 1, 301–8.

Ghiselli, E. E. (1966). *The Validity of Occupational Aptitude Tests*. New York: Wiley.

Ghiselli, E. E. (1973). The validity of aptitude tests in personnel selection. *Personnel Psychology*, 26, 461–77.

Gilligan, P., and Long, J. (1984). Videotex technology: an overview with special reference to transaction processing as an interactive service. *Behaviour and Information Technology*, 3, 41–71.

Glendon, A. I., Tweedie, D. P., and Behrend, H. (1975). Pay negotiations and income policy: a comparison of the views of managers and trade unions lay negotiations. *Industrial Relations Journal*, 6(3), 4–19.

Glowinkowski, S. P., and Cooper, C. L. (1985). Current issues in organizational stress research. *Bulletin of the British Psychological Society*, 38, 212–16.

Glueck, W. F. (1973). Recruiters and executives: how do they affect job choice? *Journal of College Placement*, 33, 77–8.

Goldberg, D. P. (1972). *The Detection of Psychiatric Illness by Questionnaire*. Oxford: Oxford University Press.

Goldsmith, W., and Clutterbuck, D. (1984). *The Winning Streak*. London: Weidenfeld and Nicolson.

Goldstein, I. L. (1974). *Training: Program Development and Evaluation*. Monterey, Calif.: Brooks/Cole.

Goldthorpe, J. H., Lockwood, D., Bechhofer, F., and Platt, J. (1968). *The Affluent Worker*. Cambridge: Cambridge University Press.

Goodale, J. C., and Hall, D. T. (1976). Inheriting a career: the effects of sex, values and parents. *Journal of Vocational Behavior*, 8, 19–30.

Goodman, P. S. (1982). *Change in Organizations*. San Francisco, Calif.: Jossey-Bass.

Goodman, P. S., and Argote, L. (1984). Research on the social impacts of robotics: issues and some evidence. In S. Oskamp (ed.), *Applied Social Psychology Annual 5*. Beverly Hills, Calif.: Sage.

Gopher, D., and Braune, R. (1984). On the psychophysics of workload: why bother with subjective measures? *Human Factors*, 26, 519–32.

Gore, S. (1978). The effect of social support in moderating the health consequences of unemployment. *Journal of Health and Social Behavior*, 19, 157–65.

Gorman, C. D., Clover, W. H., and Doherty, M. E. (1978). Can we learn anything about interviewing real people from 'interviews' of paper people? Two studies of the external validity of a paradigm. *Organizational Behavior and Human Performance*, 22, 165–92.

Gowler, D., and Legge, K. (1975). Occupational role integration and the retention of labour. In B. O. Pettman (ed.), *Labour Turnover and Retention*. Aldershot: Gower.

Gowler, D., and Parry, G. (1979). Professionalism and its discontents. *New Forum*, 5, 54–6.

Grandjean, E. (ed.) (1984). *Ergonomics and Health in Modern Offices*. London: Taylor and Francis.

Grayson, L. (1984). *The Social and Economic Impact of New Technology 1975–84: a Selected Bibliography*. Letchworth: Technical Communications.

Green, B. F., and Anderson, L. K. (1956). Color coding in a visual search task. *Journal of Experimental Psychology*, 51, 19–24.

Gregory, R. (1971). Skinner boxes. *New Society*, 9 September.

Griffin, R. W. (1983). Objective and social sources of information in task design: a field experiment. *Administrative Science Quarterly*, 28, 184–200.

Groot, A. D. de, (1961). *Methodologie*. The Hague: Mouton.

Groot, A. D. de, (1969). *Methodology: Foundations of Inference and Research in the Behavioral Sciences*. The Hague: Mouton.

Gruijter, D. N. M. de, and Kamp, L. J. Th. van der (1984). *Statistical Models in Psychological and Educational Testing*. Lisse: Swets and Zeitlinger.

Guilford, J. P. (1959). *Personality*. New York: McGraw-Hill.

Guion, R. M. (1965). *Personnel Testing*. New York: McGraw-Hill.

Gulliksen, H. (1950). *Theory of Mental Tests*. New York: Wiley.

Gulowsen, J. (1972). A measure of work-group autonomy. In L. E. Davis and J. C. Taylor (eds.), *Design of Jobs*. Harmondsworth: Penguin.

Haan, N. (1981). Common dimensions to personality development: early adolescence to middle life. In D. H. Eichdorn, J. A. Clausen, N. Haan, M. P. Honzik and P. H. Mussen (eds.), *Present and Past in Middle Life*. London: Academic Press.

Hackman, J. R. (1983). The design of work teams. In L. Lorsch (ed.), *Handbook of Organizational Behavior*. Englewood Cliffs, NJ: Prentice-Hall.

Hackman, J. R., and Lawler, E. E. (1971). Employee reactions to job characteristics. *Journal of Applied Psychology*, 55, 259–86.

Hackman, J. R., and Oldham, G. R. (1975). Development of the Job Diagnostic Survey. *Journal of Applied Psychology*, 60, 159–70.

Hackman, J. R., and Oldham, G. R. (1976). Motivation through the design of work: test of a theory. *Organizational Behavior and Human Performance*, 16, 250–79.

Hackman, J. R., and Oldham, G. R. (1980). *Work Redesign*. Reading, Mass.: Addison-Wesley.

Hackman, J. R., Pearce, J. L., and Wolfe, J. C. (1978). Effects of change in job characteristics on work attitudes and behaviors: a naturally occurring quasi-experiment. *Organizational Behavior and Human Performance*, 21, 289–304.

Haire, M., Ghiselli, E. E., and Porter, L. W. (1966). *Managerial Thinking: An International Study*. New York: Wiley.

Hakel, M. D., and Schuh, A. J. (1971). Job applicant attributes judged important across seven divergent occupations. *Personnel Psychology*, 24, 45–52.

Hall, D. T. (1968). Identity changes during the transition from student to professor. *School Review*, 76, 445–469.

Hall, D. T. (1976). *Careers in Organizations*. Pacific Palisades, Calif.: Goodyear.

Hall, D. T., and Hall, F. (1980). Stress and the two-career couple. In C. L. Cooper and R. Payne (eds.), *Current Concerns in Occupational Stress*. Chichester: Wiley.

Hall, D. T., and Schneider, B. (1973). *Organizational Climates and Careers: the Work Lives of Priests*. New York: Seminar Press.

Halpin, A. W., and Winer, B. J. (1957). A factorial study of the leader behavior descriptions. In R. M. Stogdill and A. E. Coons (eds.), *Leader Behavior: Its Description and Measurement*. Columbus, Ohio: Ohio State University, Bureau of Business Research.

Halton, J. (1985). The anatomy of computing. In T. Forester (ed.), *The Information Technology Revolution: the Complete Guide*. Oxford: Blackwell.

Hamblin, A. C. (1974). *Evaluation and Control of Training*. London: McGraw-Hill.

Hammond, N., and Barnard, P. (1984). Dialogue design: characteristics of user knowledge. In A. Monk (ed.), *Fundamentals of Human–Computer Interaction*. London: Academic Press.

Handy, C. (1984). *The Future of Work*. Oxford: Blackwell.

Hankim, C. (1979). *Occupational Segregation*. Research Paper No. 9, Department of Employment. London: HMSO.

Harman, R. L. (1974). Goals of Gestalt therapy. *Professional Psychology*, 5, 178–84.

Harn, T. J., and Thornton, G. C., III (1985). Recruiter counselling behaviours and applicant impressions. *Journal of Occupational Psychology*, 54, 165–73.

Harrington, J. M. (1978). *Shift-work and Health: a Critical Review of the Literature*. London: HMSO.

Hartley, J. (1984). Industrial relations psychology. In M. M. Gruneberg and T. D. Wall (eds.), *Social Psychology and Organizational Behaviour*. Chichester: Wiley.

Hartley, J. (1985). *Designing Instructional Text*. (2nd ed.) London: Kogan Page.

Hartley, J., and Davies, I. K. (1976). Preinstructional strategies: the role of pretests, behavioural objective, overviews and advance organizers. *Review of Educational Research*, 46, 239–65.

Hayes-Roth, F., Waterman, D. A., and Lenat, D. B. (eds.) (1983). *Building Expert Systems*. Reading, Mass.: Addison-Wesley.

Haynes, S. G. and Feinleib, M. (1980). Women, work and coronary heart disease; Prospective findings from the Framingham Heart Study. *American Journal of Public Health*, 70, 133–41.

Hedberg, B., and Mumford, E. (1975). The design of computer systems. In E. Mumford and H. Sackman (eds.), *Human Choice and Computers*. New York: North-Holland.

Heinich, R., Molenda, M., and Russell, J. D. (1982). *Instructional Media: The New Technologies of Instruction*. New York: Wiley.

Heiss, R. (1963). *Handbuch der Psychologie, Band 6: Psychologische Diagnostik*. Göttingen: Verlag für Psychologie.

Hemphill, J. K. (1950). *Leader Behavior Description*. Columbus, Ohio: Ohio State University, Personnel Research Board.

Hendrie, H. C. (1981). Depression in the course of physical illness. In G. Salvendy and M. J. Smith (eds.), *Machine Pacing and Occupational Stress*. London: Taylor and Francis.

Heneman, H. G. (1975). The impact of interviewer training and interview structure on the reliability and validity of the selection interview. *Proceedings of the Academy of Management*, 1975, 231–3.

Henning, M., and Jardim, A. (1979). *The Managerial Women*. London: Pan Books.

Hepworth, S. J. (1980). Moderating factors of the psychological impact of unemployment. *Journal of Occupational Psychology*, 53, 139–45.

Herman, S. M. (1972). A Gestalt orientation to organization development. In W. W. Burke (ed.), *Contemporary Organization Development: Conceptual Orientations and Interventions*. Arlington: NTL Institute.

Herman-Taylor, R. (1985). Finding new ways of overcoming resistance to change. In M. Pennings (ed.), *Organizational Strategy and Change*. San Francisco Calif.: Jossey-Bass.

Herriot, P. (1968). The comprehension of sentences as a function of grammatical depth and order. *Journal of Verbal Learning and Verbal Behavior*, 7, 938–41.

Herriot, P. (1981). Towards an attributional theory of the selection interview. *Journal of Occupational Psychology*, 54, 165–73.

Herriot, P. (1984). *Down From the Ivory Tower: Graduates and Their Jobs*. Chichester: Wiley.

Herriot, P. and Rothwell, C. (1983). Expectations and impressions in the graduate selection interview. *Journal of Occupational Psychology*, 56, 303–14.

Herzberg, F. (1966). *Work and the Nature of Man*. Chicago, Ill.: World Publishing Company.

Hickson, D. J., and McMillan, C. J. (1981). *Organization and Nation: the Aston Programme IV*. Aldershot: Gower.

Hildebrandt, G., Rohmert, W., and Rutenfranz, J. (1974). Twelve and 24-hour rhythms in error frequency of locomotive drivers and the influence of tiredness. *International Journal of Chronobiology*, 2, 97–110.

Hinrichs, J. R. (1972). Value adaptation of new Ph.D.s to academic and industrial environments: a comparative longitudinal study. *Personnel Psychology*, 25, 545–65.

Hofstede, G. (1980). *Culture's Consequences: International Differences in Work-Related Values*. Beverly Hills, Calif.: Sage.

Hofstede, G. (1986). The usefulness of the 'organizational culture' concept. *Journal of Management Studies*, 23, 253–7.

Hofstee, W. K. B. (1983). *Selectie*. Utrecht/Antwerp: Het Spectrum.

Holding, D. H. (1981). *Human Skills*. Chichester: Wiley.

Holland, J. L. (1973; 2nd ed., 1985). *Making Vocational Choices: A Theory of Careers*. Englewood Cliffs, NJ: Prentice-Hall.

Hollandsworth, J. G. Jr., Kazelskis, R., Stevens, J., and Dressel, M. E. (1979). Relative contributions of verbal articulative and non-verbal communication to employment decisions in the job interview setting. *Personnel Psychology*, 32, 359–67.

Hopson, B., and Adams, J. (1976). Towards an understanding of transition: defining some boundaries of transition dynamics. In J. Adams, J. Hayes and B. Hopson (eds.), *Transition*. London: Martin Robertson.

Horne, J. A., and Ostberg, O. (1976). A self-assessment questionnaire to determine morningness-eveningness in human circadian rhythms. *International Journal of Chronobiology*, 4, 97–110.

Horne, J. A., Brass, C. G., and Pettit, A. N. (1980). Circadian performance differences between morning and evening 'types'. *Ergonomics*, 23, 129–36.

Horner, K. (1970). *Femininity and Successful Achievement: a Basic Inconsistency*. Monterey, Calif.: Brooks/Cole.

House, J. (1981). *Work Stress and Social Support*. Reading, Mass.: Addison-Wesley.

House, R. (1977). A 1976 theory of charismatic leadership. In J. G. Hunt and L. Larson (eds.), *Leadership: the Cutting Edge*. Carbondale, Ill.: Southern Illinois University Press.

House, R. J., and Dessler, G. (1974). The path-goal theory of leadership: some *post hoc* and *a priori* tests. In J. C. Hunt and L. Larson (eds.), *Contingency Approaches to Leadership*. Carbondale, Ill.: Southern Illinois University Press.

House, R. J., and Mitchell, T. R. (1974). Path-goal theory of leadership. *Journal of Contemporary Business*, 3, 81–97.

House, R. J., Filley, A. C., and Kerr, S. (1976). Relation of leader consideration and initiating structure to R and D subordinates' satisfaction. *Administrative Science Quarterly*, 16, 19–30.

Huggett, C., Zmroczek, C., Henwood, F., and Arnold, E. (1985).

Microelectronics and the jobs women do. In W. Faulkner and E. Arnold (eds.), *Smothered by Invention*. London: Pluto Press.

Hughes, D. G., and Folkard, S. (1976). Adaptation to an 8-hour shift in living routine by members of a socially isolated community. *Nature*, 264, 232–4.

Humphreys, L. G. (1962). The organization of human abilities. *American Psychologist*, 17, 475–83.

Hunt, A. (1975). *OPCS: Survey of Management Attitudes and Practices Toward Women at Work*. London: HMSO.

Hunt, A. (1981). Women and underachievement at work. *EOC Research Bulletin*, 5, Spring.

Hunt, J. G. (1984). Organizational leadership: the contingency paradigm and its challenges. In B. Kellerman (ed.), *Leadership: Multidisciplinary Perspectives*. Englewood Cliffs, NJ: Prentice-Hall.

Hunt, J. G., Hosking, D., Schriesheim, C. A., and Stewart, R. (eds.) (1984). *Leaders and Managers*. New York: Pergamon.

Hunter, J. E., and Hunter, R. F. (1984). Validity and utility of alternative predictors of job performance. *Psychological Bulletin*, 96, 72–98.

Huse, E. F., and Cummings, T. C. (1985). *Organizational Development and Change*. St Paul: West.

Huws, U. (1984). *The New Homeworkers*. London: Low Pay Unit.

Hyman, R. (1972). *Disputes Procedure in Action*. London: Heinemann.

Iacocca, L. (1985). *Iacocca: an Autobiography*. New York: Bantam Books.

Iaffaldano, M. T., and Muchinsky, P. M. (1985). Job satisfaction and job performance: a meta-analysis. *Psychological Bulletin*, 97, 251–73.

Imada, A. S., and Hakel, M. D. (1977). Influence of non-verbal communication and rater proximity on impressions and decisions in simulated employment interviews. *Journal of Applied Psychology*, 62, 295–300.

Industrial Health Research Board (1931). *Eleventh Annual Report*. London: HMSO.

Institute for Employment Research (1983). *Review of the Economy and Employment*. Warwick: University of Warwick.

International Labour Office (ILO) (1984). *Collective Bargaining: a Response to the Recession in Industrial Market Economy Countries*. Geneva: ILO.

Irvine, S. H., and Berry, J. W. (1983). *Human Assessment and Cultural Factors*. New York/London: Plenum.

Jablin, F. M., and McComb, K. B. (1984). The employment screening interview: an organizational assimilation and communication perspective. In R. Bostrom (ed.), *Communication Yearbook*. Beverly Hills: Sage.

Jackson, D. N., Peacock, A. C., and Holden, R. R. (1982). Professional interviewers' trait inferential structures for diverse occupational groups. *Organizational Behavior and Human Performance*, 29, 1–20.

Jackson, P. R., and Warr, P. B. (1984). Unemployment and psychological ill-health: the moderating role of duration and age. *Psychological Medicine*, 14, 605–14.

Jackson, P. R., Stafford, E. M., Banks, M. H., and Warr, P. B. (1983). Unemployment and psychological distress in young people: the moderating role of employment commitment. *Journal of Applied Psychology*, 68, 525–35.

Jackson, S. E., and Maslach, C. (1982). After-effects of job-related stress: families as victims. *Journal of Occupational Behaviour*, 3, 63–77.

Jackson, S. E., and Schuler, R. S. (1985). A meta-analysis and conceptual critique of research on role ambiguity and role conflict in work settings. *Organizational Behavior and Human Decision Processes*, 36, 16–78.

Jahoda, M. (1958). *Current Concepts of Positive Mental Health*. New York: Basic Books.

Jahoda, M. (1982). *Employment and Unemployment: a Social-psychological Analysis*. Cambridge: Cambridge University Press.

Jamal, M. (1985). Relationship of job stress to job performance. *Human Relations*, 38, 409–24.

James, L. R., Demaree, R. G., and Mulaik, S. A. (1986). A note on validity generalization procedures. *Journal of Applied Psychology*, 71, 440–50.

Johansson, G., Aronsson, G., and Lindstrom, B. O. (1978). Social psychological and neuroendocrine stress reactions in highly mechanised work. *Ergonomics*, 21, 583–99.

Jones, A. P., and James, L. R. (1979). Psychological climate: dimensions and relationships of individual and aggregated work environment perceptions. *Organizational Behavior and Human Performance*, 23, 201–50.

Jones, B. (1982). Destruction or redistribution of engineering skills? The case of numerical control. In S. Wood (ed.), *The Degradation of Work?* London: Hutchinson.

Jones, G. R. (1983). Psychological orientation and the process of organizational socialization: an interactionist perspective. *Academy of Management Review*, 8, 464–74.

Jones, G. R. (1986). Socialization tactics, self-efficacy, and newcomers' adjustments to organizations. *Academy of Management Journal*, 29, 262–79.

Jones, S. (1968). Instructions, self-instructions and performance. *Quarterly Journal of Experimental Psychology*, 20, 74–8.

Joshi, H. (1984). *Women's Participation in Paid Work: Further Analysis of the Women and Employment Survey*. London: Department of Employment Research Paper No. 45.

Juralewicz, R. S. (1974). An experiment on participation in a Latin American factory. *Human Relations*, 27, 627–37.

Kabanoff, B. (1980). Work and non-work: a review of models, methods and findings. *Psychological Bulletin*, 88, 60–77.

Kahn, R. L., Wolfe, D. M., Quinn, R. P., Snoek, J. D., and Rosenthal, R. A. (1964). *Organizational Stress: Studies in Role Conflict and Ambiguity*. New York: Wiley.

Kahneman, D., and Ghiselli, E. E. (1962). Validity and non-linear heteroscedastic models. *Personnel Psychology*, 15, 1–12.

Kalin, R., and Rayko, D. S. (1978). Discrimination in evaluative judgements against foreign-accented job candidates. *Psychological Reports*, 43, 1203–9.

Kanter, R. M. (1977). *Men and Women of the Corporation*. New York: Basic Books.

Kanter, R. M. (1984). *The Change Masters*. London: Allen and Unwin.

Kantowitz, B. H., and Sorkin, R. D. (1983). *Human Factors: Understanding People–System Relationships*. New York: Wiley.

Kaplan, R. (1979). The conspicuous absence of evidence that process consultation enhances task performance. *Journal of Applied Behavioral Science*, 15, 346–60.

Karasek, R. A. (1979). Job demands, job decision latitude and mental strain: implications for job redesign. *Administrative Science Quarterly*, 24, 285–308.

Karasek, R. A., Baker, D., Marxer, F., Ahlbom, A., and Theorell, T. (1981). Job decision latitude, job demands, and cardiovascular disease: a prospective study of Swedish men. *American Journal of Public Health*, 71, 694–705.

Kassalow, E. M. (1980). Labor relations in advanced industrial societies. In B. Martin and E. M. Kassalow (eds.), *Labor Relations in Advanced Industrial Societies: Issues and Problems*. Washington DC: Carnegie Endowment for International Peace.

Katz, D., and Kahn, R. L. (1978). *The Social Psychology of Organizations*. New York: Wiley.

Katz, R. (1978). Job longevity as a situational factor in job satisfaction. *Administrative Science Quarterly*, 23, 204–223.

Katz, R. (1980). Time and work: toward an integrative perspective. In B. M.

Staw and L. L. Cummings (eds.), *Research In Organizational Behavior*, Vol. 2. Greenwich, Conn.: J A I Press.

Kaupinnen-Toropainen, K., Kandolin, I., and Mutanen, P. (1983). Job dissatisfaction and work-related exhaustion in male and female work. *Journal of Occupational Behaviour*, 4, 193–207.

Kay, H., Dodd, B., and Sime, M. (1968). *Teaching Machines and Programmed Instruction*. Harmondsworth: Penguin.

Keenan, A. (1976a). Interviewers' evaluations of applicant characteristics: differences between personnel and non-personnel managers. *Journal of Occupational Psychology*, 49, 223–30.

Keenan, A. (1976b). Effects of the non-verbal behaviour of interviewers on candidates' performance. *Journal of Occupational Psychology*, 49, 171–176.

Keenan, A. (1977). Some relationships between interviewers' personal feelings about candidates' general evaluation of them. *Journal of Occupational Psychology*, 50, 275–83.

Keenan, A. (1978). The selection interview: candidates' reactions and interviewers' judgements. *British Journal of Social and Clinical Psychology*, 17, 201–9.

Keenan, A., and Wedderburn, A. A. I. (1980). Putting the boot on the other foot: candidates' descriptions of interviewers. *Journal of Occupational Psychology*, 53, 81–9.

Keller, R. T., and Holland, W. E. (1981). Job change: a naturally occurring field experiment. *Human Relations*, 34, 1053–67.

Kellerman, B. (ed.) (1984). *Leadership: Multidisciplinary Perspectives*. Englewood Cliffs, NJ: Prentice-Hall.

Kelly, J. E. (1982). *Scientific Management, Job Redesign and Work Performance*. London: Academic Press.

Kelly, J. E., and Nicholson, N. (1980). The causation of strikes: a review of theoretical approaches and the potential contribution of social psychology. *Human Relations*, 33, 853–83.

Kemp, N. J., and Cook, J. D. (1983). Job longevity and growth-need strength as joint moderators of the task design–job satisfaction relationship. *Human Relations*, 36, 883–98.

Kemp, N. J., Wall, T. D., Clegg, C. W., and Cordery, J. L. (1983). Autonomous work groups in a greenfield site: a comparative study. *Journal of Occupational Psychology*, 56, 271–88.

Kerkhof, G. A. (1985). Inter-individual differences in the human circadian system: a review. *Biological Psychology*, 20, 83–112.

Kerr, C., and Siegel, A. (1954). The inter-industry propensity to strike. In A. Kornhauser (ed.), *Industrial Conflict*. New York: McGraw-Hill.

Kerr, S., and Jermier, J. M. (1978). Substitutes for leadership: their meaning and measurement. *Organizational Behavior and Human Performance*, 22, 375–403.

Kessler, R. C., Price, R. H., and Wortman, C. B. (1985). Social factors in psychopathology: stress, social support, and coping processes. *Annual Review of Psychology*, 36, 531–72.

Kets de Vries, M. F. R. (1977). The entrepreneurial personality: a person at the crossroads. *Journal of Management Studies*, 14, 34–57.

Kilmann, R. (1984). *Beyond the Quick Fix*. San Francisco, Calif.: Jossey-Bass.

Kilpatrick, R., and Trew, K. (1985). Life-styles and psychological well-being among unemployed men in Northern Ireland. *Journal of Occupational Psychology*, 58, 207–16.

Kinicki, A. J., and Lockwood, C. A. (1985). The interview process: an examination of factors recruiters use in evaluating job applicants. *Journal of Vocational Behavior*, 26, 117–25.

Klein, K. E., Wegmann, H. M., and Hunt, B. I. (1972). Desynchronization of body temperature and performance circadian rhythm as a result of outgoing and homegoing transmeridian flights. *Aerospace Medicine*, 43, 119–32.

Klein, L. (1976). *New Forms of Work Organization*. Cambridge: Cambridge University Press.

Klein, S. M., Kraut, A. I., and Wolfson, A. (1971). Employee reactions to attitude survey feedback. *Administrative Science Quarterly*, 16, 497–514.

Kleitman, N. (1939: Revised 1963). *Sleep and Wakefulness*. Chicago, Ill.: University of Chicago Press.

Kogi, K. (1985). Introduction to the problems of shift-work. In S. Folkard and T. H. Monk (eds.), *Hours of Work*. Chichester: Wiley.

Kohn, M. L., and Schooler, C. (1983). *Work and Personality: an Inquiry into the Impact of Social Stratification*. Norwood, NJ: Ablex.

Korman, A. K. (1966). 'Consideration', 'Initiating Structure' and organizational criteria. *Personnel Psychology*, 18, 349–60.

Korman, A. K., Wittig-Bergman, U., and Lang, D. (1981). Career success and personal failure: alienation in professionals and managers. *Academy of Management Journal*, 24, 342–60.

Kornhauser, A. (1965). *Mental Health of the Industrial Worker*. New York: Wiley.

Kreitman, N., and Platt, S. (1984). Suicide, unemployment, and domestic gas detoxification in Britain. *Journal of Epidemiology and Community Health*, 38, 1–6.

Kundi, M., Koller, M., Cervinka, R., and Haider M. (1979). Consequences of shift work as a function of age and years on shift. *Chronobiologia*, 6, 123.

Landsberger, H. A. (1955a). Interaction process analysis of mediation of labor–management disputes. *Journal of Abnormal and Social Psychology*, 57, 552–8.

Landsberger, H. A. (1955b). Interaction process analysis of professional behavior: a study of labor mediators in twelve labor–management disputes. *American Sociological Review*, 20, 566–75.

Landy, F. J. (1985). *Psychology of Work Behavior* (3rd ed.). Homewood, Ill.: Dorsey.

Landy, F. J., and Farr, J. L. (1983). *The Measurement of Work Performance: Methods, Theory and Applications*. New York: Academic Press.

Langer, E. J. (1983). *The Psychology of Control*. Beverly Hills, Calif.: Sage.

Larwood, L., and Gutek, G. (1984). Women at work in the USA. In M. J. Davison and C. L. Cooper (eds.), *Working Women – an International Survey*. Chichester: Wiley.

Larwood, L., Stramberg, A. A., and Gutek, B. A. (1985, 1987). *Women and Work – an Annual Review*. London: Sage.

Latack, J. C. (1984). Career transitions within organizations: an exploratory study of work, nonwork and coping strategies. *Organizational Behavior and Human Performance*, 34, 296–322.

Latham, G. P., and Saari, L. M. (1984). Do people do what they say? Further studies on the situational interview. *Journal of Applied Psychology*, 69, 569–73.

Latham, G. P., Saari, L. M., Pursell, E. D., and Campion, M. A. (1980). The situational interview. *Journal of Applied Psychology*, 65, 422–7.

Law, B. (1981). Careers theory: a third dimension? In A. G. Watts, D. E. Super, and J. M. Kidd (eds.), *Career Development in Britain*. Cambridge: Hobsons Press.

Lawler, E. E., Hackman, J. R., and Kaufman, S. (1973). Effects of job redesign: a field experiment. *Journal of Applied Social Psychology*, 3, 49–62.

Lawrence, D. H. (1971). Two studies of visual search for word targets with controlled rates of presentation. *Perception and Psychophysics*, 10, 85–89.

Lawshe, C. H., and Balma, M. J. (1966). *Principles of Personnel Testing*. (2nd ed.) New York: McGraw-Hill.

Lazarus, R. S., and Folkman, S. (1984). *Stress, Appraisal, and Coping*. New York: Springer.

Legge, K. (1984). *Evaluating Planned Organizational Change*. London: Academic Press.

Leonard, J. A. (1953). Advance information in sensorimotor skills. *Quarterly Journal of Experimental Psychology*, 5, 141–8.

Leonard, J. A., and Newman, C. (1964). On the formation of higher habits. *Nature*, 203, 550–51.

Lewin, K. (1951). *Field Theory in Social Science.* New York: Harper and Row.

Lewin, K. (1952). Group decisions and social change. In G. E. Swanson, T. M. Newcomb and E. L. Hartley (eds.), *Readings in Social Psychology.* (2nd ed.) New York: Holt.

Lewin, K., Lippitt, R., and White, R. K. (1939). Patterns of aggressive behavior in experimentally created social climates. *Journal of Social Psychology*, 10, 271–301.

Lewis, C. (1985). *Employee Selection.* London: Hutchinson.

Lieberman, S. (1956). The effects of changes in roles on the attitudes of role occupants. *Human Relations*, 9, 467–86.

Lienert, G. A. (1961). *Testaufbau und Testanalyse.* Weinheim: Julius Beltz.

Liker, J. K., and Elder, G. H. (1983). Economic hardship and marital relations in the 1930s. *American Sociological Review*, 48, 343–59.

Likert, R. (1961). *New Patterns of Management.* New York: McGraw-Hill.

Likert, R. (1967). *The Human Organization.* New York: McGraw-Hill.

Lippitt, G. L. (1969). *Organizational Renewal.* New York: Appleton-Century-Crofts.

Lippitt, G. L. (1970). Developing life plans: a new concept and design for training and development. *Training and Development Journal*, May, 2–7.

Lippitt, G. L., Langseth, P., and Mossop, J. (1985). *Implementing Organizational Change.* San Francisco: Jossey-Bass.

Locke, E. A., Sirota, D., and Wolfson, A. (1976). An experimental case study of the successes and failures of job enrichment in a government agency. *Organizational Behavior and Human Performance*, 5, 484–500.

Lockwood, B., and Knowles, W. (1984). Women at work in Great Britain. In M. J. Davison and C. L. Cooper (eds.), *Women at Work: an International Survey.* Chichester: Wiley.

Lofquist, L. H., and Dawis, R. V. (1969). *Adjustment to Work.* New York: Appleton-Century-Crofts.

Loher, B. T., Noe, R. A., Moeller, N. L., and Fitzgerald, M. P. (1985). A meta-analysis of the relation of job characteristics to job satisfaction. *Journal of Applied Psychology*, 70, 280–89.

Long, P. (1984). Would you put your daughter into personnel management? *Personnel Management*, April, 16–20.

Long, J., and Baddeley, A. (eds.) (1981). *Attention and Performance IX*. Hillsdale, NJ: Erlbaum.

Long, J., and Buckley, P. (1984). Transaction processing using videotex or: Shopping on Prestel. In B. Shackel (ed.), *Interact '84*. Amsterdam: North-Holland.

Long, R. J. (1984). The application of microelectronics to the office: organisational and human implications. In N. Piercy (ed.), *The Management Implications of New Information Technology*. London: Croom Helm.

Lorange, P., and Vancil, R. (1977). *Strategic Planning Systems*. Englewood Cliffs, NJ: Prentice-Hall.

Lord, F. M. (1980). *Applications of Item Response Theory to Practical Testing Problems*. Hillsdale, NJ: Erlbaum.

Lord, F. M., and Novick, M. R. (1968). *Statistical Theories of Mental Test Scores*. Reading, Mass.: Addison-Wesley.

Louis, M. R. (1980). Surprise and sense-making: what newcomers experience in entering unfamiliar organizational settings. *Administrative Science Quarterly*, 25, 226–51.

Lowin, A., and Craig, J. R. (1968). The influence of level of performance on managerial style: an experimental object-lesson in the ambiguity of correlational data. *Organizational Behavior and Human Performance*, 3, 440–58.

Luthans, F., and Kreitner, R. (1985). *Organizational Behavior Modification and Beyond*. Glenview, Ill.: Scott Foresman.

Luthans, F., Maciag, W. S., and Rosenkrantz, S. A. (1983). O. B. Mod: meeting the productivity challenge with Human Resource Management. *Personnel*, March–April, 28–36.

Maas, J. B. (1965). Patterned expectation interview: reliability studies on a new technique. *Journal of Applied Psychology*, 49, 431–3.

Maccoby, M. (1977). *The Gamesman*. London: Secker and Warburg.

McCormick, E. J. (1976). Job and task analysis. In M. D. Dunnette (ed.), *Handbook of Industrial and Organizational Psychology*. Chicago, Ill.: Rand McNally.

McCormick, E. J., and Sanders, M. S. (1982). *Human Factors in Engineering and Design*. New York: McGraw-Hill.

McGoldrick, A. (1985). *Equal Treatment In Occupational Pension Schemes*. London: EOC.

McGovern, T. V., and Tinsley, H. E. (1978). Interviewer evaluations of interviewee non-verbal behavior. *Journal of Vocational Behavior*, 13, 163–71.

McGrath, J. E. (1976). Stress and behavior in organizations. In M. D.

Dunnette (ed.), *Handbook of Industrial and Organizational Psychology*. Chicago, Ill.: Rand McNally.

McGregor, D. (1960). *The Human Side of Enterprise*. New York: McGraw-Hill.

McLean, A., Sims, D., Mangham, I. L., and Tuffield, D. (1982). *Organization Development in Transition*. Chichester: Wiley.

McMahon, J. T. (1972). The contingency theory: Logic and method revisited. *Personnel Psychology*, 25, 697–710.

Madge, N. (1983). Unemployment and its effects on children. *Journal of Child Psychology and Psychiatry*, 24, 311–19.

Magenau, J. M., and Pruitt, D. G. (1979). The social psychology of bargaining. In G. M. Stephenson and C. J. Brotherton (eds.), *Industrial Relations: a Social Psychological Approach*. Chichester: Wiley.

Magnusson, R. (1966). *Testteori*. Uppsala: University of Uppsala Press.

Mahoney, P. (1985). *Schools For Boys?* London: Hutchinson.

Mangham, I. L. (1979). *The Politics of Organizational Change*. London: Associated Business Press.

Mangham, I. L. (1986a). *Power, Passion and Performance*. Oxford: Blackwell.

Mangham, I. L. (1986b). *Essays in Organization Analysis and Development*. Chichester: Wiley.

Mann, F. C. (1961). Studying and creating change. In W. G. Bennis, K. D. Benne and R. Chin (eds.), *The Planning of Change*. New York: Holt, Rinehart and Winston.

Mansfield, R. (1984). Changes in information technology, organisational design and managerial control. In N. Piercy (ed.), *The Management Implications of New Information Technology*. London: Croom Helm.

Mant, A. (1983). *Leaders We Deserve*. London: Martin Robertson.

Marsh, A., Hackman, M., and Miller, D. (1981). *Workplace Relations in the Engineering Industry in the U.K. and Federal Republic of Germany*. London: Anglo-German Foundation for the Study of Industrial Society.

Marsh, P. (1967). *The Anatomy of a Strike*. London: Institute for Race Relations.

Marshall, J. (1984). *Women Managers – Travellers in a Male World*. Chichester: Wiley.

Marshall, J., and McLean, A. J. (1985). Exploring organisation culture as a route to organisational change. In V. Hammond (ed.), *Current Research in Management*. London: Frances Pinter.

Marstrand, P. (ed.) (1984). *New Technology and the Future of Work and Skills*. London: Pinter.

Martin, E., and Roberts, K. H. (1966). Grammatical features in sentence retention. *Journal of Verbal Learning and Verbal Behavior*, 5, 211–18.

Martin, J., and Roberts, C. (1984). *Women and Employment – A Life Time Perspective*. Department of Employment and Office of Population Censuses and Surveys. London: HMSO.

Martin, J., and Siehl, C. (1981). Organizational Culture and Counterculture: General Motors and DeLorean. Research Paper 633, Graduate School of Business, Stanford University.

Martin, M., and Jones, G. V. (1979). Modality dependency of loss of recency in free recall. *Psychological Research*, 40, 273–89.

Martin, R., and Wallace, J. (1985). Women and unemployment: activities and social contact. In B. Roberts, R. Finnegan and D. Gallie (eds.), *New Approaches to Economic Life*. Manchester: Manchester University Press.

Maslach, C., and Jackson, S. E. (1981). The measurement of experienced burnout. *Journal of Occupational Behaviour*, 2, 99–113.

Maslow, A. H. (1943). A theory of human motivation. *Psychological Review*, 50, 370–96.

Maslow, A. H. (1973). *The Farther Reaches of Human Nature*. Harmondsworth: Penguin.

Maurice, M. (1979). A study of the societal effect: universality and specificity in organization research. In C. J. Lammers and D. J. Hickson (eds.), *Organizations Alike and Unlike*. London: Routledge and Kegan Paul.

Mayer, R. E. (1977). The sequencing of instruction and the concept of assimilation-to-schema. *Instructional Science*, 6, 369–88.

Mayfield, E. C., Brown, S. H., and Hamstra, B. W. (1980). Selection interviewing in the life-insurance industry: an update of research and practice. *Personnel Psychology*, 33, 725–40.

Meers, A. (1975). Performance on different turns of duty within a three-shift system and its relation to body temperature – two field studies. In P. Colquhoun, S. Folkard, P. Knauth and J. Rutenfranz (eds.), *Experimental Studies of Shift Work*. Opladen: Westdeutscher Verlag.

Meili, R. (1961). *Lehrbuch der Psychologischen Diagnostik*. (4th ed.) Stuttgart.

Merton, R. K. (1957). *Social Theory and Social Structure*. Glencoe, Ill.: Free Press.

Metal Working Production (1983). *The Fifth Survey of Machine Tools and Production Equipment in Britain*. London: Morgan-Grampian.

Meyer, J., and Rowan, B. (1977). Institutionalized organizations: formal structure as myth and ceremony. *American Journal of Sociology*, 83, 340–63.

Michelson, M. (1897). Ueber die Tiefe des Schlafes. *Psychol. Arbeiten.*, 2, 84–117.

Miles, R. E. (1965). Human relations or human resources? *Harvard Business Review*, 43, 148–63.

Miles, R. E. (1975). *Theories of Management*. New York: McGraw-Hill.

Miller, G. A. (1956). The magical number seven plus or minus two: some limits on our capacity for processing information. *Psychological Review*, 63, 81–97.

Miner, J. B. (1975). The uncertain future of the leadership concept: an overview. In J. G. Hunt and L. Larson (eds.), *Leadership Frontiers*. Carbondale, Ill.: Southern Illinois University Press.

Minors, D. S., and Waterhouse, J. M. (1981a). *Circadian Rhythms and the Human*. Bristol: Wright PSG.

Minors, D. S., and Waterhouse, J. M. (1981b). Anchor sleep as a synchronizer of rhythms on abnormal routines. In L. C. Johnson, D. I. Tepas, W. P. Colquhoun and M. J. Colligan (eds.), *Advances in Sleep Research, Vol. 7: Biological Rhythms, Sleep and Shift Work*. New York: Spectrum Publications.

Minsky, M. (1975). A framework for representing knowledge. In P. Winston (ed.), *The Psychology of Computer Vision*. New York: McGraw-Hill.

Mintzberg, H. (1973). *The Nature of Managerial Work*. Englewood Cliffs, NJ: Prentice-Hall.

Mintzberg, H. (1979). *The Structure of Organizations*. Englewood Cliffs, NJ: Prentice-Hall.

Mintzberg, H. (1983). *Structure in Fives: Designing Effective Organizations*. Englewood Cliffs, NJ: Prentice-Hall.

Mintzberg, H. (1985). The organization of the political arena. *Journal of Management Studies*, 22, 133–54.

Mirvis, P., and Berg, D. (1977). *Failures in Organization Development and Change*. New York: Wiley.

Misumi, J. (1984). Decision-making in Japanese groups and organizations, *International Yearbook of Organizational Democracy*, Vol. 2. Chichester: Wiley.

Mobley, W. H., Griffeth, R. W., Hand, N. H., and Meglino, B. M. (1979). Review and conceptual analysis of the employee turnover process. *Psychological Bulletin*, 86, 493–522.

Mohrman, J., Mohrman, A., Cooke, R., and Duncan, R. (1977). Survey feedback and problem solving intervention in a school district: 'We'll take the survey but you can keep the feedback'. In P. Mirvis and D. Berg (eds.), *Failures in Organization Development and Change*. New York: Wiley.

Monk, A. (ed.), (1985). *Fundamentals of Human–Computer Interaction*. London: Academic Press.

Monk, T. H., and Embrey, D. E. (1981). A field study of circadian rhythms in actual and interpolated task performance. In A. Reinberg, N. Vieux and P. Andlauer (eds.), *Advances in the Biosciences, Vol. 30: Night and Shift Work: Biological and Social Aspects*. London: Pergamon.

Monk, T. H., and Folkard, S. (1985). Shiftwork and performance. In S. Folkard and.T. H. Monk (eds.), *Hours of Work*. Chichester: Wiley.

Moore, L. M., and Rickel, A. (1980). Characteristics of women in traditional and non-traditional managerial roles. *Personnel Psychology*, 3, 317–33.

Moore-Ede, M. C., Sulzman, F. M., and Fuller, C. A. (1982). *The Clocks That Time Us*. Cambridge, Mass., and London: Harvard University Press.

Moray, N. (1979). *Mental Workload: Its Theory and Measurement*. New York: Plenum.

Moreland, R. L., and Levine, J. M. (1983). Socialization in small groups: temporal changes in individual–group relations. *Advances in Experimental Social Psychology*, 15, 137–92.

Morgan, G. (1986). *Images of Organization*. Beverly Hills, Calif.: Sage.

Morley, I. E. (1981). Negotiation and bargaining. In M. Argyle (ed.), *Social Skills and Work*. London: Methuen.

Morley, I. E., and Hosking, D. M. (1984). Decision-making and negotiation. In M. Gruneberg and T. Wall (eds.), *Social Psychology and Organizational Behaviour*. Chichester: Wiley.

Morley, I. E., and Stephenson, G. M. (1977). *The Social Psychology of Bargaining*. London: Allen and Unwin.

Mortimer, J. T., and Lorence, J. (1979). Work experience and occupational value socialization: a longitudinal study. *American Journal of Sociology*, 84, 1361–85.

Morton, J., Barnard, P., Hammond, N., and Long, J. (1979). Interacting with the computer: a framework. In E. J. Boutmy and A. Danthine (eds.), *Teleinformatics '79*. Amsterdam: North-Holland.

Moser, K. A., Fox, A. J., and Jones, D. R. (1984). Unemployment and mortality in the OPCS longitudinal study. *Lancet*, 2, 1324–29.

Mowday, R. T., Porter, L. W., and Steers, R. M. (1982). *Employee–Organization Linkages*. London: Academic Press.

Mulder, M. (1971). Power equalization through participation. *Administrative Science Quarterly*, 16, 31–8.

Murrell, K. F. H. (1965). *Ergonomics*. London: Chapman and Hall.

National Council for Civil Liberties (1982). *Sexual Harassment at Work*. London: NCCL.

Near, J. P., Rice, R. W., and Hunt, R. C. (1980). The relationship between work and nonwork domains: a review of empirical research. *Academy of Management Review*, 5, 415–29.

Neisser, U. (1967). *Cognitive Psychology*. New York: Appleton-Century-Crofts.

Nelson, D. L., and Quick, J. C. (1985). Professional women: are distress and disease inevitable? *Academy of Management Review*, 10, 206–18.

New South Wales Anti-Discrimination Board (1978). *Discrimination in Government Policies and Practices*, Part 2. Sydney: NSW Government.

New Zealand Department of Statistics (1981). *New Zealand Census of Population and Dwellings*. Wellington: Government Printer.

Nicholas, I., Warner, M., Sorge, A., and Hartmann, G. (1983). Computerised machine tools, manpower training and skill polarisation: a study of British and West German manufacturing firms. In G. Winch (ed.), *Information Technology in Manufacturing Processes*. London: Rossendale.

Nicholas, J. (1982). The comparative impact of Organization Development interventions on hard criteria measures. *Academy of Management Review*, 7, 531–42.

Nicholson, J. (1984). *Men and Women – How Different Are They?* Oxford: Oxford University Press.

Nicholson, N. (1979). Industrial relations climate: a case study approach. *Personnel Review*, 8 (3), 20–25.

Nicholson, N. (1984). A theory of work role transitions. *Administrative Science Quarterly*, 29, 172–91.

Nicholson, N. (1987). The transition cycle: a conceptual framework for the analysis of change and human resources management. In K. M. Rowland and G. R. Ferris (eds.), *Research in Personnel and Human Resources Management*, Vol. 5. Greenwich, Conn.: JAI Press.

Nicholson, N., and West, M. A. (1987). *Managerial Job Change*. Cambridge: Cambridge University Press.

Nicholson, N., West, M., and Cawsey, T. F. (1985). Future uncertain: expected vs. attained job mobility among managers. *Journal of Occupational Psychology*, 58, 313–20.

NIP (Netherlands Instituut van Psychologen) (1976). *Beroepsethiek voor Psychologen*. Zaanijk: Heijnis.

Norman, D. A., and Bobrow, D. (1975). On data-limited and resource-limited processes. *Cognitive Psychology*, 7, 44–64.

Norman, D. A., and Bobrow, D. (1976). On the analysis of Performance Operating Characteristics. *Psychological Review*, 83, 508–10.

Northcott, J., Rogers, P., and Zeilinger, A. (1982). *Micro-electronics in Industry: Survey Statistics*. London: Policy Studies Institute.

Nunnally, J. C. (1978). *Psychometric Theory*. (2nd ed.) New York: McGraw-Hill.

Oakley, A. (1981). *Subject Women*. Oxford: Martin Robertson.

Oborne, D. J. (1982). *Ergonomics at Work*. Chichester: Wiley.

O'Brien, G. E. (1983). Skill-utilization, skill-variety and the job characteristics model. *Australian Journal of Psychology*, 35, 461–8.

Ogden, G. D. Levine, J. M., and Eisner, E. J. (1979). Measurement of workload by secondary tasks. *Human Factors*, 21, 529–48.

Oldham, G. R., and Brass, D. J. (1979). Employee reactions to an open-plan office: a naturally occurring quasi-experiment. *Administrative Science Quarterly*, 24, 267–84.

Oldham, G. R., and Rotchford, M. (1983). Relationships between office characteristics and employee reactions: a study of the physical environment. *Administrative Science Quarterly*, 28, 542–56.

Ong, C. N., and Hong, B. T. (1982). Shiftwork in manufacturing industries in Singapore. Proceedings of the 6th International Symposium on Night and Shift Work. *Journal of Human Ergology*, 11, Suppl.

O'Reilly, C., and Caldwell, D. F. (1981). The commitment and job tenure of new employees: some evidence of post-decisional justification. *Administrative Science Quarterly*, 26, 597–616.

Orpen, C. (1979). The effects of job enrichment on employee satisfaction, motivation and performance: a field experiment. *Human Relations*, 32, 189–217.

Osburn, H. G., Timmreck, C., and Bigby, D. (1981). Effect of dimensional relevance on accuracy of simulated hiring decisions by employment interviewers. *Journal of Applied Psychology*, 66, 159–65.

O'Shea, T., and Self, J. (1983). *Learning and Teaching with Computers*. Brighton: Harvester.

Parasuraman, R., and Davies, D. R. (eds.) (1984). *Varieties of Attention*. New York: Academic Press.

Parkes, K. R. (1981). Occupational stress among student nurses: a natural experiment. *Journal of Applied Psychology*, 67, 748–96.

Patrick, J. (1980). Job analysis, training and transferability: some theoretical and practical issues. In K. D. Duncan, M. M. Grunberg and D. Wallis (eds.), *Changes in Working Life*. Chichester: Wiley.

Patrick, J., and Stammers, R. B. (1981). The role of computers in training for problem diagnosis. In J. Rasmussen and W. B. Rouse (eds.), *Human*

Detection and Diagnosis of System Failures. New York: Plenum Press.

Payne, R. L., and Fletcher, B. C. (1983). Job demands, supports, and constraints as predictors of psychological strain among school-teachers. *Journal of Vocational Behavior*, 22, 136–47.

Payne, R. L., and Jones, J. G. (1987). Measurement and methodological issues in social support. In S. V. Kasl and C. L. Cooper (eds.), *Stress and Health: Issues in Research Methodology*. Chichester: Wiley.

Payne, R. L., and Pugh, D. S. (1976). Organizational structure and climate. In M. D. Dunnette (ed.), *Handbook of Industrial and Organizational Psychology*. Chicago, Ill.: Rand McNally.

Payne, R. L., Warr, P. B., and Hartley, J. (1984). Social class and the experience of unemployment. *Sociology of Health and Illness*, 6, 152–74.

Pearlman, K., Schmidt, F. L., and Hunter, J. E. (1980). Validity generalization results for tests used to predict job proficiency and training success in clerical occupations. *Journal of Applied Psychology*, 65, 373–406.

Pennings, J. M. (1985). *Organizational Strategy and Change*. San Francisco, Ill.: Jossey-Bass.

Perrow, C. (1972). *Complex Organizations: A Critical Essay*. Glenview, Ill.: Scott Foresman.

Peters, L. H., Harthe, D. D., and Pohlmann, J. T. (1985). Fiedler's contingency theory of leadership: an application of the meta-analysis procedures of Schmidt and Hunter. *Psychological Bulletin*, 97, 274–85.

Peters, T. J., and Austin, N. (1985). *A Passion for Excellence: the Leadership Difference*. London: Collings.

Peters, T. J., and Waterman, R. H. (1982). *In Search of Excellence: Lessons from America's Best-run Companies*. New York: Harper and Row.

Pettigrew, A. (1973). *The Politics of Organizational Decision-Making*. London: Tavistock.

Pew, R. W. (1966). Acquisition of hierarchical control over the temporal organization of a skill. *Journal of Experimental Psychology*, 71, 764–71.

Pfeffer, J. (1977). The ambiguity of leadership. *Academy of Management Review*, 2, 104–12.

Pfeffer, J. (1981a). Management as symbolic action. In L. L. Cummings and B. M. Staw (eds.), *Research in Organizational Behavior*, Vol. 3. Greenwich, Conn.: J A I Press.

Pfeffer, J. (1981b). *Power in Organizations*. Marshfield, Mass.: Pitman.

Phillips, J. S., and Lord, R. G. (1981). Causal attribution and perceptions of leadership. *Organizational Behavior and Human Performance*, 28, 143–63.

Pinder, C. C. (1977). Multiple predictors of post-transfer satisfaction: the role of urban factors. *Personnel Psychology*, 30, 543–56.

References

Piotrkowski, C. S. (1978). *Work and the Family System.* New York: Free Press.

Platt, S. (1984). Unemployment and suicidal behaviour: a review of the literature. *Social Science and Medicine,* 19, 93–115.

Platt, S., and Kreitman, N. (1985). Unemployment and parasuicide in Edinburgh 1968–1982. *Psychological Medicine,* 15, 113–23.

Pondy, L. R. (1967). Organization conflict: concepts and models. *Administrative Science Quarterly,* 12, 296–320.

Poole, M. (1974). Towards a sociology of shop stewards. *Sociological Review,* 22, 57–82.

Posner, B. Z. (1981). Comparing recruiter, student, and faculty perceptions of important applicant and job characteristics. *Personnel Psychology,* 34, 329–40.

Poulton, E. C. (1957). On prediction in skilled movements. *Psychological Bulletin,* 54, 467–78.

Povall, M. (1983). *Managing or Removing the Career Break.* Sheffield: Manpower Services Commission.

Povall, M. (1984). Overcoming barriers to women's advancement in European organizations. *Personnel Review,* 13(1), 32–40.

Pratten, C. F. (1976). *A Comparison of the Performance of Swedish and U.K. Companies.* Cambridge: Cambridge University Press.

Premack, S. L., and Wanous, J. P. (1985). A meta-analysis of realistic job preview experiments. *Journal of Applied Psychology,* 70, 706–19.

Prinz, W., and Sanders, A. F. (1984). *Cognition and Motor Processes.* Berlin: Springer.

Pritchard, R. D., and Karasick, B. W. (1975). The effects of organizational climate on managerial job performance and job satisfaction. *Organizational Behavior and Human Performance,* 9, 126–46.

Prokop, O. and Prokop, L. (1955). Ermudung und Einschlafen am Steuer. *Zentralblatt für Verkehrs-Medizin, Verkehrs-Psychologie und angrenzende Gebiete,* 1, 19–30.

Pruitt, D. G. (1981). *Negotiation Behavior.* New York: Academic Press.

Pruitt, D. G., Kimmel, M. J., Britton, S., Carnevale, P. J. D., Magenau, J. M., Peragallo, J., and Engram, P. (1978). The effect of accountability and surveillance on integrative bargaining. In H. Saverman (ed.), *Contributions to Experimental Economics,* Vol. 7. Tübingen: Mohr.

Pugh, D. S. (1985). *Managing in Organizations: International Perspectives.* Milton Keynes: The Open University.

Pugh, D. S., and Hickson, D. J. (1976). *Organizational Structure in its Context.* Farnborough: Saxon House.

Pugh, D. S., and Hinings, C. R. (1976). *Organizational Structure: Extensions and Replications*. Farnborough: Saxon House.

Pugh, D. S., and Payne, R. L. (eds.) (1977). *Organizational Behaviour in its Context*. Farnborough: Saxon House.

Pugh, D. S., Hickson, D. J., and Hinings, C. R. (1983). *Writers on Organizations*. (3rd ed.) Harmondsworth: Penguin.

Purcell, J. (1979). The lessons of the Commission on Industrial Relations' attempts to reform workplace industrial relations. *Industrial Relations Journal*, 10, 4–22.

Rabinowitz, S., and Hall, D. T. (1977). Organizational research on job involvement. *Psychological Bulletin*, 84, 265–88.

Rand, T. M., and Wexley, K. N. (1975). Demonstration of the effect 'similar to me' in simulated employment interviews. *Psychological Reports*, 36, 535–44.

Rapoport, R. (1970). *Mid-Career Development*. London: Tavistock.

Read, S. (1982). *Sexual Harassment at Work*. London: Hamlyn.

Reason, J., and Mycielska, K. (1982). *Absent-Minded?* Englewood Cliffs, NJ: Prentice-Hall.

Reber, A. S. (1967). Implicit learning of artificial grammars. *Journal of Verbal Learning and Verbal Behavior*, 5, 855–63.

Rehmann, J. T., Stein, E. S., and Rosenberg, B. L. (1983). Subjective pilot workload assessment. *Human Factors*, 25, 297–307.

Reigeluth, C. M. (ed.) (1983). *Instructional Design Theories and Models: an Overview of Their Current Status*. Hillsdale, NJ: Erlbaum.

Reigeluth, C. M., Merrill, M. D., Wilson, B. G., and Spiller, R. T. (1980). The elaboration theory of instruction: a model for sequencing and synthesizing instruction. *Instructional Science*, 9, 195–219.

Reilly, R. R., and Chao, G. T. (1982). Validity and fairness of some alternative employee selection procedures. *Personnel Psychology*, 35, 1–62.

Reinberg, A. (1983). Chronobiology and nutrition. In A. Reinberg and M. H. Smolensky (eds.), *Biological Rhythms and Medicine: Cellular, Metabolic, Physiopathologic, and Pharmacologic Aspects*. New York: Springer.

Reinberg, A., Andlauer, P., De Prins, J., Malbec, W., Vieux, N., and Bourdeleau, P. (1984). Desynchronisation of the oral temperature circadian rhythm and intolerance to shift work. *Nature*, 308, 272–4.

Reuchlin, M. (1969). *Méthodes d'analyse factorielle à l'usage des psychologues*. Presses Universitaires de France.

Rice, R. W. (1984). Organizational work and the overall quality of life. In S.

Oskamp (ed.), *Applied Social Psychology Annual*, Vol. 5. Beverly Hills, Calif.: Sage.

Richards, E. W. (1984). Undergraduate preparation and early career outcomes: a study of recent college graduates. *Journal of Vocational Behavior*, 24, 279–304.

Richie, J., and Barrowclough, R. (1983). *Paying for Equalisation: a Survey of Pension Age Preferences and their Costs*. London: Equal Opportunities Commission.

Rim, Y., and Mannheim, B. F. (1964). Factors related to attitudes of management and union representatives. *Personnel Psychology*, 17, 149–65.

Robarts, S., Coote, A., and Ball, E. (1981). *Positive Action for Women – The Next Step*. Nottingham: National Council for Civil Liberties.

Roberts, K. H. and Glick, W. (1981). The job characteristics approach to job task design: a critical review. *Journal of Applied Psychology*, 66, 193–217.

Robertson, I. T., and Kandola, R. S. (1982). Work sample tests: validity, adverse impact, and applicant reaction. *Journal of Occupational Psychology*, 55, 171–84.

Roe, R. A. (1983). *Grondslagen der Personeelsselektie*. Assen: Van Gorcum.

Roethlisberger, F. G., and Dickson, W. J. (1939). *Management and the Worker*. Cambridge, Mass.: Harvard University Press.

Rogers, C. R., and Skinner, B. F. (1956). Some issues concerning the control of human behavior. *Science*, 124, 1057–66.

Rogers, D. P., and Sincoff, M. Z. (1978). Favourable impression characteristics of the recruitment interviewer. *Personnel Psychology*, 31, 495–504.

Ronen, S. (1978). Job satisfaction and the neglected variable of job seniority. *Human Relations*, 31, 297–308.

Rosen, N. (1970). *Leadership Change and Work Group Dynamics*. London: Staples Press.

Rosenbrock, H. H. (1983). Robots and people. *Work and People*, 9, 14–18.

Rosenbrock, H. H. (1985). Designing automated systems: need skill be lost? In P. Marstrand (ed.), *New Technology and the Future of Work and Skills*. London: Pinter.

Ross, L. (1977). The intuitive psychologist and his shortcomings: distortions in the attribution process. *Advances in Experimental Social Psychology*, 10, 174–220.

Rothstein, M., and Jackson, D. N. (1980). Decision making in the employment interview – an experimental approach. *Journal of Applied Psychology*, 65, 271–83.

Rothstein, W. G. (1980). The significance of occupations in work careers: an empirical and theoretical review. *Journal of Vocational Behavior*, 17, 328–43.

Rothwell, S. (1984). Positive action on women's career development: an overview of the issues for individuals and organisations. In C. L. Cooper and M. J. Davidson (eds.), *Women in Management*. London: Heinemann.

Rousseau, D. M. (1977). Technological differences in job characteristics, employee satisfaction and motivation: a synthesis of job design research and socio-technical systems theory. *Organizational Behavior and Human Performance*, 19, 18–42.

Rubin, J. Z., and Brown, B. R. (1975). *The Social Psychology of Bargaining and Negotiation*. New York: Academic Press.

Rulon, P. J., Tiedeman, D. V., Tatsuoka, M. M., and Langmuir, C. R. (1967). *Multivariate Statistics for Personnel Classification*. New York: Wiley.

Rumelhart, D. E., and Norman, D. A. (1978). Accretion, tuning, and restructuring: three modes of learning. In J. W. Cotton and R. Klatzky (eds.), *Semantic Factors in Cognition*. Hillsdale, NJ: Erlbaum.

Rumelhart, D. E. and Norman, D. A. (1982). Simulating a skilled typist: a study of skilled cognitive-motor performance. *Cognitive Science*, 6, 1–36.

Rush, M. F., and McGrath, P. S. (1973). Transactional analysis moves into corporate training: a new theory of interpersonal development becomes a tool for personal development. *The Conference Board Record*, 10, 38–44.

Rutenfranz, J., and Helbruegge, T. (1957). Über Tagesschwankungen der Rechengeschwindigkeit bei 11-jährigen Kinder. *Zeitschrift fuer Kinderheilkunde*, 80, 65–82.

Rutenfranz, J., Aschoff, J., and Mann, H. (1972). The effects of a cumulative sleep deficit, duration of preceding sleep period and body temperature on multiple choice reaction time. In *Aspects of Human Efficiency: Diurnal Rhythm and Loss of Sleep*. London: English Universities Press.

Rutenfranz, J., Colquhoun, W. P., Knauth, P., and Ghata, J. N. (1977). Biomedical and psychological aspects of shift work. *Scandinavian Journal of Work and Environmental Health*, 3, 165–82.

Rutenfranz, J., Knauth, P., and Angersbach, D. (1981). Shift work research issues. In L. C. Johnson, D. I. Tepas, W. P. Colquhoun and M. J. Colligan (eds.), *Advances in Sleep Research, Vol. 7: Biological Rhythms, Sleep and Shift Work*. New York: Spectrum Publications.

Rutenfranz, J., Haider, M., and Koller, M. (1985). Occupational health measures for nightworkers and shiftworkers. In S. Folkard and T. H. Monk (eds.), *Hours of Work*. Chichester: Wiley.

Rutter, M. (1972). *Maternal Deprivation Reassessed*. Harmondsworth: Penguin.

Rychlak, J. F. (1982). *Personality and Life Style of Young Male Managers*. New York: Academic Press.

Rynes, S. L., and Miller, H. E. (1983). Recruiter and job influences on candidates for employment. *Journal of Applied Psychology*, 68, 147–54.

Rynes, S. L., Heneman, H. G., and Schwab, D. P. (1980). Individual reactions to organizational recruiting: a review. *Personnel Psychology*, 33, 529–42.

Sackett, P. R., Harris, M. M., and Orr, J. M. (1986). On seeking moderator variables in the meta-analysis of correlational data: a Monte Carlo investigation of statistical power, and resistance of Type I error. *Journal of Applied Psychology*, 71, 302–10.

Salaman, G., and Thomson, K. (1980). *Control and Ideology in Organizations*. Milton Keynes: Open University Press.

Saunders, D. S. (1977). *An Introduction to Biological Rhythms*. London: Blackie.

Sawyers, L. (1984). Microcomputers in retailing: a case study. In N. Piercy (ed.), *The Management Implications of New Information Technology*. London: Croom Helm.

Sayles, L. R., and Chandler, M. K. (1971). *Managing Large Systems*. New York: Harper and Row.

Scarborough, H., and Moran, P. (1985). How new tech won at Longbridge. *New Society*, 71, 207–9.

Schein, E. H. (1967). Attitude change during management education: a study of organizational influences on student attitudes. *Administrative Science Quarterly*, 11, 601–28.

Schein, E. H. (1969). *Process Consultation: Its Role in Organization Development*. Reading, Mass.: Addison-Wesley.

Schein, E. H. (1971). The individual, the organization, and the career: a conceptual scheme. *Journal of Applied Behavioral Science*, 7, 401–26.

Schein, E. H. (1978). *Career Dynamics: Matching Individual and Organizational Needs*. Reading, Mass.: Addison-Wesley.

Schein, E. H. (1985). *Organizational Culture and Leadership*. San Francisco, Calif.: Jossey-Bass.

Schelling, T. C. (1960). *The Strategy of Conflict*. Oxford: Oxford University Press.

Schmidt, F. L., and Hunter, J. E. (1981). Employment testing: old theories and new research findings. *American Psychologist*, 36, 1128–37.

Schmidt, F. L., and Kaplan, L. B. (1971). Composite vs. multiple criteria: a review and resolution of the controversy. *Personnel Psychology*, 24, 419–34.

Schmidt, F. L., Hunter, J. E., McKenzie, R., and Muldrow, T. (1979). The impact of valid selection procedures in work force productivity. *Journal of Applied Psychology*, 64, 609–26.

Schmitt, N. (1976). Social and situational determinants of interview decisions: implications for the employment interview. *Personnel Psychology*, 29, 79–101.

Schmitt, N., and Coyle, B. W. (1976). Applicant decisions in the employment interview. *Journal of Applied Psychology*, 61, 184–92.

Schmitt, N., Gooding, R. Z., Noe, R. A., and Kirsch, M. (1984). Meta-analyses of validity studies published between 1964 and 1982 and the investigation of study characteristics. *Personnel Psychology*, 37, 407–22.

Schneider, B. (1985). Organizational behavior. *Annual Review of Psychology*, 36, 573–611.

Schneider, W., and Shiffrin, R. M. (1977). Controlled and automatic human information processing: I. Detection, search, and attention. *Psychological Review*, 84, 1–66.

Scholl, R. W. (1983). Career lines and employment stability. *Academy of Management Journal*, 26, 86–103.

Schriesheim, C. A., and Hosking, D. (1978). Review essay of Fiedler, F. E., Chemers, M. M. and Maher, L., Improving Leadership Effectiveness: The Leader Match Concept. *Administrative Science Quarterly*, 23, 496–505.

Schriesheim, C. A., and Kerr, S. (1974). Psychometric properties of the Ohio State leadership scales. *Psychological Bulletin*, 81, 756–65.

Schriesheim, C. A., and Kerr, S. (1977). R.I.P. LPC: a response to Fiedler. In J. G. Hunt and L. L. Larson (eds.), *Leadership: the Cutting Edge*. Carbondale, Ill.: Southern Illinois University Press.

Schriesheim, C. A., House, R. J., and Kerr, S. (1976). Leader initiating structure: a reconciliation of discrepant research results and some empirical tests. *Organizational Behavior and Human Performance*, 15, 297–321.

Schulz, J. W., and Pruitt, D. G. (1978). The effects of mutual concern on joint welfare. *Journal of Experimental Social Psychology*, 14, 480–91.

Sekaran, U. (1985). The paths to mental health: an exploratory study of husbands and wives in dual-career families. *Journal of Occupational Psychology*, 58, 129–137.

Seligman, M. E. P. (1975). *Helplessness: On Depression, Development, and Death*. San Francisco, Calif.: Freeman.

Sell, R. R. (1983). Transferred jobs: a neglected aspect of migration and occupational change. *Work and Occupations*, 10, 179–206.

Selznick, P. (1957). *Leadership in Administration*. New York: Harper and Row.

Seymour, W. D. (1966). *Industrial Skills*. London: Pitman.

Shackel, B. (ed.) (1974). *Applied Ergonomics Handbook*. Guildford: IPC Science and Technology Press.

Shaffer, L. H. (1973). Latency mechanisms in transcription. In S. Kornblum (ed.), *Attention and Performance IV*. New York: Academic Press.

Shaiken, H. (1979). Impact of new technology on employees and their organizations. Research report: International Institute for Comparative Social Research, Berlin.

Shaiken, H. (1980). Computer technology and the relations of power in the workplace. Research report: International Institute for Comparative Social Research, Berlin.

Sharlt, J., Chang, T. L., and Salvendy, G. (1986). Technical and human aspects of computer-aided manufacturing. In G. Salvendy (ed.), *Handbook of Human Factors*. New York: Wiley.

Sheldon, M. E. (1971). Investments and involvements as mechanisms producing commitment to the organization. *Administrative Science Quarterly*, 16, 143–50.

Shepherd, A. (1985). Hierarchical task analysis and training decisions. *Programmed Learning and Educational Technology*, 22, 162–76.

Sherif, M. (1966). *Group Conflict and Cooperation*. London: Routledge and Kegan Paul.

Shiffrin, R. M. (in press). Attention. In R. C. Atkinson, R. J. Herrnstein, G. Lindzey, and R. D. Luce (eds.), *Stevens' Handbook of Experimental Psychology*. (2nd ed.) New York: Wiley.

Shinar, D., and Acton, M. B. (1978). Control-display relationships on the four-burner range: population stereotypes versus standards. *Human Factors*, 20, 13–17.

Shneiderman, B. (1980). *Software Psychology*. Cambridge, Mass.: Winthrop.

Siffre, M. (1964). *Beyond Time*. (Edited and translated by H. Briffault.) New York: McGraw-Hill.

Silverman, D. (1970). *The Theory of Organisations*. London: Heinemann.

Silverstone, R., and Towler, R. (1983). *Secretarial Work in Central London 1970–1981*. London: Manpower Services Commission.

Simons, G. (1981). *Women in Computing*. Manchester: National Computing Centre.

Singleton, W. T. (ed.) (1978). *The Analysis of Practical Skills*. Lancaster: MTP Press.

Singleton, W. T. (ed.) (1981). *Management Skills*. Lancaster: MTP Press.

Singleton, W. T. (ed.) (1982). *The Body at Work*. Cambridge: Cambridge University Press.

Skinner, B. F. (1971). *Beyond Freedom and Dignity*. New York: Knopf.

Sloan, A. (1964). *My Years With General Motors*. New York: Doubleday.

Smith, A. (1776). *On the Wealth of Nations*. Harmondsworth: Penguin.

Smith, D. J. (1980). How unemployment makes the poor poorer. *Policy Studies*, 1, 20–26.

Smith, F. J., Scott, K. D., and Hulin, C. L. (1977). Trends in job-related attitudes of managerial and professional employees. *Academy of Management Journal*, 20, 454–60.

Smith, H., and Green, T. (eds.) (1980). *Human Interaction with Computers*. London: Academic Press.

Smith, P. (1980). *Small Groups and Personal Change*. London: Methuen.

Smith, R., and Quinlan, T. (1983). Hand in hand with technology. *Employment Gazette*, 91, 213–16.

Snyder, G. H., and Diesing, P. (1977). *Conflict among Nations: Bargaining, Decision-Making and System Structure in International Crises*. Princeton: Princeton University Press.

Snyder, M. and White, P. (1981). Testing hypotheses about other people: strategies of verification and falsification. *Personality and Social Psychology Bulletin*, 7, 39–43.

Social Trends (1985). London: HMSO.

Social Trends (1987). London: HMSO.

Softly, E. (1985). Word processing: new opportunities for women office workers? In W. Faulkner and E. Arnold (eds.), *Smothered By Invention*. London: Pluto Press.

Sonnenfeld, J., and Kotter, J. P. (1982). The maturation of career theory. *Human Relations*, 35, 19–46.

Sorge, A., Hartmann, G., Warner, M., and Nicholas, I. (1983). *Microelectronics and Manpower in Manufacturing*. Aldershot: Gower Press.

South, S. J. (1985). Economic conditions and the divorce rate: a time-series analysis of the post-war United States. *Journal of Marriage and the Family*, 47, 31–41.

Sowa, J. F. (1984). *Conceptual Structures: Information Processing, Mind and Machine*. Reading, Mass.: Addison-Wesley.

Spearman, C. (1927). *The Abilities of Man, their Nature and Measurement*. New York: MacMillan.

Spector, P. E. (1985). Higher-order need strength as a moderator of the job scope – employee outcome relationship: a meta-analysis. *Journal of Occupational Psychology*, 58, 119–27.

Spencer, H. (1873). *The Study of Sociology*. London: Routledge and Kegan Paul.

Staehle, W. H. (1984). Job design and automation in the Federal Republic of Germany. In F. Butera and J. E. Thurman (eds.), *Automation and Work Design*. Amsterdam: North-Holland.

Stagner, R., and Rosen, H. (1956). *The Psychology of Union–Management Relations*. London: Tavistock.

Stammers, R. B. (1981). The computer terminal as a simulator. *European Journal of Industrial Training*, 5(7), 27–9.

Stammers, R. B. (1982). Part and whole practice in training for procedural tasks. *Human Learning*, 1, 185–207.

Stammers, R. B. (1983). Simulators for training. In T. O. Kvalseth (ed.), *Ergonomics of Workstation Design*. London: Butterworth.

Stammers, R. B., and Patrick, J. (1975). *The Psychology of Training*. London: Methuen.

Stead, B. A. (1978). *Women in Management*. London: Prentice-Hall.

Stephenson, G. M. (1978). The characteristics of negotiation groups. In H. Brandstatter, J. H. Davis and H. Schuler (eds.), *Social Decision Processes*. Beverly Hills, Calif.: Sage.

Stephenson, G. M. (1981). Intergroup bargaining and negotiation. In J. C. Turner and H. Giles (eds.), *Intergroup Behaviour*. Oxford: Blackwell.

Stephenson, G. M., and Brotherton, C. J. (eds.) (1979). *Industrial Relations: a Social Psychological Approach*. Chichester: Wiley.

Stephenson, G. M., Kniveton, B. H., and Morley, I. E. (1977). Interaction analysis of an industrial wage negotiation. *Journal of Occupational Psychology*, 50, 231–41.

Stephenson, G. M., Brotherton, C. J., Skinner, M. R., and Delafield, G. (1983). Size of organization and attitudes at work. *Industrial Relations Journal*, 14(2), 28–40.

Sternberg, R. J. (1985). *Beyond IQ*. Cambridge: Cambridge University Press.

Sterrett, J. H. (1978). The job interview: body language and perceptions of potential effectiveness. *Journal of Applied Psychology*, 63, 388–90.

Stewart, R. (1982). *Choices for the Manager: a Guide to Managerial Work and Behaviour*. London: McGraw-Hill.

Stinson, J. E., and Tracy, L. (1974). Some disturbing characteristics of the LPC score. *Personnel Psychology*, 24, 477–85.

Stogdill, R. M. (1948). Personal factors associated with leadership: a survey of the literature. *Journal of Psychology*, 25, 35–71.

Strauss, A. (1978). *Negotiations*. San Francisco, Calif.: Jossey-Bass.

Student, K. R. (1968). Supervisory influence and work group performance. *Journal of Applied Psychology*, 52, 188–94.

Super, D. E. (1980). A life-span, life-space approach to career development. *Journal of Vocational Behavior*, 16, 282–98.

Super, D. E. (1981). Approaches to occupational choice and career development. In A. G. Watts, D. E. Super and J. M. Kidd (eds.), *Careers Development in Britain*. Cambridge: Hobsons Press.

Sydiaha, D. (1962). Bales' interaction process analysis of personnel selection interviews. *Journal of Applied Psychology*, 46, 344–9.

Tajfel, H., Flament, C., Billig, M. G., and Bundy, R. P. (1971). Social categorization and intergroup behaviour. *European Journal of Social Psychology*, 1, 149–78.

Tannenbaum, A. S., Kavcic, B., Rosner, M., Vianello, M., and Wieser, G. (1974). *Hierarchy in Organizations*. San Francisco, Calif.: Jossey-Bass.

Taylor, F. W. (1911). *The Principles of Scientific Management*. New York: Harper.

Taylor, J. C. (1979). Job design criteria twenty years later. In L. E. Davis and J. C. Taylor (eds.), *Design of Jobs*. (2nd ed.) Santa Monica, Calif.: Goodyear.

Tepas, D. I., Walsh, J. K., Moss, P. D., and Armstrong, D. (1981). Polysomnographic correlates of shift work performance in the laboratory. In A. Reinberg, N. Vieux and P. Andlauer (eds.), *Night and Shift Work: Biological and Social Aspects*. Oxford: Pergamon Press.

Terborg, J. R. (1985). Working women and stress. In T. A. Beehr and R. S. Bhagat (eds.), *Human Stress and Cognition in Organizations*. Chichester: Wiley.

Terborg, J. R., and Shingledecker, P. S. (1983). Employee reactions to supervision and work evaluation as a function of subordinate and manager sex. *Sex Roles*, 9, 813–24.

Terkel, S. (1972). *Working: People Talk about What they Feel about What they Do*. New York: Pantheon Books.

Tessler, R., and Sushelsky, L. (1978). Effects of eye contact and social status on the perception of a job applicant in an employment interviewing situation. *Journal of Vocational Behavior*, 13, 338–47.

Thomas, L. E., McCabe, E., and Berry, J. E. (1980). Unemployment and family stress: a reassessment. *Family Relations*, 29, 517–24.

Thompson, J. D., and Tudeau, A. (1959). Comparative studies in administration. Abridged in H. J. Leavitt and L. Pondy (eds.), *Readings in Managerial Psychology*. Chicago, Ill.: University of Chicago Press.

Thorndike, E. (1900). Mental fatigue. *Psychological Review*, 7, 466–82.

Thorndike, R. L. (ed.) (1971). *Educational Measurement*. (2nd ed.) Washington DC: American Council on Education.

Thornton, G. J., and Byham, W. C. (1982). *Assessment Centers and Managerial Performance*. New York: Academic Press.

Thorsrud, E. (1972). Job design in the wider context. In L. E. Davis and J. C. Taylor (eds.), *Design of Jobs*. Harmondsworth: Penguin.

Thurstone, L. L. (1930). Primary mental abilities. *Psychometric Monographs*, No. 1.

Thurstone, L. L. (1931). *Reliability and Validity of Tests*. Michigan: University of Michigan Press.

Tilley, A. J., Wilkinson, R. T., Warren, P. S. G., Watson, B., and Drud, M. (1982). The sleep and performance of shift workers. *Human Factors*, 24, 629–41.

Tkach, H. (1980). The female executive. *Managing*, 1, 13–19.

Tom, V. R. (1971). The role of personality and organizational images in the recruiting process. *Organizational Behavior and Human Performance*, 6, 573–92.

Toops, H. A. (1944). The criterion. *Educational and Psychological Measurement*, 4, 271–98.

Travers, R. W. (1951). Rational hypotheses in construction of tests. *Educational and Psychological Measurement*, 11, 128–35.

Treisman, A. M., and Gelade, G. (1980). A feature integration theory of attention. *Cognitive Psychology*, 12, 97–136.

Trist, E. L., Higgin, G. W., Murray, H., and Pollock, A. B. (1963). *Organizational Choice*. London: Tavistock.

Trist, E. L., Susman, G., and Brown, G. W. (1977). An experiment in autonomous group working in an American underground coal mine. *Human Relations*, 30, 201–36.

Tucker, D. H., and Rowe, F. M. (1977). Consulting the application form prior to the interview: an essential step in the selection process. *Journal of Applied Psychology*, 62, 283–7.

Turner, A. N., and Lawrence, P. R. (1965). *Industrial Jobs and the Worker*. Cambridge, Mass.: Harvard University Press.

Turner, J. C. (1975). Social comparison and social identity; some prospects for intergroup behaviour. *European Journal of Social Psychology*, 5, 5–24.

Upton, R. (1984). The 'home office' and the new homeworkers. *Personnel Management*, September, 39–43.

Urwick, L. (1943). *The Elements of Administration*. New York: Harper.

US Department of Labor (1978). *Women in Traditionally Male Jobs: the*

Experiences of Ten Public Utility Companies. Washington DC: US Government Printing Office.

US Department of Labor (1980). *Perspectives on Working Women: a Databook*. Washington, DC: Bureau of Labor Statistics.

US National Academy of Sciences (1983). *Children of Working Parents*. Washington DC: National Academy Press.

Vaill, P. B. (1984). The purposing of high performance systems. In T. J. Sergiovanni and J. E. Corbally (eds.), *Leadership and Organizational Culture*. Chicago, Ill.: University of Illinois Press.

Vance, R. J., Kuhnert, K. W., and Farr, J. L. (1978). Interview judgments: using external criteria to compare behavioral and graphic scale ratings. *Organizational Behavior and Human Performance*, 22, 279–94.

Van Maanen, J. (1976). Breaking-in: socialization to work. In R. Dubin (ed.), *Handbook of Work, Organization and Society*. Chicago, Ill.: Rand McNally.

Van Maanen, J., and Schein, E. H. (1979). Toward a theory of organizational socialization. In B. M. Staw (ed.), *Research in Organizational Behavior*, volume 1. Greenwich, Conn.: JAI Press.

Vecchio, R. P. (1983). Assessing the validity of Fiedler's contingency model of leadership effectiveness: a closer look at Strube and Garcia (1981). *Psychological Bulletin*, 93, 404–508.

Veiga, J. F. (1983). Mobility influences during managerial career stages. *Academy of Management Journal*, 26, 64–85.

Vernon, P. E. (1956). *The Measurement of Abilities*. London: University of London Press.

Vernon, P. E. (1963). *Personality Assessment*. London: Methuen.

Vernon, P. E. (1971). *The Structure of Human Abilities*. London: Methuen.

Vidaček, S., Kaliterna, L., Radoševič-Vidaček, B., and Folkard, S. (1986). Productivity on a weekly rotating shift system: circadian adjustment and sleep deprivation effects? *Ergonomics*, 29, 1583–90.

Visick, D., Johnson, P., and Long, J. (1984). A comparative analysis of keyboards and voice recognition in a parcel sorting task. In E. Megaw (ed.), *Contemporary Ergonomics 1984*. London: Taylor and Francis.

Vroom, V. (1966). Organization choice: a study of pre- and post-decision processes. *Organizational Behavior and Human Performance*, 1, 212–25.

Vroom, V. (1976). Leadership. In M. D. Dunnette (ed.), *Handbook of Industrial and Organizational Psychology*. Chicago, Ill.: Rand McNally.

Vroom, V., and Deci, E. (1971). The stability of business school graduates: a follow-up study of job attitudes of business school graduates. *Organizational Behavior and Human Performance*, 6, 36–49.

Vroom, V., and Jago, A. G. (1978). On the validity of the Vroom-Yetton Model. *Journal of Applied Psychology*, 63, 151–62.

Vroom, V., and Yetton, P. W. (1973). *Leadership and Decision-Making*. Pittsburgh, Penn.: University of Pittsburgh Press.

Walker, C. R., and Guest, R. H. (1952). *Man on the Assembly Line*. Cambridge, Mass.: Harvard University Press.

Walker, J. (1985). Social problems of shiftwork. In S. Folkard and T. H. Monk (eds.), *Hours of Work*. Chichester: Wiley.

Walker, K. F. (1959). Conflict and mutual misunderstanding: a survey of union leaders' and business executives' attitudes to industrial relations. *Journal of Industrial Relations*, 1, 20–30.

Walker, K. F. (1962). Executives' and union leaders' perception of each other's attitudes to industrial relations. *Human Relations*, 15, 183–96.

Walker, K. F. (1979). Psychology and industrial relations: a general perspective. In G. M. Stephenson and C. J. Brotherton (eds.), *Industrial Relations: a Social Psychological Approach*. Chichester: Wiley.

Wall, T. D., and Clegg, C. W. (1981). A longitudinal field study of group work redesign. *Journal of Occupational Behaviour*, 2, 31–49.

Wall, T. D., and Martin, R. (1987). Job and work design. In C. L. Cooper and I. T. Robertson (eds.), *International Review of Industrial and Organizational Psychology 1987*. Chichester: Wiley.

Wall, T. D., Clegg, C. W., and Jackson, P. R. (1978). An evaluation of the Job Characteristics Model. *Journal of Occupational Psychology*, 51, 183–986.

Wall, T. D., Burnes, B., Clegg, C. W., and Kemp, N. J. (1984). New technology, old jobs. *Work and People*, 10, 15–21.

Wall, T. D., Kemp., N. J., Jackson, P. R. and Clegg, C. W. (1986). An outcome evaluation of autonomous working groups: a long-term field experiment. *Academy of Management Journal*, 29, 280–304.

Wall, T. D., Clegg, C. W., and Kemp, N. J. (1987). *The Human Side of Advanced Manufacturing Technology*. Chichester: Wiley.

Walton, R. E., and McKersie, R. B. (1965). *A Behavioral Theory of Labor Negotiations*. New York: McGraw-Hill.

Wanous, J. P. (1980). *Organizational Entry*. Reading, Mass.: Addison-Wesley.

Warner, M., and Sorge, A. (1980). The context of industrial relations in Great Britain and West Germany. *Industrial Relations Journal*, 11(1), 41–9.

Warr, P. B. (1973). *Psychology and Collective Bargaining*. London: Hutchinson.

Warr, P. B. (1978). A study of psychological well-being. *British Journal of Psychology*, 69, 111–21.

Warr, P. B. (1984). Reported behaviour changes after job loss. *British Journal of Social Psychology*, 23, 271–5.

Warr, P. B. (1987). *Work, Unemployment, and Mental Health*. Oxford: Oxford University Press.

Warr, P. B., and Jackson, P. R. (1984). Men without jobs: some correlates of age and length of unemployment. *Journal of Occupational Psychology*, 57, 77–85.

Warr, P. B., and Jackson, P. R. (1985). Factors influencing the psychological impact of prolonged unemployment and of re-employment. *Psychological Medicine*, 15, 795–807.

Warr, P. B., and Parry, G. (1982). Paid employment and women's psychological well-being. *Psychological Bulletin*, 91, 498–516.

Warr, P. B., and Payne, R. L. (1983). Social class and reported changes in behavior after job loss. *Journal of Applied Social Psychology*, 13, 206–22.

Warr, P. B., and Wall, T. (1975). *Work and Well-being*. Harmondsworth: Penguin.

Warr, P. B., Fineman, S., Nicholson, N., and Payne, R. (1978). *Developing Employee Relations*. Westmead: Saxon/Gower.

Warr, P. B., Banks, M. H., and Ullah, P. (1985). The experience of unemployment among black and white urban teenagers. *British Journal of Psychology*, 76, 75–87.

Washburn, P. V., and Hakel, M. D. (1973). Visual cues and verbal content as influences on impressions formed after simulated employment interviews. *Journal of Applied Psychology*, 58, 137–41.

Watson, D., and Clark, L. A. (1984). Negative affectivity: the disposition to experience aversive emotional states. *Psychological Bulletin*, 96, 465–90.

Watts, A. G., Super, D. E., and Kidd, J. M. (1981). *Career Development in Britain*. Cambridge: Hobsons Press.

Weaver, C. N. (1980). Job satisfaction in the United States in the 1970s. *Journal of Applied Psychology*, 65, 364–7.

Weber, R. M. (1947). *The Theory of Social and Economic Organization*. New York: Free Press.

Weick, K. (1979). *The Social Psychology of Organizing*. Reading, Mass.: Addison-Wesley.

Weiss, H. W. (1978). Social learning of work values in organizations. *Journal of Applied Psychology*, 63, 711–18.

Werbel, J. D. (1983). Job change: a study of an acute job stressor. *Journal of Vocational Behavior*, 23, 242–50.

Wernimont, P. F., and Campbell, J. P. (1968). Signs, samples and criteria. *Journal of Applied Psychology*, 52, 372–6.

West, D. J., Horan, J. J., and Games, P. A. (1984). Component analysis of occupational stress inoculation applied to registered nurses in an acute care hospital setting. *Journal of Counseling Psychology*, 31, 209–18.

Wever, R. A. (1979). *The Circadian System of Man: Results of Experiments under Temporal Isolation.* New York: Springer.

Wever, R. A. (1983). Fractional desynchronization of human circadian rhythms: a method of evaluation entrainment limits and functional interdependencies. *Pflugers Archiv*, 396, 128–37.

Wexley, K. N., Sanders, R. E., and Yukl, G. A. (1973). Training interviewers to eliminate contrast effects in employment interviews. *Journal of Applied Psychology*, 57, 233–6.

White, M. (1985). Life stress in long-term unemployment. *Policy Studies*, 5, 31–49.

White, M., and Trevor, M. (1983). *Under Japanese Management.* London: Heinemann.

Whitefield, A. (1984). A model of the engineering design process derived from Hearsay-II. In B. Shackel (ed.), *Interact '84*. Amsterdam: North-Holland.

Whitefield, A. (1985). A qualitative analysis of knowledge use in designing with and without CAD. In *CAD '86*. Guildford: IPC Science and Technology Press.

Whyte, W. (1956). *The Organization Man.* New York: Simon and Schuster.

Wickens, C. D. (1984). *Engineering Psychology and Human Performance.* Columbus: C. E. Merrill.

Wiener, Y., and Schneiderman, M. L. (1974). Use of job information as a criterion in employment decisions of interviewers. *Journal of Applied Psychology*, 59, 699–704.

Wilkinson, B. (1983). Technical change and work organization. *Industrial Relations Journal*, 14(2), 18–27.

Wilkinson, R. T. (1965). Sleep deprivation. In O. G. Edholm and A. L. Bacharach (eds.), *The Physiology of Human Survival*. New York: Academic Press.

Williams, R., and Guest, D. (1969). Psychological research and industrial relations. *Occupational Psychology*, 43, 201–11.

Williams, S. (1985). *A Job to Live: the Impact of Tomorrow's Technology on Work and Society*. Harmondsworth: Penguin.

Willis, P. E. (1977). *Learning to Labour*. Farnborough: Saxon House.

Winefield, A. H., and Tiggemann, M. (1985). Psychological correlates of employment and unemployment: effects, predisposing factors, and sex differences. *Journal of Occupational Psychology*, 58, 229–42.

Winnubst, J. A. M. (1984). Stress in organizations. In P. J. D. Drenth, H. Thierry, P. J. Willems and C. J. de Wolff (eds.), *Handbook of Work and Organizational Psychology*. Chichester: Wiley.

Wojtczak-Jaroszowa, J. and Pawlowska-Skyba, K. (1967). Night and shift work I: circadian variations in work. *Medycyna Pracy*, 18, 1.

Wood, S. (ed.) (1982). *The Degradation of Work?* London: Hutchinson.

Woodward, J. (1965). *Industrial Organization: Theory and Practice*. Oxford: Oxford University Press.

Yetton, P. (1984). Leadership and supervision. In M. Gruneberg and T. Wall (eds.), *Social Psychology and Organizational Behaviour*. Chichester: Wiley.

Zaleznik, A. (1977). Managers and leaders: are they different? *Harvard Business Review*, May–June, 1977, 67–78.

Zedeck, S., Tziner, A., and Middlestadt, S. E. (1983). Interviewer validity and reliability: an individual analysis approach. *Personnel Psychology*, 36, 355–70.

Zulley, J., Wever, R., and Aschoff, J. (1981). The dependence of onset and duration of sleep on the circadian rhythm of rectal temperature. *Pflugers Archiv*, 391, 314–18.

Author Index

Authors appearing within '*et al.*' in the course of the text are
referenced here through page numbers printed in italics.

Subject Index

FOR THE BEST IN PAPERBACKS, LOOK FOR THE 🐧

In every corner of the world, on every subject under the sun, Penguin represents quality and variety – the very best in publishing today.

For complete information about books available from Penguin – including Puffins, Penguin Classics and Arkana – and how to order them, write to us at the appropriate address below. Please note that for copyright reasons the selection of books varies from country to country.

In the United Kingdom: Please write to *Dept E.P., Penguin Books Ltd, Harmondsworth, Middlesex, UB7 0DA*.

If you have any difficulty in obtaining a title, please send your order with the correct money, plus ten per cent for postage and packaging, to *PO Box No 11, West Drayton, Middlesex*

In the United States: Please write to *Dept BA, Penguin, 299 Murray Hill Parkway, East Rutherford, New Jersey 07073*

In Canada: Please write to *Penguin Books Canada Ltd, 2801 John Street, Markham, Ontario L3R 1B4*

In Australia: Please write to the *Marketing Department, Penguin Books Australia Ltd, P.O. Box 257, Ringwood, Victoria 3134*

In New Zealand: Please write to the *Marketing Department, Penguin Books (NZ) Ltd, Private Bag, Takapuna, Auckland 9*

In India: Please write to *Penguin Overseas Ltd, 706 Eros Apartments, 56 Nehru Place, New Delhi, 110019*

In the Netherlands: Please write to *Penguin Books Netherlands B.V., Postbus 195, NL–1380AD Weesp*

In West Germany: Please write to *Penguin Books Ltd, Friedrichstrasse 10–12, D–6000 Frankfurt/Main 1*

In Spain: Please write to *Longman Penguin España, Calle San Nicolas 15, E–28013 Madrid*

In Italy: Please write to *Penguin Italia s.r.l., Via Como 4, I-20096 Pioltello (Milano)*

In France: Please write to *Penguin Books Ltd, 39 Rue de Montmorency, F-75003 Paris*

In Japan: Please write to *Longman Penguin Japan Co Ltd, Yamaguchi Building, 2–12–9 Kanda Jimbocho, Chiyoda-Ku, Tokyo 101*